ASSEMBLIES AND REPRESENTATION IN LANGUEDOC IN THE THIRTEENTH CENTURY

Assemblies and Representation in Languedoc in the Thirteenth Century

THOMAS N. BISSON

PRINCETON UNIVERSITY PRESS · PRINCETON, N J · 1964

Publication of this book has been aided by
the Ford Foundation program to support
publication, through university presses, of
works in the humanities and social sciences.

Printed in the United States of America
by Vail-Ballou Press, Inc., Binghamton, N.Y.

To My Mother and Father

◈ Preface

The studies on which this volume rests were begun in 1955 at the suggestion of Professor Joseph R. Strayer. To him, above all, I am indebted for guidance and interest which, continuing long after my graduate work was finished, have been unfailingly learned, stimulating, and patient. I venture to hope that his confidence in the significance of early institutional history may find some small justification in my results.

Many other persons have helped me, although no one but myself is responsible for errors or shortcomings that remain. The late Professor Theodor E. Mommsen provided exemplary criticism at an early stage of the work. His teaching and friendship are among my treasured memories. Philippe Wolff, Professor of Medieval History at Toulouse, introduced me to the life and riches of the Midi and he has given generously of his learning and interest. Professor Gaines Post not only made valuable criticisms of my interpretations but furnished me with copious references to legal sources in manuscript. While I cannot flatter myself that he agrees with all my conclusions, I remain very much in his debt. His distinguished *Studies in Medieval Legal Thought*, recently published by the Princeton University Press, will greatly facilitate reference to the numerous articles I have cited in their original form. My manuscript also benefited from a characteristically perceptive reading by Professor William F. Church, my senior colleague at Brown University.

The library staffs of Amherst College, Brown University, and the great repositories of London and Paris have done much to assist my work. I am also grateful to the archivists of southern France, and especially, among them, to Messrs. Blaquière, Bousquet, Burias, Gérard (formerly of Toulouse), Gouron, Prat, Sablou, and Saint-Blanquat.

A year of study in France in 1956–57 was made possible by the renewal of a Charlotte Elizabeth Procter Fellowship by the Graduate School of Princeton University. The American Philosophical Society supported archival research in the summer of 1961, and Brown University provided a summer stipend in 1962. To the Princeton University Press I am obliged for a subsidy in aid of publication as well as for courtesy and skill in the editing.

The material dealing with the general court of Agenais originally appeared, in a different form, in *Speculum,* and it is reprinted in this book by permission of the Mediaeval Academy of America.

Finally, I would like to express gratitude to my friend George Kateb for his intellectual stimulation and interest; and to my wife for much encouragement and help.

T.N.B.

July 1964

℥ Contents

Contents

ASSEMBLIES AND REPRESENTATION IN LANGUEDOC IN THE THIRTEENTH CENTURY

ABBREVIATIONS

A.D.	Archives Départementales
A.H.R.	*American Historical Review*
A.M.	Archives Municipales
A.N.	Paris, Archives Nationales
B.É.C.	*Bibliothèque de l'École des Chartes*
B.M.	Bibliothèque Municipale
B.N.	Paris, Bibliothèque Nationale
C.,D.	*Code* and *Digest* of Justinian's *Corpus Juris Civilis*
Extra	*Liber Extra,* i.e., *Decretales D. Gregorii Papae IX* . . . (Venice, 1600)
H.F.	*Recueil des Historiens des Gaules et de la France* (Paris, 1738–)
H.L.	Devic and Vaissete, *Histoire Générale de Languedoc* . . . , Privat ed., 16 vols. (Toulouse, 1872–1904)
I.A.C.(D.)	*Inventaire des Archives Communales (Départementales)*
Layettes	*Layettes du Trésor des Chartes,* ed. Teulet, *et. al.,* 5 vols. (Paris, 1863–1909)
P.R.O.	London, Public Record Office
R.H.	*Revue Historique*

ᕯI᠊ᕯ *Introduction*

Medieval representation in assemblies has usually been treated as a part of constitutional history.[1] This is not surprising. The most important European assemblies, historically, were those which acquired constitutional powers and attributions, such as the English parliament, the Spanish Cortes, and the French assemblies of Estates. Moreover, the study of representative institutions, though it originated before the French Revolution, was nourished and flourished in the liberalism of the nineteenth century. Hallam and Guizot were fascinated by the rights of medieval assemblies.[2] Their successors concentrated on legislative powers and the grant of taxes; and William Stubbs, writing the greatest *Constitutional History* of the century, concluded that the parliament of England originated in the

[1] The literature is too extensive to cite fully. But, in addition to the works mentioned below in this paragraph, see the following: B. Wilkinson, *The Constitutional History of England, 1216–1399,* 3 vols. (London, 1948–1958), II, 6–7, 53–54, 204–269; and III, chs. 5–7; R. B. Merriman, "The Cortes of the Spanish Kingdoms in the Later Middle Ages," *A.H.R.*, XVI (1911), 479–495; A. Luchaire, *Manuel des Institutions Françaises* (Paris, 1892), pp. 487–504; F. Lot and R. Fawtier, *Histoire des Institutions Françaises au Moyen Age,* II (Paris, 1958), 547–577. See also n. 11 below; and cf. C. H. McIlwain, chapter on "Medieval Estates," *Cambridge Medieval History,* VII (1932); and R. S. Hoyt, "Recent Publications in the United States and Canada on the History of Representative Institutions before the French Revolution," *Speculum,* XXIX (1954), esp. 356–364.

[2] See H. Hallam's *View of the State of Europe during the Middle Ages* (London, 1818; many later editions); F. Guizot's *Histoire des Origines du Gouvernement Représentatif en Europe* (Paris, 1851), a famous set of lectures delivered in 1820–1822; and see generally for this paragraph and the next, C. Stephenson, *Mediaeval Institutions: Selected Essays,* ed. B. Lyon (Ithaca, 1954), pp. 105–109.

recognition of national authority by a king who, though pressed, was responsive to the political capabilities of his people.[3] This view contained an important element of truth, which has stood the test of time. There is general agreement today that financial necessity largely explains the original representative parliament; and taxation has been recognized as a fundamental factor in the rise of other institutionalized medieval assemblies.[4] The constitutional point of view has found further support in the results of new work on Roman and canon law, which indicate a significant understanding of legal rights, counsel, and consent.[5]

The discovery that assemblies had obligations as well as rights was the signal achievement of revisionist scholarship at the end of the last century. According to Riess, the summons of town and county deputies in England was to be explained rather by the king's need of them in judicial and administrative work than by a requirement to obtain

[3] *The Constitutional History of England*, II, 4th ed. (Oxford, 1896), ch. 15.

[4] See generally G. L. Haskins, *The Statute of York and the Interest of the Commons* (Cambridge, Mass., 1935); Hoyt, "Recent Publications," 364–369; McIlwain, in *Camb. Med. Hist.*, VII, 683–686, 702. There had been a reaction against the original tendency to emphasize finance (see next paragraph), and Stephenson's careful reappraisal of the problem, *Mediaeval Institutions*, pp. 104–125 ("Taxation and Representation in the Middle Ages," reprinted from the *Haskins Essays* [1929]), and pp. 126–138, doubtless helped to restore taxation to a just place in the total picture. (In England, to be sure, that picture is more complex today, for writers like Lapsley, Plucknett, and F. M. Powicke believe that early parliaments functioned in various ways, according to circumstances.)

[5] G. Post, "Plena Potestas and Consent in Medieval Assemblies: A Study in Romano-Canonical Procedure and the Rise of Representation, 1150–1325," *Traditio*, I (1943), 355–408; "A Romano-Canonical Maxim, 'Quod Omnes Tangit,' in Bracton," *Traditio*, IV (1946), 197–251; see also B. Tierney, *Foundations of the Conciliar Theory* . . . (Cambridge, 1955), esp. pp. 87–127.

their consent to taxation.[6] This view led to a broader current of synthesis which, continuing today, emphasizes the utility of assemblies to kings and princes, and minimizes the pressures of self-conscious subject communities. England has remained the chief testing-ground. Maitland and McIlwain set forth the influential judicial interpretation of the parliament;[7] and recent work has drawn attention to the administrative uses of fourteenth-century parliaments.[8] Even finance is seen in a different light. The right to be consulted on taxation did not necessarily mean that consent could be withheld. Professor Gaines Post has shown how the reviving ideas of public necessity and the state enabled princes to control the assemblies they convoked; and he has argued that deputies bore "full powers" to assemblies in response to imperious, judicial-conciliar commands.[9]

[6] L. Riess, *Geschichte des Wahlrechts zum Englischen Parlament im Mittelalter* (Leipzig, 1885); "Der Ursprung des Englischen Unterhauses," *Historische Zeitschrift*, LX (1888), 1–33.

[7] F. W. Maitland, introduction to *Memoranda de Parliamento, 1305* (London, 1893); McIlwain, *The High Court of Parliament and its Supremacy* (New Haven, 1910); in various studies on the origins of parliament, H. G. Richardson and G. O. Sayles have presented a significant refinement of this view. Their results are summarized in *Parliaments and Great Councils in Medieval England* (London, 1961).

[8] T. F. T. Plucknett, "Parliament," in *The English Government at Work, 1327–1336*, eds. Willard, Morris, Strayer, Dunham, 3 vols. (Cambridge, Mass., 1940–1950), I, 117; J. R. Strayer, "The Statute of York and the Community of the Realm," *A.H.R.*, XLVII (1941), 5–8; but cf. Wilkinson, *Constitutional History*, esp. II, 6–7, 53–54, 204–269; and III, *passim*.

[9] "Plena Potestas and Consent in Medieval Assemblies"; and see also the important essays on "The Theory of Public Law and the State in the Thirteenth Century," *Seminar* (annual extraordinary number of *The Jurist*), VI (1948), 42–59; and "A Romano-Canonical Maxim, 'Quod Omnes Tangit,' in Bracton." Post's arguments concern the Continent as well as England; and, for France, see also Strayer's study cited in next note.

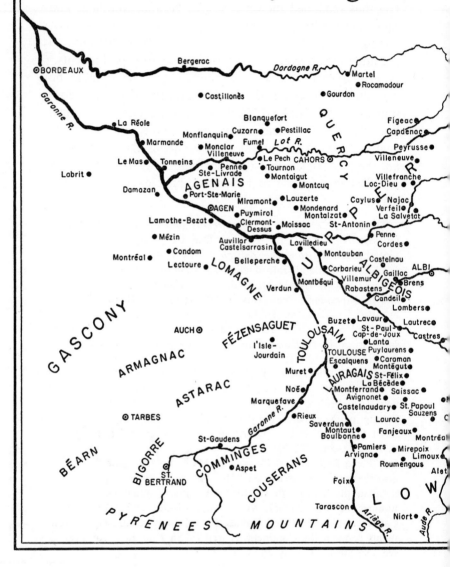

Thirteenth Century Languedoc

BORDEAUX

Bergerac

Dordogne R.

Martel

Rocamadour

Garonne R.

Castillonès

Gourdon

QUERCY

Blanquefort

Figeac

La Réole

Cuzorn

Pestillac

Capdénac

Monflanquin

Fumel

Lot R.

Peyrusse

Marmande

Monclar

Villeneuve

Le Pech

CAHORS

Villeneuve

Le Mas

Tonneins

Pennes

Tournon

Villefranche

Labrit

Ste-Livrade

Montaigut

Loc-Dieu

AGENAIS

Montcuq

Damazan

Port-Ste-Marie

Miramont

Lauzerte

Caylus

Najac

AGEN

Puymirol

Mondenard

Verfeil

Lamothe-Bezat

Clermont-

Montalzat

La Salvetat

Dessus

Moissac

St-Antonin

Mézin

Auvillar

Lavilledieu

Penne

Castelsarrasin

Cordes

Condom

Montauban

Montréal

Lectoure

Belleperche

Corbarieu

Castelnau

LOMAGNE

Montbéqui

Villemur

Gaillac

ALBI

Verdun

Rabastens

Brens

Candeil

Lombers

Buzet

Lavaur

Lautrec

AUCH

FÉZENSAGUET

St-Paul-

Cap-de-Joux

Castres

l'Isle-

Jourdain

TOULOUSAIN

Lanta

TOULOUSE

Puylaurens

GASCONY

Escalquens

Caraman

Montégut

Muret

AURAGAIS

St-Félix

ARMAGNAC

Noé

La Bécède

Montferrand

Saissac

Marquefave

Avignonet

St. Papoul

ASTARAC

Garonne R.

Rieux

Castelnaudary

Sauzens

TARBES

Saverdun

Laurac

Montaut

Fanjeaux

Montréal

St-Gaudens

Boulbonne

Pamiers

Mirepoix

BÉARN

BIGORRE

Arvigna

Limoux

ST.

COMMINGES

Aspet

Roumengous

Alet

BERTRAND

COUSERANS

Foix

LOW

PYRENEES

MOUNTAINS

Tarascon

Niort

Ariège R.

Aude R.

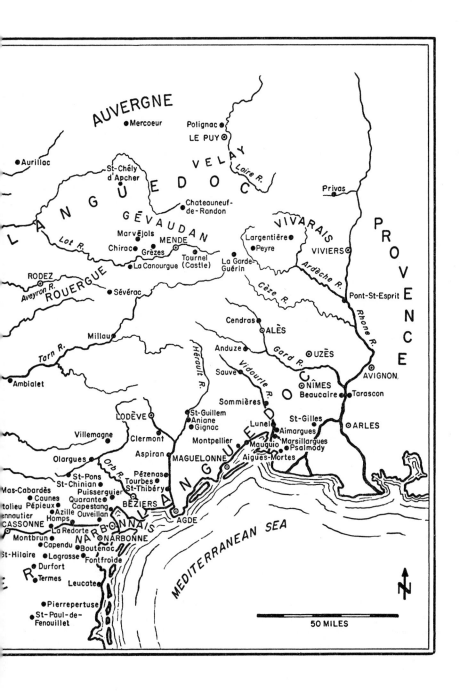

Early representation in France has not yet received adequate attention from an administrative point of view.[10] French historians have never wholly abandoned their original disposition to emphasize the powers of assemblies. Once it had been realized that the national assemblies called by Philip the Fair were consultative and not constitutional,[11] interest shifted to a later period. Similar con-

[10] Professors J. R. Strayer and C. H. Taylor have pointed the way in their *Studies in Early French Taxation* (Cambridge, Mass., 1939), emphasizing problems of government, and then determining how various national, regional, and local assemblies were used to solve them; see also Taylor's articles on French assemblies of the early 14th century in *Speculum*, xiii (1938), 295–303; xiv (1939), 275–299; and xxix (1954), 433–459; and Post, "Plena Potestas and Consent," 379ff. See too, in the same connection, R. Fawtier, "Parlement d'Angleterre et États Généraux de France au Moyen-Age," *Académie des Inscriptions & Belles-Lettres, Comptes Rendus*, 1953, esp. pp. 276–279. Strayer, Taylor, and Fawtier are all concerned with the peculiar and decisive tension between centralization and provincialism in France.

[11] There are no recent comprehensive works on these assemblies, which were much studied for more than a century after the Revolution: see the bibliography in P. Viollet, *Histoire des Institutions Politiques et Administratives de la France*, 3 vols. (Paris, 1890–1903), iii, 245. The first important books were E. Boutaric, *Les Premiers États Généraux, 1302–1314* (Paris, 1860); and H. Hervieu, *Recherches sur les Premiers États Généraux et les Assemblées Représentatives Pendant la Première Moitié du Quatorzième Siècle* (Paris, 1879); a still useful introduction is C. V. Langlois, "États Généraux," *La Grande Encyclopédie*, xvi, 510–523. The principal documents, mostly letters of summons and procurations, were printed by G. Picot, *Documents Relatifs aux États Généraux et Assemblées Réunis sous Philippe le Bel* (Paris, 1901). It is now clear that the king used these assemblies in his national emergencies to influence and consolidate public opinion; but when taxation was involved, negotiations for grants proceeded locally. For recent opinion, besides the works cited in previous note, see Lot and Fawtier, *Institutions Françaises*, ii, 550–557 (this passage occurs in a chapter entitled "le Contrôle [i.e., of the Monarchy] par les Assemblées"). The wholly negative results of

siderations diverted attention from the courts and local assemblies of the thirteenth century. To French writers, representation meant assemblies of Estates, and on this basis they devoted themselves assiduously to descriptive analysis of the Estates-General and provincial Estates from the time of their organization in the fourteenth century.[12] Many of them accepted as a working hypothesis, if only implicitly, the definition of provincial Estates given by Léon Cadier in 1888: "la réunion des trois ordres d'une province en assemblée regulièrement constituée, périodiquement convoquée, et possédant certaines attributions politiques et administratives dont la principale est le vote de l'impôt." [13]

M. Parent, "Les Assemblées Royales en France au Temps de Saint Louis," *École Nationale des Chartes: Positions des Thèses . . . de 1939*, pp. 155–161, followed naturally from the conception that assemblies must be constitutional bodies.

[12] The major account of the Estates-General is Picot's *Histoire des États Généraux Considérés au Point de Vue de leur Influence sur le Gouvernement de la France de 1355–1614*, 4 vols. (Paris, 1872; 2d ed., 1888). There are many works on the regional Estates; some of the more important titles may be found in libraries under the following names: L. Cadier (Béarn), J. Billioud (Burgundy), A. Thomas (central France), A. Coville and H. Prentout (Normandy), and É. Delcambre (Velay). For Languedoc see works by Dognon and Gilles, cited below, nn. 25, 38. A convenient bibliography of the Estates may be found in É. Lousse, *La Société d'Ancien Régime, Organisation et Représentation Corporatives*, I, nouv. éd. (Louvain, 1952), 10–11. Professor J. R. Major is reworking the whole field of the French Estates: see his books on *Representative Institutions in Renaissance France, 1421–1559* and *The Deputies to the Estates General in Renaissance France* (Madison, 1960); other volumes are promised.

[13] *Les États de Béarn* (Paris, 1888), p. 1; cf. Prentout, *Les États Provinciaux de Normandie*, 3 vols. (Caen, 1925–1927), who justly evaluates this idea as it relates to the question of origins (I, 35–36) but then introduces his own subject with an implicit acceptance of it (though in a suitably flexible form, I, 38–82); cf. R. Busquet, "La Provence," in Lot and Fawtier, *Institutions Françaises*, I (Paris, 1957), 257.

The origins of such assemblies were generally sought in the immediate circumstances of their establishment.

Only in one sense have scholars recognized—or been unable to deny—that assemblies of the twelfth and thirteenth centuries have significance in the history of French representation. This was the period when representative elements began to appear occasionally in feudal and royal courts. The old theory that the Estates were in line of descent from these expanded courts may be hard to demonstrate, but it is even harder to disprove. This idea still prevails, though sometimes in modified form.[14] Recently Professor G. I. Langmuir has given reasons for doubting that Capetian courts had the institutional identity which has been attributed to them.[15] Yet even if this is so, and even if it holds true for provincial "courts" as well, one might still argue that later attendance in Estates was derived from the feudal obligation of counsel.[16]

Certain studies that are more concerned with law and theory than assemblies have also directed attention to the age before the Estates. Some of these have shown that ideas both constitutional and authoritarian were being worked out in the two laws as the thirteenth century dawned, and that these ideas were soon influencing ecclesiastical prac-

[14] See, e.g., M. Bloch, "Pour une Histoire Comparée des Sociétés Européennes," *Revue de Synthèse Historique*, XLVI (1928), 27; Major, *The Estates General of 1560* (Princeton, 1951), p. 3; R. Busquet, in (Lot and Fawtier) *Institutions Françaises*, I, 257; cf. F. Olivier-Martin, *Histoire du Droit Français* (1948), pp. 223–224, 365, 393.

[15] G. I. Langmuir, "Counsel and Capetian Assemblies," *Études Présentées à la Commission Internationale pour l'Histoire des Assemblées d'États*, XVIII (1958), 21–34; see also his " 'Judei Nostri' and the Beginning of Capetian Legislation," *Traditio*, XVI (1960), 203–239, which has the importance, among other things, of suggesting that much work remains to be done on Capetian consultation and consent in the 13th century.

[16] As Olivier-Martin seems to think, *Droit Français*, p. 365.

tice. Just how they came to affect secular institutions remains one of the difficult questions in the investigation of medieval representation.[17] Then there is the work of the historians sometimes spoken of as the "corporatists." They have been examining the evidence for emergent juridical estates in order to determine a point of transition from the "individualism" of feudalism to the "corporate state" in which representation flourished.[18] This approach, whatever its defects, has the merit of recognizing how political centralization and specialization worked to create new *cadres* and new administrative instruments for the confrontation of prince and community.[19] Moreover, the corporatists, like the specialists on written law, rightly treat the rise of representation as an international European phenomenon. A generation ago Marc Bloch suggested that it would be well to study the history of representation comparatively,[20] and the legal and corporatist work constitutes

[17] See works of Post cited above, notes 5 and 9. I do not mean to deny that his studies go far toward answering this question.

[18] See É. Lousse, "Parlementarisme ou Corporatisme? Les Origines des Assemblées d'États," *Revue Hist. Droit Franç. et Étranger* (cited hereafter as *R.H.D.F.É.*), XIV (1935), 683–706; *La Société d'Ancien Régime*, I (nouv. éd.); G. de Lagarde, "Individualisme et Corporatisme au Moyen Age," in *L'Organisation Corporative du Moyen Age à la Fin de l'Ancien Régime: Études Présentées à la Commission Internationale pour l'Histoire des Assemblées d'États,* II (1937), 1–59; and numerous other works printed in this and other volumes of the same series.

[19] See, e.g., Lousse, *Société d'Ancien Régime*, I (nouv. éd.), esp. 95–97; cf. Strayer, "The Laicization of French and English Society in the Thirteenth Century," *Speculum,* XV (1940), esp. 80–85.

[20] Bloch, "Pour une Histoire Comparée," *Rev. Synth. Hist.,* XLVI (1928), 27–29. The work of other historians was pointing independently to the same need at about the same time: e.g., Richardson, "The Origins of Parliament," *Trans. Royal Hist. Society,* 4th ser., XI (1928), 137–183; Stephenson, "Taxation and Representation in the Middle Ages" (1929, *loc. cit.*); McIlwain, "Medieval Estates," in *Camb. Med. Hist.,* VII (1932).

the best response to that requirement yet to appear. But we are still lacking the factual basis for a sound general account of early assemblies. Bloch himself knew this, and with the characteristic injunction that the wider scene be kept in view, he called for more research on local problems.[21] Much remains to be done today. The study of local developments should be especially illuminating in a country like France, where mature representative institutions were organized chiefly at the provincial level.

From a comparative standpoint, it would be curious to find that France had no history of assemblies and representation in the thirteenth century. The remarkable Cortes of Spain can be traced in their representative character to the twelfth century, for as early as 1188 we hear of the addition of town delegates to the usual curial groups of clergy and nobles in Leon. During the next century similar assemblies appeared in the other peninsular kingdoms. In Italy town magistrates occasionally attended imperial diets from the 1150's. By the early years of the thirteenth century, the pope (Innocent III) was calling empowered deputies of cities to his Curia to provide counsel, swear fealty, and accept papal enactments. Frederick II instituted general courts of prelates, nobles, and town delegations in his Italian provinces in 1234. For Germany there is sporadic evidence of communities of vassals and towns, which convened in local assemblies, and sometimes held a balance against their overlords.[22]

Older discussions of parliamentary origins in France drew attention to numerous "feudal assemblies" attended

[21] "Pour une Histoire Comparée," 27–29. See also Post, "Roman Law and Early Representation in Spain and Italy," *Speculum,* xviii (1943), 211–232; a good comparative survey of medieval representative institutions, avowedly provisional, may be found in Fawtier's *L'Europe Occidentale de 1270 à 1380,* pt. 1 (Paris, 1940), pp. 233–259.

[22] McIlwain, in *Camb. Med. Hist.,* vii, 696–697, 704–706.

by men of the several orders from the eleventh to the thirteenth century.[23] Most of those assemblies that included townsmen had occurred in southern France, a fact which Achille Luchaire attributed to the relative importance of the urban element in the Midi throughout the Middle Ages.[24] Some of these gatherings were obviously of considerable interest as precedents, and they have been mentioned regularly in standard works: Simon de Montfort's "parliament" of Pamiers in 1212, in which townsmen joined prelates and barons in approving an important regional settlement; a meeting of nobility and town magistrates of Agenais in 1263 to deliberate on the local coinage; and, most important, a series of assemblies attended by individuals and delegates of the three orders in the *sénéchaussées* of Beaucaire and Carcassonne between 1258 and 1275; there have been references to various other meetings.[25] These assemblies have never been studied in detail, either individually, or in connection with other assemblies and administrative institutions of the Midi.

[23] See the list compiled by A. Callery, "Les Premiers États Généraux, Origine, Pouvoirs et Attributions," *Revue des Questions Historiques*, XXIX (1881), 111–117, from older and often uncritical accounts (I have found mistaken, for example, his notation of a general assembly of Rouergue in 1243).

[24] "Une Théorie Récente sur l'Origine des États-Généraux," *Annales de la Faculté des Lettres de Bordeaux*, III–IV (1881–1882), 55–56. Luchaire was criticizing Callery's argument that the Estates were the logical and juridical outgrowth of "legislative" Capetian assemblies that approved progressive alterations in the rigidly contractual framework of feudal law. The discrediting of this view, which Callery put in rather extreme terms, probably helped to turn attention away from the 13th century.

[25] Viollet, *Institutions*, III, 180; É. Chénon, *Histoire Générale du Droit Français Public et Privé* . . . , 2 vols. (Paris, 1926–1929), I, 827–828; P. Dognon, *Les Institutions Politiques et Administratives du Pays de Languedoc du XIIIᵉ Siècle aux Guerres de Religion* (Toulouse, 1895), pp. 195–201; A. Fliche, "L'État Toulousain," in (Lot and Fawtier) *Institutions Françaises*, I, 89, 95.

Other facts, too, point to southern France as a region in which thirteenth-century assemblies and representation might profitably be examined. We find evidence there, on the one hand, of continuous feudal development, and on the other, of unprecedented political disruption. Scattered through the area were small communities of nobles, and even of towns. Some dioceses and *pays* included in larger feudal units evolved distinguishable central institutions of their own. Many districts, including Béarn, Comminges, Quercy, Albigeois, and Gévaudan, subsequently had their own Estates. Close study of the extreme southwest may some day illuminate the important question of the relationship between French and Spanish assemblies. Many years ago Léon Cadier showed that the viscounty of Béarn had a plenary court which even in the late twelfth century may occasionally have included town delegates.[26] We find indications of similar development in neighboring Bigorre; and the fact that these principalities shared with Aragon and Navarre a peculiar form of written custom, the *fors* (Spanish: *fueros*), suggests the possibility of mutual influence in the matter of assemblies in this "western Pyrenean world."[27] But no effort has been made to relate these courts to those of the Gascon seigneuries of Armagnac, Fézensac, Fézensaguet, and Lomagne, although there is evidence that the latter assemblies likewise included townsmen in the thirteenth century.[28]

In Languedoc, to the east, this feudal evolution seems to have been less precocious, but in other respects we have there a field of investigation both more complex and more instructive. It was in this area that those unusual southern

[26] *États de Béarn*, pp. 51–63.
[27] *Ibid.*, pp. 19–24, 31; see P. Tucoo-Chala, "Les Institutions de la Vicomté de Béarn (X⁰–XV⁰ Siècles)," in (Lot and Fawtier) *Institutions Françaises*, I, 323.
[28] Dognon, *Institutions de Languedoc*, p. 196.

assemblies, mentioned above as interesting but unstudied precedents, took place. There too we can observe the institutions of important lordships, notably the county of Toulouse and the viscounties of Béziers and Narbonne, during the period when they lost their autonomy and power. The independent development of Gascony and the southwest may be attributed in part to the continued immunity of that area from the authority of the French crown; whereas to Languedoc the thirteenth century brought the Albigensian crusade, with its stern heritage of royal conquest. By dealing with this region in transformation, it is possible not only to observe the normal state of its feudal assemblies, but also to consider the possible influences of native institutions on the practices of an externally imposed administration; furthermore, it provides an opportunity to examine the earliest royal assemblies in the Midi.

The proximity of Languedoc to the springs of revived Roman law may be thought to be a special key to the rise of representation there.[29] Montpellier in the twelfth century, and Toulouse, in the thirteenth, became important centers for the teaching of law.[30] Trained lawyers occupied an increasingly exalted position in the public life of Languedoc.[31] Roman law, with its characteristic procedures and precision

[29] See Post, "Roman Law and Early Representation in Spain and Italy," 213ff.

[30] See É. Jarriand, "L'Évolution du Droit Écrit dans le Midi de la France," *Rev. Quest. Hist.*, XLVIII (1890), 208–209.

[31] They were often called upon as arbiters, e.g., *Gallia Christiana* . . . , 16 vols. (Paris, 1715–1865), XIII, *inst.*, 38–40; *I.A.C., Narbonne, Annexes de la Série BB*, ed. G. Mouynès (Narbonne, 1879), II, i, 1–6; or for advice, *Layettes*, III, no. 3939; A.M. Albi, FF.14, no. 1. No need to cite the numerous appearances of lawyers in charter witness lists. Cf. A. Gouron, ". . . Pénétration du Droit Romain au XII° Siècle dans l'Ancienne Septimanie," *Annales du Midi*, LXIX (1957), 108–116.

of documentary formulas, worked its way into regional custom, though less rapidly than is sometimes supposed.[32] By the turn of the thirteenth century, some of the leading towns were at least occasionally being regarded as corporations. In 1206 the magistrates and community of Montpellier employed an "actor seu syndicus" for litigation.[33] The next year a bishop of Saint-Bertrand-de-Comminges granted his townsmen the right to appoint syndics.[34] Evidently a corporate theory adequate for a sophisticated form of municipal representation in assemblies was already understood. This theory was developing apace in ecclesiastical communities,[35] as were, presumably, the related notions of legal rights, corporate decision, and consent. A comprehensive Roman-canonical law of procedure was taking

[32] *Lo Codi*, a 12th-century Provencal *summa* of the *Code*, must have facilitated the reception of Roman law in the Midi. Several times translated, it had measurable influence on the *fors* of Béarn. See the edition of the *dauphinois* text by L. Royer and A. Thomas, *Notices et Extraits des Manuscrits . . .* , XLII (1933), 1–138; and P. Rogé, *Les Anciens Fors de Béarn . . .* (Toulouse, 1908). Examples of renunciations of Roman *exceptiones,* and Roman arbitration, are legion in documents of Languedoc. But H. Richardot, "Le Fief Roturier à Toulouse aux XIIe et XIIIe Siècles," *R.H.D.F.É.*, 4e sér., XIV (1935), 310–311, has shown that formulas from the revived Roman law are not clearly traceable in documents relating to land tenure in the Toulouse area before the second half of the 13th century.

[33] *H.L.,* VIII, 534–538.

[34] *I.A.D., Haute-Garonne, Série E. Supplément,* ed. F. Pasquier (Toulouse, 1913), p. 6.

[35] *Archives Municipales d'Agen: Chartes d'Agen, Première Série (1189–1328)*, eds. A. Magen, G. Tholin (Villeneuve-sur-Lot, 1876), no. 4; *Cartulaire et Archives . . . de Carcassonne,* ed. M. Mahul, 6 vols. in 7 (Paris, 1857–1882), V, 552, 554, 556–557, 560; VI, ii, 393–394; etc. For canonist theory see O. Gierke, *Das Deutsche Genossenschaftsrecht,* 4 vols. (Berlin, 1868–1913), III, 336–342. For representation in civil procedure in Languedoc in the mid-13th century, see Nepos de Montauban, *De Exceptionibus Liber . . .* (Lyon, 1577), pp. 40–75.

shape,[36] and it was maneuvering into position to affect secular and customary practice. On the other hand, there is much to suggest the continuity of informal patterns of activity.[37] Not until the reign of Louis IX does formal corporate procuration become common in Languedoc. Even then older modes of representation continued. Other legal tenets corresponded to points of customary or practical wisdom. It will be seen that the effect of Roman-canonical theory on practice is not always very easy to measure.

The foregoing considerations explain the present book. It is an account of the origins of representation in Languedoc; but it is not, except incidentally, a study of the origins of Estates in Languedoc.[38] My interest is not to determine whether assemblies of the thirteenth century resemble the later Estates, but rather to see what was new and notable about them in their own age. The main emphasis is placed

[36] See the treatises on procedure edited by L. Wahrmund, *Quellen zur Geschichte des Römisch-Kanonischen Processes im Mittelalter*, 5 vols. (Innsbruck, 1905–1931), esp. *Summa Minorum* of Arnulph, *"Curialis," Rhetorica Ecclesiastica* (I, ii, iii, iv), and *Summa Aurea* of William of Drogheda (II, ii).

[37] Informal representation shown by chapter records at Nîmes, A.D. Gard, G.245; G.300, nos. 63, 30, 36; etc.; and Toulouse, A.D. Haute-Garonne, 4G239, xxx,3; 4G230, xxvii,4,1; 4G233, xxviii,8; etc. For abbeys, A.D. Tarn, H.7, last piece; *H.L.* VIII, 1595–1596,ii, *et passim*.

[38] For this distinction, see my essay on "The General Court of Agenais in the Thirteenth Century," *Speculum*, XXXVI (1961), 254–281. On the beginnings of the Estates of Languedoc, see H. Gilles, "Les États de Languedoc au XVᵉ Siècle," *École . . . des Chartes: Positions des Thèses . . . 1952*, pp. 51–54.

The word "represent," in its various forms, is used in different ways in this book, as it is in common parlance (cf., e.g., pp. 45–46, 152, 304). The reader who is attentive to the context will not find, I trust, that the word is misused. In its most precise sense, "representation" means conscious deputations by individuals and communities, especially the latter.

on the administration of regional assemblies: the uses and functions of meetings summoned by lords and kings, or their deputies, in districts larger than towns. Within this scope two topics receive special attention: the power of summons and the introduction of corporate deputations into assemblies. The latter is the key element in the beginnings of French representation. The summons is an important factor too, but thus far it has been largely overlooked by historians of assemblies. This may be one reason why the earliest period of continental representation remains so little understood. If some of the "assemblies" here discussed do not seem like assemblies to readers, I can only suggest that medieval governors probably had a less restricted conception of assemblies than we do. For the same reason, the study is not limited to gatherings of men of two or more orders: assemblies of nobles alone, or of town delegates, are likewise significant as administrative phenomena, and they have an important later history in France.[39] I try, wherever possible, to define local communities and spheres of political interest, not in order to find Estates where none exist, but rather to explain the composition of assemblies. While attendance is examined for general characteristics, the lack of comprehensive social histories usually prevents very thorough analyses of composition. The legal ideas of rights, representation, the summons, counsel, and consent are treated only as they are found in practice or in law known to have been in effect. References to theory are given in a few places where it seems pertinent, but otherwise this subject is excluded. I trust that this approach does not unduly underestimate the importance of what men thought, or may have thought, they were doing.

In geographical scope, this book deals with most of

[39] Little studied as yet, but see the articles by C. H. Taylor, cited above, n. 10.

historical Languedoc.[40] The term "Languedoc" refers to the region delimited roughly by the Rhone River, the Mediterranean, the western side of the Garonne valley, Quercy, and Auvergne. The feudal county of Toulouse was centered in the western part of this area,[41] in the rolling country of the middle Garonne, which, with the hills to the north and east, is sometimes spoken of as "upper" Languedoc. Included in the county of Toulouse were five distinct districts with traditions of unity that had come down from the early Middle Ages. These were the dioceses of Toulouse, Albi, Rodez (Rouergue), Cahors (Quercy), and Agen. We find the word "pays" (*patria*) [42] used frequently to refer to them, particularly in documents dating from the earlier years of the period under consideration; and it should also be noted that "dioecesis" was a secular administrative designation as well as an ecclesiastical one. In the first half of the thirteenth century the counts of Toulouse instituted seneschals in these districts, which thereafter, even under changed lordship, continued to be administered and denoted as *sénéchaussées*; but this usage did not supersede the other appellations. Agenais lay at the western limit of Languedoc, or beyond it, and its institu-

[40] For the following paragraphs, see generally A. Longnon, *Atlas Historique de la France* (Paris, 1912), plates 12, 13; and A. Molinier, "Sur la Géographie de la Province de Languedoc au Moyen Age," *H.L.*, XII, esp. 225ff., 312–346.

[41] The *comtat* Venaissin (marquisate of Provence) on the Rhone, a Toulousan dependency, was administered separately and is excluded from this study; see E. Boutaric, *Saint Louis et Alfonse de Poitiers* (Paris, 1870), pp. 65, 68, 141–142, 179. In the 12th century the counts (called Counts of St-Gilles) had focussed their political attentions on the east, but by 1200, the western domains were again taking precedence; see Y. Dossat, "Le Comté de Toulouse et la Féodalité Languedocienne à la Veille de la Croisade Albigeoise," *Revue du Tarn*, n.s., IX (1943), reprint, 6–8.

[42] See G. Dupont-Ferrier, "De Quelques Synonymes du Terme 'Province' dans le Langage Administratif de l'Ancienne France," *R.H.*, CLXI (1929), 282–283, 286.

tions conformed to the Gascon pattern in many respects. But it is included in this study because it belonged to the county of Toulouse during most of the thirteenth century. I sometimes use the expression "western Languedoc" in reference to the belt of lands running roughly northwest up the Aude River and down the Garonne. The Aude valley, dominated by the houses of Béziers and Narbonne before the crusade, became the *sénéchaussée* of Carcassonne in 1226 at the royal conquest. The suzerainty of Toulouse, and, later, of the crown extended over the important principalities of Foix, Comminges, Astarac, and Lomagne,[43] which are mentioned in that connection; but their internal histories lie beyond my limits.

"Lower" or coastal Languedoc, an area encompassing the viscounties of Béziers, Narbonne, and Nîmes, was subject to Toulousan overlordship, with competition from Aragon, in the early thirteenth century. The right bank of the Rhone was a political complex of small baronies, where, along with Toulouse and Aragon, the Empire claimed certain rights of suzerainty. There were three important territories in northeastern Languedoc, the dioceses of Mende (Gévaudan), Viviers (Vivarais), and Le Puy (Velay).[44] Besides these cities, the important towns of the east were Montpellier, Nîmes, Beaucaire, Uzès, and Alès. This area was organized as the *sénéchaussée* of Beaucaire after the conquest of Languedoc.[45] Imperial power declined during the thirteenth century, and Aragon lost virtually all but its lordship over Montpellier.

[43] Though not necessarily over all of them at the same time, or in the same degree for each; the statement applies best to the period after about 1240.

[44] The dioceses did not always correspond exactly to the territories, the original *pagi*: see Molinier, "Géographie de Languedoc," *H.L.*, xii, 169–171, 219–221.

[45] See R. Michel, *L'Administration Royale dans la Sénéchaussée de Beaucaire au Temps de Saint Louis* (Paris, 1910), pp. 1–19.

Apart from the crusade and royal conquest, two events chiefly determine the chronological divisions of this study: the acquisition of the county of Toulouse in 1249 by Alfonse of Poitiers, the king's brother, and the transfer of that county to the king himself, when Alfonse and his wife died without heirs in 1271. Developments in the reigns of Philip III and Philip IV are treated in a final chapter. But no detailed account is given of the general royal assemblies that began to meet in 1302–1303 in consequence of national issues. They are not unknown, and they are a subject in themselves.

❧II❧ *Feudal and Provincial Assemblies* (1180-1271)

BEFORE THE ALBIGENSIAN CRUSADE

There were no assemblies associating the men of all or much of Languedoc before the crusade.[1] This was chiefly because Languedoc had little effective political unity at that time. No one lord was strong enough to impose his will on his vassals or his neighbors. The Toulousan domains and fiefs constituted the most extensive feudal system. Count Raymond VI (1194–1222) was theoretically entitled to summon men from places as far separated as Agenais, Foix, and Provence. In practice, however, he was quite unable to hold his feudatories together in any unified territorial politics. A "Toulousan state," such as had existed in the mid-twelfth century, was no longer a reality in 1200. The count's power had declined relatively if not absolutely.[2] The most serious opposition came from the kings of Aragon, whose aspirations in southern France enabled them to wean the seigneuries of Carcassonne, Foix, and Narbonne from support of Toulouse and bring them into their own sphere of influence. In 1204 Peter of Aragon got control of Montpellier by a fortunate marriage. This was, however, the high tide of his fortunes in the Midi. A balance was achieved between king and count in which the

[1] For general narrative of events in the period covered by this chapter, see Vaissete's account in *H.L.*, VI, and P. Belperron's *La Croisade contre les Albigeois et l'Union du Languedoc à la France, 1209–1249* (Paris, 1942).

[2] For want of study of the acts after 1194, this is not yet wholly clear. See A. Fliche, "L'État Toulousain," in (Lot and Fawtier) *Institutions Françaises*, I, 73–88; J. H. Mundy, *Liberty and Political Power in Toulouse, 1050–1230* (N.Y., 1954), p. 59, *et passim*; Y. Dossat, "Comté de Toulouse et la Féodalité," 7–12.

latter obtained a lien on important Aragonese holdings in Rouergue and Gévaudan; he also received the homage of the viscount of Narbonne.[3] But the politics of Aragon had assured the power of Béziers-Carcassonne, an uncontrollable enclave in the Toulousan domains extending from Albi to the coast. The lower Rhone fiefs were virtually cut off from Toulouse, while the county holdings in Vivarais lay far across the mountains of upper Languedoc, and within those mountains the episcopal lands of Gévaudan were wholly independent of Toulouse. Even in the west the constituent Toulousan territories were lacking in common feudal experience.

The divisive effect of political factors was probably intensified by religious conflict. The cathar heresy, long existent in Languedoc, had evoked official ecclesiastical opposition from the 1160's. This heresy was concentrated geographically in the southern parts of the dioceses of Toulouse and Albi and throughout the diocese of Carcassonne. Viscount Roger II of Béziers (1167–1194) was quite certainly a partisan of the unorthodox doctrines, and he left the tutelage of his son to an undoubted cathar.[4] Raymond VI seems to have been more tolerant than unorthodox, and the same can perhaps be said of his nominal vassal, Raymond-Roger of Foix (1188–1223). But their position was sufficiently equivocal to hinder satisfactory relations and cooperation with the churchmen of their estates. It is tempting to offer a similar explanation for the absence

---

[3] *H.L.*, VI, 210–214; and A. Molinier in XII, 272–276. Aragon's new leadership in the early crusade years, definitively checked at Muret in 1213, can be explained by Raymond VI's desperation at that juncture.

[4] H. C. Lea, *A History of the Inquisition of the Middle Ages,* 3 vols. (N.Y., 1887–1888), I, 118–128; Belperron, *Croisade,* pp. 105–109; L. de Lacger, "L'Albigeois pendant la Crise de l'Albigéisme . . . ," *Revue d'Histoire Ecclésiastique,* XXIX (1933), 301–302.

of the unswervingly orthodox viscounts of Lautrec from the councils of their Toulousan lords.[5] Political and religious divisions helped to prevent the development of such general regional issues as might have encouraged the formation of a sizeable feudal community. Languedoc had not outgrown the localism of the early feudal age. There was no custom of all Languedoc (apart from the vague allegiance to principles of Roman law which it shared with the entire South); and there was no public law with an application extended much beyond the limits of the central town, barony, or *pays*.

Regional and local assemblies prior to the crusade must be sought within the various seigneuries, or, as in the case of Toulouse, within their constituent districts. Most assemblies can be explained by reference to feudal theory and administrative practices. In the Middle Ages, the feudal obligation of *consilium* was prevalent in Languedoc as elsewhere. This does not necessarily mean that we should speak of the feudal *curia* as a recognized institution.[6] The lords summoned; they took counsel; and the documents refer frequently to gatherings of the lords' advisers and favorites, supplemented on occasion by vassals and notables who presumably owed suit at court. In plenary form, these bodies—"courts" if not meetings of "the Court"—usually served purposes of justice and consultation. However, they were not so active as to develop specialized judicial and administrative organs, as happened in some other areas. Moreover, in most parts of Languedoc the word "curia" is

---

[5] The only such meeting that a viscount of Lautrec certainly attended in the two decades before the crusade was an extra-feudal assembly with regional clergy in 1191, discussed below, p. 107.

[6] As does A. Molinier, "Étude sur l'Administration Féodale dans le Languedoc (900–1250)," *H.L.*, vii, 144; see generally, for this view, A. Luchaire, *Manuel des Institutions*, pp. 201–203. I am, of course, considering the *curia* only as a judicial or political assembly, not as a social institution or household.

rarely used to describe feudal gatherings. Counsel is mentioned in recognitions and acts of homage, but often in a
rather formal way; it does not clearly appear that counsel
in the sense of obligatory suit was much insisted upon or
seriously regarded in the later twelfth and early thirteenth
centuries. The charters speak of *consilium et auxilium* [7] and
the vassal's support *in guerris et placitis*.[8] And while a distinction between "aid and advice" or between "war and
plea" seems always to be implied, the feudal summons in
Languedoc had a predominantly military character. A
document of 1165 says that a vassal summoned to court
should bring his knights, as if he were going to war.[9] In
1204 the viscount of Narbonne promises the count of
Toulouse "counsel and aid in suits and wars against all men
and women in the world." [10] The lord of Anduze tells
another count of Toulouse in 1224 that he will perform
"war and plea for you and your successors against all
men." [11] Not all acts, it is true, were so abbreviated and
stereotyped. We find a wordy recognition of homage to the
abbot of Lagrasse in 1208 which distinguishes clearly
between military and conciliar service, and even between

---

[7] *H.L.*, vIII 441–442, 490, 666; A.N., JJ.13, fol. 41v (acts of
years 1197–1218).

[8] *H.L.*, vIII, 335, 695; *Le Fonds Thésan aux Archives . . . de
Léran*, eds. F. Pasquier, S. Olive (Montpellier, 1913), p. 72; *Layettes*, II, nos. 1658, 1680 (acts of 1179–1224).

[9] Molinier, *H.L.*, vII, 144; he also cites a Spanish piece of 987
(*ibid.*, v, 303) that speaks of a lord and vassals as *commilitones*;
see also P. Guilhiermoz, *Essai sur l'Origine de la Noblesse en
France au Moyen Age* (Paris, 1902 [1960]), pp. 247–248, 255ff.;
cf. F. L. Ganshof, *Feudalism*, tr. P. Grierson, 2nd Eng. ed. (N.Y.,
1961), pp. 87–93.

[10] *Layettes*, I, no. 709.

[11] *Ibid.*, II, no. 1658: "quod guerram et placitum pro vobis et
successoribus vestris contra omnes homines faciam."

judgment and advice; it also speaks explicitly of a feudal *curia*.[12] But this is quite exceptional.

When the count of Toulouse's court is mentioned, it usually appears as a delegated, local, and specialized tribunal. Disputes and other judicial business not settled privately wound up ordinarily in the regular courts of the vicars and bayles.[13] It must have been rare for magnates to attend these courts as vassals, although one text seems to mean that they did.[14] We find only one example of a major feudal issue that came before a tribunal of great men. This was a dispute of about 1201 between the counts of Toulouse and Foix over the latter's homage for the fortified town of Saverdun. It was settled at Toulouse—"in curia Tolosana"—by a panel of judges who were mostly prominent nobles of western Languedoc: Count Bernard of Comminges, seven knights of the Toulousain-Foix region, and several notables of Toulouse. This attendance can be explained by the exigencies of the case, with which most of the judges were familiar.[15] Only in the loosest sense was

[12] *Ibid.*, I, no. 852: ". . . et deffensionem contra omnes homines. . . . Et si vocati essemus, ego vel aliquis de dominis de Termino, ab abbate Crasse, debebamus venire sine mora ad ejus curiam et interesse, si ipse abbas vellet, judiciis et consiliis ejus, et ei obedire et servire ibi, sicuti domino."

[13] On the vicar's court at Toulouse, see Mundy, *Toulouse*, pp. 37–38, 100–103; the court of the comital bayle at Le Caylar is mentioned in *Layettes*, I, no. 708 (1204); cf. Molinier, "L'Administration Féodale," *H.L.*, VII, 196–199; E. Boutaric, "Organisation Judiciaire du Languedoc au Moyen Age." *B.É.C.*, XVI (1855), 207–211.

[14] *H.L.*, VIII, 443, comital privilege of 1197 for clergy of Nîmes: ". . . ut quandocumque in curia nostra coram nobis vel vicariis & baronibus nostris . . . placitare voluerint. . . ."

[15] *H.L.*, VIII, 267–271. In July 1201 Raymond VI granted Saverdun to Arnaud de Villemur (*Layettes*, I, no. 612), probably in consequence of the count of Foix's refusal to recognize Toulousan suzerainty (see *H.L.*, VI, 193–194); hence the *placitum* at Toulouse. Four of the judges had witnessed the enfeoffment in July, which took place at Montbrun, in Toulousain.

this a court of peers.[16] There is no other evidence of county nobility assembled in judicial session in this period.[17] The personal retinue of the count was sometimes supplemented by local clergy and nobles to witness his acts or to solemnize important transactions. In these meetings the Raymonds were acting as regional or local seigneurs—as counts of Toulousain, or overlords of Rouergue or Alès, for example.[18] In October 1190 Raymond V and the abbot of Aurillac entered upon agreements whereby the abbot was to receive the count's support, especially against his rebellious townsmen in Aurillac, in exchange for the cession of territorial rights in Albigeois. The pact was concluded at Capdenac, on the borders of Quercy and Rouergue, in the presence of many lay and ecclesiastical notables of those districts. Among them were the count and the bishop of Rodez, the viscount of Saint-Antonin, the prior of Capdenac, and Bernard d'Arpajon, an important knight of Rouergue. They and some twenty others may be classified roughly as followers of either the count or the abbot; and it may be remarked in passing that other such witness lists

---

[16] Mundy, *Toulouse*, pp. 143, 353, n. 43, argues that this case shows that the principle of trial by peers was recognized in Toulouse. Molinier, *H.L.*, vii, 207, is quite mistaken in saying that the judges are termed *pares* in the document. B. C. Keeney finds little evidence of judgment by peers in the Midi, *Judgment by Peers* (Cambridge, Mass., 1949), p. 13.

[17] Private agreement and arbitration were probably common even in major feudal issues. We find the count of Toulouse in the 1190's, as *dominus de unoquoque eorum*, arbitrating disputes between the count of Comminges and Jourdain de l'Isle, *H.L.*, viii, 408–411.

[18] That is to say, men in these regions were within their sphere of influence, if not actually vassals. For lack of evidence it is often impossible to say whether any particular knight of late 12th-century Languedoc was bound to the regional overlord by precisely defined bonds of homage and fidelity. In most cases it is probably safer to assume that they existed. By the second quarter of the 13th century, lords were trying to get feudal obligations in writing.

could be similarly analyzed.[19] The viscount of Saint-Antonin and another knight present, Pons de Saint-Privat, had attended another meeting of nobles held by the count of Toulouse in Albigeois in the same year, and they were possibly both vassals of the county.[20] Count Hugo of Rodez, and probably the bishop too, were vassals of Raymond V for rights and properties in Rouergue.[21] Raymond VI was in Rouergue in later years trying to extend his territorial control in that direction. In April 1204 he received the rights to Millau and parts of Gévaudan from the king of Aragon, a notable transaction which was the occasion for an assembly of nobles and townsmen at Millau. The instrument of mutual recognition preserves the names of *curiales* and professional men in the count's retinue and of some followers of the king.[22] But according to testimony given many years later, Count Guillaume of Rodez, "many other knights and barons," and townsmen of Millau were gathered together at some point of the proceedings.[23] In March 1208 the bishop and the count of Rodez engaged important demesne rights to Raymond VI in the presence of regional clergy and nobility.[24]

Numerous meetings of the same sort occurred in eastern Languedoc, at Montpellier, Nîmes, Uzès, Pont-St-Esprit,

[19] *Layettes*, I, no. 374. See also *H.L.*, VIII, 307, an act recording guarantees made to the viscount of Nîmes by the count of Toulouse about 1174 before 21 named witnesses "& multi alii tam de terra comitis quam de terra vicecomitis"; also col. 598.

[20] *H.L.*, VIII, 404–405. This assembly is discussed below, p. 33.

[21] At least they were vassals in 1208, when Raymond VI visited Rouergue, *Layettes*, I, nos. 839, 840; cf. Molinier, *H.L.*, XII, 273.

[22] *H.L.*, VIII, 518–522. The identity of the count's men can be determined by checking the index of *ibid.* The list is incomplete.

[23] *Layettes*, V, no. 558, an *enquête* of 1251 on the comital *pezade* at Millau in which the witness remembered the count's promise, when he received title to the town from the king of Aragon about 45 years before, "ut extimat," to hold the town free from *tailles* and exactions.

[24] *Ibid.*, I, nos. 839, 840.

and elsewhere.[25] Western knights were not normally summoned to the Rhone area, but some of the more notable eastern barons, like the lords of Sauve and Uzès, may sometimes have followed the counts as they moved about the Rhone valley.[26] Nowhere in the county are these assemblies called "courts," and it is evident that their composition was determined as much by the availability of local notables as by the feudal obligation of suit. Often they were gatherings of witnesses to acts of feudal recognition, homage, and fealty.[27]

In the more compact viscounty of Béziers-Carcassonne,[28] we find something much more like a central "court" or assembly of nobles. The spirited Roger II, continuously at odds with the count of Toulouse, was doubtless very dependent on the support of his regional knights. A number of great men seem to have been in attendance regularly, witnessing his acts and providing counsel.[29] The viscount's formal transfer of allegiance to Alfonse of Aragon in November 1179 took place at Carcassonne in the presence of his *barones* and *fideles*.[30] His ability to control the nobles

[25] *Ibid.*, no. 417 (probably at Montpellier; cf. *H.L.*, VIII, 400–402); *Layettes*, I, no. 844; *H.L.*, VIII, 591–592, 592–598, 590–591 (St-Gilles).

[26] See *H.L.*, VIII, 402, 427–429; no. 151, 591; 592.

[27] *Layettes*, I, no. 612, local knights of southern Toulousain attend the homage of Arnaud de Villemur to Raymond VI in 1201; no. 844, local officials and knights of Nîmes, notice of enfeoffment and fealty by Rostaing de Marguerittes in 1208; also *H.L.*, VIII, 591–592, at Uzès; etc.

[28] Theoretically two viscounties administered by one lord (who also held titles to Razès and Albi); see, e.g., *H.L.*, VIII, 467.

[29] E.g., Hugues de Roumengous, Bertrand de Saissac, Guillaume de St-Félix, Pierre-Raymond d'Hautpoul, *ibid.*, 278–279, 313–314, 339–340, 364; *Layettes*, I, no. 297.

[30] *Layettes*, I, nos. 297, 298. By a document of 2 November 1179, Petrus de Marca, *Marca Hispanica, sive Limes Hispanicus* . . . (Paris, 1638), *app.*, 1371–1372, we learn that *magnates terrae* swore to this pact.

is shown by two assemblies held in May 1191.[31] Gathering in *colloquium* "on the order of lord Roger" at Sauzens, a few miles west of Carcassonne, twenty-eight knights promised perpetual faith and support to the viscount's son and heir. Possibly this meeting-place was chosen in deference to the location of the knights, for most of them can be associated by their names with places to the west of Carcassonne.[32] Soon afterward, perhaps the same day, thirty-three other nobles swore to the same pact in the city of Carcassonne.

Roger II convoked another large assembly of nobles in March 1194. It approved his final testament and his plan for a council of regency. By the latter plan, the control of three districts of the viscounty was left in the hands of certain loyal notables. The bishop of Béziers, Étienne de Servian, Elzéar de Castries, and Déodat de Boussagues were responsible for domains in the dioceses of Béziers and Agde; the bishop of Albi, Guillaume Vassal, Bérenger de Bonfils de Lavaur, and Guillaume de Saint-Paul, for possessions in Albigeois, Rouergue, and Toulousain; while the vicars of Carcassonne and Razès were to care for Carcassonais, Razès, Termenais, and Lauragais.[33] From 1199 to 1205 the young viscount Raymond-Roger (1194–1209) acted a number of times with the "advice and volition" of his *proceres*. In August 1199 he granted to Étienne de Servian a certain building site in the environs of Béziers.[34] Early in 1201 the lord of Faugères obtained the castle of Lunas in fief and received pledges on a debt from the vis-

[31] *H.L.*, VIII, 411–412.

[32] E.g., Bertrand and Aymery-Olivier de Saissac, Arnaud-Raymond de Pennautier, Guillaume and Jourdain de St-Félix, Raymond-Arnaud de Vintron, Elesiarius (junior and senior), Arnaud and Pierre d'Aragon, Raymond de Niort, etc.

[33] *Ibid.*, VI, 153–155. Bertrand de Saissac was named tutor and the organization was to continue for five years. See also VIII 429–431.

[34] *Ibid.*, VIII, 453–454,iii.

count.[35] The latter authorized the canons of Béziers to fortify their churches in 1203, and in May of the next year he mortgaged his extensive rights over the canons for a large sum of money.[36] It is fairly clear that these consultative actions were in part a survival of the regency. The viscount had attained the age of majority by 1201, as acts of that year definitely state, but the names of individual regents continue to appear in the documents. In April 1201 Étienne de Servian, the bishop of Albi, the vicar of Carcassonne, and Guillaume Vassal were in attendance; and the latter three served as pledges for Raymond-Roger in an important feudal transaction a year later.[37]

On certain occasions the viscount referred explicitly to his feudal "court of barons," [38] and it is likely that some of the other meetings were also understood to be sessions of the court. They were sometimes of considerable size, for the

[35] *Ibid.*, 468–471,ii,iii.

[36] *Cartulaire de Béziers*, ed. J. Rouquette (Paris, 1918), pp. 513–518, 518–523.

[37] *H.L.*, viii, 468, 470–471,ii,iii; 473,i. The same vicars named in Roger's will were still in business in 1201–1202. No names are given at heads of the instruments of 1201, but since the witness lists are composed exclusively of names of great men in the viscounty, it is clear that they were the *proceres* mentioned. Cf. below, n. 52.

[38] *Cartulaire de Béziers*, p. 518 (May 1204): "sit manifestum quod ego Raimundus Rotgerius, vicecomes Biterris . . . consilio et voluntate baronum curie mee, scilicet Petri Rotgerii de *Cabaretz* vicarii Carcassensis, et Bernardi Pelapulli vicarii Biterrensis, et Amblardi Vassalli, et Guillelmi Bernardi, et Samuelis judei, bajuli et secretarii mei, et burgensium Biterris, scilicet Aimerici Bofati, et . . . [4 others], et aliorum quamplurimum, et omnium curialium curie mee deserviencium, pro magna et evidenti utilitate mea et totius vicecomitatus . . ."; pp. 513–518 (October 1203), reference to counsel and will "procerum curie mee, videlicet . . . et aliorum plurium curie mee baronum . . ."; see also *H.L.*, vi, 208, mention of the viscount's act in 1206 *"du conseil des grands de sa cour."* There was reference in 1194 to an act of Roger's court in 1185, *Gallia Christiana*, vi, *inst.*, 142–143.

regents were by no means the only men of the viscounty to assemble.[39] Four or five barons are named as attending and advising in the meetings of 1203 and 1204, but in each case "many more" unnamed were said to be present. Assemblies of 1185 and 1204 included townsmen of Béziers and *curiales* among whom, presumably, were lawyers and scribes. Other notables of the viscounty witnessed the solemn instruments that issued from these meetings and added weight to the decisions made in them. Béziers was apparently the usual place of assembly in this period.[40]

The viscounty of Narbonne also had central courts. They convened sometimes as judicial bodies to settle suits,[41] on other occasions to solemnize important seigneurial transactions.[42] In size and composition they varied considerably. Viscountess Ermengarde met with three judges-adjunct and others at Ouveillan in 1188 to settle a local dispute over marsh rights. Apart from the judges, one of whom (a *magister*) served in the same capacity on at least one other occasion, two men present can be identified as regional knights; a third was probably a local notable, while three others cannot be placed.[43] A somewhat larger court was held by Viscount Aymery III (1192–1239) at Narbonne in February 1203, when he made a major ecclesiastical donation. Eleven men are named and "many others" reported to be present. Unfortunately, the names given furnish few clues as to the place of origin or social posi-

---

[39] See n. 37 above.

[40] The assembly of 1185 convened in the church of St-Nazaire, Béziers. The place is not given in the other documents cited, but they were written by notaries of Béziers, and most of the negotiations concerned Béziers or the environs. The viscount's summons of vassals in 1209 is reported by Guillaume de Tudèle, *La Chanson de la Croisade Albigeoise*, ed. and tr. E. Martin-Chabot, 3 vols. (Paris, 1931–1961), i, 32, 44, 46.

[41] *H.L.*, viii, 390–391; 418–419,ii.

[42] *Ibid.*, 487–490,i-iii.   [43] *Ibid.*, 390–391, and index.

tion of those assembled. Only one of them is known to have attended the viscounts previously. Probably all were notables of Narbonne and the environs.[44] There was an important assembly in March 1204 to observe and approve the viscount's homage to Raymond VI of Toulouse. The meeting place was Capestang, a few miles northeast of Narbonne. Those in attendance included great prelates, notably the archbishop and the papal legate, three advisers of the viscount, knights, "good men" and "citizens" of Narbonne, as well as certain followers of the count of Toulouse.[45]

Less can be said about other baronies in Languedoc, time having dealt less kindly with their records. What we have suffices to show that there were occasional gatherings of vassals and notables for feudal and administrative purposes in many districts, including the bishoprics of Maguelonne and Nîmes, the lordships of Montpellier and Uzès, the county of Melgueil, and the viscounties of Nîmes, Saint-Antonin, and Lautrec.[46] A large assembly, described as a *comune colloquium,* convened at Montpellier in June 1204 when King Peter of Aragon recognized himself to be the bishop of Maguelonne's vassal for the lordship of Montpellier. Among those present were the counts of Toulouse and Provence, and the lords of Anduze and Orange; sixty-seven names are listed in the written act, but "very many others" are not.[47] Seigneurial instruments of Uzès speak of the "convocation" of witnesses. In 1205 the lord of Uzès

[44] *Ibid.,* 487–489,i. See also 489,ii.

[45] *Ibid.,* 489–490,iii.

[46] *Ibid.,* 522–523; *Layettes,* I, no. 330; *H.L.,* VIII, 303–305,iii (cf. *Layettes,* I, no. 935); *H.L.,* VIII, 530–531; 293–295; 400–402; 354–355,vi (cf. *Layettes,* I, no. 844, count of Toulouse acting as viscount of Nîmes in 1207); *Layettes,* I, no. 476; *H.L.,* VIII, 385–386,ii; etc. The counts of Toulouse held Melgueil from 1172, and Nîmes from 1187, VI, 48–49, 122–123.

[47] *H.L.,* VIII, 522–523 (*Layettes,* I, no. 718).

made a pious donation to the Carthusians of Vallebonne, and confirmed gifts by nobles described as "my feudal knights." This was done in the presence of knights and clergy, including a former bishop of Uzès and the papal legate.[48] But there is no clear evidence of baronial courts in these smaller fiefs.

In respect to their functions, the convocations of nobles and notables just discussed do not present very remarkable features. Most of them occurred because the lords found it useful to summon them. Their composition, in size and range, was consistent with the importance of the business at hand and the prestige of the seigneur or his title. Very rarely were assemblies of regional nobles organs of consent. The smaller seigneurial councils may have served occasionally as sounding boards for local complaints. But the great men of the *pays* formed no united front, and, except possibly in the viscounty of Béziers, they had no constitutional role. Nor do we often see them providing counsel, though inadequacy of the sources may be accountable for this. Counsel was less likely to be recorded than consent. The prevalent feudal imperatives regarding counsel as a way to wisdom were doubtless recognized in Languedoc, at least in some degree.

There remains a question about counsel and consent in the viscounty of Béziers. A reference to curial consent in 1185, when the viscount granted rights in Béziers city to Aragon, can hardly be mistaken.[49] This was an important enactment directly touching the interests of parties who were said explicitly to have given consent. But Raymond-Roger's acts *consilio et voluntate* from 1199 on are less easy to interpret. The terms recur at least five times, and

---

[48] *H.L.*, viii, 530–531,i,ii.

[49] *Gallia Christiana*, vi, *inst.*, 142–143. The act apparently remained inoperative until after Roger's death in 1194; see J. Azais, "De Roger II, Vicomte de Béziers . . . ," *Bull. Soc. Arch. Béziers*, i (1836), 51–66.

were probably not confused.[50] If nothing more, they suggest a responsible common solicitude on the part of the vassals for the viscounty at a serious juncture in its history. In March 1202 the young viscount pledged his fiefs to the count of Foix in case of his death without heirs, and while there was no formal notice of a consultation, many of the vassals were named as sureties.[51] In certain other acts the "advice and will" of the knights seem to express a concern for the integrity of the patrimony. In fact they were probably taking the initiative. *Voluntas* has a more positive connotation than *consensus*. It is hard to see how the viscount could have done without them in important matters. Legally, however, the clauses may signify no more than the continued advisory activity of the former regents. The viscount does sometimes act without their formal approval,[52] and the consultations may have been understood as a courtesy instead of a right.

On one or two other occasions, seigneurial actions involving the rights of notables of a particular area seem to have been the cause of their summons and collective consultation. About the year 1191 the count of Toulouse, the viscount of Béziers, and the bishop of Albi, who were coseigneurs of Albigeois, granted extensive judicial privileges to Cistercian abbeys of the region. They did this "with the counsel and assent of many noble men." Just who were

[50] *H.L.*, VIII, 453,iii; 468,ii; 470,iii; *Cartulaire de Béziers*, pp. 513, 518.

[51] *H.L.*, VIII, 473–474,i. In 1224 it was said that the pact had been made "in presentia domini Raimundi . . . comitis Tholosani [this is surely wrong: see 474,ii], & plurium aliorum virorum nobilium," 787.

[52] *Ibid.*, 467,i; 483–485; cf. 473–474,i. There was possibly some influence here of the Roman law of *auctoritatis interpositio* in tutelage. Cf. *C.* v, 59, 5, and W. Buckland, *A Manual of Roman Private Law*, 2nd ed. (Cambridge, 1953), pp. 97–99. *C.* I, 14, 8, on consultation with *proceres*, might also point to the recognition of some right to be consulted.

among the "many" is not made clear. The witness list, un-fortunately incomplete, includes the names of ten important regional notables, vassals or followers of one or the other of the contracting suzerains. Two knights present were with Raymond V at Capdenac in October 1190, two others figure subsequently as *curiales* of the viscount of Béziers, and there were two ecclesiastics of Albi.[53] Another event that affected the rights and interests of a considerable com-munity was Aymery's homage for the viscounty of Nar-bonne in 1204, which ended a long series of wars against the count of Toulouse. The viscount claimed to have acted with the counsel of great men, knights, "good men," and citizens of Narbonne. This group is distinguished from the large body of men "present and witnessing," including the legate and followers of Raymond VI, although the more notable men of Narbonne were among the witnesses too.[54] It is not clear that all of the Narbonne people were present in the meeting, which took place at Capestang, and doubt-ful that any large number of them influenced the viscount's decision. Yet, however constituted and whatever its role, the support of a community of Narbonne was invoked in an important political step. In most of Languedoc extraor-

---

[53] *H.L.*, viii, 404–405,i. The four knights mentioned were re-spectively Isarn de St-Antonin, Pons de St-Privat, Pierre-Ermen-gaud, and Sicard de Boissezon; see *ibid.*, index. The absence of Sicard de Lautrec from the list is conspicuous but not proof that he did not attend; cf. below, pp. 107–108, for his presence in an-other meeting of 1191.

[54] *Ibid.*, 489–490,iii: "habito consilio B. Narbonensis archiepi-scopo (*sic*) & B. Narbonensis archidiaconi & P. preceptoris Nar-bonensis & G. de Redorta & G. M[o]netarii & P. Raimundi de Bos, & militum ac proborum hominum & civium Narbonensium. . . ." G. Monetarii, G. de Redorta, and P. Raimundi de Bosco were witnesses. Several others can be identified as members of Ray-mond's company; consult names in index. Note also Viscount Roger's homage to the king of Aragon in November 1179, which was done in assembly, "laude et consilio baronum et fidelium hominum suorum . . . ," *Layettes,* i, no. 298.

dinary taxation was still unknown and general legislation very uncommon. Only when such issues arose could we expect to find consent clearly registered in assemblies.[55] The troubled peace of the Midi was being recognized as an urgent problem in several areas during this period. Ways of dealing with it in nonfeudal assemblies are considered in the next chapter.

Towns and townsmen already had a certain place in assemblies of Languedoc before the Albigensian crusade. Some *prosomes* of Saint-Gaudens attended a county court of Comminges in 1176.[56] Notables of Toulouse, perhaps consuls, were among the judges in the "Toulousan court" of about 1201; and it has also been noted that many "good men" of Millau were said to have approved the transfer of their lordship in an assembly of 1204. Townsmen of Béziers appeared in the viscount's courts in 1185 and 1204; and in the former instance we are told that besides the notables and "other barons of the land," the "whole populace of the city" was present. This must not, of course, be taken too literally. It probably means that many notables of city and bourg were on hand to hear the decision and spread the word. But three *cives* are mentioned explicitly as consulting with the bishop, chapter, and viscount, who decided what Roger II might alienate in the town.[57] Burghers of Carcassonne and Limoux, with other "good men" and magnates of the viscounty lands, swore their fidelity to Alfonse of Aragon when Roger submitted to him

[55] How far the rights in cases cited above were really legal rights is hard to say. Lawyers and clergy were probably becoming aware of the applicability of *C.* v, 59, 5 (". . . quod omnes similiter tangit, ab omnibus comprobetur") to various situations in these years; see G. Post, in *Traditio,* IV, 202.

[56] C. Higounet, *Le Comté de Comminges . . . ,* 2 vols. (Toulouse, 1949), I, 33; but no further trace of such representation is found in Comminges for nearly two more centuries, 393–394.

[57] *Gallia Christiana,* VI, *inst.,* 142–143. See also Bellaud Dessalles, *Histoire de Béziers* (Béziers, 1929), p. 53.

in 1179, and it is not unlikely that at least some of them attended the baronial assembly on that occasion.[58] Most of the knights who promised support to Roger's son at Carcassonne in 1191 must have been residents of the city [59] and presumably dominated its councils. Town *parlamentum* and *curia* very likely sat together at times, though it is not until 1224 that a full assembly of that kind is mentioned in Carcassonne.[60] At Nîmes the urban knights and citizens certainly met together.[61]

The participation of the greater towns in these seigneurial assemblies was a consequence of their peculiar importance in the constitution of the *pays*. Regional nobles as well as the leading commercial and industrial elements were becoming concentrated in places like Toulouse, Car-

---

[58] P. de Marca, *Marca Hispanica, app.*, 1371–1372: "facio [Roger] vobis jurare homines de Carcassona & de Limoso & multos alios probos homines & magnates terrae meae . . . ." It is tempting but dangerous to infer from this that men representing other towns were present. See the list of about 400 men who, "mandato expresso . . . Rodgerii," subscribed an oath of fealty to their new overlord, *Layettes*, I, no. 298.

[59] This is suggested by the following considerations: (1) Carcassonne is known to have had a numerous urban nobility in the twelfth century; see J. Poux, *La Cité de Carcassonne . . . L'Épanouissement (1067–1466)* (Toulouse, 1931), pp. 10–14; *H.L.*, v, 924–925,xi. (2) Of the 33 names, only 7 can be readily associated with places outside Carcassonne (which is not proof that they were not resident in that city), e.g., Saissac, Cailhau, Leprade, Agen, Montréal; 24 are characteristically urban names, e.g., Roger Ferrol (and four others of the same surname; a Bernard and a Hugues *Feirollus* figure among the town leaders in 1226, *H.L.*, VIII, 846–847,iv), Arnaud Morlan, Guillaume Hugues, Raymond Mir. (3) No less than 12 of the names figure among the first 80-odd names of those who swore fidelity to the king of Aragon in November 1179, *Layettes*, I, no. 298.

[60] Discussed below, pp. 54–55. Urban parliaments are considered in detail in Appendix I.

[61] *H.L.*, VIII, 567–571; also at Lautrec, knights and *barrias*, 582–583 (both acts of 1209).

cassonne, Béziers, Narbonne, and Nîmes.[62] The surrounding countryside took its name and its law from the leading towns.[63] Its communities—few of them can be called towns —were subordinate, politically and economically, to the neighboring cities and their overlords. In the first years of the thirteenth century Toulouse acted independently of the count to reduce much of Toulousain to submission by force of arms in its quest for commercial and political privileges.[64] At a later time, with its citizen moving out of town, Narbonne's parliament legislated for Narbonnais.[65]

It is hardly possible as yet to speak of representation. Many urban nobles doubtless retained rights and properties in outlying rural districts. In summoning them as well as knights of the *pays,* a lord might be indirectly in touch with men not on his own domain. But the burghers of Toulouse or Béziers or Narbonne were in no sense agents of a "third estate" of the countryside, where the bourgs and *castra* were only beginning to assume a juridically definite status as *universitates.* Effectively subject to their seigneurs, wholly localized and agricultural, the villages had little in common with the larger towns and cities, and they con-

[62] See reference to "baros de la vila" at Béziers, *Chanson de la Croisade,* ed. Martin-Chabot, I, 52. On rural knights moving into Toulouse, see Mundy, *Toulouse,* pp. 134–135. For Narbonne, see *I.A.C., Narbonne, Annexes de la Série AA,* ed. G. Mouynès (Narbonne, 1871), p. 31; *H.L.,* VIII, 960. On the origin of the urban nobility of Languedoc as a movement from the countryside see A. Dupont, *Les Cités de la Narbonnaise Première* (Nîmes, 1942), p. 667; Mundy, *Toulouse,* pp. 133–134 and references.

[63] See customs for nobles of *Narbonensis patria, H.L.,* VIII, 960; the usages of Toulouse were being adumbrated in the thirteenth century, and were referred to in rural communities of Toulousain before they were reduced to writing, e.g., Fonsorbes, P. Ourliac, *Les Sauvetés de Comminges: Étude et Documents . . .* (Toulouse, 1947), p. 126.

[64] Mundy, *Toulouse,* pp. 68, 70–71. Even some rural knights seem to have come under its sway.

[65] See Appendix I, pp. 306–307.

stituted no community among themselves. Even in the great towns, the *cives* or *burgenses* who joined with nobles did so not as special delegates of their social class, but as prominent members of town councils or parliaments which were themselves often responsible to the regional lord. Everywhere the significant distinction was between "good men" (*probi homines*), whether nobles or *bourgeois*, and the "little people," usually sharing in civil rights, but devoid of political influence.[66]

Therefore, the claim of lords to services from their townsmen—it is occasionally specified as feudal counsel and aid [67]—did not result in convocations of urban representatives. It meant rather that the count, viscount, vicar, or bayle could convoke townsmen or notables *in the towns* as a court of law or counsel as well as summon them in time of war. To be sure, the early customs of Carcassonne speak of the use of townsmen in both the bayle's court and the lord's court. By the latter we should perhaps understand a feudal *curia,* and since this body might meet anywhere in the viscounty, the article in question could conceivably justify the summons of deputies from Carcassonne to some other place. But this charter was probably patterned on that of Montpellier, which contains the same articles.[68] And a court of the barony of Montpellier would ordinarily meet in the city.

[66] See Dognon, *Institutions*, pp. 68–70; the *populus magnus et parvus* is mentioned in the customs of Mirepoix (1207), *H.L.,* VIII, 547; for the three classes at Toulouse, see *Chanson*, ed. Martin-Chabot, II, 6, 14, 22, *et passim.* Mundy, *Toulouse,* pp. 161–162, points out that it is not before the early thirteenth century that noble titles, suggestive of a new importance attached to knightly status, begin to figure prominently in Toulousan documents.

[67] E.g., *H.L.,* VIII, 442, Moissac promises *consilium et auxilium* to Raymond VI; cf. Dognon, *Institutions*, pp. 83–84, 138–139, 196; see also C. Petit-Dutaillis, *Les Communes Françaises* (Paris, 1947), p. 111.

[68] *Layettes,* I, nos. 743 (272-273), 721 (255-256). The distinction seems to be a little sharper in the Montpellier charter. But the

CRUSADE AND ROYAL CONQUEST
1209–1229

Regional assemblies in Languedoc are better attested for the period of the Albigensian crusade than before. The evidence of charters becomes fuller, and in addition we have the accounts of the chroniclers Pierre des Vaux-de-Cernay, Guillaume de Tudèle and his anonymous continuator, and Guillaume de Puylaurens. They refer often to courts, councils, and parliaments in which the Montforts, the king of Aragon, and the counts of Foix and Comminges were participants; there is some information, too, about assemblies of the Raymonds of Toulouse and the viscounts of Béziers and Narbonne. The events of the war involved all of these men in a game of shifting territorial politics in Languedoc. While the component districts of the county of Toulouse, notably Toulousain, Quercy, and Rouergue, remained intact, their overlordship was contested, with consequent political disruption. Count Raymond VI came quickly to the support of the crusaders in 1209. He hoped thereby not only to retain his estates but to add to them at the expense of the hostile and heretical viscount of Béziers. Raymond's enthusiasm waned, however, and turned to opposition when the armies of the French (*Francigene*) moved from conquests in the viscounty of Béziers to the extirpation of heresy in his own lands in upper Languedoc. The dispossessed viscount Raymond-Trencavel (1209–1247) of Béziers lost all authority in his domains. Aymery of Narbonne seconded the crusaders' campaign from the start, but, along with his townsmen, he subsequently maintained a somewhat independent position in accordance with self-interest.

During the first decade of intermittent war and negotiation, the Montforts and crusaders held notable assemblies.

---

bayle's court was, of course, the "lord's court," and it is possible that no differentiation is meant.

In composition they were both ecclesiastical and feudal. They were meetings of a seigneurial army engaged in a "holy war" guided by papal legates and prelates of Languedoc.[69] At the siege of Lavaur in April 1211, Roger of Comminges solemnly promised to be the liege man of Simon de Montfort in the presence of the abbot of Combelongue, the bishops of Couserans, Toulouse, and Paris, the viscount of Donges, Guy de Lucy, Guy de Lévis, and "many other *proceres* and barons of the army of God."[70] A few weeks later two legates, the archbishop of Narbonne, the bishops of Toulouse and Uzès, and the abbot of Vaux attended the concession of all of Trencavel's rights in the viscounty of Béziers to Simon de Montfort.[71] The parliament of Pamiers in 1212 was in many respects an ecclesiastical council, and the invariable presence of prelates in Montfort's counsels on other occasions shows plainly his dependence on ecclesiastical approval.[72] The effective strength of his army was the contingent of northern barons and their followers, campaigning each year for their required forty days. Whether motivated by promise of rewards, love of adventure, or uncommon fidelity, some twenty of the feudal army remained with Montfort in Languedoc for a number of years, and they are frequently mentioned by name as members of his advisory council.[73] Some

[69] Cf. H. Pissard, *La Guerre Sainte en Pays Chrétien* (Paris, 1912), pp. 44–49.

[70] *H.L.*, viii, 608–609; see also 571–572, a donation to Citeaux "ad instantiam tam baronum exercitus Domini, quam & legati & prelatorum, qui presentes erant"; and, for the army-assembly analogy, *Chanson*, ed. Martin-Chabot, i, 34, 204; (cf. below, n. 254).

[71] *H.L.*, viii, 609–611.

[72] See below, p. 44; *H.L.*, viii, 571–572, 688; etc.

[73] See *Petri Vallium Sarnaii Monachi Hystoria Albigensis*, eds. P. Guébin, E. Lyon, 3 vols. (Paris, 1926–1939), i, 119, 187; Belperron, *Croisade*, pp. 179–180, 187; also *H.L.*, viii, 655–657; 670–673; *Layettes*, i, no. 1119; etc.

of them appeared in a court "of vassals and *curiales* of the lord count," which convened in the palace at Carcassonne in March 1212 to approve Montfort's donation of the fortified town of Pézenas to Raymond of Cahors, a faithful supporter and financier of the crusade.[74] The lists given in charters usually trail off into the abbreviation "and many others,"[75] so that we cannot know the names of all those who attended these baronial courts. But it is clear that they remained basically the company of French knights and ecclesiastics. Some of the knights were invested with conquered heretical seigneuries, such as Castres, Termes, Montréal, and Limoux.[76] The old vassals of the viscounty of Béziers were not ordinarily present in Montfort's councils, whose composition thus bore little relation to the disposition of native elements in lower Languedoc. As the conquering count of Toulouse, Montfort encountered general hostility, and though he placed seneschals in Agenais, Rouergue, and Toulousain, he probably could not count on assemblages of barons in those areas.[77] Occasionally, local nobility or even townsmen supplemented his ordinary council. After the capitulation of Moissac in 1212, the abbot and Simon de Montfort reached an agreement on mutual rights in Moissac in a gathering of knights and burghers in the abbey.[78] In November 1214 Henry of Rodez did homage to Montfort in the presence

[74] *H.L.*, VIII, 604–608. The act is extraordinarily verbose and repetitious: "auctoritate & consilio domini . . . & aliorum procerum & curialium meorum . . . in presencia vassallorum & curialium domini comitis, publice & manifeste, scilicet [mostly same names]," who counselled the donation.

[75] *Ibid.*, 608, 609; A.N., JJ.13, fols. 20v–21; etc. For the chronicles, see *Chanson*, ed. Martin-Chabot, III, 262; cf. I, 280.

[76] Belperron, *Croisade*, p. 249, gives a useful list.

[77] But for Agenais, see below, pp. 73ff.

[78] *H.L.*, VIII, 621–625; also A.N., JJ.13, fols. 20v–21 (cf. J.896, no. 33), at least one burgher, and probably several, of Figeac attend a feudal convention in October 1214.

of twenty-six notables. Six or seven of these were members
of the ecclesiastical-baronial group that accompanied
Montfort, eight were definitely nobles and clergy of the
Quercy-Rouergue area, while twelve others cannot be identified and were presumably mostly local notables.[79] Regional knights were on hand in considerable numbers when
Amaury de Montfort renewed his father's *paréage* with
the abbot of Saint-Antonin for Pamiers in 1218.[80] Feudal
agreements and homages all around Languedoc received
publicity in similar meetings.[81]

It is not surprising that Simon de Montfort frequently
consulted his barons.[82] He was in the unusual position of
being an elected lord. The notables of the army, convening
in a council, or "parlament," had chosen him viscount of
Béziers just after the capture of Béziers and Carcassonne
in 1209. According to the *Chanson*, Montfort accepted
the commission on condition that the "princes" there present should swear to aid him, upon his summons, in time of
danger.[83] Thereafter his status in the seething South was

---

[79] *H.L.*, VIII, 655–657; for the names, *ibid.*, index.

[80] *Ibid.*, 578–579,ii.

[81] A.N., JJ.13, fols. 20v–21; *Layettes*, V, no. 211; *H.L.*, VIII,
651–653; 686-687; 704-706,iii; *Hystoria Albigensis*, II, 25; 120,
122–123, ceremonial feudal assembly of Languedoc in 1213 when
Amaury de Montfort was knighted.

[82] In addition to instances already cited, see *Hystoria Albigensis*,
I, 119, 152, 171, 212; II, 144; and cf. Belperron, *Croisade*, pp.
188–189. For eastern analogies see S. Runciman, *A History of
the Crusades*, 3 vols. (Cambridge, 1951–1954), I, 178, 184, *et
passim*; and see esp. G. Langmuir, "Counsel and Capetian Assemblies," *Études Présentées . . . Commission . . . l'Hist. des Assemblées d'États*, XVIII (1958), 27, who cites the very numerous
references to councils and counsel in Villehardouin.

[83] Ed. Martin-Chabot, I, 86–88; Pierre des Vaux-de-Cernay, *Hystoria*, I, 101, gives other details, and says that the army-assembly's
power was delegated to ("Eliguntur igitur de toto exercitu") two
bishops, the legate, and four knights, who then chose Simon de
Montfort. It is a remarkable instance of political awareness. A

often precarious. Agreement on important matters was necessary for military solidarity, politic when donations were made as rewards to individuals. Decisions about military strategy were no doubt reached regularly in small conferences, although the *Chanson* refers to gatherings of fifteen or thirty barons who attended Montfort on critical occasions.[84] Enactments in large meetings were endowed with extra ceremonial importance, and Montfort probably understood that his own prestige was enhanced in them. Of all his assemblies, none is so important or so well known as the "parliament of Pamiers."[85] It convened late in November 1212 with the object of drafting and approving a political settlement and constitution for the lands conquered by, and at least nominally subject to, the new viscount of Béziers. Montfort was not as yet count of Toulouse, and important places in upper Languedoc—notably Toulouse, Montauban, and Rouergue—were still beyond his control. But his most recent campaigns had left him master of the old Trencavel domains, comital Albigeois, Agenais, much of Quercy and Toulousain, and parts of the county of Foix. It was for the inhabitants of these relatively populous areas that the legislation of Pamiers was produced.

Two-thirds of the statutes were devoted to the setting of fixed reciprocal ties between lord and vassal, and the establishment of a civil and adminstrative code based on the

---

similar commission functioned in the parliament of Pamiers in 1212, below, p. 46.

[84] Ed. Martin-Chabot, II, 176, 130.

[85] So called by Guillaume de Tudèle (*Chanson*). The chief sources are: (1) text of the statutes, *H.L.*, VIII, 625–635 (orig., A.N., J.890, no. 6; numerous copies and editions, and at least one variant version: see "Catalogue des Actes de Simon et d'Amauri de Montfort," ed. A. Molinier, *B.É.C.*, XXXIV (1873), 463–464; cf. P. Timbal, *L'Application de la Coutume de Paris au Pays d'Albigeois* [Toulouse, 1950], p. 16); (2) *Hystoria Albigensis*, II, 62–64; (3) *Chanson*, ed. Martin-Chabot, I, 280.

custom of the Ile-de-France.[86] The likelihood of continuing
war made it necessary to include provisions insisting on
knight service, an obligation that was poorly observed in
pre-crusade Languedoc.[87] A whole series of articles can be
interpreted as an effort to tighten the ruler's control of his
vassals, both French and meridional. Certain provisions
concerning the administration of justice tended to favor
the courts of the viscount and his castellans against local
seigneurial jurisdictions. The regulation of seigneurial
rights and duties, payments of rents and *tailles*, rules concerning serfs and villains, and particularly the law of succession, were all patterned "according to the custom and
usage around Paris."[88] Fifteen of the forty-six articles, notably the first eleven, embodied Montfort's concession to
the Church, in recognition of its indispensable support of
his campaigns in Languedoc. These articles inveighed
against heresy and the protection of heretics, and prohibited heretics from serving in public office. To confirm a
promise made by Simon de Montfort in 1209, but probably
ill kept, an annual three-penny hearth tax was to be paid
henceforth to the papacy. The regular payment of tithes
and first fruits was guaranteed, privileges of churches and
abbeys upheld, while clergy received assurance of the *pri-
vilegium fori* and exemption from *tailles* and *péages*.[89]

The ecclesiastical provisions were those of a typical provincial reform synod, and the assembly of Pamiers can indeed be described as a church council.[90] The great prelates
of the Midi, among them the archbishop of Bordeaux, and

[86] On the sequel of the legal settlement in Languedoc, see generally Timbal, *Coutume de Paris*; he gives an analysis of the statutes, pp. 16–27.

[87] A. Molinier, "Étude sur l'Administration de Louis IX & d'Alfonse de Poitiers," *H.L.*, VII, 543; Timbal, pp. 19–20.

[88] See Timbal, pp. 21–22.

[89] *H.L.*, VIII, 625–634; VI, 311.

[90] See Hefele, *Histoire des Conciles*, tr. Leclercq, 11 vols. (Paris,
1907–1952), V,ii, 1292, with references to Labbe, Mansi.

the bishops of Toulouse, Carcassonne, Agen, Périgueux, Couserans, Comminges, and Tarbes, were conspicuous in the assembly. But in its fundamental character and over-all composition, the meeting was much more like a plenary feudal *curia.* The chroniclers agree in depicting Simon de Montfort as the central figure at Pamiers, even to the point of stating that it was he who issued the summonses.[91] The statutes were published in Montfort's name alone. The rhetorical preamble to the text shows him acting as high justiciar to right wrongs against God and the Roman Church, and against justice; and to provide for the peace of his land, the honor of God, Church, and king, and for the benefit of all his subjects.[92] Here we have a characteristic instance of medieval legislation issuing from a high court of justice.

The plenary assembly that counseled the statutes of Pamiers was somewhat representative of those lands where they were to be applied. Oddly, neither the text nor the chronicles mention names of men in attendance, aside from nine of the prelates. From hints and internal evidence, as well as from contemporary documents, it would be possible to construct a considerable list of knights who were probably there. But it is enough to note that the sources convey an unmistakable impression of an exceptionally large gathering of men from all parts of Montfort's territories.[93] The

---

[91] *Hystoria Albigensis*, II, 62; *Chanson*, ed. Martin-Chabot, I, 280. See also *Thesaurus Novus Anecdotorum*, eds. E. Martène, U. Durand, 5 vols. (Paris, 1717), I, 837, art. 48.

[92] *H.L.*, VIII, 625–626: "In nomine Domini . . . per ipsum enim ad hoc sumus in sede justicie non modica constituti, ut ea que contra Deum & ecclesiam Romanam atque contra justiciam attemptantur, . . . revocemus . . . cupiens omnia supradicta adimplere & pacatam & quietam terram habere & retinere ad honorem Dei & sancte Romane ecclesie & domini regis Francorum & ad utilitatem omnium subjectorum nostrorum. . . ."

[93] *Ibid.*, 626: ". . . de consilio venerabilium dominorum, scilicet archiepiscopi Burdegalensis & Tolosani, Karcassensis, Agenensis, Petragoricensis, Coseranensis, Convenarum, Bigorrensis episco-

full session was too unwieldy to cooperate in the discussion and drafting of the statutes. Pierre des Vaux-de-Cernay tells us that a special twelve-man commission was chosen for this purpose. It was composed of four churchmen—the bishops of Toulouse and Couserans, one Templar, and one Hospitaller—four northern knights, and four men of Languedoc—two knights and two burghers. This representation closely conformed to the juridical estates of society recognized in the statutes and to political realities in Languedoc. "It was not without cause," wrote the chronicler, "that some were Frenchmen and others natives who were chosen to establish these oft-mentioned customs, for thus would be removed from the hearts of men all such suspicion as might arise if one or the other group should have some lawmakers of their own."[94] Many of the Pamiers articles were quite as applicable to townsmen as to nobles and churchmen, and they refer frequently to *burgenses*.[95] But it is wholly uncertain whether the two burghers in the commission of twelve correspond to a like proportion in the plenary assembly. The sources refer to the latter as a general *colloquium* or *parlemen* of clergy and nobility. The *Chanson* mentions "many other good men," while the text of the statutes speaks of other "wise men" with prelates and bar-

---

porum, & sapientum virorum & aliorum baronum & procerum nostrorum tales generales consuetudines in tota terra nostra ponimus . . ."; the *Chanson* tells of "many barons, bishops, and other good men," and adds: "Trastuit li castela de son païs i son," ed. Martin-Chabot, I, 280. The archdeacon of Paris is mentioned in a somewhat different text of the statutes, B.N., Doat, CLIII, 53rv; his seal is preserved on an original, *Layettes*, V, no. 197. The names of other clergy and knights in Montfort's army can be found in various contemporary documents, e.g., *H.L.*, VIII, 604–608; 621–625.

[94] *Hystoria Albigensis*, II, 63–64.

[95] E.g., nos. 24, 25, 43.

ons as composing the assembly.[96] Undoubtedly there were
a good many more than two townsmen in the parliament
of Pamiers. We may be fairly sure, however, on the negative grounds of lack of evidence and lack of precedent, that
they did not come in uniform delegations from many towns
subject to Montfort. Men of Pamiers must have been there,
perhaps also burghers of Béziers and Carcassonne. But the
assembly seems to have been more like those previously
considered in which local men sat with nobles gathering in
their town.

The parliament of Pamiers functioned in several different
ways. It was primarily a consultative body. The full assembly "counseled" the legislation. Reduced to the proportions of a manageable committee, it did much or all of the
legislative work. To what extent the assembly was legally
constitutive is hard to say, since we do not know just how
the committee was chosen. Nor is it clear whether the full
assembly approved or ratified the finished statutes, though
it probably did.[97] But we can hardly speak of "consent" in
this case, unless in the sense of consultative consent, which
could be given but not withheld.[98] It is possible that the ecclesiastical law enjoining the convocation of men to participate in decisions touching their rights had some influence in this assembly. The rule that laity should be sum-

[96] *Hystoria Albigensis*, II, 62: ". . . convocavit nobilis comes
Montis Fortis episcopos et nobiles terre sue apud castrum Apami-
arum, celebraturus colloquium generale"; the *Chanson*'s reference
is paraphrased above, n. 93, where the appropriate part of the
statutes is also given; and see *Thes. Novus Anecd.*, I, 837, art. 48.

[97] See again n. 93.

[98] Cf. the canonical theory of counsel that must be sought but
need not be followed, e.g. *glossa ordinaria* to *Extra*, I, 43, 7*Cum
olim*, ad vv. *sive discordet*; I, 6, 41*Ne pro*, ad v. *consilio*; cf. Innocent IV, *Apparatus super Libros Decretalium* (Venice, 1481),
to *Extra*, III, 5, 29*Grave*. And see F. Olivier-Martin, *Histoire de la
Coutume . . . de Paris*, 2 vols. (Paris, 1922–1930), I, 72, who believes that the assent was constitutive and effected a "contract."

moned to councils dealing with such matters of the faith as heresy was certainly applicable.[99] No doubt many of the secular statutes involved the rights of knights and townsmen present. Yet the canonical theory linked with *quod omnes tangit . . .* was not invoked in this connection, and no corresponding secular law was in force. So it must be doubted that the laymen at Pamiers, working as an administrative body at the lord's command, sat by right. There is not the slightest reason to suppose that the embryonic estates—least of all the "third estate"—had any political program or cohesion; nor had they a vote, collective or divided. Unquestionably, however, the size of the assembly was related to the importance of the *negotium.* To associate the men of Languedoc in the task of their political and legal reorganization was to ensure against opposition born of localism and ignorance. If the inner assembly did the work, the larger body doubtless did considerable listening. The program embodied in the statutes must have required some justification, especially to natives of the Midi. In one of its aspects, then, the parliament of Pamiers was a propagandistic device for influencing regional opinion. It also served to register oaths. At the close of the meeting, Montfort and the knights swore in solemn religious terms to observe the statutes.[100]

Simon de Montfort died in a skirmish under the walls of Toulouse in June 1218, an event which assured that town of its autonomy. Shortly afterward, his son Amaury summoned his barons and advisers to a *cort complida* to determine how the remainder of his territories might best

[99] *Extra,* iii, 10, 10, and glosses; Post, " 'Quod Omnes Tangit,' in Bracton," *Traditio,* iv, 202–203. Tancred, Apparatus to *Compilatio Prima,* v, t. *De hereticis,* c. *Ad abolendam* (Lucius III), ad. v. *principum*: "Laici enim vocari debent ad concilium ubi questio fidei agitari debet . . .", Rome, Biblioteca Apostolica, MS Vat. Lat. 1377, fol. 84vb.

[100] *H.L.,* viii, 634; *Hystoria Albigensis,* ii, 64. Cf. *Extra,* v, 7, 9*Ad abolendam.*

be preserved in the face of revitalized meridional opposition. Just where and when this assembly took place we do not know, but it was almost certainly made up of the notables of his army. In addition to Amaury's, the *Chanson* reports speeches by Bishop Foulques of Toulouse, the cardinal legate Bertrand, and the count of Soissons. It was agreed to renew appeals for a royal campaign with papal support.[101] Prince Louis arrived in 1219 but accomplished little. Neither then, it seems, nor on the occasion of his earlier activity in Languedoc, did he summon local assemblies. As King Louis VIII he invaded Languedoc in 1226, to gain finally for the crown the great inheritance in lower Languedoc that Amaury had been unable to secure. Many writers have asserted that at this time Louis convoked an assembly of men of the three orders to advise on the establishment of royal administration at Béziers.[102] They refer to an ordinance of 1340 which says that when the viscounty and town of Béziers were incorporated in the royal domain, "it was ordained with the common counsel and assent of prelates, barons, nobles, communities, and other subjects of the region" that there should be a royal vicar and judge in Béziers. This passage is apparently anachronistic, and certainly vague, failing even to give the name of the king.[103] Nor is there any other mention of this assembly,

101 *Chanson*, ed. Martin-Chabot, iii, 228–234; *Hystoria Albigensis*, ii, 319–320.

102 Boutaric, *Saint Louis et Alfonse*, p. 529; he is followed, even to the point of reproducing a wrong reference, by Cadier, *États de Béarn*, p. 25; Viollet, *Institutions*, iii, 180; Chénon, *Droit Français*, i, 827; cf. Callery, "Premiers États Généraux," *R.Q.H.*, xxix, 115.

103 *Ordonnances des Roys de France . . .*, 22 vols. (Paris, 1723–1849), iii, 168–169: "attentisque utilitatibus tam Reypublice & nostris quam etiam subjectorum, communi consilio & assensu Prelatorum, Baronum, Nobilium, Communitatum & aliorum subjectorum illarum partium quorum intererat, ordinatum fuerit quod. . . ."

whose supposed proportions would surely have attracted
contemporary notice. In fact we have evidence only for
occasional convocations of the barons and clergy of the
king's army. In April 1226 Louis promulgated an ordinance "with the counsel of great men and prudent," which
regulated the punishment of convicted heretics and de-
prived supporters of heresy of their property and civil
rights.[104] The next October, at Pamiers, a gathering "of all
the prelates and barons of France who were with him" approved an ordinance whose effect was to reaffirm the ecclesiastical sanction of excommunication, adding monetary
amends payable by recalcitrants to the secular arm.[105]
Prelates of the Narbonne province may have done fealty to
the king in this assembly, or some other one, in 1226.[106]

We know less about the courts or assemblies of the native barons who opposed the French warriors. The chroniclers rarely explain things from their point of view. But
Raymond VI probably consulted his vassals and followers
frequently. Knights of Toulouse and Toulousain were generally faithful to him and fought for him. The counts of
Foix and Comminges were among the greater nobles who
rallied to his support. And in 1213 King Peter of Aragon
brought his strong feudal levies to supplement Raymond's
forces. Many leaders and knights of the two armies met in a

[104] C. Petit-Dutaillis, *Étude sur la Vie et le Règne de Louis VIII
(1187–1226)* (Paris, 1894), Catalogue des Actes de Louis VIII, p.
497, no. 362; *Ordonnances*, xii, 319.

[105] Confirmed by a council of Narbonne in 1227, J. Mansi,
Sacrorum Conciliorum Nova et Amplissima Collectio (Florence,
1759–1798; new series, Paris, 1901—), xxiii, 21; also mentioned by Guillaume de Puylaurens, *Cronica*, ed. Beyssier, *Bibliothèque de la Faculté des Lettres de l'Univ. de Paris,* xviii (1904),
150, who suggests that the counsel was rather that of the cardinal
Romanus than of prelates and barons of France. I follow Petit-
Dutaillis, *Louis VIII*, p. 505, no. 425, in this dating, but cannot
find proof for it.

[106] *H.L.*, viii, 860–861, ii. Molinier's criticism of Vaissete on
this point, vi, 615, does not seem well founded.

parliament in September 1213 before the fatal battle of Muret, which ended Aragon's hopes for a transpyrenean empire and cost Peter his life. The discussions, confined to questions of military strategy, were led by the king, who directed the campaign. The *Chanson* represents him as offering a bold plan of attack on Montfort's forces in Muret, while Raymond's cautious scheme of entrenchment was scorned and discredited by an Aragonese baron. The counts of Foix and Comminges, Hugues d'Alfaro, Raymond's son-in-law, burghers and artisans of Toulouse, and other unnamed knights were present with Raymond. A considerable number of Aragonese and Catalonian knights sat with the king.[107]

The disastrous defeat at Muret ended serious active resistance to Montfort's occupation for some time. We have no acts of Raymond VI from summer 1213 to January 1217.[108] But he and his son made a triumphal return to Languedoc through Provence in 1216, and the young Raymond won a reputation with his vigorous and successful defense of Beaucaire. Thereupon Toulouse, chafing under its severe foreign administration, entered into negotiations with Raymond VI, who easily regained the town in 1217. The result was a second siege of Toulouse by Simon de Montfort which lasted for nine months and was only terminated by Montfort's death. The *Chanson* reports another parliament at an uncertain date during the siege, this time led by Raymond. It served to rally the knights and townsmen to a vigorous defense against their assailants. The attendance is described thus: the counts of Foix and Comminges, Roger and Bernard of Comminges, Dalmatz de Creixell, an important Catalonian knight, "and many other great barons and counselors, with the richest and best barons of the town, and knights, burghers, and consuls." Men of Toulousain, like Roger de Montaut, Guillaume

---

[107] *Chanson*, ed. Martin-Chabot, II, 22, 24.
[108] *H.L.*, VIII, 1950.

Unaud, and Roger d'Aspet, who had been in the comital
army that recovered Toulouse, probably attended this assembly.[109] The townsmen were undoubtedly on hand in
large numbers, for they were the heart of the resistance. We
hear of an exhortation by a lawyer named Master Bernard,
who spoke on behalf of the consulate, of which he was a
member, and "for all the rest of the populace great and
small."[110] The clergy, of course, were conspicuously absent
from Raymond's military councils. Otherwise, the latter
seem similar in character to the army-assemblies of the
Montforts. There are a few references to military convocations of Raymond VI and his son, and it is worth noting
that the contingents commonly included town militia.[111]

Only after 1218 do we find the Raymonds again holding
courts like those of the prewar period.[112] As before, these
meetings drew men of particular regions in which the count
was operating, and their size was related to the importance
of the matter at hand. In March 1222 the count-associate
Raymond VII (1222–1249) recovered the town of Moissac and swore to observe its liberties. In accordance with
an old custom, ten of the count's barons took the oath with
him, and their names are preserved. One of them was Raymond's brother Bertrand; at least six others were knights
of Quercy-Agenais; only one figures in contemporary charters as regularly attendant on the count.[113] In December

[109] See *Chanson*, ed. Martin-Chabot, ii, 264ff.

[110] *Ibid.*, iii, 50–60.

[111] *Ibid.*, i, 186, 204, 206, 208; ii, 14; cf. 16, 98; *Hystoria
Albigensis*, ii, 268–269, 272.

[112] *H.L.*, viii, 718–720,i; 747–748,ii, acts of Raymond VI; but
most of the evidence relates to Raymond VII: see 1950–1956. A
feudal recognition of August 1213 in Quercy, A.N., JJ.19, fol.
179rv, stands alone, and follows a notarial form that came into
use after the crusade.

[113] *H.L.*, viii, 749–750,iv, and cf. index. The custom in question
was specified in an early 12th-century charter granted to Moissac
by Gausbert de Fumel, A. Lagrèze-Fossat, *Études Historiques sur
Moissac*, 3 vols. (Paris, 1870–1874), i, 68, art. 2.

1224 a somewhat larger gathering of regional nobles solemnized an important exchange of rights to fortified places in Albigeois between Raymond VII and Matfred de Rabastens. The viscount of Lautrec and lords of Rabastens, Penne (Albigeois), Gaillac, and Tauriac were among those present.[114] Comparable assemblies occurred at Toulouse and elsewhere, in the Rhone valley domains as well as in the west.[115] But Toulouse remained the focal point of comital activity. It maintained its independence even in the wake of Louis VIII's invasion in 1226.[116] Various acts of the 1220's show Raymond VII performing transactions at Toulouse in the presence of such important barons as the counts of Foix, Comminges, and Astarac, Géraud de Gourdon, Raymond Unaud, Hugues d'Alfaro, Guillaume-Bernard de Najac, and Pelfort de Rabastens. These men assembled, with other knights of Toulousain, on 21 September 1222, when Raymond obtained formal recognition as lord of Toulouse and promised to observe its municipal liberties.[117] Later in the same year some of these nobles convened again on the occasion of further concessions by the count to the town.[118] And when Raymond gave the *castrum* of Saint-Félix-du-Lauragais to the count of Foix in May 1226, the witnesses included Bernard-Jourdain and Bertrand de l'Isle, Géraud

[114] *H.L.*, VIII, 811–815, probably somewhere in Albigeois or the Tarn area.

[115] *Ibid.*, 746–747; 798–800; A.N., JJ.19, fols. 177v, 178, 180v–181.

[116] See Mundy, *Toulouse*, pp. 88–90. As he remarks, 88, "The Raymonds fought the war [of 1217–1229] not as princes of a Mediterranean state but as chiefs of the Toulousan Fatherland."

[117] R. Limouzin-Lamothe, *La Commune de Toulouse . . .* (Toulouse, 1932), Cartulaire du Bourg, no. 80, pp. 417–419. This writer offers the reasonable hypothesis, p. 207, that the barons rendered homage to the new count on this occasion.

[118] *Ibid.*, no. 79, pp. 415–416; no. 81, pp. 419–420; no. 82, pp. 421–422.

de Gourdon, Sicard de Puylaurens, and lesser knights of Toulousain.[119]

This "court" of barons gravitating about the count of Toulouse undoubtedly lent a certain weight and prestige to his acts. The nobles were a strong element of regional support at a time when the young Raymond VII was much in need of it. Yet the assemblies they attended were more like town councils than baronial courts. Knights, notables, and consuls of Toulouse were dominant in them, the consuls in particular having achieved a virtual ascendancy over the count even in his business outside the city. They alone advised and approved the donation of Saint-Félix in 1226, even though, as noted above, a good many regional knights attended the meeting on this occasion. In 1228 Count Raymond promised to ratify the decisions of his proctor in the peace negotiations with the king, "having taken full counsel on this matter of our barons and especially of the consuls of Toulouse."[120] Aside from the consuls, the participants in this court cannot be identified. Like other town-meeting courts, it probably included a few knights of the county, nobles of Toulouse and the surrounding *pays*, and other town notables.

In lower Languedoc, Trencavel of Béziers profited temporarily from the inability of Amaury de Montfort to maintain Simon's conquests. With the cooperation of his strong kinsman and tutor, the count of Foix, the viscount governed his inherited domains until the royal invasion of 1226. The most remarkable assembly in that period took place early in 1224. Reminded—"by prudent men, both knights and burghers"—of his father's promise, in the event of his death without legitimate posterity, to leave the viscounty to the count of Foix, Trencavel renewed this pact in a combined *curia* and town parliament at Carcassonne.

---

[119] *H.L.*, VIII, 832–834.

[120] *Ibid.*, 879,i. A consular list for 1227–1228 may be found in Mundy, *Toulouse*, p. 187.

This is a clear instance of counsel and consultative approval. We have the names of many of the knights and town notables. Most of the knights can be associated with northern and western Carcassonais, bordering on Lauragais and the county of Foix.[121] For general feudal assemblies held by the viscount of Narbonne there is little evidence. The constitutional position of his *curia* as one of the three regular courts of Narbonne became better defined during the war years. By the 1220's, it had the appearance of a specialized judicial institution centering in the town. The viscount had the right to summon the consuls, town councils, or general parliament into session in his *curia*.[122] Nobility of the countryside might also gather there on occasion. In May 1229 *milites Narbonesii* assembled with the consuls, "good men," and people at Narbonne "in the court of the lord Aymery" to take an oath of fidelity to the king.[123] Ceremonial as-

[121] *H.L.*, VIII, 787–789; "relatione videlicet virorum prudentium, tam militum quam burgensium . . . in nostro palatio Carcassone, in pleno colloquio omnium hominum ipsius ville & plurium militum ipsius terre nostre, concedimus. . . ." Among the knights were Jourdain de Cabaret and Pierre de Laure, vicars of the viscounty, Isarn d'Aragon, Pierre de Fenouillet, Pierre-Roger de Mirepoix, Jourdain and Guillaume de St-Félix, Isarn de Prouille, and Guillaume-Pierre de Fanjeaux. Further grants to the count of Foix were made at Limoux in June 1227, in presence of vassals and notables, but without explicit mention of consultation, *ibid*, 863–865.

[122] See *I.A.C., Narbonne, Annexes de la Série AA*, no. 8, pp. 9–11, the *consilium proborum hominum* of city and bourg is assembled in 1221 by the three courts to make a town statute.

[123] *H.L.*, VIII, 896–897,i: "Acta fuerunt haec solemniter . . . apud Narbonam, in curia domini Aymerici, convocato & congregato ibi populo Narbonae in generali colloquio, & praesentibus omnibus supradictis" (consuls, knights, and "good men"). Thirty-three knights are named, and doubtless many were resident in Narbonne; but most of them can be associated with places outside the town. That one must distinguish between knights of Narbonne and Narbonnais is clear from the customs of nobles of the *pays*, October 1232, *ibid*., 960.

semblies took place in Rouergue, Gévaudan, and Velay during these years, with men of Le Puy figuring prominently in convocations held in their city.[124]

No detailed study of the councils and church-directed assemblies of the crusading period can be made here. But it should be noted that they were seldom exclusively clerical in composition. Laity of Narbonne were present with suffragan bishops and abbots in meetings of 12 and 13 March 1212 which solemnized the election of an archbishop of Narbonne and witnessed Viscount Aymery's homage to him.[125] The utility of an assembly of clergy, nobles, and townsmen for consultative and propagandistic purposes, on a matter of concern to much of Languedoc, had occurred to Pope Innocent III. Early in 1213, during the complicated negotiation the failure of which was to result in Muret, he directed the legates to convoke "in a secure and fitting place, archbishops, bishops, abbots, counts, barons, consuls and rectors, and other prudent men who may seem necessary and suitable for this," to work out a peaceful settlement.[126] No such assembly met, however, and the final deliberations at this moment of crisis occurred in the winter at the council of Lavaur, which was composed exclusively of prelates.[127]

In some cases the lay element in councils can be explained by church law. It was now required that laymen be

[124] Vassals of the count of Rodez are named in a pact between the latter and Millau in 1223, printed and discussed by J. Bousquet in *Annales du Midi*, LXXII (1960), 25–42. Also A. Philippe, *La Baronnie du Tournel . . . Documents* (Mende, 1903), no. 1; *Preuves de la Maison de Polignac . . .* , ed. A. Jacotin, 5 vols. (Paris, 1898–1906), I, nos. 106, 115; IV, no. 643.

[125] *Gallia Christiana*, VI, *inst.*, 52–53.

[126] *H.F.*, XIX, 567–568.

[127] *Hystoria Albigensis*, II, 66–95; Belperron, *Croisade*, p. 260. See also *H.F.*, XIX, 530–531; *Hystoria*, I, 167, and notes, parallel course of events in 1210. For notice of other mixed assemblies between 1209 and 1215, see G. de Puylaurens, *Cronica*, ed. Beyssier, 131; *Hystoria*, I, 196–199; II, 255.

sworn to cooperate actively against heretics; and canonists held that laity were entitled to be summoned when the agenda concerned faith and heresy.[128] Submissions and promises made by the counts of Foix and Comminges and the town of Toulouse in April 1214 were received "publicly" in the archiepiscopal palace at Narbonne in the presence of clergy, nobles, "and many others, both of the city of Narbonne and from elsewhere."[129] And the council of Toulouse in July 1229, which reaffirmed and strengthened the old diocesan inquisition, was attended by important meridional nobles and deputies of Toulouse, as well as the archbishops of Narbonne, Auch, and Bordeaux, and many other prelates. Guillaume de Puylaurens describes the lay element as comprising Raymond VII and other counts (except Roger-Bernard of Foix), barons, the seneschal of Carcassonne, and two consuls of Toulouse, one representing the city and the other the bourg.[130] The council dealt with matters concerning the whole area of Languedoc—indeed, of virtually all southern France.[131] Assuming that the secular attendance had some correspondence to this territorial scope, the council was more than a court of barons of the county of Toulouse. Once again we are reduced to conjecture on the meaning of a phrase, in this case: "alii comites,

[128] *Extra*, V, 7, 9*Ad abolendam*; Tancred, Appar. to this decretal as in *Comp. Prima*, v, t. *De heret.*, ad v. *principum* (quoted above, n. 99), MS Vat lat. 1377, fol. 84vb; also Brit. Mus., MS Royal 11 C. vii, fol. 246b, Jacobus de Albenga to *Comp. Quinta*, t. 1, c. *Cunctis*, ad v. *presente*, citing the same decretal and others: ". . . Et merito vocandi sunt laici quando tractatur causa fidei et matrimonii, quoniam omnes tangit, quare ab omnibus comprobari debet . . ."; cf. Appar. "Ius Naturale" to *Decretum*, dist. 96, c. 4*Ubi nam*, B.N., MS Lat. 15393, fol. 70a.

[129] This phrase is used to describe the meeting of 25 April, *H.L.*, viii, 651; see also 643–646.

[130] *Cronica*, 154–155.

[131] Mansi, *Sacrorum Conciliorum . . . Collectio*, xxiii, 194: ". . . in Tolosana diocesi, & Narbonensi provincia, & circumjacentibus diaecesibus [*sic*], & terris vicinis. . . ."

preter Fuxensem, et barones";[132] this might well mean the inclusion of the counts of Comminges, Astarac, and Rodez, the viscounts of Narbonne, Lautrec, and Lomagne, as well as lesser nobles. Except for the parliament of Pamiers, the council of Toulouse was probably the most important assembly, even in its purely secular aspect, of the crusading period. Laymen were summoned because their cooperation was necessary in the procedure of uprooting heresy that was enacted. Bishops were to designate laymen in each parish to work with priests in reporting heretics and their supporters; seigneurs were required to act vigorously against heretics hidden in their lands; and all persons who had reached the age of majority were to swear to their orthodoxy. Other articles were intended to ensure the peace and public security: they included injunctions against confraternities and the construction or rebuilding of castles.[133] According to Guillaume de Puylaurens, the whole assembly and eventually the "whole land" approved these "statutes of the peace."[134]

AFTER THE CONQUEST
1229–1249

Feudal courts continued to meet during the reign of Louis IX. In seigneuries that survived the shufflings of the treaty of Paris in 1229 there was no sudden change in the composition or activities of baronial assemblies. As before, their size varied with the importance of the business at hand, the usual entourage consisting of a few favorites and councillors. This group was often supplemented by men of

[132] G. de Puylaurens, *Cronica*, 155.

[133] Cc. 1, 3, 4, 12, 38, 41, etc.

[134] *Cronica*, 155. The counts of Toulouse and Foix and the viscount of Béziers had made peace with the Church in a council at Montpellier in August 1224, and other barons were evidently present, Mansi, *Conciliorum . . . Collectio*, xxii, 1205–1208; A.D. Lot-et-Garonne, MS d'Argenton, iii, 17, no. 28.

the particular locality where the overlord held court. Knights and notables advised and approved in ordinary seigneurial matters, such as homages and land transactions. They rarely served as a court of justice. These points are best illustrated by the situation in the county of Toulouse. Despite the loss of most of his possessions and influence in lower and eastern Languedoc,[135] Raymond VII was still the strongest single baron in the Midi. No other principality offers so extensive a documentation as Toulouse for the period 1229–1249. Politically, Raymond's acts tell a story of retrenchment and consolidation in his western domains. A long series of seigneurial transactions, notably in the Garonne valley and environs of Toulouse, worked almost uniformly to the advantage of the count. Feudal ties with the regional nobles were created or reestablished, the acts of homage becoming particularly numerous in the late 1230's.[136] Raymond found ample support in the western nobility for his league with Henry III and Hugues de Lusignan; and even the failure of their rising against the crown in 1242 seems not to have seriously weakened him.[137]

This increase in power is reflected in the size and composition of Raymond's feudal courts. Witness lists tend to be longer, and the names of greater barons in the Toulousan sphere of influence occur in them with some regularity. This group included the counts of Comminges, Foix, Armagnac, and Astarac, the viscounts of Narbonne and Lau-

[135] Raymond VII regained Venaissin in 1234. Roughly 10 per cent of his subsequent acts concern Provence, where, as in the west, he tried to add to his feudal power. See next note.

[136] Most of Raymond's documents are catalogued in *H.L.*, VIII, 1950ff. Not all of them are in print, and there is no modern study of them. See also Boutaric, *Saint Louis et Alfonse*, pp. 67–68.

[137] *H.L.*, VI, 741–742, 745–752. Raymond had to relinquish a few places, VIII, 1104,v. See generally C. Bémont, "La Campagne de Poitou, 1242–1243," *Annales du Midi*, V (1893), 289–314.

trec, and Jourdain de l'Isle.[138] Count Bernard V of Comminges was especially faithful in attendance. He was present when the lord of Isle did homage and fealty to Raymond VII in July 1229; he witnessed other comital transactions at Toulouse in the 1230's; he followed Raymond
to Provence in 1239, and in 1240 and 1241 he again attended the count in acts at Toulouse.[139] The orientation of
Comminges toward Toulouse, one of the major tendencies
in the feudal politics of this period, culminated in November 1244 with the young Bernard VI's surrender of the
entire county to the count of Toulouse as a fief. The gathering at Toulouse on this occasion was impressive in solemnity and numbers: the bishops of Toulouse and Comminges
headed a list of witnesses that included some thirty-five
followers and advisers of both counts.[140] A notable absentee
was the count of Rodez, who seems not to have attended
gatherings in the vicinity of Toulouse. A considerable
number of nobles and notables of Rouergue, Quercy, and
Albigeois, including the count of Rodez, met with Raymond at Millau in 1237 to witness the homage of a local
knight.[141] Admixtures of regional nobles of Agenais and
Albigeois can also be found in comital acts in those areas.
There is little evidence that Raymond's eastern vassals fol-

---

[138] A.N., JJ.19, fols. 178rv, 175v, 19v, 79v–80; *H.L.*, VIII,
932–933, 1076–1077, 1093–1094; *Layettes,* II, nos. 2457, 2742,
2875, 2938, 2939, 3205; G. de Puylaurens, *Cronica,* 166.

[139] A.N., JJ.19, fols. 175v, 81–82; Higounet, *Comté de Comminges,* I, 115.

[140] Higounet, I, 118–119; *H.L.,* VIII, 1165–1167.

[141] *Ibid.,* 1009–1010,ii; cf. G. Lacoste, *Histoire Générale de la
Province de Quercy,* new ed., 4 vols. (Cahors, 1883–1886), II,
248–249. Of the 16 names, 10 at least are local, 2 others possibly
so.

lowed him in his western lands.[142] His relatively few acts in eastern Languedoc require no special comment.[143] Raymond VII convoked a particularly important county assembly at Toulouse in April 1233. On this occasion he promulgated numerous statutes intended to induce greater vigilance against heretics in his lands and to enforce the papal regulations against heretics and peace-breakers. The background for this was the count's engagement in 1229 to cooperate fully with the Church in extirpating heresy. Charged with being "tepid and remiss" in this task, he had been haled before the king at Melun, where the papal legate and southern prelates directed that articles of reform be drafted. These articles became the basis for the statutes of Toulouse which Raymond published in the assembly in his own name.[144]

The composition of this meeting can only be known in the general terms of the preamble to the statutes. It says that they were issued "with the advice and assent of bishops and other prelates, of counts and barons, of knights and many other prudent men of our land."[145] Guillaume de Puylaurens speaks of "many barons," and makes it clear that the papal legate and seneschal of Carcassonne were present.[146] Undoubtedly the bishop of Toulouse was

[142] A.N., JJ.19, fols. 174–175; *Layettes*, II, no. 2938; *H.L.*, VIII, 1250–1251.

[143] The most remarkable of these is the grant of rights to the count by Marseille in 1230 in a combined parliament and comital court, including western vassals, *H.L.*, VIII, 934–938 (cf. VI, 664–665); see also VIII, 993–997; 1027–1030; *et passim*.

[144] *Ibid.*, VIII, 963–969; G. de Puylaurens, *Cronica*, 158; *H.L.*, VI, 675–677; Y. Dossat, *Les Crises de l'Inquisition Toulousaine* . . . (Bordeaux, 1959), pp. 105–111.

[145] *H.L.*, VIII, 963.

[146] *Cronica*, 158: "et ea [statuta] in presentia legati et plurium baronum et senescalli Carcassone . . . publicavit. . . ."

among the other churchmen.[147] If the categories of counts, barons, and knights[148] were all represented, as the preamble states, then it is probably safe to interpret the chronicler's "plures" in a liberal sense. The "other prudent men" surely included Raymond's councillors and men of Toulouse, but there is no reason to think that other towns were represented in any regular way. Like the parliament of Pamiers, which it resembles in some respects, the Toulouse assembly of 1233 *included* men of the two or three orders; but again this does not mean that it was an assembly of estates.[149] It was likewise a consultative and advisory body, useful for spreading word of the renewed campaign, but without sovereign legislative character.[150]

At Christmas 1244 Count Raymond convoked a "great court" at Toulouse. Guillaume de Puylaurens says that some two hundred nobles received recognition of knighthood on this occasion, which he further describes as "extremely sumptuous and pompous." But he names only seven of those present: the count of Comminges, the viscount of Lautrec, Guy de Sévérac, Sicard Alaman, Jourdain de l'Isle, Guillaume de Bonneville, and Bernard de la Tour.[151] Other names could be supplied for the "many others " not identified by the chronicler, for we have record of neighboring knights in attendance on the count in the weeks just before and after Christmas.[152] Raymond VII was

[147] G. de Puylaurens says that he and a royal knight, Gilles de Flagac, were entrusted with the supervision of Raymond's reforms.

[148] The charter's usage here (and cf. statutes of Pamiers, *H.L.*, VIII, 626, 628, 634) is different from Puylaurens' reference to *barones* (above, n. 146), perhaps equivalent to "nobles."

[149] Cf. Dognon, *Institutions*, p. 197.

[150] *H.L.*, VIII, 963: "matura deliberatione habita & diligenti studio precedente, hec statuta salubria in terra nostra & nostrorum duximus ordinanda"; see n. 146 for the chronicler's phrase.

[151] *Cronica*, 165–166.

[152] Including a feudal recognition at Toulouse on 31 December 1244, *H.L.*, VI, 772–773; *Layettes*, II, no. 3222; see also nos. 3203–3206, 3225–3229.

at the height of his power, capable of summoning men from areas well outside Toulousain. So large an assembly as Puylaurens describes must have included knights from distant seigneuries, although Guy de Sévérac, a prominent lord of eastern Rouergue, is the only one of whose presence we can be certain. Further hints of this wider community may be found in references to a gathering at Millau where the count lay dying in 1249. This was an advisory council which included the bishops of Toulouse, Agen, Cahors, Rodez, and Albi, "magnates and many knights of his land, and the consuls of Toulouse."[153]

There are other indications besides this one that the consulate of Toulouse remained influential in Raymond's affairs. Consuls were present at agreements of 1231 and 1232 pertaining to rights at Dourgne and Montauban.[154] The town apparently acquired interests in Agenais, for we find consuls of Toulouse attending general assemblies there around mid-century.[155] The importance of Toulousain, the county heartland, can be seen in the frequent attendance of minor regional knights in the count's public acts in the Garonne valley. Records of these acts refer to members of the noble families of Rabastens, Marquefave, Noé, Castelnau, Escalquens, Toulouse, Lanta, Montégut, Miremont, and Montaut.[156] Sicard Alaman, Pons Grimoard, Pons Astoaud, and Guy Foucois (the later Pope Clement IV),

---

[153] G. de Puylaurens, *Cronica*, 168; cf. *Layettes*, v, no. 568, *enquête* concerning the validity of Raymond's will; *H.L.*, viii, 1257–1259. The persons mentioned had administrative rights or interests in the count's dispositions; and the officials of Toulouse and several other magnates were named executors. Professor Post suggests to me here the procedural relevance of *quod omnes tangit* . . . ; cf. his " 'Quod Omnes Tangit,' in Bracton," *Traditio*, iv, 200–209.

[154] *H.L.*, viii, 940–943; vi, 671.

[155] *Layettes*, iii, no. 3833; and see below p. 100.

[156] A.N., JJ.19, fols. 177rv, 179, 171–172, 81–82; *H.L.*, viii, 932–933, 949–954, 1039–1040, 1076–1077; *Layettes*, ii, nos. 2166, 2171, 2875, 2938, 2939, 2997.

whose names appear even in enactments at a distance from Toulouse, were leading members of an inner circle of councillors.[157]

Many recognitions and homages from the 1220's on specify the obligation of suit at court as well as military service (*guerra et placitum*).[158] The count was evidently insisting on these services in practice. In most parts of the county they continued to be understood primarily as personal obligations. The petty nobles of Montaigut (Albigeois), Najac, and Fanjeaux made collective professions to the count on different occasions, but except in Agenais, obligations were not yet associated with the wider countryside or diocese.[159] Assemblies of nobles were ceremonial or advisory, manifestations of Raymond's authority and political sense. In October 1229, "deliberato consilio baronum nostrorum," the count rewarded previous service of the house of Foix by restoring certain valuable holdings in the county to Roger-Bernard of Foix.[160] Their knowledge of matters concerning their own districts explains why local notables were summoned as witnesses on various occa-

[157] A.N., JJ.19, fols. 174–175, 19v; *H.L.*, VIII, 1059,i; *Layettes*, II, nos. 2742, 2787, 2455.

[158] A.N., JJ.19, fols. 180v–181, 178rv, 179v–180, 81–82; *H.L.*, VIII, 1039,iv; 1076; *Layettes*, III, no. 3718. It is true that these acts are all patterned on a single notarial form (traceable at least as far back as 1213, JJ.19, fol. 179, and continuing in documents written by Johannes Aurioli, count's notary); but it is significant that the count almost always used this form (for exceptions see JJ.19, 162v–163, 173v, 21rv, 65). Raymond complained to the king that the seneschal of Carcassonne had summoned some of the count's vassals, contrary to custom, *H.L.*, VIII, 1193,viii (letter of January 1247); see also *Layettes*, III, no. 4208, similar complaint by the bishop of Lodève about 1255.

[159] A.N., JJ.19, fols. 178rv, 179v–180, 177rv, acts of 1228–1229. On Agenais, see below, pp. 77, 82–83.

[160] *H.L.*, VIII, 923–924,i. But the barons are not named, and the term *barones nostri* does not recur. Cf. *Layettes*, V, no. 568.

sions.[161] The connection between military and advisory service can be seen in an interesting document of 1242. Asked to provide counsel, the count of Foix, Raymond's strongest vassal, advised his lord to wage war against the king, with a promise to support the campaign.[162] Western knights sometimes attended judgments or compromises involving the count of Toulouse,[163] but there seems to be no evidence of a tribunal of peers of the county during these years.

Feudal assemblies and courts convened in other major baronies of Languedoc, such as Comminges and Foix. Bernard VI of Comminges, before doing homage to Raymond VII in 1244, had deliberated with his councillors and had taken the advice of "[the bishop of Comminges], Boniface de Fauga, Arnaud-Guillaume de Barbazan, Gaillard and Bernard de Sazos, Bernard de Benque, and many others." Together with those named, a good many other Commingian knights figure in the long witness list.[164] In June 1241 Count Roger of Foix made concessions to the church of Foix after consultation with the count of Pailhès, Raymond de Niort "and our barons standing about, namely Arnaud de Marquefave, Guillaume-Bernard d'Arnave, Loup de Foix, Raymond-Batalha de Chateauverdun, [and] Pierre-Guillaume d'Arvigna."[165] We have some evidence for relations between the count and the knights and burgh-

---

[161] See, among many such, *Layettes*, II, no. 2997, at Saverdun, 1242, a witness list including local knights, preceded by the formula: "ad hoc vocati et rogati."

[162] *H.L.*, VIII, 1087: "nos Rogerius . . . requisiti a vobis domino nostro R. . . . ut demus vobis consilium, utrum facietis guerram . . . [etc.]"; cf. G. de Puylaurens, *Cronica*, 160.

[163] See, e.g., *H.L.*, VIII, 949–954; cf. A.N., JJ.19, fol. 144rv.

[164] *H.L.*, VIII, 1165–1167.

[165] *Ibid.*, 1061–1063,ii.

ers of his towns, particularly Saverdun.[166] But there was no town representation in assemblies either in Foix or Comminges in the time of Louis IX. In the county of Rodez, the viscounty of Lautrec, and other minor principalities of upper and eastern Languedoc, no courts or communities of knights can be clearly distinguished.[167]

Of the important feudatories of coastal Languedoc, only the submissive viscount of Narbonne retained his domains intact in the aftermath of royal conquest. And it is possible to speak of the feudal court of Narbonne as an institution. We find continuity from the 1220's of a fairly well defined community of nobles of the *pays*. Most of the "knights of Narbonnais" who assembled in Aymery's *curia* in May 1229 reappear in November 1242 as witnesses to an act of homage by the viscount of Fenouillet; following their names is the phrase: "isti omnes sunt milites dicti domini Amalrici [Amaury (1239–1270)]."[168] This group included members of the regional families of Boutenac, Pierrepertuse, La Redorte, Bessan, Ouveillan, and Montbrun. In 1232 countryside knights joined the town nobility of Nar-

---

[166] See *ibid.*, 1075, 1548–1549,ii; the count addressed a statute against heretics to the county as follows, 1479,i; "Rogerius . . . universis bailivis, consulibus, universitatibus & populis Appamiarum, Fuxi, Savarduni, Tarasconis, de Ax, Lordati & aliis universitatibus totius comitatus Fuxi, salutem. . . ."

[167] There are a few scattered documents for the period to 1271, e.g., the foundation charter for Ribouisse, granted by Guy de Lévis in 1271, *ibid.*, 1724: "Nos igitur . . . militum & quorumdam hominum nostrorum habito diligenti concilio, volentes . . ."; the witness list for conventions between Philippe de Montfort and the abbot of Candeil records names of a few local notables, B.N., Doat, cxv, 123–133; for knights of Lautrec and vicinity, see *H.L.*, viii, 1432; C. Portal, "Chartes de Labruguière (Tarn), 1266," *Bull. Hist. et Philol. du Comité des Travaux Hist. et Scient.* (1897), 830; for Rouergue, *H.L.*, viii, 1201–1202; and for the east, *Layettes*, ii, no. 2471 (Maguelonne, 1236); *H.L.*, viii, 1228,iii (Clermont, 1247); vi, 868; viii, 1501 (Montpellier, 1260, 1262); etc.

[168] *H.L.*, viii, 897,i; 1097; cf. above, p. 55.

bonne in petitioning the viscount Aymery III to draw up
and publish their customs.[169] In addition to local nobles, a
royal lieutenant, the viscount of Lautrec, and Pierre-Roger
de Mirepoix had attended an assembly at Narbonne in
January 1232, when the viscounty was engaged to the
house of Foix in case of extinction of the legitimate line.[170]
Also continuing from the earlier thirteenth century was the
confusion between seigneurial courts and town meetings.
Most lists include the names of town notables, both knights
and burghers.[171] On an important occasion in 1265 Amaury summoned the general parliament to session *in curia
sua.*[172] The viscount ordinarily convoked his knights at
Narbonne, although they might sometimes meet elsewhere.[173]

In its function and competence the *curia* had various
aspects. First, it was a permanent civil and criminal court
with a judge and officials, the highest court of the viscounty.[174] The customs of 1232, very Roman in character,
do not speak explicitly of judgment by peers in Narbonnais, and we find no other evidence of it.[175] The court was
also a consultative and advisory body, usually including a
relatively small group of councillors and officials.[176] While
it cannot be sharply distinguished from his judicial competence, the viscount's administrative and legislative power

169 *Ibid.*, 960; cf. above, n. 123.

170 *Ibid.*, 956–957,ii.

171 *Ibid.*, 957,ii; 1007–1008,iv; *I.A.C., Narbonne, Annexes de la
Série AA*, no. 20, p. 34; B.N., Doat, L, 89–92.

172 A.M. Narbonne, AA.109, fol. 34 (Appendix II, no. 3).

173 A.M. Narbonne, AA.24.

174 *H.L.*, VIII, 1107,iv; *I.A.C., Narbonne, Annexes de la Série
AA*, no. 33, pp. 47–48.

175 *H.L.*, VIII, 960–963, and art. 8: "Item si questio vertatur
inter dominum vicecomitem Narbone & aliquem militem ejus
feudatarium, ipse vicecomes debet ei statuere judices sine omni
suspicione."

176 *Ibid.*, 960, 1007–1008,iv; B.N., Doat, L, fol. 89; A.M.
Narbonne, AA.24.

centered in his court, which occasionally issued statutes jointly with the coseigneurial court of the archbishop.[177] Finally, the *curia* could be a strictly ceremonial and feudal body, as in the homage of 1242, already mentioned, which was subscribed only by knights. The same act shows that Amaury's vassal, the viscount of Fenouillet, had his own group of knights in Fenouilhedès, south of Narbonne.[178]

The old viscounties of Béziers and Carcassonne did not retain autonomous or legitimate feudal communities after 1226. But Trencavel II abandoned neither titles nor pretensions, and in 1240 he headed a last pathetic, unsuccessful revolt of the lesser barons of the region.[179] Many of the latter had never acknowledged royal authority, while others had been proscribed for heresy and forced to flee their domains. Among the leaders were Olivier de Termes, the lords of Barbaira, Cabardès, Durfort, Niort, Pépieux, Raymond d'Orzals, Raymond-Hugues de Serrelongue, Raymond de Villeneuve, Hugues de Roumengous, and Jourdain de Saissac.[180] These men and others of the *petite noblesse* were uprooted forever in the royal and ecclesiastical reprisals of the following years.[181] The only assemblies even remotely resembling "courts" of the viscounty—indeed they were much more like town parliaments—occurred in 1247, when Trencavel made his definitive submission to the crown. One meeting, at Béziers on 7 April, was composed of major prelates, royal officials, "very numerous" clergy and laity—townsmen probably among the latter—and regional knights who had remained loyal or

---

[177] *I.A.C.*, Narbonne, *Annexes de la Série AA*, no. 33, pp. 47–48.

[178] *H.L.*, VIII, 1097; cf. 898, a donation of "dominia militum totius terrae Fenoletensis. . . ."

[179] *Ibid.*, VI, 718–719; A. Molinier, "Sur l'Expédition de Trencavel & le Siège de Carcassonne, en 1240," *ibid.*, VII, 448–453.

[180] G. de Puylaurens, *Cronica*, ed. Beyssier, 160; *H.L.*, VIII, 1043; VII, 450, 452.

[181] As Molinier pointed out, *H.L.*, VII, 448.

reverted to orthodoxy.[182] With reference to his rights at Lombers, the former viscount published a nearly identical renunciation at Castres on 12 May in a similar gathering of ecclesiastics, knights, and local notables.[183] These documents refer to a *universitas* of knights and people of the two cities and of the whole viscounty of Béziers-Carcassonne.[184] Yet one finds no evidence of assemblies corresponding in composition to the corporation of estates in the old viscounty.

The only ecclesiastical councils or courts that concern us are those attended by laymen. But there is no reason to suppose that such meetings had any influence on the form and function of secular assemblies during the reign of Louis IX. Political, administrative, or judicial in purpose, "mixed" assemblies were strictly *ad hoc*, without institutional character. Their secular composition was determined rather by the availability of individual notables than by territorial organization.[185] The new inquisition by joint commissions of clerics and laymen was an important innovation, to be sure, but it would carry us too far from the present subject to enter into its relationship with procedures of secular *enquête* in the Midi. Varying in size from a dozen or fifteen to fifty, these committees were usually both local and specialized in composition. Their *de facto* power was considerable, because their recommendations usually went far toward settling cases.[186] Occasionally an investiga-

---

[182] *Layettes*, III, no. 3588.

[183] *Ibid.*, no. 3599.

[184] *Ibid.*, no. 3588; Trencavel gave up "totum vicecomitatum Biterris et Carcassone et universitatem, milites seu populum, dictarum civitatum et tocius vicecomitatus Biterrensis et Carcassonensis. . . ."

[185] *H.L.*, VIII, 1121–1122, 1138, 1272–1273, 1547,i.

[186] See Lea, *Inquisition in the Middle Ages*, I, 387–391; A. P. Evans, "Hunting Subversion in the Middle Ages," *Speculum*, XXXIII (1958), 20; also Dossat, *L'Inquisition Toulousaine*, pp. 152ff; and C. Douais, "La Formule 'Communicato Bonorum Virorum Con-

tion was regional in scope, as, for example, in 1243, when "many knights and other men" of royal and Toulousan lands were condemned as heretics. We are told that the Dominican inquisitor conferred with the archbishop of Narbonne, the bishop of Albi, other prelates and other "prudent men"; but the latter are not identified.[187]

Placing the whole period 1180–1249 in review, the conclusion seems warranted that the seigneurial *curia* was not a very stable or well-defined institution in Languedoc. Doubtless the crusade and conquest upset the older feudal order. But Dognon misleads us when he suggests that a pre-existent feudal court of Toulouse survived the war.[188] To be sure, the duty of suit was taken more seriously in the county of Toulouse after the 1220's. Possibly this was true of other lordships too. In the same years we find a feudal court of Narbonne, and it may have existed earlier; there was certainly such a body in the viscounty of Béziers for a few years before the crusade. Yet the prevailing impression remains that assemblies were irregular events. The summons of vassals was beyond the order of routine. Nobles of the countryside may sometimes have attained some minimal sense of corporate identity. We hear of "knights of the land" meeting with viscounts of Béziers in 1194 and 1224, and the lords of Narbonnais, mingling with urban knights, acted as a community in 1232 when they requested that their regional custom be put in writing. But such meetings of the estate of nobility were rare enough in the lesser baronies, and probably unknown in the larger ones.

Acts of summons, if they were ever in writing, have not survived from this period. Hence we know very little about the administration of feudal assemblies. Nor can we know

silio' des Sentences Inquisitoriales," *Le Moyen Age,* XI (1898), 157–160.

[187] *H.L.,* VIII, 1143–1144.

[188] *Institutions,* p. 197.

how systematically "representative" the larger convocations were intended to be. Of their predominantly aristocratic character the evidence is sufficient to leave no doubt.
Townsmen frequently appear in them, but they are invariably men of leading towns where the meetings are held.
Moreover, they are men of quality—knights, officials, or
notables; the little people are only occasionally in evidence,
as included in the parliament of the *universitas* or militia.
Indeed, it can hardly be said that town representation
makes any progress in Languedoc in the first half of the
thirteenth century.[189] Multiple deputations of towns may
sometimes have occurred but were not noted as such in the
records. The lords do not manifestly summon towns or villages to central places. The third estate of non-nobles—
cives, burgenses—has its definite juridical existence, but its
nascent interests do not as yet find expression in any regional community.

Corporate delegation was becoming known in ecclesiastical assemblies, as is shown by the presence of chapter heads
in the Fourth Lateran Council in 1215 and proctors of
chapters in the legatine council of Bourges in 1225.[190] It is
worth noting that the only hint of a corporate municipal
representation in the Languedoc assemblies here surveyed
relates to mixed gatherings sponsored by the Church. At
Narbonne in 1214, seven consuls of the city and bourg of
Toulouse swore that they had the authority of proctors to
take the oath against heresy on behalf of the urban *universitas,* which might thus regain its good standing in the

[189] But for special situations in Agenais and Quercy see next
section and next chapter.

[190] *Patrologiae Cursus Completus . . . Latinae,* ed. J. Migne, 221
vols. (Paris, 1844–1864), ccxvi, 825 (xvi,30); A. Luchaire, *Innocent III: Le Concile de Latran . . .* (Paris, 1908), pp. 8–10;
Matthew Paris, *Chronica Majora,* ed. H. R. Luard, 7 vols., *R.S.*
(London, 1872–1883), iii, 105–109; *The Register of S. Osmund,*
ed. W. H. Rich Jones, 2 vols., *R.S.* (*London,* 1883–1884), ii,
51–54; etc.; cf. *H.L.,* viii, 866,i.

Church.[191] Again, in the council of 1229, two Toulousan consuls, one of the city and the other of the bourg, swore to observe the statutes of peace on behalf of the whole community.[192]

Most regional assemblies in Languedoc to 1249 were advisory, acclamatory, or propagandistic in their function. The inner seigneurial councils could usually be depended upon to provide the information that enabled lords to proceed with any particular business. But it was often useful, especially in outlying districts, to have the opinion of local men on the value of a property whose transfer was contemplated or the facts about a *paréage* to be made or privileges to be confirmed. Whether as formal witnesses or as bystanders, an aggregate of men in attendance added solemnity—even legality[193]—to a pact or feudal homage and enhanced the prestige of the principals involved. The usefulness of plenary assemblies for disseminating information regarding new policies can be seen in the meetings of Pamiers in 1212 and Toulouse in 1229 and 1233. Notables and town magistrates seem sometimes to have been consulted on account of their legal or administrative rights. But this theoretical basis for a right of summons is not yet maintained consciously or explicitly. In practice, assemblies provided counsel, and even consent, if that word be taken in its usual medieval sense. They usually took no initiative. They merely approved decisions on the questions for which they were convoked, which is not to deny that in theory some of those who participated may have had rights to advise or consent.

---

[191] *Ibid.*, 647–651.

[192] G. de Puylaurens, *Cronica,* 155. These are among the earliest references to municipal procuration of any kind in Languedoc.

[193] "Praesentibus et videntibus," e.g., *H.L.*, viii, 391, 489,ii; "in presentia & testimonio," e.g., *ibid.*, 488,i; 490,iii; 581,i; "in praesentia testium," *ibid.*, 405. On the technicalities of validation see A. Giry, *Manuel de Diplomatique* (Paris, 1894), pp. 613–616.

THE GENERAL COURT OF AGENAIS
1182–1271[194]

Local nobles and notables convened in Agenais much as they did elsewhere in early thirteenth-century Languedoc.[195] In this respect the history of assemblies in this western-most Toulousan fief conforms to the pattern described in preceding pages. In other respects, however, it is a different history, and a significantly different one. We find in Agenais, for one thing, a more marked consciousness of community and association than in most districts to the east. Moreover, there existed in Agenais a somewhat institutionalized feudal court. And from a remarkably early date—at least as early as 1182—this court of Agenais could be summoned as a plenary or general body, including town deputies as well as knights.

Agenais had been a fief, or territory, of the duchy of Aquitaine, which passed under Angevin control in 1152. But subsequently, though never divided, the district had a history of its own under shifting suzerainties. It parted ways with the duchy in 1196 when Count Raymond VI of Toulouse acquired it as a dowry for his marriage to Joan, King Richard's sister. It was still part of the county when the Toulousan inheritance fell to the French crown in 1271. Raymond VI had agreed to hold Agenais as a fief of Aquitaine, but his successors tended to ignore feudal obligations. Hence, when Raymond VII died without male heirs in 1249, Henry III of England tried to recover Agenais. For another hundred years the region was involved in the larger complex of feudal disputes between the English

---

[194] This section, in its essentials, has already appeared in *Speculum*, XXXVI (1961), 254ff. It is here, and in parts of chapters 4 and 6, somewhat revised and expanded. In this chapter I sometimes overstep the limit of 1271, but emphasis remains on the prior period.

[195] *Layettes*, II, no. 2742; JJ.19, fol. 19v (orig. indicated in *Layettes*, III, no. 3776).

and French, and it was not until 1359 that Agenais came to be subjected definitively to France.[196]

The distinctiveness of Agenais goes farther back in time than we can trace it today, but it was already apparent in the twelfth century. Constituted as a border district in a major feudal aggregate, Agenais was necessarily ruled from a distance through deputies. This worked to the advantage of the bishops of Agen, strong free-holding territorial lords. Yet they never gained such mastery in Agenais as did the neighboring bishops of Cahors in Quercy, and this fact largely accounts for important institutional differences between the two dioceses.[197] Secular lordship had remained effective in Agenais because the Aquitainian dukes were well served by their agents, the omni-competent seneschals. Angevin administration was more advanced than Toulousan. It is probable that the first seneschal in the county of Toulouse was a seneschal of Agenais.[198]

The men of Agenais were understood to form a kind of regional community, with common rights and responsibilities. The earliest town charter, which Duke Richard granted to Marmande in 1182, refers to the "general custom of

[196] J. Andrieu, *Histoire de l'Agenais*, 2 vols. (Paris, 1893), I, 34–41, 62–63, 66, 69–71, 75–77, 111–117, 135, 140; M. Gavrilovitch, *Étude sur le Traité de Paris de 1259* . . . (Paris, 1899), pp. 23–24, 71–74; G. P. Cuttino, introd. to *Livre d'Agenais* (Toulouse, 1956), pp. vii–xiv; cf. P. Chaplais, "Le Traité de Paris de 1259 et l'Inféodation de la Gascogne Allodiale," *Le Moyen Age*, 4e sér., x (1955), esp. 132–133, 135.

[197] Cf. next chapter.

[198] *H.L.*, VII, 130, seneschals of Toulousain and Agenais mentioned for first time in 1210. But, unlike Toulouse, there are almost no documents on Agenais for the years preceding. It is quite possible that Agenais had had a seneschal from 1196 on, or from an earlier time, since the lord's seneschal "in Agenais" is mentioned in the charter of Marmande of 1182, A.N., JJ.72, fols. 145ff; cf. J. Momméja, "Sénéchaux du Quercy," *Recueil des Travaux de la Société* . . . *d'Agen*, 2ᵉsér., xiii,ii (1898), 231–233.

Agenais" for criminal penalties.[199] We find many later references to privileges and obligations that the people of a given place share with other villages of the countryside.[200] There was a regional law of succession, as well as feudal regulations for homage and fealty *ad consuetudinem Agennensem*.[201] A sense of community quite independent of class interests is shown by the general liability to military duty. The *Chanson de la Croisade* assures us that the army which rallied to support the count of Toulouse against Simon de Montfort's French crusaders in 1211 included "the whole Agenais, so that no one stayed behind."[202] With due allowance for enthusiastic exaggeration, this should probably be regarded as a reference to the "common" or "general army of Agenais," an institution that is often mentioned in later documents.[203] In 1232 a seneschal had occasion to address himself "to the barons, knights, townsmen, and the whole university of Agenais," and this corporate notification was something more than mere rhetoric. Another seneschal reported some years later that the *genus* of barons and knights of Agenais and the "whole people" had raised an

[199] A.N., JJ.72, fols. 145ff.

[200] *H.L.*, VIII, 1965, no. 151; *Archives Historiques du Département de la Gironde* [to be cited as *Arch. Gir.*] (1859), I, no. 182 (a register of recognitions in Agenais made in 1286–1287), 356, no. 24; 360, no. 39; etc.; also VII (1865), 67, art. 37, reference to "general costuma d'Agenes" in a late 13th-century charter.

[201] P. Ourliac, "Note sur les Coutumes Successorales de l'Agenais," *Annales de la Faculté de Droit d'Aix*, XLIII (1950), 253–258; *Arch. Gir.*, I, 352: *Livre d'Agenais*, no. 21, p. 50

[202] Ed. Martin-Chabot, I, 208.

[203] Cited regularly in the recognitions of 1286, *Arch. Gir.*, I, 352, 359, *et passim* (note the revealing expression of military obligation: "quando nobiles et alii de patria faciunt exercitum," 354, nos. 13, 15); *Livre d'Agenais*, nos. 5–11, pp. 17–20. This was an old custom: early charters refer to the army as the "ost en Agenes," A.N., JJ.72, fol. 150v; cf. H. Tropamer, *La Coutume d'Agen* (Bordeaux, 1911), p. 28. This institution should not be confused with the bishop's peace army, discussed in ch. 3.

outcry about the failure to act promptly against certain marauders. The feeling of regional solidarity was perhaps most fully articulated in fealty proceedings of Edward I in 1286, when the villagers of Damazan recognized their obligation to take the oath and perform military service together with the *tota communitas Agennensis*.[204]

Circumstances of the early thirteenth century were such as to encourage a common territorial politics. Already in 1203 King John was addressing himself to the whole populace of Agenais in opposition to his undependable vassal Raymond VI.[205] Panic and sympathy explain the massive support tendered by Agenais at Raymond's first major summons in 1211, but resistance melted when he took no personal part in the defense of Agenais in the following year. Yet the political consensus, if not the religious, remained strongly contrary to the *Francigene*. Submission was simply the expedient course, as the people of Agen recognized. Penne resisted because the seneschal had assembled a garrison force there. Other towns watched and waited. Marmande decided to stand a siege and was captured.[206] In the crisis the nobles seem to have acted more circumspectly. A certain number of them sought out Montfort at the siege of Penne, recognized him as their lord, and did homage for their fiefs. They may have appeared together, though this is not clear, and it is likely that they

---

[204] C. de Saint-Amans, "De la Monnaie dite Arnaldèse des Évêques d'Agen," *Rec. Trav. Soc. Agen*, VII (1855), 614–615, no. 3; *Layettes*, V, no. 672; *Arch Gir.*, I, 382, no. 127. As is shown in later pages, these three situations can all be associated with the general court.

[205] *Rotuli Litterarum Patentium* . . . , ed. T. Duffus Hardy, I (London, 1835), 23ab.

[206] See *Chanson*, ed. Martin-Chabot, I, 208–262; *Hystoria Albigensis*, II, 16–38. Doubtless many people at Agen approved the bishop's submissive policy in 1212; but a few years later the city joined in the regional reaction against the Montforts' rule, *H.L.*, VI, 542–544; Belperron, *Croisade*, p. 349.

had acted on the basis of a preliminary decision in common.[207]

Pierre des Vaux-de-Cernay is our lone witness for this incident, which is therefore open to critical doubt. But it is not inherently improbable, nor is there any obvious motive for falsifying the point. If the event is historical, it has the significance of being the earliest recorded instance of the knights of Agenais in a feudal posture before the regional lord. Yet homage to Montfort at such a juncture could only represent a repetition of similar acts before Raymond VI or his deputies, and probably the dukes of Aquitaine before them. Common feudal obligations were the basis for associative experience among the knights of Agenais. In 1214 a local noble recognized that he owed to Montfort "such service . . . as the other barons of Agenais owe." [208] Feudal counsel or suit at court, though infrequently specified, was surely a recognized duty.[209] And when another Agenais noble, also in 1214, acknowledges the jurisdiction of Montfort's court of Agen(ais?), we must suppose that he means a feudal court.[210] Such a court cannot have been new with Simon de Montfort, even though there is no earlier direct evidence of it. The court of nobles probably met occasionally to hear major feudal causes.

If the baronial court is rarely mentioned in the thirteenth century, this is because, at the very moment when it comes into historical view, it is being superseded by the general

[207] *Hystoria*, II, 25: "Nec pretermittendum quod, dum esset comes in obsidione Penne, venerunt ad eum omnes nobiles terre illius et, facientes ei hominium, acceperunt ab eo terras suas." But some Agenais nobles probably refrained from committing themselves. Several are included in a list of Gascon magnates who swore fealty to King John at La Réole in April 1214, *Rotuli Litterarum Clausarum . . .* , ed. T. Duffus Hardy, I (London, 1833), 201; *Hystoria*, II, 199.

[208] A.N., J.890, no. 12 (indic. *Layettes*, V, no. 206).

[209] See below pp. 81–82.

[210] A.N., JJ.13, fol. 43.

court. There can be no real doubt that the latter evolved from a pre-existent *curia* by the addition of town deputies.[211] The expanded court is first mentioned in an article of the Marmande customs of 1182: "And when the prince of the land or his seneschal shall convoke his general court, some or all of the consuls, according to the order of the lord, should go to the said court for the town of Marmande, at the expense of the town." [212] Forty years elapse before we find another reference to the general court. It is mentioned briefly in 1222 in a convention between two towns of Agenais; [213] and it receives fuller notice in the customs of Agen in an article which, though undated, probably belongs to the third or fourth decade of the thirteenth century. This article, undoubtedly reflecting earlier conditions, refers to the lord's *cort*—and the omission of the adjective is significant here—as a tribunal with cognizance of cases involving the peace of Agenais, and composed of barons, knights, consuls, and townsmen of the diocese.[214] The custumals of Fumel (1265) and Tonneins-Dessous (1301), the latter in terms repeated from the charter of Marmande, also refer to the general court.[215] The *curia generalis* had become a customary institution of the community of Agenais.[216]

[211] This was Dognon's belief, *Institutions*, p. 196.

[212] "E quant lo princep de la terra o sos senescalc mandera sa cort general, lo cosselh tot o la una partida segont lo mandament del senhor deven anar en aquela court per la vila de Marmande a mession de la vila," A.N., JJ.72 (a registral copy of the *vidimus* by Philip VI in 1341; another copy is in B.N., MS n.a.franç. 3404), fol. 150v.

[213] *Chartes d'Agen*, no. 14.

[214] Tropamer, *Coutume d'Agen*, pp. 28, 30, art. 3, partially quoted below, n. 255. For discussion of the texts, see *ibid.*, pp. 5–11.

[215] *Arch. Gir.*, VII (1865), 18, art. 12; A. Lagarde, *Notice Historique sur la Ville de Tonneins* (Agen, 1882), p. 118, art. 25.

[216] See also "Prise de Possession de l'Agenais au Nom du Roi de France en 1271," eds. G. Tholin, O. Fallières, *Rec. Trav. Soc.*

The earliest record of an actual session is a document of 1232. It relates that the seneschal of Agenais, on the instance of the count of Toulouse, had made an enactment concerning the bishop's coinage rights "by the consent of the barons, knights, townsmen, and the general court of Agenais." [217] There may have been a meeting of the general court in 1234,[218] but no other sessions are recorded in the next fifteen years. In 1249 deputies acting for Alfonse, the new count of Toulouse, had occasion to convoke an assembly composed of barons and knights of Agenais, consuls of Agen, and councillors and men of bourgs, *castra*, and villages of the diocese.[219] This gathering closely resembles another in 1271 that was explicitly termed "general court." The latter assembly was also styled *parlamentum*, however; and the terms "cort" or "curia," unqualified, continued to be used in reference to assemblies of men of two orders, or even of three.[220] Hence we must not lay too much stress on the terminology. The *curia generalis* was an institution of some commonly recognized function and composition, but other kinds of assemblies also met in Agenais, some limited to nobles, others to townsmen. We have somewhat problematical evidence of several regional meetings which may have been general courts; and we know of at least two gatherings in the later thirteenth century that included men of all three estates. All of these assemblies have a common history derived from the general tradition of community and association in Agenais.

Agen, 2ᵉ sér., xɪɪɪ (1897), to be cited as *Sais(imentum)*.
Agen(ense)., 72, summons of a *curia generalis* at Agen in 1271, "juxta usum dicte terre."
[217] *Rec. Trav. Soc. Agen*, vɪɪ, 614–615, no. 3.
[218] See below, p. 95.
[219] *Layettes*, ɪɪɪ, no. 3833.
[220] *Sais. Agen.*, 72, 85 (prelates were also summoned according to the second text); customs of Agen, art. 3 (below, n. 255); *Layettes*, ɪv, no. 4883; *Livre d'Agenais*, no. 2, p. 8.

Assemblies of Agenais were usually presided over by the seneschal.[221] Count Raymond VII sometimes summoned men of one or another order in Agenais, and he may have attended the general court of 1232.[222] But there is no record that Alfonse or, later, the kings of France or England ever appeared personally in the assemblies of their distant possession. To supplement the work of their seneschals in Agenais, these rulers sometimes had recourse to special commissioners, who used the general court to carry out their instructions.[223] The bishops of Agen, despite their important seigneurial rights in Agenais, could not convoke the assembly on their own authority. When he wished to discuss the diocesan coinage with the men of Agenais in 1263, Bishop Guillaume III asked the seneschal to convoke "his court" for that purpose.[224]

The usual place of assembly was Agen, the administrative center of the district.[225] Apparently no one place within the city was reserved. We hear of gatherings in the cathedral church, the bishop's palace, the town hall (*domus communitatis*), the house of the Templars, and the Dominicans' house and cloister.[226] Different sessions of the

[221] Cf. n. 212; and see *Rec. Trav. Soc. Agen*, VII, 614–615, no. 3; *Layettes*, IV, no. 4883; *Rôles Gascons*, eds. F. Michel, C. Bémont, 4 vols. (Paris, 1885–1906), II, no. 1428.

[222] *Chartes d'Agen*, nos. 31, 32; A.N., J.306, no. 80.

[223] *Layettes*, III, no. 3833 (Queen Blanche, acting for Alfonse); *Sais. Agen.*, 72, 85; *Livre d'Agenais*, no. 2, p. 8; cf. *Arch. Gir.*, I, no. 181, 348–349, regarding sessions of 1286, in which Edward I may have appeared (cf. below, pp. 238–239).

[224] *Layettes*, IV, no. 4883.

[225] See *ibid.*, no. 4883; *Sais. Agen.*, 72; *Chartes d'Agen*, no. 60. There is no certain instance of a general court held elsewhere (but cf. *Livre d'Agenais*, no. 17, p. 37); a meeting of Agenais nobles in 1243 took place at Castelsarrasin, on the border of Toulousain, perhaps to accommodate Raymond VII, A.N., J.306, no. 80.

[226] *Layettes*, III, no. 3833; *Enquêtes Administratives d'Alfonse de Poitiers . . . 1249–1271*, eds. P. Fournier, P. Guébin (Paris, 1959), no. 7, pp. 64–67 (not a general court); *Sais. Agen.*, 72, 85, 87; *Chartes d'Agen*, no. 60

same general court might convene in different places.[227] The method of summons is unknown. General patent letters or notification by word of mouth were probably most common.[228] Important persons or towns may sometimes have received individual letters,[229] but the fact that no such letter has survived seems to indicate that this was not the ordinary practice. There are no administrative lists for Agenais until the later thirteenth century.

Inquiry into the origins, original function, and composition of the general court is plagued by the virtual absence of evidence before the 1220's. No traces remain of the first summonses of townsmen. They must be earlier, but cannot be much earlier, than 1182, when southwestern bourgs and *castra* were just beginning to acquire juridical individuality. The principles governing attendance, for nobles as well as towns, can only be determined from materials of a later day. Yet it is improbable that those principles had changed very much in the century or so after 1180.

The attendance of nobles must have been founded ultimately on the same obligation of feudal counsel or suit that brought them together in the simple baronial court. Hence it may seem surprising that this service is so rarely specified in the thirteenth century. Up to 1250, only a few scattered acts mention it. In 1259, among 159 nobles making recognitions, only one man volunteered that he owed "court" as well as homage and knight service for his

[227] As in November 1271, *Sais. Agen.*, 72, 85–87; and August 1279, *Chartes d'Agen*, no. 60; *Livre d'Agenais*, no. 2, pp. 8–9.

[228] Both are exemplified by a curious document of 1274, *Recogniciones Feodorum in Aquitania* . . . , ed. C. Bémont (Paris, 1914), no. 174, the lone surviving instrument of general summons for the Gascon seisin of Edward I; cf. *Arch. Gir.*, I, nos. 181 (348–349), 182 (351). According to the usages of Agen, Tropamer, *Coutume d'Agen*, p. 28, the host was "cried" generally throughout Agenais.

[229] Cf. *Rot. Pat.*, I, 23ab.

fiefs.[230] Recognition rolls of 1286 show the government's concern for its jurisdiction, without stressing suit.[231] On the other hand, these acts, and others like them, invariably specify military obligations.[232] The distinction between *consilium* and *auxilium* may well have been lost in Agenais, where, as in other regions, a knightly assembly must have looked much like a knightly army. As a case in point, we may notice a political gathering in 1243 which was composed of those very nobles in Agenais who had recently supported Raymond VII in his unsuccessful revolt against the king of France.[233] The significance of the military analogy will become more fully apparent in a moment.

De-emphasis on counsel may be further explained by the fact that feudal services had lost much of their personal character in Agenais. With the long tradition of absentee lordship and delegated responsibility, feudal relations were, from an early date, "realized," to use Ganshof's word, and collectivized.[234] Like the knight in 1214, and a host of others after him, one thought of service as due for landed possessions in Agenais and defined it according to com-

[230] *H.L.*, VIII, 677; A.N., JJ.19, fol. 19v; "Hommages des Seigneurs de l'Agenais au Comte de Toulouse en 1259," eds. Tholin, Fallières, *Rec. Trav. Soc. Agen*, 2e sér., XIII (1897), 11–62, and 33.

[231] *Arch. Gir.*, I, 357, no. 30; 358; no. 31; etc.; cf. 381, no. 125, a knight recognizes "se debere facere et stare juri coram eo [lord of Agenais]"; and 386, no. 140.

[232] In addition to the recognitions of 1259 and 1286, see *Livre d'Agenais*, nos. 5–11, pp. 17–20, obligations to *exercitus et homagia* in 1279.

[233] A.N., J.306, no. 80 (Appendix II, no. 1); cf. Rymer, *Foedera, Conventiones, Litterae, et cujuscunque Generis Acta Publica . . .*, Rec. Comm. ed., 4 vols. (London, 1816–1869), I,i, 249, for their analogous act of conspiracy the preceding summer.

[234] Cf. the stimulating remarks by J. R. Strayer in *Twelfth-Century Europe and the Foundations of Modern Society*, eds. M. Clagett, G. Post, R. Reynolds (Madison, 1961), pp. 80–82; and see Ganshof, *Feudalism*, 2nd Eng. ed., p. 150.

mon custom (*de his quae habeo in diocesi Agenensi* . . .
*servicium teneor facere, quale debent alii barones Agen-
enses*).[235] And so, perhaps from its very inception, the
general court was something more than just the lord's court.
It was an institution of the countryside, attended by knights
who may have thought of themselves as vassals owing personal suit, but who are usually described as *barones,
milites*, and *domicelli* of Agenais; their attendance was determined rather by social status and holdings than by
vassalage.[236] There were many seigneurial families in the
region, and the aggregate of Agenais nobles was even larger
than the number of residents. The powerful lords of Albret,
with holdings centered elsewhere in Gascony, had interests
and possessions in Agenais that accorded them pre-eminence
there. We know that they attended general assemblies of
Agenais.[237] For similar reasons, the viscount of Lomagne
and the lord of Pestillac, in Quercy, were also accounted
nobles of Agenais.[238] The total population of nobility in
Agenais was surely more than 150 at mid-century and may
have approached twice that figure. But the records are inadequate for a dependable estimate.[239] Though useful for

[235] A.N., J.890, no. 12; "Hommages . . . en 1259," 13, 20, 22–
24, 31, 34, etc.; *Livre d'Agenais*, no. 5, pp. 17–18. The sense that
feudal obligations were collective, rather than individual, is very
clear in the recognitions of 1286, *Arch. Gir.*, I, no. 182, e.g., 354,
nos. 13, 15; 360, no. 41.

[236] See *Layettes*, III, no. 3833; *Chartes d'Agen*, no. 60, p. 84;
cf. *Livre d'Agenais*, p. 8.

[237] *H.L.*, VIII, 1039,iii; 1119; 1290; "Hommages . . . en 1259,"
54, no. 1; *Arch. Gir.*, I, 361, no. 42; cf. *Chartes d'Agen*, no. 50·,
where, in excusing himself from assembly, Amanieu d'Albret refers
to himself as "unus de diocesi Agenni vel districtu" of Count
Alfonse.

[238] *H.L.*, VIII, 1289–1290; "Hommages en 1259," 18, no. 4;
59–60, no. 1; *Livre d'Agenais*, pp. 17, 19.

[239] In 1243, 29 nobles in arms, A.N., J.306, no. 80; in 1259,
159 names of knights, *domicelli*, and others not called *burgenses*,
not counting many unnamed relatives and *parcionarii*, "Hommages

other purposes, the recognition rolls of 1259, 1271, and 1286 give little precise information about allodial titles or about the status of those "partners" (*parcionarii*) among whom Gascon fiefs could be subdivided almost endlessly.

Certain assemblies in the later thirteenth century included nearly 100 nobles.[240] But the usual or traditional attendance in the general court must have been smaller than this, limited in some way to the more notable barons and knights of Agenais. We have no clear evidence of the identity and size of this group.[241] The important nobles, at least, were under some special obligation to attend when summoned. They had to show cause in order to excuse failure to appear in person. In an assembly of 1263 the barons asked postponement of an important decision "on account of the absence of certain nobles who were unable to come to the said court, hindered by legitimate impedi-

---

. . . en 1259," 11–62; in 1271, 92 nobles swore fealty at Agen, and we know of others who did not appear, *Sais. Agen.*, 85–87, cf. 67, 72; a list of 1279 shows at least 118 nobles owing knight service and homage, *Livre d'Agenais*, pp. 17–20; the roll of 1286 includes 81 persons specifically designated as nobles, but certainly refers to many more than that. On the nobility see generally Tholin, "Notes sur la Féodalité en Agenais au Milieu du XIIIᵉ Siècle," *Rev. de l'Agenais*, XXIII–XXVI (1896–1899), esp. XXIII, 543–546; XXVI, 64–78, 173–185; and cf. E. Lodge, *Gascony under English Rule* (London, 1926), pp. 193–204.

[240] Meetings of 1271 and 1286, mentioned in preceding note. The total attendance was in each case probably larger than the number of recorded names.

[241] Cf. n. 239. To the military list of 1279 may be added a catalogue of 35 Agenais nobles whose service Edward I sought in 1294, *R.G.*, III, no. 3882; but the two sets of names are not readily comparable. (An accompanying list of Gascon nobles in 1294 is marked "de curia Sancti Severi," one of the four regular courts of Gascony proper.) Twenty-two important nobles in an assembly in 1279 are known by name, but the texts indicate that the number present was still larger, *Chartes d'Agen*, no. 60; *Livre d'Agenais*, no. 2, p. 9.

ment." [242] Amanieu d'Albret, "detained by arduous business," named a personal deputy for a certain assembly in 1253.[243] Representation was, therefore, not unknown, and it was sometimes extended from individuals to small groups of partners; [244] but attendance in person was the rule. We do not find an estate of nobility represented in the general court, though the knights of Agenais could consolidate when they had a cause.[245]

The summons of townsmen was based on seigneurial rather than feudal prerogative. Nothing is said about *consilium* in the charters and recognitions. The latter, indeed, show plainly that towns and villages of Agenais were not vassals. Among numerous demesne communities that conceded seigneurial rights, dues, fealty, and military service in 1271, 1279, and 1286, not one recognized homage. Nor do the villagers indicate that service is due for fiefs and tenures, as do the nobles.[246] The king is said to have the right of *exercitus* "on" the men of a given place.[247] This need occasion no surprise, of course, but it must also be noticed that in some respects the military service of towns in Agenais was under the influence of feudal usage in the thirteenth century. The troops of Agen, like the nobles, were obligated only for forty days a year.[248] In 1271 the community of Sainte-Livrade, held in *paréage* by the king,

[242] *Layettes,* IV, no. 4883.

[243] *Chartes d'Agen,* no. 50; a knight was represented in 1271 on account of sickness, *Sais. Agen.,* 87.

[244] *Ibid.,* 86–87; *Arch. Gir.,* I, 364–365, nos. 60, 63; 383, nos. 128, 130.

[245] Cf. *Enquêtes d'Alfonse,* no. 7.

[246] *Sais. Agen.,* 66–84; *Livre d'Agenais,* nos. 5–11, pp. 17–20, where the distinction between urban and knightly obligations is very clear in the rubrics; *Arch. Gir.,* I, 356, no. 24; 360, nos. 39, 40; 372–373, no. 89; 374, no. 96; 376, no. 103; 377–378, no. 110; 382, no. 127; 384–385, nos. 135, 136; cf. 355, no. 18; 357, no. 26.

[247] *Arch. Gir.,* I, 378, no. 110; cf. 360, no. 39.

[248] Tropamer, *Coutume d'Agen,* p. 28; *Arch. Gir.,* I, 381, no. 124; 384, no. 132.

recognized its obligation to furnish two knights for forty days according to the custom of Agenais.[249] Not even the smallest royal village could be called to service arbitrarily.[250] Nevertheless, the town levies seem to have been predominantly extra-feudal in nature. It was the practice at Agen for heads of homesteads, or their substitutes, to serve in the ranks, and the same system doubtless prevailed elsewhere in the region.[251]

But the general levy was inconvenient for most purposes, and so, with the recognition of consular towns as collectivities, there developed some alternative devices of token or representative service or financial commutation. By the fourteenth century, Agen had obtained a customary quota of 200 sergeants, and may sometimes have fined for military service.[252] Now it is very significant that this principle was already known in 1182 when we first hear of the general court. The consuls of Marmande were obliged to take the field when the lord called out the host. The townsmen had to finance this service, just as they had to pay the expenses of their consuls as deputies in the general court.

[249] *Sais. Agen.*, 77; cf. 76.

[250] *Arch. Gir.*, I, 384–385, nos. 135, 136; the formulas of 1286 invoke occasion of need (*tempore necessitatis*), and community of obligations, 360, no. 40; 373, no. 89; 385, no. 136; etc.; but this principle is much older, B.N., MS Lat. 6009, fols. 507–510; Tropamer, *Coutume d'Agen*, p. 28.

[251] Tropamer, pp. 28, 30; *Arch. Gir.*, I, 372–373, no. 89; *R.H.D.F.É.*, VI (1860), 440.

[252] *Chartes d'Agen*, nos. 98, 145 (p. 281); "Chartes d'Agen se rapportant au Règne de Philippe de Valois," ed. Tholin, *Arch. Gir.*, XXXIII (1898), no. 48, 113. The *communitas Agenni* was represented in the feudal army which joined Raymond VII in swearing support to Henry III in 1242, *R.G.*, I, no. 592; and cf. *Enquêtes d'Alfonse*, p. 350, no. 502; *Correspondence Administrative d'Alfonse de Poitiers,* to be cited as *C.A.*, ed. A. Molinier, 2 vols. (Paris, 1894–1900), II, no. 1531. Commutation of *ost et chevauchée* was known in Bordelais at least as early as 1208, *Arch. Gir.*, I, no. 16.

And these two provisions occur in the *same article* of their charter.[253] The theoretical connection between military and conciliar activity is confirmed by later charters. We find it most explicit, and in the same context, in the customs of Fumel, which speak of the right of the local lords to tallage the villagers "per ost mandada o per cort generale."[254] In these circumstances it seems likely that the general court had its origins in military procedures. This hypothesis derives strong support from the important privileges of Agen, which were known throughout Agenais. They prescribe that, in the event of an issue between the regional lord and a town, a general court should hear the case, if possible, before an army is summoned.[255] In other words,

[253] A.N., JJ.72, fol. 150v, in the context of administrative duties at public expense. Such representative military service does not necessarily mean that other townsmen were not liable at their own expense.

[254] *Arch. Gir.*, VII, 18, art. 12, with the rubric: "Cum sia facha ost e cort." Simon de Montfort's *ost* in 1211 was termed *cort* in the *Chanson*, ed. Martin-Chabot, I, 204, c. 87, 1. 2. I doubt that the editor's emendation here is correct.

[255] Tropamer, *Coutume d'Agen*, p. 28 (printed from other texts by Moullié in *Rec. Trav. Soc. Agen*, v [1850], 241–244; and H. Barckhausen, *Archives Municipales de Bordeaux: Livre des Coutumes* [Bordeaux, 1890], 219–220): "[Men of city and suburbs of Agen are obligated to annual *ost* of 40 days in the diocese.] En aital manera quel senher, si hom lo fa tort en Agenes o deforas lo meiss hebescat, deu mandar e far cridar la ost generalment per tot Agenes, e deu far assaber a Agen sobre cui volra cavalgar o metre seti: e si en alcu loc d'Agenes vol metre seti o cavalgar, lo coselhs tot prumerament avant que home d'Agen isco en ost deu enquerre lo senhor els habitans d'aquel loc. E sil senher e li habitant d'aquel loc volo far drech a esgart del senher e de sa cort, lo senhor los deu dregh prendre. E home d'Agen d'aqui en la no son tengutz ni devo far ost al senhor sobre aquel o aquelhs, pero que sion en l'abescat d'Agenes, que, aissi cum predigh es, volran far dregh a esgart del senher e de sa cort, ea cals corts deu estre dels baros e dels cavoers d'Agenes e dels coselhs e dels proshomes de la ciutat d'Agen e dels borcs d'Agenes: mas en autre loc que sia foras l'ebescat d'Agenes, lo coselhs no home d'Agen no an enquesta."

townsmen should convene with knights as a court in disputes that may result in their convocation as an army. Further illustration of this theory may be found in an agreement of 1222 between Agen and Le Mas "for the common profit of Agenais, of the city, and of the bourgs and of the barons." The two communities recognized that quarrels between them should be in the jurisdiction of barons and consuls of regional towns.[256] Interurban disputes were evidently regarded as threatening the peace of Agenais. Let us now observe that the two passages just cited seem to refer to the conciliar procedure in question as a privilege of a responsible community of Agenais. Townsmen and nobles, the former probably motivated in part by commercial concerns, and both groups burdened with military obligations, had developed a common interest in maintaining the regional peace. Such responsibility in the community of men of the two orders was hardly inconsistent with the feudal and seigneurial authority of the overlord, and it may have been fostered by him. It might be added that the holding of fiefs by non-nobles in Agenais (as elsewhere in the Midi) tended to blur class lines.[257] This may have facilitated an assimilation of towns as seigneuries in the feudal regime. In most respects, to be sure, the estates re-

---

[256] *Chartes d'Agen,* no. 14: "A honor de Deu trastot poderos, lo paire el fil el sanch esperit, e pel profech comunal d'Agenes, de la ciutad e dels borcs e dels baros. . . . Pero si contrast fo que ja no sia, ni rancura forzia entre vos e nos, que aco fos determenad per acordir o per drech, a coneguda dels baros e dels cosels dels borcs d'Agenes, [e aquo que devant lo senhor deuria anar, que per lui sia determenad]." (Done in the presence of the seneschal.) It is hard to say whether the bracketed words have the effect of a saving clause, or imply a real division of jurisdiction.

[257] See Molinier in *H.L.,* VII, 133–134; "Hommages . . . en 1259," 16, 20, 51; cf. H. Richardot, "Le Fief Roturier à Toulouse aux XII° et XIII° Siècles," *R.H.D.F.É.,* 4° sér., XIV (1935), 312–317, 322ff. Also Tropamer, *Coutume d'Agen,* p. 86, on right of townsmen to act as lords.

mained distinct, and we must not exaggerate the strength or endurance of bonds between them. But the early recognition of military need by the associated men of Agenais must have made it easier in practice to muster the assembly. Hence the conclusion may be drawn that the early development of the general court resulted from a combination of the military obligation imposed by the overlord and military necessity recognized by the community of Agenais.[258]

Town and village representation in the assembly was apparently not enforced as an obligation. In principle, however, the summons of townsmen remained seigneurial. Most of the consulates in Agenais were directly subject to the territorial lord, and we do not know that places other than these were ever convoked. Mediate lords might make their own summons to the general court the occasion for taxing their peasants, as was customary at Fumel, but the regional prince had no part in that sort of local arrangement.[259]

[258] In the absence of evidence, we cannot link the military theory of communal foundations (Petit-Dutaillis, *Communes Françaises,* esp. pp. 103–123) with the origins of the general court. The charters of Marmande and Agen refer to the army only in judicial contexts, without suggesting any administrative policy of strengthening or extending military obligations. Certain bastides were organized for military reasons, but most such foundations belong to a period when the general court was in decline.

[259] *Arch. Gir.*, VII, 18, art. 12. The villagers were then said to be "quiti de cort," meaning, literally, that they had "paid court." This is the seigneurial aid in support of feudal service, discussed by C. Stephenson, *Mediaeval Institutions*, pp. 2–4. Tonneins-Dessous obtained customs of Marmande from mediate lords in 1301, but this does not mean that the provision for attendance in the *cort generale* was honored in practice, Lagarde, *Tonneins*, p. 118, art. 25. In view of the military analogy, it is significant that we know of the exemption of baronial towns from the army, e.g., Caumont (1289), B.N., MS n.a. franç. 3391, fol. 85; Lafox was tallaged for its lords' service, customs of 1254, ed. Cabié, *Rec. Trav. Soc. Agen,* VIII (1883), 267.

The number of communities that were ordinarily represented, and their identity, cannot be determined very precisely. Only one list, pertaining to an assembly in 1279, has
survived. It includes Agen, Condom, Port-Sainte-Marie,
Mézin, Penne, Monflanquin, Villeneuve, Marmande,
Montréal, and Tournon; but there follows a reference
to "many other places" of the diocese of Agen.[260] As we
have seen, an assembly in 1249 was described as including
delegates of the city, bourgs, *castra*, and villages; and to this
may be added a directive of King Edward I in 1289 which
requests the summons to a general court of "consuls of all
the villages." [261] But the number of chartered rural communities was increasing rapidly in the later thirteenth century, and by 1300, among some fifty consulates in Agenais,
there were more than thirty royal towns and villages.[262]
One may doubt that all or even very many of them were
ever represented together in assemblies. Probably the larger
places sent deputies more often than the smaller ones, but
there was no juridical distinction in this regard between
commercial towns, *castra*, bastides, and villages.

As the charters indicate, the representatives of townsmen
in the general court were the consuls, ex officio. The customs of Agen add that "good men," meaning councillors,
might also attend the assembly, and we have record that
they sometimes did so.[263] There were no special elections.
This representation was indirect, the more so for the fact

[260] A composite list, drawn from *Chartes d'Agen*, no. 60 (p.
84), and *Livre d'Agenais*, no. 2, p. 9; the quoted formula is identical in the two documents.

[261] *R.G.*, II, no. 1428.

[262] *Livre d'Agenais*, nos. 6, 8, 10, pp. 18–20; "Les Coutumes de
l'Agenais: Monclar, Monflanquin (1256–70), Saint-Maurin
(1358)," ed. H. Rébouis, *N.R.H.D.F.É.*, XIV (1890), 388–397;
also M. Curie-Seimbres, *Essai sur les Villes fondées dans le Sud-
ouest de la France aux XIIIe et XIVe Siècles* . . . (Toulouse
1880), pp. 225–238.

[263] Above, n. 255; *Layettes*, III, no. 3833; IV, no. 4883.

that lords, bayles, notables, or consuls themselves controlled the choice of officials in many places in Agenais.[264] Of special delegates or empowered syndics in assembly we hear nothing until late in the century. Deputations were invariably from individual towns; there is no evidence that a third estate as such was represented.

The clergy had no regular place in the early general court. There is no mention of prelates as a group in assemblies before 1271, and the charters of customs are equally silent. Churchmen ordinarily attended assemblies as individual notables or witnesses; they never attended as representatives of clergy in Agenais. The bishop of Agen appeared frequently, and we also find evidence of abbots, canons, archdeacons, and *magistri* attending. But the total number of different clerics whose names are recorded is very small; and it includes men of other dioceses, such as the bishops of Toulouse and Lectoure, and the abbots of Moissac and Figeac.[265]

The absence of the clerical estate may be viewed as a consequence of the allodial status of Agenais churches and hence, indirectly, as an indication of the feudal ancestry of the general court. It was not merely that lords had had little reason to consult the clergy, or that the latter, for their part, had developed no tradition or cause in common with the laity.[266] More fundamental was the fact that few ecclesiastics in Agenais were vassals (or admitted that they

[264] See Dognon, *Institutions*, pp. 75, 80, 89; in charters granted by Alfonse and copied (for the most part) by Edward I, the lord or bayle appointed consuls, but a council for finance was chosen "by the people," e.g., *N.R.H.D.F.É.* xiv, 405, art. 13; xii (1888), 88–89, art. 13.

[265] *Layettes*, iii, no. 3833; *Chartes d'Agen*, no. 60 (pp. 84, 89); *Arch. Gir.*, i, no. 182.

[266] The bishop doubtless had clerical support in favoring the crusade in Agenais. Extraordinary taxation, when extended to clergy at all, was negotiated individually: see, e.g., Brit. Mus., Cotton. MS Julius E.1, fol. 39; cf. *R.G.*, ii, nos. 1610, 1793.

were).[267] They were far outnumbered by nobles and towns in the feudal recognition sessions of the later thirteenth century. Moreover, such rare recognitions as they made show that the higher clergy ordinarily held temporalities in free alms; they were exempt from regional military service.[268] This ecclesiastical independence was not calculated to please a new generation of strong rulers, and it was challenged toward the end of the century.[269] One indication of the changing situation is the summons of clergy to the general court. But since this occurs under the royal governments after 1271, when the assembly was being altered in other ways as well, the subject may be deferred to later chapters.

The general court of Agenais retained its original military and judicial functions in the thirteenth century. A case of the year 1255 may be cited. The seneschal had led a successful military expedition against some Gascon nobles who had done violence to "men and burghers" of Agenais.

[267] R. Boutruche notes the same situation in Bordelais and Bazadais, *Une Société Provinciale en Lutte contre le Régime Féodal: L'Alleu en Bordelais et en Bazadais du XIᵉ au XVIIIᵉ Siècle* (Rodez, 1947), p. 45. He explains it by the act of 1137 by which Louis VII, piously motivated by the Gregorian reform, had freed the episcopal and abbey churches of the province of Bordeaux, which included Agenais, from their obligations of homage and fealty.

[268] Two prelates recognized fiefs in 1259, "Hommages . . . en 1259," 43, no. 14; *The Gascon Calendar of 1322*, ed. G. P. Cuttino (London, 1949), no. 1016; and three in 1286, *Arch. Gir.*, I, 361, no. 45; 362–363, no. 51; 374–375, no. 97. The prior of Port-Sainte-Marie admitted obligation to fealty and *exercitus* in 1271, *Sais. Agen.*, 80, but the whole act is canceled. The abbot of Condom in 1285 owed only fealty and recognition of feudal holdings to the king, "sine alio deverio, sicut est hactenus observatum," *R.G.*, II, no. 938 (275).

[269] See Boutruche, *L'Alleu en Bordelais*, pp. 112–113; *R.G.*, II, no. 1428. At Agen the consuls disputed clerical immunity from common expenses for properties that had previously paid *taille, Chartes d'Agen*, nos. 101, 102, 104–106, 108, 109, 74 (p. 122).

According to the act of submission, the seneschal took the field "(fecit exercitum) de consilio baronum et militum et proborum hominum dyocesis Agenensis."[270] This phrase probably refers to a meeting of the general court, for the issue in question resembles that military contingency which the customs of Agen had specified as the occasion for assembly. To put it in general terms, the townsmen make of their injury a regional issue, which is discussed in plenary session, and results in the proclamation of a general army. In the circumstances it is clear that *consilium* means "advice" or even "judgment," but it does not imply "consent," for the military campaign was wholly to the advantage of the men of Agenais. Indeed, we know of protests in this very period against a seneschal who hesitated in calling the army when needed.[271] It would appear from the recognitions of 1286 that the general army was still a flourishing institution a generation later. And when the nobles and villagers state that they will serve in the ranks when others of Agenais do likewise, we may perhaps infer that the decision was supposed to be made in assembly.[272] But there is no further evidence of this in practice.

Meetings of this kind must be characterized as judicial, and certain other deliberative sessions of the general court

[270] *Layettes*, III, no. 4199. One of the offenders disclaimed financial liability for the expedition because "paratus fuerit et sit stare juri, in curia dicti senescalli, omnibus de se querelantibus"; cf. *H.L.*, VI, 844, n. 3 (Molinier).

[271] *Layettes*, V, no. 672, the seneschal entreats Alfonse to advise him promptly in regard to the depredations of certain knights which have aroused such great indignation in Agenais "contra me quare non statim invado eosdem et eos [men of Agenais] similiter per se invadere non permitto, et quare non congrego excercitus contra ipsos, quod nescio consilium quod apponam . . . [dated 1256–1258]."

[272] *Arch. Gir.*, I, 354, nos. 13, 15; 356, no. 24; etc.; and esp. 373, no. 91, a noble's obligation to serve "quando mandatur et fit exercitus communiter in Agenezio per barones, milites et universitates diocesis Agennensis"; also B.N., MS n.a.franç. 3404, fol. 199.

(to be discussed presently) had a similar nature. Of ordinary litigation there is no direct evidence, but it seems
likely that the court occasionally heard major suits, perhaps on appeal. In 1270 the barons of Agenais petitioned
Count Alfonse for the right to convene in general court
four times a year, without summons, in order to hear appeals. This showed their discontent with certain novel procedures which were making it possible for the count's
officials to do without the old feudal tribunal. Their petition
was rejected, partly on the grounds that the holding of such
frequent courts would be inconsistent with law and custom.[273] In May 1270, in a conciliatory gesture before
embarking on crusade, Alfonse conceded the right of the
nobles of Agenais to be tried by their peers under the
presidency of the seneschal, but he said nothing about the
plenary court.[274] The government was undoubtedly trying
to curtail its activity. The decline of the general court as a
judicial institution dates from the later years of Alfonse.

Reluctance to depend on the court may have resulted
partly from the recognition by administrators that certain
privileges of the Agenais community were becoming associated with it. Seneschals had to swear to uphold the re-

[273] A.N., J.1031, no. 11, now printed in *Enquêtes d'Alfonse*, pp.
349–350, nos. 493, 498: "Super petitione baronum de Agenesio
. . . de sexto articulo super quatuor curiis generalibus habendis in
Agenesio certis temporibus sine mandato cuiuscumque et appellationibus interponendis per curiam decidendis.—Videtur consilio
domini comitis quod, cum ista [?, perhaps *iste*; but the editors'
reading is better than mine given in *Speculum*, xxxvi, 269, n. 97]
non competant eis de consuetudine nec de iure . . . , non videtur
eorum petitio admitenda." See also *H.L.*, viii, 1352–1356, 1715–
1723, Alfonse's administrative ordinances of about 1254 and 1270
(which do not mention the general court); B.N., Doat, cxvii, 266v–
272v; Boutaric, *Saint Louis et Alfonse*, pp. 412–414, 497–501;
Molinier in *H.L.*, vii, 520–528. The latter writers, rather vaguely
and implausibly, find the influence of recent English events in the
petition of 1270.

[274] B.N., Doat, cxvii, 266vff.

gional custom before the assembly.[275] Moreover, on at least one standing issue, the integrity of the diocesan coinage, the general court had achieved a certain right of its own. In Agenais, as elsewhere in feudal France, the seigneur had enjoyed the privilege of altering his coinage. The money of Agen belonged to the bishop, who held it in fief from the lord of the land in the thirteenth century.[276] And by that time, through a comprehensible but obscure evolution, the bishop was losing his right of arbitrary mutation, so disadvantageous for a trading community. In 1234, on the petition of men of Agen and barons and knights of the diocese, Bishop Raoul served public notice that he would preserve the money unchanged in weight and alloy during his lifetime.[277] We do not know of an assembly on this occasion, but there may have been one. For it had already been recognized that the bishop could make only one mutation, at the time of his accession; and in 1232, Raoul's predecessor had obtained the financial equivalent of such a mutation with the consent of the general court of Agenais, summoned by the seneschal. The assembly granted him a twelve-penny *fouage* in return for confirmation of the coinage.[278] We know of at least one other gen-

---

[275] See below, pp. 235ff.

[276] *Gallia Christiana,* II, *inst.*, 431–432, the important *paréage* between Simon de Montfort and the bishop in 1218; *Gascon Calendar*, no. 1000.

[277] *Chartes d'Agen*, no. 24 (*H.L.*, VIII, 970-971). It is significant that canon lawyers were taking note of monetary mutations at about the same time. See *Extra*, II, 24, 18*Quanto*, and *glos. ord.* Innocent IV, *Apparatus*, to this decretal (followed by Hostiensis) argued that a king could not impair the coinage "sine consensu populi."

[278] *Rec. Trav. Soc. Agen*, VII, 614–615, no. 3, an inadequate text; the existing MS copies are A.D. Lot-et-Garonne, MS d'Argenton (2J54), III, no. 33, p. 19; and, much older, new G.2, no. 1, from which my quotation is taken: "Guillem A. de Tantalon, senescal d'Agenes, als baros e als cavalers e als borzes e a tota la universitat d'Agenes, salut et amistad. A saber vos fara que per

eral court, in 1282, which approved the same levy for the same purpose. It was said at that time that this practice was customary; [279] and there are numerous references to the *fouage* of the money.[280]

This meant that the assembly, in its broadly judicial capacity, had gained control of a form of seigneurial taxation. The levy of a shilling per household could be expected to bring in more than a monetary debasement, which was becoming increasingly unpopular and difficult to accomplish. The preference for the direct tax and the limitation of episcopal prerogative are both well illustrated by a case of the year 1263. Bishop Guillaume III wanted to obtain recognition of his right to take "redemption" of the money "universally from the whole diocese of Agen," and caused a general court to be summoned for that purpose. On 23 November, after the session, he wrote to the count of Toulouse that a "great part" of the assembled barons and town deputies had acknowledged his claims, but that the barons had requested a delay on account of the absence of certain nobles. Accordingly, another assembly of barons and consuls was scheduled to meet on 3 January 1264, in

---

coseil e per commandament de nostre senhor lo conte de Tolosa e per voluntat dels baros e dels cavalers e dels borzes et de la cort general d'Agenes aven establid e pausat e per lo [*sic,* Argenton *co*] que la moneda no sia abatuda ni cambiada, car lo senhor avesque la a cofermada a sa vita com le ne [? Argenton *ce ne*] de rada ung fug de l'avesquad d'Agenes .xij. d. arnaudencs los cals dont hom al sobredichs senhor avesque d'Agen. . . ."

[279] *Livre d'Agenais,* no. 17, p. 37 (quoted in *Speculum,* xxxvi, 276, n. 130).

[280] *Chartes d'Agen,* no. 44 (p. 62), "fogatge que convenga levar per lo fagh de la moneda" (1248); A.D. Lot-et-Garonne, MS d'Argenton, iii, no. 72, 43; new G.2, no. 5, evidence of a *fouage* levied in 1292; A. Ducom, *La Commune d'Agen* (Paris, 1892), pp. 283–284, no. 2.

order: "to do whatever should be done about these matters."[281] Unfortunately, we have no information on the outcome of the case. Other forms of taxation remained independent of the general court. The crusading subsidies of Alfonse were negotiated entirely at the local level.[282]

No other area of the county of Toulouse—possibly none in all of France—could show so relatively developed a provincial assembly as Agenais in the middle of the thirteenth century. It is not very surprising that Agenais was also the scene of the earliest recorded assemblies of associated towns in Languedoc. A defensive league was formed in 1224 between Agen and five neighboring communities.[283] From then on, townsmen of the Garonne valley frequently dealt collectively with their interests: the maintenance of free and open routes, procedures for regulating disputes, the disposition of tolls and subsidies, mutual defense, and the like. The towns were represented in these negotiations and activities by their consuls or councillors, or by individual notables.[284] This evidence takes on added importance in view of the fact that the practice of consular representation in the general court cannot be directly documented before 1249. The first mention of corporate Roman-canonical procedures among associated communities of Agenais occurs in 1254, when Alfonse speaks of distributing a certain indemnity to Garonne towns through their proctors.[285]

Town and village delegates sometimes assembled with

[281] *Layettes*, IV, no. 4883 (quoted in *Speculum*, XXXVI, 276, n. 132). Molinier's account of this episode, *H.L.*, VII, 509, is extremely inaccurate. Cf. Y. Dossat, "Dates de Décès de Deux Évêques d'Agen . . . ," *Bull. Philol. et Hist.* (1958), pp. 84–85.

[282] *C.A.*, II, nos. 1532, 1840, 1962, 1968; etc.

[283] *Chartes d'Agen*, no. 16; cf. nos. 14, 15.

[284] *Ibid.*, nos. 18, 30–34, 41, 72, 77, 80.

[285] *C.A.*, II, no. 2092; cf, below, p. 99.

the count of Toulouse. In 1239, when he was deeply indebted to financiers of Bordeaux, Raymond VII sought to raise revenue by imposing a toll on wine and grain which passed the port of Marmande; and in the next year he levied a special *taille* on Garonne towns to support the work of restoring the river channel. This *taille* was to be assessed and collected "per consules et consilia villarum de riparia," and it seems likely that the count had consulted the consuls and councillors in this matter.[286] He had imposed the earlier toll of Marmande "de consilio burgensium et proborum hominum de riparia." This evidently refers to a meeting of councillors, and perhaps consuls, and notables. They resorted to the administrative device of appointing two "good men" to act as collectors for the association of valley communities. Only the seven leading towns (whose bankers had already advanced a part of the debt and were to be repaid from proceeds of the toll) are specified: Agen, Le Mas, Marmande, Port-Sainte-Marie, Castelsarrasin, Moissac, and Montauban.[287] This list includes four notable towns of Agenais, but the three last-named places were in Quercy. There is other evidence, too, that common commercial interests which were centered in Agenais involved mercantile towns well outside the district.[288] But none of these external towns had a place in the general court. Indeed, it is quite impossible to show that prior experience in the court had any influence in creating a sense of community among valley towns. The only feature that the general court certainly shared with the assemblies of associated towns was the form of representation. One other point should be noted. The documents relating to this associative activity often take the form of conventions. For example, in May 1240 the seneschal of

[286] *Chartes d'Agen*, no. 32.

[287] *Ibid.*, no. 31.

[288] *Ibid.*, nos. 18, 41; *Calendar of the Patent Rolls, 1247–1258* (London, 1908), pp. 251–252.

Agenais, the consuls of Agen, Le Mas, Marmande, and Moissac, and men of La Réole issue public notice of their agreement for the security of roads.[289] The count of Toulouse may sometimes summon townsmen *ex potestate*, in tacit conformity with the legal theory of consultation in matters touching common or administrative rights. But the initiative and authority of the commercial community go even further to explain these assemblies.

There is evidence of procuration and the corporate representation of both towns and estates in Agenais.[290] By the middle of the thirteenth century, these devices were being used occasionally in assemblies. Especially notable is the case of an individual procuration which is, in fact, the earliest surviving mandate for any assembly of Agenais or Languedoc. On 3 June 1253 the Gascon baron Amanieu d'Albret granted an agent "potestatem faciendi et ordinandi" in a gathering that was to deal with a certain unspecified *negocium*. Besides stating that he was kept from attending personally by "arduous business," the principal obligated himself to recognize decisions made by his deputy in assembly. It is possible that in constituting his proctor, the lord of Albret was complying with some governmental imperative, perhaps embodied in a summons; but it seems more likely that he was acting voluntarily.[291]

---

[289] *Chartes d'Agen*, no. 34; cf. no. 35; and cf. G. Langmuir, "'Judei Nostri' and the Beginning of Capetian Legislation," *Traditio*, XVI (1960), 210ff., on royal conventions of the early thirteenth century.

[290] E.g., *Gascon Calendar*, nos. 997, 1013, 1023; P.R.O., E.36, vol. 275, fols. 256v-257v; etc. The procuration of individual towns in Agenais was known at least as early as 1216, *Chartes d'Agen*, no. 4. Charters of Port and Fumel prescribe procedure for constituting syndics, B.N., Baluze, XXVI, 341/350; *Arch. Gir.*, VII, 16, art. 5.

[291] A.M. Agen, AA. 2 (*Chartes d'Agen*, no. 50): "Viris venerabilibus et discretis domino Symone Clareti, senescallo Agenni, et baronibus Agennensibus, capitulo Tolosano et aliis probis hominibus sub potestate domini comitis Pictavensis constitutis, Amaneus

This mandate was addressed to the seneschal and barons of Agenais, consuls of Toulouse, and "other good men" subject to Count Alfonse, so that the assembly in question was apparently not a general court.[292] It was probably a special advisory session called by the seneschal to study problems raised by the administration of the new overlord. We know of one such conference at an uncertain earlier date. The seneschal had undertaken to construct new bastides, an enterprise that needed to be regulated according to the custom of Agenais. To that end, probably in 1252, he took counsel with consuls and notables of Agenais and men of Toulouse.[293] Their decisions were incorporated in an ordi-

de Lebreto, salutem. . . . Cum, arduis negociis retardati, ad vos, quod displicet, accedere non possimus, venerabili nostro domino Arnaldo de Montepesato damus potestatem faciendi et ordinandi vobiscum, super eo negocio pro quo convenistis, quod sibi, pro nobis, videbitur faciendum, obligantes nos per presentes quod vobiscum, sicut unus de diocesi Agenni vel districtu dicti domini comitis, exequamur, secundum quod nomine nostro ordinabit dominus Arnaldus de Montepesato predictus. Datum Lingone [Langon], feria tercia post assensionem Domini, anno Domini M.CC.L.III. [3 June 1253]." (In *Speculum*, xxxvi, 266, I mistakenly followed the editors' dating.) Boutaric and Molinier overlooked this document, and its editors missed its significance. Regarding Albret's preoccupations, see C. Bémont, *Simon de Montfort, Earl of Leicester, 1208–1265*, new ed., tr. E. F. Jacob (Oxford, 1930), pp. 118–120.

[292] For evidence of relations between Toulouse and Agen in this period, some of it seeming to show Agen following the lead of the consuls of Toulouse in internal matters and jurisdiction, see *Chartes d'Agen*, nos. 3, 10, 11, 40; *Enquêtes d'Alfonse*, no. 7, p. 66. At least two consuls of Toulouse attended the general court of 1249 as witnesses, *Layettes*, iii, no. 3833.

[293] *Enquêtes d'Alfonse*, no. 7, pp. 65–66: "consilium fuit datum a consulibus et ab aliis urbis Agennensis, presentibus nobili viro domino Sicardo Alamanni et probis hominibus Tholosanis jurisperitis et aliis etiam Condomii et Penne et Portus Sancte Marie et de Medicino et de Grandi Castro et de Marmanda et Mansi, Agennensis diocesis [who all gave counsel according to the custom of Agenais]." See also no. 8, pp. 67–68.

nance for regional administrative reform, promulgated by county investigators in March 1253 in the bishop's residence at Agen in the presence of four prominent nobles of Agenais. One of these four was the same person who later received Albret's mandate, and he may have been acting as a proctor on this occasion. However that may be, it is important to notice that the four nobles are said to be in attendance "pro se et aliis baronibus et militibus Agennesii." [294] Whether they had been explicitly summoned as delegates of an estate of nobility cannot be determined, nor can we be sure that their acquiescence was legally binding on the regional baronage. But the phraseology suggests that the representation of an order in assembly was already becoming a practical possibility.

[294] *Ibid.*, no. 7; cf. nos. 9, 10, pp. 69–72; Molinier, in *H.L.*, vii, 509, 568, for reform ordinances of this period.

〘III〙 *Diocesan Assemblies in*
Upper Languedoc (1170-1270)

The half-century commencing about 1170 was an unusually turbulent age in Languedoc. The progress of heresy and the feudal power struggles, which continued in the Albigensian crusade, undermined the precarious basis of peace and stability. Private wars were still causing trouble enough, but the ravages of irresponsible mercenary hordes, if not actually worse, were the more spectacular for their novelty in the twelfth century. The city of Mende stood a siege by Brabantines and Spaniards between 1165 and 1170.[1] In 1179 the stern anathemas of the Third Lateran Council were extended to include Brabantines, Basques, Navarrais, and other brigands, as well as heretics. Though these measures had special reference to Languedoc,[2] it is doubtful that they had much effect there. The papal legate ordered Raymond VI in 1209 to rid his domains of mercenaries,[3] but there is evidence of ill-controlled foreigners serving on both sides during the Albigensian wars. Pierre des Vaux-de-Cernay describes conditions of extreme insecurity in eastern Languedoc, the Béziers area, and Rouergue in 1213–1214.[4]

[1] *Chronicon Breve de Gestis Aldeberti* in *Les Miracles de Saint Privat*, ed. C. Brunel (Paris, 1912), p. 126.

[2] J. Mansi, *Sacrorum Conciliorum . . . Collectio*, XXII, 231–232. See Pissard, *Guerre Sainte*, pp. 28–40.

[3] Mansi, *Collectio*, XXII, 770–771.

[4] *Hystoria Albigensis*, II, 179, 185, 230–231. The pious chronicler sometimes echoes the prevailing orthodoxy in linking heretics with peace-breakers, e.g., 232: "ruptarii, pacis et fidei turbatores." See also R. Michel, *Sénéchaussée de Beaucaire*, p. 113; and, generally, H. Géraud, "Les Routiers au Douzième Siècle," *B.É.C.*, III (1841–42), 126–147, an account followed by A. Luchaire, *La Société Française au Temps de Philippe-Auguste* (Paris, 1909), pp. 11–22, which should be read with caution.

Measures for maintaining the peace figure prominently in many provincial church councils of the early thirteenth century, notably the parliament of Pamiers in 1212, the council of Montpellier in 1215, and the council of Toulouse in 1229.[5] The Montpellier program of 1215 was especially comprehensive. It provided for sworn commitments to the peace in the dioceses, with overseers or guardians of the peace (*paciarii*), local armies against peace-breakers, and other procedures or penalties for violations. A tax (*compensum*) to support this work is mentioned; and there were to be annual assemblies to hear complaints and deal with other matters relating to the peace.[6]

By this time, however, the worst was over. Lower Languedoc soon came under the firm control of the king, and when Raymond VII submitted to the Church and crown in the 1220's, he made engagements to maintain the peace. Assemblies and armies of the sort envisioned in 1215 do not seem to have been summoned in lower Languedoc afterwards. The legislation of Montpellier should therefore be regarded as standing near the end of a long tradition of diocesan peace measures as old as the Peace of God itself. These procedures had had a notable history in southern France in the eleventh and twelfth centuries. The episcopal peace and truce were at least theoretically operative in some areas in the later twelfth century. In Comminges the count or bishop could proclaim the peace and obtain the service of townsmen.[7] A royal privilege of 1156 guarantees to the bishop of Uzès the pro-

[5] Mansi, *Conciliorum Collectio*, xxii, (667–669 [Montpellier, 1195]), 771, 775, 789, 861, 947–949; xxiii, 201–202; and L. Huberti, *Studien zur Rechtsgeschichte der Gottesfrieden und Landfrieden* (*Ansbach*, 1892), pp. 509–529.

[6] Mansi, *Conciliorum Collectio*, xxii, 947–949.

[7] "La Grande Charte de Saint-Gaudens (1203)," ed. S. Mondon, *Revue de Comminges*, xxv (1910), 42.

ceeds of the peace tax, or *compensum,* in his diocese.[8]
Some years later Bishop Bernard of Béziers (1167–1184)
summoned Viscount Roger and "knights of the land" to
swear to maintain the peace of clergy, peasants, and other
defenseless persons, and to observe the Truce of God
between Thursday evening and Monday morning. Peace
oaths were to be sworn in the parishes, and parishioners
were obligated "to follow the peace," that is, to assemble as
a peace army, at the bishop's summons.[9] There was no
mention of taxation, which perhaps already existed, and
thus this gathering had no constitutive role. It is the last
peace assembly in coastal Languedoc of which we have
record.

In the hilly regions of upper Languedoc the situation was
different. Violence and banditry were even worse there than
in the south and continued longer. Toulousan authority,
unknown in Velay, was relatively weak in Quercy, Gévaudan, and Vivarais. Royal power made but slow progress.
Except in Gévaudan it was not seriously felt in these areas
until the later thirteenth century. This left the bishops and
minor lay lords in contention for local supremacy. In these
contests the bishops had all the advantages: their spiritual
powers, or pretensions, their regalian rights derived from
the ancient county functions they claimed to hold, their
landed endowments, and their expanding feudal lordship.
By the thirteenth century, the bishops of Mende, Le Puy,
and Viviers had become the virtual temporal rulers of their
dioceses. Episcopal power was also strong in Agenais,
Quercy, Albigeois, and Rouergue, though somewhat diluted
by the suzerainty of the counts of Toulouse and the prox-

[8] *H.L.,* v, 1201.

[9] *Ibid.,* vIII, 275–276. The document is dated "about 1170" in
this edition; Huberti, *Gottesfrieden,* p. 454, says "about 1168"; no
reasons are given in either place. Nor is our knowledge of it advanced by H. Vidal, *Episcopatus et Pouvoir Épiscopal à Béziers à
la Veille de la Croisade Albigeoise, 1152–1209* (Montpellier,
1951), p. 70.

imity of other influential lay rulers.[10] Most of the assemblies considered in this chapter were summoned by bishops or dealt with matters within the range of episcopal prerogatives. Usually, but not always, they were concerned with the bishops' maintenance of the diocesan peace, the institutions of which continued to function in some parts of upper Languedoc until well into the thirteenth century. These developments seem to have been too localized to find a place in the general law of the Church. While pronouncements on the peace and truce were recorded, neither they nor the law of synods have much to contribute to our knowledge of assemblies for the peace. It is doubtful that laymen attended synods regularly, or were expected to. Nevertheless, canon law specified occasions for their summons, such as when statutes were to be published, or when matters of the faith, touching common interests and hence subject to common consideration, were to be discussed.[11] The peace was presumably understood locally to be a religious question concerning clergy and laity alike.

ROUERGUE AND ALBIGEOIS

Apparently the peace movement was not known in any

[10] See generally J. Regné, *Histoire du Vivarais*, II (Largentière, 1921), 29–97; É. Delcambre, "Le Paréage du Puy," *B.É.C.*, XCII (1931), 122–149; C. Porée, *Études Historiques sur le Gévaudan* (Paris, 1919), pp. 347–385, 415–464; M. A. F. de Gaujal, *Études Historiques sur le Rouergue*, 4 vols. (Paris, 1858–1859), I, 176–179; G. Lacoste, *Histoire . . . de Quercy*, II, 155ff.; A. Ducom, *Commune d'Agen*, pp. 140–168; *H.L.*, VII, Note 52 (Molinier), 284–295.

[11] *Decretum*, dist. 63, c. 2*Hadrianus;* dist. 96, c. 4*Ubi nam;* and *glos. ord.*; dist. 18, c. 17*Decernimus; Extra*, V, 1, 25*Sicut olim*; C. Cheney, *English Synodalia of the Thirteenth Century* (Oxford, 1941), pp. 4–25.

In most cases laymen probably had only a "consultative" vote. See D. Bouix, *Du Concile Provincial . . .* (Paris, 1850), pp. 176–187. Hostiensis, *In Quinque Libros Decretalium Commentaria* (Venice, 1581), to *Extra, III*, 10, 10*Et si membra*, makes the point clear for provincial councils.

organized form in Rouergue and Albigeois until the later twelfth century. In that period important measures against the ravages of warfare were promulgated in both districts. The "peace" was proclaimed, as a kind of religious venture in regional cooperation by the people of these areas. Maintenance of the peace was recognized as a public work, to be supported by capitations on clergy and laity, graduated according to agricultural wealth. The monetary tariffs were virtually the same for the two districts, although the dues could be acquitted partly in kind in Albigeois. There the count of Toulouse and the bishop of Albi were to divide the proceeds, and a similar arrangement came to prevail in the diocese of Rodez. It was specified in the case of Rouergue that the taxation should be administered in the parishes by persons designated by the curate with the approval of archpriest and parishioners; they were to render account to the cathedral church of Rodez.[12]

The interest of these programs, from our point of view, is that they were instituted in general assemblies. Unfortunately, little is known about these meetings. The first occurred in Rouergue, most likely at Rodez, some time between 1166 and 1170, and is mentioned only in a bull of confirmation given by Pope Alexander III on 14 May 1170. The bishop of Rodez had notified the pope that he had acted on the counsel of abbots, *prévôts,* and archdeacons of the diocese, and "barons of the land," with his brother Hugo, count of Rodez, to establish a diocesan peace with supporting taxation.[13] The meeting so described must

[12] *H.F.*. xv, no. 266, 886–887; *Gallia Christiana*, i, *inst.,* 6. On the peace taxation in general see Molinier, "L'Administration Féodale," *H.L.,* vii, 161–163; and J. Poux, "Essai sur le Commun de Paix ou Pezade dans le Rouergue et dans l'Albigeois," *École . . . des Chartes: Positions des Thèses . . . 1898*, pp. 107–116.

[13] *H.F.,* xv, 886–887: "Ex quodam siquidem rescripto a tua nobis fraternitate transmisso, ad audientiam nostram pervenit quod tu, habito consilio abbatum, praepositorum et archidiaconorum tuo-

have been at once a synod and a great lordly court. The religious attendance is fully explained by the traditions of the piously motivated peace movements, as is the seeking of papal approval, and the provisions for ecclesiastical control of the finances. The lay barons had a much more important part here than in ordinary church councils.[14] Their function was to advise and consent to a regional measure which could succeed only with their support and good will; doubtless they received clerical admonitions at the same time. Other than the count and bishop, it is impossible to identify the men present.

A similar assembly convened in Albigeois, almost certainly at Albi, in 1191. Very likely the reform-minded bishop Guillem Peire took the initiative. Our one source, a document evidently drafted at the time of the meeting, indicates that Raymond V and the bishop acted jointly, with the advice of Roger of Béziers, Sicard, viscount of Lautrec, and "barons and illustrious men of Albigeois."[15] Nothing

---

rum, et baronum terrae, cum nobili viro Hugone fratre tuo Comite Ruthenae, hujusmodi pacem et concordiam statuisti, quod . . ."; see also G. Molinié, *L'Organisation Judiciaire, Militaire et Financière des Associations de la Paix* . . . (Toulouse, 1912), pp. 118–133; but his view that there were regular organizations has been refuted (though too sweepingly) by R. Bonnaud-Delamare, "La Légende des Associations de la Paix en Rouergue et en Languedoc au Début du XIII° Siècle (1170–1229)," *Bull. Philol. et Hist.* (1936–1937), pp. 47–78.

[14] Mixed diocesan assemblies were not, of course, an innovation; laity had attended the "peace councils" from their inception late in the tenth century. See Huberti, *Gottesfrieden*, pp. 37, 123, *et passim*.

[15] *Gallia Christiana*, I, *inst.*, 6: ". . . dominus Raimundus comes Tolosae, & Guillelmus Petri Albiensis episcopus, consilio domini Rogeri Biterrensis vicecomitis, & Sicardi, vicecomitis de Lautrec, & Albiensium baronum, & illustrium virorum, in Albiensi diocesi pacem constituerunt." Now lost, the document, as we have it, is probably incomplete; it existed in a medieval copy in the archives of Saint-Salvi, Albi, whence it was copied by Doat (B.N., Doat,

else is said about the attendance. The gathering probably included some of the men—the viscount of Saint-Antonin, Pons de Saint-Privat, Guillaume de Saint-Paul, and others —who met with the same lords at about this time to concede judicial privileges to the Cistercians of Albigeois.[16]

The bull of 1170 refers to the tax in Rouergue as the *commune,* and so it is often designated in later documents; but the usual term for the imposition in the two dioceses was *pazagium,* or *pezade.*[17] To describe the *pezade* as a tax "freely consented by an assembly of clergy and laity representing the entire diocese"[18] is probably going beyond the evidence. The peace was a community enterprise dependent on the cooperation of clergy and local strong men. Only through them, it seems, were townsmen, artisans, and peasants participants in a decision that was to be costly to them for more than six centuries. In form these gatherings resembled many previous diocesan assemblies of notables, though they may have been the first such in Rouergue and Albigeois to deal with the peace. Once the procedure had been agreed upon in assemblies, further deliberations were unneeded. There is no record of peace meetings in the thirteenth century in these districts. Payment of a few pennies annually in return for security from banditry was no doubt regarded a fair bargain by the suffering rural population in the twelfth century. In these circumstances

---

cv, 113v–115v) and by the editors of the *Gallia.* On this pact see also L. de Lacger, "L'Albigeois pendant la Crise de l'Albigéisme," *Rev. d'Hist. Ecclés.,* xxix, 593–595.

[16] Above, ch. 2, pp. 33–34.

[17] See Poux, "Pezade," *Pos. des Thèses . . . 1898,* pp. 107–116; Molinié, *Associations de la Paix,* p. 116. *Commune* was distinct from *communia* (meaning peace army, as in Agenais; see p. 134 below); but it was easy to confuse these related terms. See *Documents sur l'Ancien Hôpital d'Aubrac,* eds. J. Rigal, P. Verlaguet, 2 vols. (Rodez, 1913–1934), i, no. 12, 19–20; and cf. *Miracles de Saint Privat,* ed. Brunel, p. 135.

[18] Molinié, *Associations de la Paix,* p. 120.

the contractual basis for the *pezade*, such as it was, could easily be obscured by the regional overlords, who rapidly contrived to make it a seigneurial due or *taille*, heedless of its original purpose. Bishops, counts, and, as successors of the latter, kings of France, collected it in the two dioceses until the Revolution.

Indeed, the history of the peace movement in Rouergue and Albigeois is reduced to the history of this tax.[19] Many individuals, especially nobles, and some local communities gained exemption in the earlier thirteenth century;[20] and rights to *pezade* were often sold or divided.[21] By 1250, the counts of Toulouse and Rodez and the bishop were sharing the bulk of the proceeds in Rouergue, but the administration seems to have been lax.[22] The accession of Alfonse of Poitiers brought a reaction, and numerous complaints in the next two decades show how assiduously the new count's agents were serving him. They tried to collect from men outside the district,[23] and they encroached on the shares of the count and bishop of Rodez.[24] The men of Millau, alleging that their charter of 1187 freed them from all arbitrary exactions, campaigned unsuccessfully in 1251 for immunity from *pezade*.[25] Najac, on the other hand, had obtained liberty from this particular tax under Raymond

[19] Poux, "Pezade," *Pos. des Thèses . . . 1898*, pp. 108ff.

[20] See Molinié, *Associations de la Paix*, pp. 131–133; A. Molinier, "L'Administration Féodale," *H.L.*, vii, 162; A.D. Aveyron, G.10, fol. 15.

[21] *C.A.*, i, nos. 157, 167; B.N., Doat, cvi, 151–152v, 179–180; cxv, 39, 118v; A.D. Tarn-et-Garonne, A.297, fols. 543v–544v, bishop of Albi sells Sicard Alaman the product of *pezade* in Albigeois for six years.

[22] See Molinié, *Associations de la Paix*, p. 136. Millau reported exactions by Raymond vii (*Layettes*, iii, no. 3961; iv, no. 5743; v, no. 558), but there is little other evidence.

[23] *C.A.*, i, no. 150; ii, no. 2071.

[24] *Ibid.*, i, nos. 186, 391, 392; ii, no. 1624.

[25] *Layettes*, v, no. 558; Molinié, *Associations de la Paix*, p. 139.

VII, and Alfonse guaranteed the franchise in a charter of 1255.[26]

The effort of towns to get free of this onerous and misdirected taxation is especially evident in Albigeois in the later thirteenth century.[27] Gaillac, for example, purchased exemption from the bishop's half of the *pezade* in 1252, and four years later bought off Alfonse as well.[28] The case of 1252 arose from the refusal of the town to pay the episcopal *pezade*, and the consuls' arguments in the dispute which followed are of considerable interest. They claimed that in the past the revenues had been diverted from their proper objectives, the repression of peace-breakers and repair of their damages; also, at present, the area was enjoying peace, "wherefore *cessante causa debuit cessare effectus*." Furthermore, they questioned the legality of the *pezade*, as not having been established "by those who ought to have constituted it, nor yet with the consent of the consuls or *universitas* of Gaillac." [29] This may be indicative of an old sentiment that the assembly which approved the peace tax some sixty years before had not been adequately representative. But we cannot conclude that the men of Gaillac now envision the possibility of collective consultation of diocesan towns on regional taxation. The *pezade* has

[26] Gaujal, *Rouergue*, I, 328.

[27] B.N., Doat, CVI, 111; Réalmont gained exemption in 1280 (*H.L.*, V, 1354, no. 137), Rabastens and Cordes by 1300 (É. Rossignol, *Étude sur . . . Gaillac* [Toulouse, 1886], p. 54).

[28] *H.L.*, VIII, 1310–1312, 1393.

[29] *Ibid.*, 1310–1311: "tum quia si constitutum fuit pazagium, nunquam fuit constitutum ab eis a quibus constitui debuit nec etiam de voluntate consulum vel universitatis Galliaci. . . ." The *cessante causa* phrase (see *Extra*, II, 28, 60; William of Drogheda, *Summa Aurea*, ed. Wahrmund, *Quellen zur Geschichte des Römisch-Kanonischen Processes . . .* , II, ii, 351–352, 363, cites it as a maxim) suggests a legal understanding of the theory of "just cause," meaning here taxation justified only in time of necessity.

degenerated into a local imposition and has become a matter for individual negotiation.

GÉVAUDAN

Peace institutions were known in Gévaudan much earlier than in Rouergue or Albigeois, and they remained operative in Gévaudan much longer. We hear of keepers or judges of the peace in Gévaudan before 1100,[30] and there are occasional references to regional assemblies and military expeditions led by the bishop of Mende in the twelfth century. A council in the period 1102–1112 is said to have dealt with the peace.[31] Possibly the obligations and procedures of the peace in Gévaudan were instituted in this meeting,[32] somewhat as they were in the later assemblies in Rouergue and Albigeois. By mid-century or a little later Bishop Aldebert III (1151–1187) was acting "by religious censure and military force" to discipline local marauders. On one occasion the notorious castle-bandits of La Garde-Guérin, having been reduced to submission, were brought to Mende to make solemn professions of their amendment in a general assembly.[33] Quite likely the peace was associated with the regional cult of Saint Privat, which was much stimulated, to the bishop's advantage, by the alleged miraculous discovery of the martyr's remains in 1170. The turbulent diocese was soon pacified.[34] In the same period

[30] C. Brunel, "Les Juges de la Paix en Gévaudan . . . ," *B.É.C.*, CIX (1951), 32–41.

[31] *Miracles de Saint Privat*, ed. Brunel, pp. 20–21, 38, and n. 2; cf. "Vita, Inventio et Miracula Sanctae Enimiae," ed. C. Brunel, *Analecta Bollandiana*, LVII (1939), 281–284.

[32] As Porée believes, *Gévaudan*, pp. 352, 354.

[33] *Chronicon de Gestis Aldeberti*, in *Miracles de Saint Privat*, pp.132–133; also p. 130; and (*Miracles*), pp. 58–59, 105; and see generally Porée, *Gévaudan*, pp. 355–363.

[34] Brunel, *Miracles de Saint Privat*, pp. xxxii-xxxvi; Porée, *Gévaudan*, pp. 361–362. A capitation known as the "penny of Saint Privat" was paid by individual men of Gévaudan in the 12th cen-

there is mention of a customary meeting place in the
suburb of Mende where the clergy and people of Gévaudan
gathered "at suitable times" to honor the saint and recognize measures made by the bishop and his advisers "for
peace and good customs." [35] It is wholly probable that the
peace tax, parish militia, peace oaths sworn in assemblies,
and related practices were in existence during the episcopate of Aldebert III.[36] But we have no direct evidence of
them before the second decade of the thirteenth century.
From then on, until about mid-century, the record is fairly
abundant. Much of it is in the form of sworn testimony
taken in the course of official investigations into political
authority in Gévaudan beginning in 1269.[37] The witnesses,
some of whom remembered events of a half-century or
more before, were remarkably explicit on many important
points. Their reports show that the right to summon was
recognized very early in Gévaudan as an attribute of episcopal power, and they provide the earliest surviving evidence for the administration of regional assemblies in
Languedoc.

---

tury and after, "ratione servitutis quam suberant homines beato
Privato," down to the 14th century. It was administered somewhat
like the peace tax but seems to have remained quite distinct from
it; see A.N., J.894, no. 9, *testes* 30, 32, 41; *Mémoire relatif au
Paréage de 1307 conclu entre l'Évêque Guillaume Durand II et le
Roi Philippe-le-Bel* (Société d'Agriculture, Sciences & Arts de la
Lozère, I, Mende, 1896), 212–216.

[35] *Miracles de Saint Privat*, p. 105.

[36] A.N., J.894, no. 9, *t.* 48, reference to "forma pacis ab antiquo
constituta," in use in early 13th century; Porée, *Gévaudan, p.j.*,
no. 5, p. 489. A. Molinier, in *H.L.*, VII, 161, overlooked this material.

[37] Porée, *Gévaudan*, pp. 281–331, gives a good account of the
documents and procedures leading to the *paréage* of 1307. The
main pieces for my purposes are A.N., J.894, no. 9 (partly dupli-
cated in A.D. Lozère, G.735–736); and A.D. Lozère, G.730,
largely printed as the *Mémoire Relatif au Paréage de 1307*.

Under Bishop Guillaume IV (1187–1223) there were two kinds of summons "for the peace": for swearing the peace, and for preserving it.[38] The peace oath was normally sworn by the nobles of Gévaudan in ceremonial asssemblies summoned by the bishops at the time of their accession. The first such assembly definitely remembered was that of Bishop Étienne II (1223–1247), held probably in 1223;[39] and Odilo I (1247–1273) likewise required the oath in an inaugural session.[40] But peace oaths were also taken in other assemblies, and they were collected by priests in the parishes. A witness reported that Étienne II had required the oath from the barons "and then from everyone in Gévaudan." [41] Probably the usual occasion for these sworn commitments was when " a peace" was proclaimed and a military expedition undertaken. Parishioners convened in central places for these purposes.[42]

It was understood that the bishop "held the peace" in the diocese.[43] He could summon the peace army on his own authority in time of need. But necessity had to be explained, and negotiations with malefactors might well eventuate in a settlement before the army had gathered, or while it waited to march. A summons of representative parishioners to Mende "for carrying on business of the peace" is reported by one witness with such perfect ambiguity as to remind us again that we must not distinguish very sharply

---

[38] A.N., J.894, no. 9, *t.* 14: "Interrogatus qua ex causa vocabantur barones ab episcopis dixit se nescire, set audivit dici quod pro contentionibus quas habebant inter se et pro pace juranda et servanda et hec au. dici de domino G. de Petra . . . [etc.]."

[39] A.N., J.894, no. 9, *testes* 13, 25, 34, 41, 45, 50; see also *Mémoire,* 221–222.

[40] A.N., J.894, no. 9, *t.* 42; *Mémoire,* 222.

[41] A.N., J.894, no. 9, *t.* 34*bis* (J. lo Troter).

[42] *Ibid., testes* 6, 26, 27, 48.

[43] *Ibid., t.* 42: "dominus Stephanus episcopus Mimatensis tenuit pacem in Gaballitano. . . ."

between military and deliberative assemblies.[44] The "peace," in one sense of the word, was a temporary association, or "community," of soldiers and peace-guardians (*pasiarii*).[45] The soldiers would perform the required field operations and then disband; but the *pasiarii*, who were responsible to the bishop, might continue in service for some time. They may have been appointed in assemblies. Their "office" is clearly described by one witness, who says that they received complaints and warned violators to make amends. If the warning were disregarded, the guardians would summon "everybody in the land, in such manner that each household provided one man, and they [the *pasiarii*] accompanied them all against the malefactors." [46] It may be noted that an army so composed for such a purpose bore some resemblance to the general army of Agenais. The men of Mende were obliged "to follow" the *communias* under certain conditions that are comparable to the privileges of Agen relative to the army of their district.[47] But apparently the *pax* in Gévaudan varied in com-

[44] *Ibid., t.* 13: ". . . Stephanus episcopus mandavit per parochias Gaballitanas quod mitterentur ad eum homines de una .x., de alia .xx., secundum quod plus vel minus erant in eis et hec mandabat pro prosequendis negociis pacis; et quadam vice, cum irent paces versus Monistrol, ipse testis . . . ivit cum aliis vicinis suis et cum essent apud Mimatam fuit compositum et homines fuerunt remissi."

[45] *Ibid., testes* 15, 16, 26, *et alii.* The bishops were said "to use the peace," e.g., *testes* 41, 7, 14. See also *testes* 4, 6, 41, and *Mémoire*, 223–224; *Miracles de Saint Privat*, p. 135; G. de Burdin, *Documents Historiques sur la Province de Gévaudan*, 2 vols. (Toulouse, 1846–1847), ii, 199. Bonnaud-Delamare, "Légende des Associations de la Paix," *Bull. Hist. et Philol.* (1936–1937), 47–48, disregarded the evidence for Gévaudan.

[46] A.N., J.894, no. 9, *t.* 4; *Mémoire*, 223–224. Also *testes* 6, 49. *Pasiarii* were said to have been appointed in Bishop Odilo's inaugural meeting, *t.* 42.

[47] *Miracles de Saint Privat*, p. 135; Burdin, *Documents sur Gévaudan*, ii, 199; cf. H. Tropamer, *Coutume d'Agen*, pp. 28, 30.

position. On one occasion, at least, Bishop Étienne II convoked token levies from the parishes, ten men from the smaller ones, and twenty from the larger.[48] The *pax* was clearly distinguished from the nobles who accompanied it on the peace expeditions: the bishops campaigned *cum pace et baronibus*, it was said.[49]

To meet the expenses of the peace, the bishops levied a tax called the *compensum pacis*, or *compessum*. It seems to have been collected on an annual basis, though not every year. No assembly was required to grant it. As part of the pre-existent *forma pacis*, it may have been agreed upon once and for all in some much earlier meeting. The *compensum* resembled the Rouergue *pezade* in being at once an assessment on persons and on agrarian property. It was administered like the *pezade*, too. Clerical supervisors worked with local laymen in the parishes. The sums they collected were sent to the cathedral church at Mende and deposited in a chest, the keys to which were held by the bishop and several barons acting as trustees.[50]

The episcopal summons changed in character with the coming of the thirteenth century. Its religious basis was weakened. The peace was dissociated from the cult of Saint Privat and came to be regarded as an attribute of *major dominatio*, or the bishop's regalian rights in Gévaudan. King Louis VII had sanctioned the episcopal *regalia* in a

[48] Above, n. 44.

[49] A.N., J.894, no. 9, *testes* 15, 31; or "cum comtoribus et pacibus," *t*. 49, and for the plural *paces*, see also *testes* 13, 27. *Paces* is surely not synonymous with *pasiarii* (cf. Porée, *Gévaudan*, pp. 363–364); the former word probably means parish regiments, or sub-divisions of the *pax*.

[50] A.D. Lozère, G.25; Michel, *Beaucaire, p.j.*, no. 7, pp. 384–386; A.N., J.894, no. 9, *testes* 7, 11, 26, 34, 41, 48; *Mémoire*, 224–229. Also *t*. 27 (*Mémoire*, 313), men of certain remote parishes paid an annual tax in chestnuts instead of serving in the peace army.

diploma of 1161 known as the "golden bull." [51] Since that time, the bishops Aldebert III and Guillaume IV had been striving to make their regalian claims effective. They had also been building up their feudal lordship. Already by the middle of the twelfth century a number of great barons in Gévaudan were the bishop's vassals;[52] but other lords remained independent, notably the holders of the viscounty of Gévaudan, or Grèzes, successively the kings of Aragon, counts of Toulouse, and the king of France. Lordships in the vicinity of Grèzes, west of Mende, resisted episcopal power until the second quarter of the thirteenth century.[53]

The Albigensian wars served to enhance the bishop's authority. Guillaume IV gained prestige as Simon de Montfort's lieutenant, and he was the effective ruler of Grèzes during the years when Aragon was at odds with the papacy.[54] Moreover, he was able to get explicit recognition of his lordship from certain nobles for the first time. Curiously enough, the bishop was absent from the diocese when this happened. On 5 July 1219, and again about two weeks later, his vicar held assemblies at Mende to obtain homages and fealties. These were solemn procedures according to a prescribed form that continued in use afterward in the thirteenth century: they took place in the cathedral before the relics of Saint Privat "in the presence of the chapter and of a great part of the barons and castellans of the diocese." This conventional phrase is not discrepant with the actual attendance as shown by lists of names in the several surviving documents. Twelve canons and seventeen notables of the diocese are named in the act of the lord of

---

[51] *Layettes*, I, no. 168; Porée, *Gévaudan*, pp. 359–361. Though *major dominatio* might mean overlordship or suzerainty, it was usually interpreted as meaning regalian power, A.N., J.894, no. 9, *testes* 3, 27, 29, etc.; Porée, pp. 463–464.

[52] Porée, *Gévaudan*, pp. 355–357.

[53] *Ibid.*, pp. 197–227, 366–368, 370–374, 379–385.

[54] *Ibid.*, pp. 205–221.

Tournel on 5 July; and while the same twelve canons were again present on 18 July, the attendance of lay magnates seems to have been somewhat larger in the second meeting.[55] The most remarkable thing about these occasions is that the barons did homage and fealty not on account of the bishop's feudal lordship, but rather because of his regalian rights.[56] This confusion of suzerainty and "sovereignty" was acceptable to the bishop as a practical means of extending his authority. The nobles performed homage and fealty in numerous later gatherings, notably in those inaugural assemblies in which the peace oaths were also sworn. Often enough these obligations were undertaken on account of fiefs, in a strictly feudal manner; but it continued to be recognized that the bishops had lordship over certain nobles by reason of the *regalia*.[57] Some of the testimony in the investigations indicates that the extra-feudal nature of fealty, as distinct from homage, was understood in Gévaudan. This was in conformity to the bishops' claims to judge and distrain all individuals in Gévaudan.[58]

Various witnesses, when questioned about the *regalia* or *major dominatio*, defined it by reference to the episcopal

[55] A. Philippe, *La Baronnie du Tournel . . . Documents . . .* , no. 1; "Documents Linguistiques du Gévaudan," ed. C. Brunel, *B.É.C.*, LXXVII (1916), 22–29; Porée, *Gévaudan*, pp. 382–383, and n. 3. For mention of this assembly in the *enquêtes*, see A.N., J.894, no. 9, *testes* 41, 48, *et alii*; *Mémoire*, 442–443.

[56] *B.É.C.*, LXXVII, 23: "eu, W. de Castelnou sobredigs, per la reconoisensa de la sobredicha regalia, faz homenesc e jure fedeltat . . ."; cf. Philippe, *Tournel*, no. 1; Porée, *Gévaudan*, pp. 382, and n. 1, 383.

[57] A.N., J.894, no. 9, *testes* 13, 28, 30, 31, 33, 34, 34*bis*, 38, 40, 42, 45, 50; *Mémoire*, 443ff.

[58] A.N., J.894, no. 9, *t.* 28: "Deodatus de Caniliaco dixit dicto domino episcopo seu electo [Odilo] hec verba: 'Domine, ego nichil teneo a vobis, set vobis tanquam maiori domino Gaballitano facio fidelitatem pro regalia'"; also *t.* 30 (but cf. *t.* 42); *testes* 29, 34*bis*, 42, 49, and *passim*; *Mémoire*, 324–325.

summons.[59] Like the obligations, the right of summons had a feudal aspect. The bishops certainly convoked vassals for judicial purposes, and they seem to have led some strictly feudal military campaigns.[60] Their appellate jurisdiction was of more doubtful character. Appeals must sometimes have passed simply from lord to overlord, but the *Mémoire* relating to the *paréage*, written just after 1300, sweepingly interprets the testimony on appeals as evidence of the bishop's regalian authority.[61] Perhaps it is safe to say that most summonses after about 1220, whether for deliberative, judicial, or military purposes, were based on some measure of extra-feudal authority. Convocations for the peace certainly were regalian during the episcopate of Guillaume IV, when we first get clear evidence of them; and this was true of the participation of the barons as well as the peace regiments.[62] And one witness stated unequivocally that it was because of temporal rather than spiritual domination that the bishops summoned.[63]

Independent episcopal authority in Gévaudan reached its peak in the decade from about 1217 to 1227. The *compensum* was frequently levied in this period. A number of expeditions for the peace occurred, notably one against Marvéjols in 1220, which ruined Aragonese power and prestige in Gévaudan.[64] But in this case, and probably in others, the peace force was being used for political ends. The barons were not disposed to serve the bishop's temporal interests. Moreover, the next bishop, Étienne II, was less astute and less authoritative than Guillaume. Though Étienne II convoked assemblies and armies and levied the

[59] A.N., J.894, no. 9, *testes* 1, 4, 14, 30; cf. *t.* 28.

[60] *Ibid.*, *testes* 14, 25, 28; Porée, *Gévaudan*, pp. 435–441.

[61] A.N., J.894, no. 9, *testes* 4, 29, etc.; *Mémoire*, 328–329.

[62] A.N., J.894, no. 9, *testes* 27, 32, 41, 48.

[63] *Ibid.*, *t.* 14.

[64] *Ibid.*, *testes* 6, 13, 26, 27, 32, 34*bis*, 41, 48; *Mémoire*, 224–229; Porée, *Gévaudan*, pp. 213–214.

compensum, he eventually felt it necessary to associate the royal seneschal of Beaucaire in the work of maintaining the peace in Gévaudan. This marked a new era in the political life of the diocese.

In 1227 the bishop temporarily granted half of the peace tax and certain other revenues to a royal official in exchange for his service in defense of the church.[65] The next year a group of lords south of the Tarn tried to shake off the obligation of their men to the *compensum,*[66] a sure sign that there had been frequent recent levies. The bishop also had to fight a war with his vassal, the lord of Tournel, in 1228; and in 1229 French royal power moved into Gévaudan as the king replaced the chastened count of Toulouse in the rights to the viscounty of Grèzes. By 1232, the bishop had so far lost control of the diocesan peace that he sought out the seneschal, Pèlerin Latinier, at Nîmes and asked for his assistance.[67] It is significant that the bishop acted without the barons' advice. Though they probably had the right to be consulted on a measure that would alter the peace machinery, at the moment they were quite ungovernable and had forfeited their place in the bishop's confidence.

The exact terms of this first request are not known. After receiving instructions from the king, the seneschal responded affirmatively. He marched into Gévaudan in 1233 and, in a prearranged meeting at Mende, presented the recalcitrant nobles of the region with a *fait accompli.* It was said that in this assembly, or possibly in another of about the same time, the bishop made a public plea for the seneschal's help, offering him half the proceeds and a third of the peace fines. Full regalian right in Gévaudan was reserved to the bishop. The cooperative arrangement was to last for three years, and the terms were recorded in instruments to which

---

[65] A.D. Lozère, G.25; *Mémoire,* 413–414.
[66] Porée, *Gévaudan, p.j.,* no. 5, pp. 488–490.
[67] See *ibid.,* pp. 224, 417; *Mémoire,* 414–415.

the seneschal, bishop, and chapter of Mende were party.[68]
The barons present, except the lord of Tournel, "consented
to" or approved this measure.[69] The seneschal then appointed one Mercadier as his bayle or lieutenant to keep
the peace in Gévaudan. There are ample reports of Mercadier's expeditions in the next few years; and cooperative
peace campaigns were also undertaken.[70]

These agreements relating to the peace were renewed
three times by Étienne II: in about 1237, again with Pèlerin; in 1239 with his successor, Pierre d'Athies; and in 1241
with the next seneschal, Pierre d'Ernancourt.[71] Some of
the barons, the archdeacon, and the *prévôt* opposed the first
renewal, and the concession was revoked. When a refrac-
tory baron then broke the peace (at Mercadier's suggestion,
according to one report), the bishop asked the barons to
help him. Their refusal caused him to make the second
agreement with Pèlerin.[72] In 1241 the bishop once again
convoked the barons and asked for their counsel whether to
grant the rights of the peace to Pierre d'Ernancourt; whereupon, it was recalled, the proud lord of Anduze exclaimed:
"We are of great blood, and it is not right that we should
be sold like a cow or sheep!"[73] We can discern in these

[68] A.N., J.894, no. 9, *testes* 1, 13, 26, 27, 29, 31, 34, 41, 42,
48, etc.; and see Porée, *Gévaudan*, pp. 417–421; cf. Michel, *Beaucaire*, pp. 146–148; J.894, no. 9, *t.* 41; *Mémoire*, 414–422.

[69] According to *t.* 48, A.N., J.894, no. 9.

[70] *Ibid.*, *t.* 13 says that Mercadier was appointed in the assembly. Porée, *Gévaudan*, pp. 421–425; J.894, no. 9, *passim*. Both
Michel, *Beaucaire*, p. 148, and Porée identify this Mercaderius
with the famous mercenary chief of Richard the Lion-Hearted,
but this is impossible. H. Géraud, "Mercadier. Les Routiers au
Treizième Siècle," *B.É.C.*, III (1841), 422, 437 (an article cited
by Michel) shows that Richard's Mercadier died in 1200.

[71] A.N., J.894, no. 9, *testes* 27, 28, 34, 41; Michel, *Beaucaire*,
p.j., no. 7, pp. 384–386; *Mémoire*, 423–424; Porée, *Gévaudan*, pp.
425–426.

[72] A.N., J.894, no. 9, *t.* 27.

[73] *Ibid.*, *t.* 34.

events a continuing recognition of baronial rights in the peace institutions; but these rights were meaningless without the responsibilities that the nobles refused to assume.

The history of the peace tax in Gévaudan ends abruptly in the 1240's. By this time people generally believed that, whatever the rights involved, *de facto* the royal forces were keeping the peace.[74] When the bishop of Clermont took over the supervision of Gévaudan for the king in 1243, he promptly declared the *compensum* abolished, in episcopal as well as royal domains.[75] This clever stroke, well calculated to undermine the bishop's political support, was evidently based on the principle that the bishop had no right to levy a tax for a function now performed by the crown with its own resources. Nor could the bishops revive their rights. Nothing more is said about the *compensum*, and a number of witnesses stated explicitly that Odilo I (1247–1273) did not "use the peace."[76] It was reported, however, that Odilo had required the peace oath from the barons in his inaugural assembly, and that *pasiarii* had been elected in that meeting.[77]

Odilo was, in fact, a much abler ruler than his predecessor. His efforts in a long struggle against royal encroachments largely explain why episcopal complaints were given a thorough airing in the investigations after 1269. Without abandoning claims to sovereignty, Odilo acted vigorously on the basis of the feudal lordship he still possessed. He insisted on the feudal services, and most of his convocations were feudal in nature.[78] One assembly, held at St-Chély

[74] *Ibid.*, *t.* 47, *pro rege*: "dixit se scire pro certo quod postquam dominus rex fuit dominatus in terris istis tenuit pacem in Gaballitano et deffendit guerras, dicens quod etiam hodie occiderat [sic] se barones nisi timore regis cessarent."; *testes* 14, 15.

[75] *Layettes*, II, no. 3047; A.N., J.894, no. 9, *testes* 19 (?), 20, 21; cf. 18, 29, 31, *et alii;* Porée, *Gévaudan*, pp. 433–434.

[76] A.N., J.894, no. 9, *testes* 13, 15, 16, 20, *et alii.*

[77] *Ibid.*, *t.* 42.

[78] *Ibid.*, *testes* 1, 4; A.D. Lozère, G.71, no. 2; see Porée, *Gévaudan*, pp. 435–452.

d'Apcher in October 1263, was especially remarkable. It was occasioned by mounting grievances against the seneschal, whose agents had been acting in the bishop's fiefs, and had summoned episcopal vassals to distant towns in the *sénéchaussée* of Beaucaire. The preceding May they had gone so far as to prohibit the circulation of the bishop's coinage in his own fiefs. So the bishop convoked his vassals, including the lords of Apcher, Tournel, Chateauneuf, Peyre, and Mercoeur, the lord Randon, the count of Rodez, and others. They discussed affairs in the diocese, notably the recent monetary ruling. Moreover, they acted in association to constitute two proctors to carry their cause to the Parlement of Paris.[79]

Some administrative details about this assembly are known to us. One of the witnesses in 1270, a canon of Mende, said that he himself had dictated the episcopal letter of summons. He added that all the vassals who were convoked appeared "or else excused themselves by letter,"[80] which warrants the conclusion that the bishop's feudal summons was more imperious than a mere invitation. The epistolary summons was not new in 1263. The earliest record of it in Gévaudan pertains to the inaugural assembly of Étienne II in about 1223.[81] The peace force was convoked in the same way. One witness remembered seeing Bishop Étienne's messengers carrying letters to certain parish chaplains, directing them to call out the regiments;

---

[79] A.N., J.894, no. 9, *testes* 4, 30, 43, 44; Porée, *Gévaudan, p.j.*, no. 12, pp. 503–504; 448; cf. T. Bisson, "Coinages and Monetary Policy in Languedoc during the Reign of Saint Louis," *Speculum*, XXXII (1957), 461. No other clear instances of Languedoc assemblies sending deputies to Parlement in this period have come to light.

[80] A.N., J.894, no. 9, *t.* 43. For another letter of feudal summons, in 1259, see A.D. Lozère, G.71, no. 2.

[81] A.N., J.894, no. 9, *t.* 34*bis*: "vidit quod quando dominus Stephanus fuit factus episcopus, aiornavit barones Gaballitanos per litteras quas ipse testis tulit ad eos."

"and he saw people of the said parishes going toward the lord bishop to follow him in the peace."[82] The king's officials also summoned by letter;[83] but the story of royal assemblies in Gévaudan may be postponed to a later chapter. Representation became known as a concept in Gévaudan. The first extant use in Languedoc of the word "to represent" (*representare*) occurs in testimony about a legal investigation made for the bishop some time after mid-century.[84] Townsmen and villagers, however, had no specified place, except as parishioners, in the episcopal assemblies of Gévaudan. Notables of the city sometimes appeared in gatherings at Mende, but not as representatives.[85] Mende was the only town of consequence in this backward rural area. Few charters of privileges were granted in Gévaudan in the thirteenth century; and there is no evidence of collective interests on the part of a third estate.[86] Nor do we find any concern to control the bishop's monetary rights. The *mendois* was not an important coinage. Odilo I wished to maintain it in circulation, as an attribute of his temporal authority, but it does not appear that he or other bishops of

---

[82] *Ibid., t.* 16.

[83] *Ibid., t.* 1, *pro rege*. Roman-canonical practice undoubtedly influenced these procedural developments. On the epistolary summons and excuses, see *Decretum*, dist. 18, esp. cc. 10, 13; "*Curialis*," ed. Wahrmund, *Quellen* . . . , I, iii, 19ff.; Magister Aegidius, *Summa, ibid.*, vi, 21–22; Wm. of Drogheda, *Summa Aurea, ibid.*, II, ii, 14–19, 24-25, 157–159.

[84] A.N., J.894, no. 9, *t.* 42: "ipse testis, ut baiulus domini episcopi, aiornavit predictos dominum A. de Petra et Garinum Abcherii ut venirent personaliter coram eo et representarent homines suos qui predictis interfuerant, qui et venerunt et representaverunt multos de dictis hominibus et tunc judex domini episcopi inquisivit cum illis hominibus. . . ."

[85] Philippe, *Tournel*, no. 39, p. 144; no. 4, p. 28; Porée, *Gévaudan*, p. 382, n. 3.

[86] See Porée, pp. 333–335; and cf. G. Atger, *Les États du Gévaudan* (Montpellier, 1957), p. 2.

Mende abused, or even used, their right to change the coinage.[87]

QUERCY

Peace institutions in the diocese of Cahors resembled those of Gévaudan. The first trace of them dates to about 1200, but doubtless they were older. As in the case of Gévaudan, we know about the peace in Quercy chiefly through a royal investigation, this one made in the 1250's.[88] The king was concerned about his rights in Quercy after Raymond VII's death. Though the witnesses invariably stated that the king alone could adequately maintain the peace, their testimony pointed unmistakably to underlying episcopal rights. The aged prior of Cahors remembered seeing Bishop Géraud Hector (d. 1199?)[89] levy the peace tax, or *comune*, on two different occasions.[90] According to another witness, the count of Toulouse was associated in the task of keeping the diocesan peace in the first decade of the thirteenth century;[91] and the king and Simon de Montfort were soon afterwards claiming the comital rights of lordship over Quercy. Bishop Guillaume IV (1208–1234) required the peace tax at different times, both alone, and jointly with Montfort and the royal seneschal. There were various allusions to later impositions by the bishops alone, even in the time of Géraud de Barasc (1237–1250).[92]

[87] See Bisson, "Royal Monetary Policy in Languedoc," 449, 461.

[88] A.N., J.896, no. 33, printed by E. Albe, *Cahors: Inventaire . . . des Archives Municipales, Première Partie, XIII⁰ Siècle (1200–1300)* (Cahors, n.d.), pp. 46–50.

[89] *Gallia Christiana*, I, 130; Albe, *op. cit.*, p. 45, says 1202, without giving reasons. Cf. G. de Lacroix, *Series & Acta Episcoporum Cadurcensium . . .* (Cahors, 1626), pp. 73–78.

[90] A.N., J.896, no. 33; Albe, p. 46, no. 1.

[91] *Ibid.*, p. 47, no. 6 (but this may possibly be another reference to Simon de Montfort).

[92] *Ibid.*, pp. 46–50.

Apparently the bishop could proclaim a peace whenever he thought it necessary. Whether the diocesan community had a hand in this decision we do not know. But it is clear that the bishop took counsel when the *comune* was levied. Several witnesses testified that the diocese was taxed "for the preservation of peace . . . by the bishop's authority with the consent of barons and great towns and then amends were made and wages paid to those performing military service."[93] This seems to have been a standard operation in Quercy for at least half a century before the investigation. We hear of peace oaths and *paciarii*, just as in Gévaudan, and it is likely that the oaths were sworn, and the guardians appointed, in assemblies. The tax was levied by priests in the parishes and then brought to central treasuries at Cahors and Figeac.[94] Little else is known about the tax in Quercy, or indeed about the military duty for which it was intended. The nobles and *paciarii* served, and the towns were required to furnish militia. The provision *De patz segre* in the charter of Cahors states that the "custom of Cahors is such" that the men of the city accompany the bishop when the latter has established a peace in Quercy. All the other towns do likewise, but they are not obliged to follow him beyond the limits of the diocese.[95]

Unlike the situation in Albigeois, Rouergue, and Gévaudan, the community of barons and towns in Quercy maintained control of its peace taxation. Each episcopal

[93] *Ibid.*, p. 46, no. 1, testimony confirmed by subsequent witnesses; also p. 47, no. 11; p. 49, no. 16; cf. p. 50, no. 24.

[94] *Ibid.*, pp. 47–49, and especially p. 48, no. 11: "episcopus convocabat barones apud Caturcum, et in manu sua jurabatur pax"; and p. 50, no. 30. Albe reads *pactarii* for *paciarii* throughout. The latter spelling prevails in Quercy, while it is *pasiarii* in Gévaudan.

[95] *Ibid.*, p. 46, no. 1; p. 49, no. 16. É. Dufour, *La Commune de Cahors* (Cahors, 1846), pp. 202–204; *Le 'Te Igitur,'* eds. P. Lacombe, L. Combarieu (Cahors, 1874), p. 160 (two versions of a text which, to my knowledge, has never received the careful attention it warrants).

peace required separate negotiation. Decisions were presumably made in assemblies, with some sort of town representation. The term "great towns" undoubtedly means Cahors and Figeac, and probably places like Gourdon and Rocamadour as well.[96] At least one of these partially representative episcopal assemblies met in the period before 1200.[97] This is the earliest recorded instance of multiple deputations of towns for any assembly in Languedoc (though, as previously remarked, it can hardly be doubted that the general court of Agenais had convened before 1182). The representation of townsmen, as distinct from parishioners, in assembly and army, links Quercy with Agenais rather than Gévaudan. The Quercynois were less remote than the upland people to the east, more diversified in economic pursuits, and more generally enfranchised.

The bishop's *ad hoc* peace mechanism was inadequate to cope with disorder in Quercy after the Albigensian wars. Again the comparison with Gévaudan is instructive. At the very time when the bishop of Mende was calling in the royal seneschal for help, the people of Quercy were resorting to supplementary measures of their own. The men of Cahors and Figeac took the initiative. They proposed to cooperate with the viscount of Turenne, the lord of Gourdon, and the abbot of Tulle as guarantors of the peace. In February 1233 they assembled at Rocamadour, a shrine that overshadowed Cahors in sanctity, with many other notables of Quercy, and made a solemn conjuration of peace.[98] They agreed to suppress brigandage and to protect

[96] Cf. Albe, *Cahors: Inventaire*, p. 48, nos. 11, 15; p. 49, nos. 16, 17; p. 50, no. 24.

[97] *Ibid.*, p. 46, no. 1, *et seq.*; cf. p. 48, no. 15.

[98] A.M. Cahors, AA.1. The piece is correctly dated (February 1232–1233) by Albe, *Cahors: Inventaire*, pp. 23–24; cf. Géraud, "Routiers au Treizieme Siècle," *B.É.C.*, III, 434, 442; Lacoste, *Quercy*, II, 230; Lacroix, *Acta Episcoporum Cadurcensium*, pp. 94–95. Also C. Justel, *Histoire Généalogique de la Maison d'Auvergne . . .* (Paris, 1645), *preuves* (Turene), 43–45, who prints

churches and religious houses of the region. Strictly a military-judicial enterprise, the pact was to remain in effect for eight years. There was no mention of special taxation. Twelve consuls represented Cahors in the assembly, and seven acted for Figeac.[99] This was the familiar sort of ex officio agency, which probably prevailed in episcopal peace assemblies just as it did in Agenais. Some twenty-nine villages, most of them informally represented by their lords or notables, and many knights were associated in the pact and swore to it; and provision was made for others to join in the future. Whatever the history of this arrangement, it certainly did not put an end to disturbances in Quercy. New security measures were made or envisaged from time to time thereafter.[100]

The interests of the diocesan community were not limited to the peace. Just as in Agenais, though not in Gévaudan, the episcopal money came under the surveillance of the nobles and townsmen. As early as 1211 we hear of a bishop's engagement to the men of Cahors to maintain a stable coinage. And in July 1212 the petition of "barons of Quercy and burghers of Cahors" led to a detailed mone-

---

a privilege given by the viscount of Turenne to Cahors dispensing it from service north of the Dordogne, unless voluntarily.

[99] A.M. Cahors, AA.1, acts "a consulibus Caturcensibus . . . pro se et tota universitate civitatis Caturci, salvo dominio domini episcopi Caturcensis; et a consulibus Figiacensibus . . . pro se et tota communitate ville Figiacensis, salvo dominio domini abbatis Figiacensis, facta fuit pacis confederatio et amoris concordia et reformatio. . . ."

[100] B.N., Doat, cxviii, 60–62v, agreement of January 1238 between the bishop and men of Cahors, but having nothing, apparently, to do with the Rocamadour pact, despite Lacoste, *Quercy*, ii, 248 (he may have been misled by MS Fouilhac, A.D. Lot, F.136, fol. 233, which wrongly speaks of a diocesan confederation); also Lacroix, *Acta Episc. Cadurc.*, p. 133, Pope Alexander IV authorizes bishop to act against *colligationes* against the "liberty of the church" and the "peace of . . . city and diocese"; *C.A.*, ii, no. 2033.

tary convention. Its most notable provision was that, in return for assurances of non-mutation by the present bishop,
the nobles and townsmen recognized the right of his successors to change the money once "on account of lordship
and his jurisdiction."[101] The manipulation of monetary
rights remained thereafter an important source of extraordinary income. In acts of 1224 and 1230, Bishop Guillaume
sold his rights to the consuls of Cahors in order to raise
needed money.[102] Subsequent bishops regained the privilege along with the right to one mutation.[103]

It is clear that the wider community of Quercy, including men of towns other than Cahors, acquired some control
over the right to alter the money. The bishops may have
had to deal with general assemblies for this purpose. They
were certainly familiar with the procedures in Agenais.[104]
But the record of assemblies in Quercy is veiled behind
continued references to petitions, more so than in Agenais
where the institutionalized general court is sometimes mentioned. The lack of such an established body in Quercy
may sufficiently explain the want of specific allusions to

[101] Lacroix, *Acta Episc. Cadurc.*, pp. 87–88; B.N., Doat, cxviii,
7–8v; J. Malinowski, "Notice sur les Monnaies des Évêques et des
Consuls de Cahors . . . ," *Rev. Agenais*, ii (1875), 266.

[102] A.M. Cahors, DD.1; Malinowski, "Monnaies," 267. The
chapter, however, continued to enjoy certain rights to the coinage,
A.M. Cahors, DD.1; DD.5.

[103] See A.M. Cahors, FF.4 (Lacroix, pp. 105–106); Malinowski,
"Monnaies," 268–269.

[104] A bishop of Agen arbitrated a compromise between the
bishop and people of Cahors over rights to the money, including
mention of the right of mutation, A.M. Cahors, FF.4 (February
1250). But I cannot argue, in the fragmentary state of the documentation, that Agenais had priority. Indeed, the Quercy agreement of 1212 might almost have been a model for the Agenais
charter of 1234 (above, ch. 2, p. 95); in both, the petition is made
by men of the city (only) and nobles of the diocese.

The nascent canonist theory of popular right to consent to monetary mutations, cited above, ch. 2, n. 277, should be borne in
mind.

assemblies. On two occasions we catch a glimpse of a diocesan community acting through the agency of the consuls of Cahors. In November 1251 Bishop Barthélemi confirmed the money in agreements with the city consuls, acting for themselves, the *universitas* of Cahors, and "the whole land of Quercy."[105] What the latter phrase meant is made clearer in an act of the same bishop some years later. In 1265 he promised to restore the coinage to the weight and alloy at which it had been minted by his predecessor. The petition which led to this decision is described thus: "consules Caturci, pro se ipsis et universitate Caturci et pro consulatibus et villis nec non et pro tota terra Caturcinii, ipsis consulatibus seu maiori parte ipsorum consencientibus, nos requisiverunt et cum instancia rogaverunt, quod pro communi utilitate et evidenti tocius Caturcinii necessitate . . . [etc.]"[106] In this case the consuls of Cahors represented not only the city but also men of other consulates and villages in Quercy. And the passage suggests that the agreement to present their cause to the bishop in this way had been reached in some kind of preliminary meeting of communities and possibly of nobles. The legal character of the consent in question is emphasized by the reference to common utility and necessity of the land as a basis for common action. Again as in Agenais, the underlying reali-

[105] B.N., Doat, cxviii, 124–125v (Appendix ii, no. 2).

[106] Preserved in documents of September 1265 (A.M. Montauban, AA.2, fols. 47v–48, but lacking mention of chapter's seal) and 5 December 1265, A.M. Cahors, DD.5 (badly and incompletely printed by Lacroix, *Acta*, pp. 134–135; see my Appendix ii, no. 4). Curiously enough, the petition (which was granted) was for a *lowering* of the weight and alloy. Malinowski's account of this matter is erroneous and garbled, "Monnaies," 271.

See, for *maior pars*, Gierke, *Genossenschaftsrecht*, iii, 220–223, 321ff.; and cf. *glos. ord.* to *Extra*, i, 6, 41*Ne pro*, ad v. *consilio* (relating to bishops' provision to vacancies): ". . . Credo quod hoc facere debuit consentiente capitulo vel maiori parte. . . ." G. Post, *Traditio*, i, 372, n. 8, cites the Roman law on public utility and necessity.

ties were probably economic. The bishop recognized that
he had no right to change the money or innovate, except
one time at accession. He gave assurances to the consuls
that his alteration of the money at their request would constitute no precedent to be turned to the advantage of future
bishops.

The bishops had vassals in Quercy,[107] but we know
nothing about their feudal assemblies. In 1211 Simon de
Montfort fully assumed the authority that counts of Toulouse had enjoyed in Quercy, including suzerainty over the
bishop.[108] Nobles "of the territory of Cahors" are first mentioned collectively in the same year, when, according to
Pierre des Vaux-de-Cernay, they deputed the bishop to
Montfort to request that he come and assume lordship
over them. Montfort went to Cahors and he probably held
an assembly to receive their submissions.[109] Later, in the
fall of 1214, he spent some time in Quercy with his entourage. He is said to have acted as a judge-delegate for the
king at Figeac. Montfort then subdued the unruly lords of
Capdenac, "long a nest and refuge of brigands," and they
made peace and did fealty in a gathering of religious and
lay notables at Figeac.[110] Neither in this act, nor in others
of the same month at Figeac and Cahors,[111] nor at any
other time in 1214, is there evidence of a major summons
of men of Quercy. The point needs to be made only because it was held by older historians that an "assembly of
estates of Quercy" met in the year 1214.[112] Other alleged

[107] Lacroix, *Acta*, pp. 75–76, 100; Lacoste, *Quercy,* II, 204.

[108] *H.L.*, VIII, 611–612; *Chanson de la Croisade*, c. 85 (Martin-
Chabot, I, 202); Pierre des Vaux-de-Cernay, *Hystoria Albigensis*,
I, 245.

[109] *Hyst. Albig.*, I, 245–247; cf. ch. 2, p. 76, for a comparable
event in Agenais in 1211.

[110] *Hyst. Albig.*, II, 230–231; *Layettes*, V, no. 208.

[111] *Ibid.*, no. 207; A.N., JJ.13, fol. 38v.

[112] A. de Cathala-Coture, *Histoire Politique, Ecclésiastique et
Littéraire du Querci*, 3 vols. (Montauban, 1785), I, 189. J. Cham-

meetings of Estates in Quercy turn out to be equally ficti-
tious: an assembly said to have granted Louis IX 500
marks for crusade in 1245,[113] and another in 1251, sup-
posedly to deal with the Albigensian heresy.[114] No evidence of these gatherings exists today and probably none
ever existed. On the other hand, we cannot safely assume
that our knowledge of the developing associative life in
Quercy is very complete. By mid-century, nobles and notables were probably accustomed to being summoned to central towns. Shortly after their similar enactment at Agen
in March 1253, Alfonse's investigators set forth a reform
ordinance for Agenais-Quercy at Montauban in the presence of the bishops of Toulouse and Cahors, the abbot of
Montauban, the seneschal and other county officials, "and
many others publicly convoked there."[115] And in March

---

pollion-Figeac, *Documents Historiques* . . . , 4 vols. (Paris, 1841–
1848), III, 55, refers to a "compte-rendu d'une assemblée des états
de Quercy, du 24 février 1214." I have found no trace of this document. The supposed meeting may be identical with that of October
1214 at Figeac, which J. Baudel, "Notes pour Servir à l'Histoire
des États Provinciaux de Quercy," *Annuaire* . . . *du Département
du Lot* (1881), part 3, pp. 2–3, calls the first meeting of estates
"that the chroniclers cite" (?). But other works, including unprinted local histories (B.M. Cahors, MS 79; A.D. Lot, F.136),
say nothing of such an assembly.

[113] Baudel, "États . . . de Quercy," 3ff. (followed by Callery,
"Premiers États-Généraux," *R.Q.H.*, XXIX [1881], 79, n. 1). No
source is cited; older works are again silent; and it is significant
that Baudel himself not only made no mention of this meeting,
but gave up the idea of Estates in the 13th century, in a note on
the Quercy Estates read before the Congrès des Sociétés Savantes
in 1889, *Bull. Hist. et Philol.* (1889), 135.

[114] Cathala-Coture, *Histoire du Querci*, I, 219, who cites no
evidence, but is followed by Baudel, "États . . . de Quercy," 11–12,
and Callery, *R.Q.H.*, XXIX, 79, n. 1. The assembly was said to have
met at Rocamadour, and may have been confused with the confederation there in 1233, sometimes wrongly dated 1231. Cf. MS
chronicle of Fouilhac, A.D. Lot, F.136, fol. 237.

[115] *Enquêtes d'Alfonse*, pp. 69–71; cf. ch. 2, pp. 101–102.

1259 the consuls of Cahors called on or summoned the consuls of Moissac and Montauban, the abbot of Figeac, and a prominent noble, to join them in a protest against flagrant nepotism on the part of the bishop.[116]

AGENAIS, VELAY, AND VIVARAIS

Institutions of the peace were known, or memories of them survived, in Agenais, Velay, and Vivarais in the thirteenth century. Little more than this can be said. In all three districts we find mention of the episcopal peace in charters of the second decade of the century;[117] and in Agenais the bishops were still claiming their rights forty years or so later;[118] but in no case is there evidence of actual assemblies or armies for the peace or levies of the peace tax. Proclamations of the peace must have been rare in these areas. The privilege is not even mentioned in the associative treaties between Philip the Fair and the bishops of Le Puy and Viviers.

Most obscure is the situation in Vivarais. When in 1215 the bishop granted Simon de Montfort half the proceeds of the *compensum pacis*, whenever it should be levied, he was probably affirming the prior existence of this tax and the right of the count of Toulouse to share it; yet it is possible that Montfort simply insisted on the clause *pro forma*.[119] In Velay a dispute between the bishop and men of Le Puy was settled in 1219 in terms that link the sworn men of the peace with the *ost et chevauchée*. Oaths to the peace were taken periodically, it seems, and the bishop could

---

[116] B.N., Doat, cxviii, 127v–130.

[117] *H.L.*, viii, 665; *Gallia Christiana*, ii, *inst.*, 431–432; Étienne Médicis, *Le Livre de Podio . . .* , ed. A. Chassaing, 2 vols. (Le Puy, 1869–1874), i, 208–210.

[118] Ducom, *Agen, p.j.*, no. 2, pp. 284–286.

[119] *H.L.*, viii, 665. Earlier that year, in a privilege for the church of Uzès, he had reserved a quarter part of the *compensum* of that diocese in fief, *Gallia Christiana*, vi, *inst.*, 305; cf. 307, same provision in a royal diploma of 1254.

summon the townsmen to join the jurors in operations against malefactors. But he reserved authority "in good faith" to a militia composed of one man per household even if the peace had not been sworn, or "if those who swore the peace were unwilling to go."[120] The latter phrase suggests that the knights of Velay were entitled to decide whether or not to take up arms for the peace, as in Agenais; and the composition of the bishop's militia closely resembles that of the general army, as defined in the customs of Agen at about the same time. The bishop in Velay was like both lords in Agenais, the count and the bishop, in having rights to amends in default of service.[121] The charter of Le Puy stresses the episcopal power to summon, but says nothing about special peace taxation.

By this time, the impetus of the peace movements in Velay, dating back to the year 990, was spent. In the later twelfth century the peace traditions had combined with devotion to the Virgin to produce a remarkable reaction against the prevailing violence. The confraternity of Notre-Dame-du-Puy originated in the supposed vision of a poor carpenter in 1182.[122] It generated enthusiasm among the local faithful, took to the roads with the pilgrims of Le Puy, and developed into a sworn association of white-garbed people of all ranks. Since the impulse was popular, leveling tendencies were soon manifest. The line between legitimate conjuration and conspiracy was characteristically indistinct, and the movement got quite out of control. The assemblies were evidently mass meetings, like many previous councils for the peace or crusade in central France. The bishop had no recognized leadership in them. In this

[120] *Livre de Podio,* I, 209–210.

[121] *Ibid.,* 209; Tropamer, *Coutume d'Agen,* pp. 28, 30; Ducom, *Agen, p.j.,* no. 2, pp. 285–286.

[122] For general accounts of this incident and its results, see *H.L.,* VI, 106–109, and 108–109, n.6 (Molinier); Géraud, "Routiers au Douzième Siècle," *B.É.C.* III, 139–145; Luchaire, *Société Française,* pp. 13–20.

respect these developments in Velay differed from the paci-
fist enthusiasm in Gévaudan in the previous decade.

In Agenais the peace militia, referred to as the *communia* in a document of 1263, was supposed to be composed in the same way as the general army.[123] The peace
tax was known as the *commune pro pace*. When we first
hear of it in 1218, the count of Toulouse already had the
right to share its proceeds and administration with the
bishop, a provision which recurs in later charters.[124] The
decision to levy the *commune* probably required some
sort of consultation with the community. In practice, however, it seems clear that the count's general army had taken
the place of the bishop's peace militia in the thirteenth century.[125] Let us recall that in somewhat the same way the
episcopal rights to the money had been drawn into the
count's domain by becoming subject to the approval of the
general court of Agenais.[126] But in Velay and Vivarais the
bishops retained their coinages exempt from the influence
or control of the diocesan communities.[127] Possibly they
exercised their prerogatives more responsibly than the bishops of Agen, but it should be borne in mind that the sees of
Le Puy and Viviers were more independent of their suzer-

[123] That is, the principle of hearth-service was common to both,
Ducom, *Agen, p.j.*, no. 2, p. 285; cf. Tropamer, *Coutume d'Agen,*
pp. 28, 30.

[124] *Gallia Christiana,* ii, *inst.,* 431–432, and 432, act of 1224;
Ducom, *Agen, p.j.*, no. 2, p. 284. They also shared amends for
violations of the peace.

[125] Cf. ch. 2, esp. pp. 75, 85–89, 92.

[126] Above, pp. 95–97.

[127] The viscounts of Polignac shared in the mint rights until
1248, when their portion was sold to the chapter. We hear of a
bishop's order to strike coins in 1269 "de consensu capituli,"
Gallia Christiana, ii, *inst.,* 236. See generally Bisson, "Coinages
and Royal Monetary Policy," *Speculum,* xxxii, 449; Delcambre,
"Paréage du Puy," *B.É.C.,* xcii, 156, and *passim*; P. Babey, *Le
Pouvoir Temporel de l'Évêque de Viviers au Moyen Age, 815–1452*
(Paris, 1956), pp. 45–46, 149.

ains than was that of Agen, and that the commercial use of money was less developed in the upland eastern dioceses.

All three bishoprics had feudal rights and vassals.[128] The bishops of Agen held court following their ceremonial entry to the city and then received homages and recognitions of fiefs from their vassals.[129] In the fourteenth century towns were invited to send deputies to these sessions,[130] and this may well have been true in earlier times. Bishops were negotiating with townsmen, probably as members of the feudal community, in the thirteenth century.[131] Feudal assemblies in Velay and Vivarais must have been more exclusively aristocratic, though attended sometimes by notables of the cities.[132] These meetings need not be considered in detail, for they present no remarkable features in the period before 1270.

Diocesan assemblies dealing with the peace and other regalian concerns were probably more important than the feudal meetings considered in the previous chapter (except

[128] A.D. Lot-et-Garonne, MS d'Argenton, *preuves* (III), nos. 31, 32, pp. 18–19; no. 51, pp. 33–34; Ducom, *Agen*, pp. 165–166; *p.j.*, no. 2, pp. 277ff; B.N., Périgord, xxix, fol. 263. For Velay, *H.L.*, viii, 638; Delcambre, "Géographie Historique du Velay du *Pagus* au Comté et au Bailliage," *B.É.C.*, xcviii (1937), 41–42; "Paréage du Puy," 122–136; and for Vivarais, *H.L.*, xii, 291; Babey, *Pouvoir Temporel*, pp. 74, 319–320.

[129] Ducom, *Agen, p.j.*, no. 2, pp. 277–281; Y. Dossat, *Bull. Phil. et Hist.* (1958), 83.

[130] *Gallia Christiana*, ii, *inst.*, 434.

[131] See, e.g., A.D. Lot-et-Garonne, MS d'Argenton, iii, 26–27, no. 42 (out of order): "Si vero aliqua generalis compositio fieret inter barones, milites et burgenses diocesis Agen. et episcopum Agen. super decimis. . . ."

[132] *Preuves de la Maison de Polignac* . . . , ed. Jacotin, i, nos. 106, 115; iv, no. 643. There is little evidence for Vivarais. In Velay the bishops apparently summoned vassals in local places for administrative reasons, Cazalède, *Répertoire Général des Hommages de l'Évêché du Puy, 1154–1744*, ed. A. Lascombe (Le Puy, 1882), pp. 137–138, 292–293, 310–311, *et passim*.

the general court of Agenais) for the history of associative and representative practices in Languedoc. Finance, for the first time, is seen as an issue for general discussion; a well organized procedure of summons comes to light in Gévaudan; while Quercy shows us some traces of constitutionalism as well as town representation in assemblies. Subsequent chapters will reveal the significance of these developments.

§IV§ The Beginnings of Capetian Administration (1226-1271)

The establishment of royal government in lower Languedoc and the accession of Alfonse of Poitiers to the county of Toulouse significantly changed the history of regional assemblies in the Midi. At the highest feudal level, the old ceremonial courts, consisting of knights and notables who witnessed and solemnized feudal transactions, virtually disappeared. In October 1250 a few southern nobles, with the royal seneschals and the bishop of Toulouse, attended Alfonse at Beaucaire when he received the homages of the counts of Rodez and Comminges.[1] The new count of Toulouse returned to the South in the next spring, and an act of June 1251 attests his presence at Montauban in the company of special advisers and several knights of Quercy.[2] Soon afterward, Alfonse left Languedoc, not to return until 1270. King Louis IX, for his part, never presided over assemblies in the Midi. So it is the activity of Capetian officials that must be investigated.

Meetings held by lieutenants and seneschals often resembled the older seigneurial courts in composition, but they tended to be smaller and more professionalized.[3] Their affinity to the feudal assembly was most obvious in time of war. Thus in 1229 papal and royal commissioners asked "counsel from prelates and barons and many others who were in the army," the question being whether to accept a political and ecclesiastical settlement agreed to by the count of Foix. Although it was a large gathering, the

[1] *H.L.*, VIII, 1277–1278; *Layettes*, III, no. 3903.

[2] *H.L.*, VIII, 1294–1296.

[3] See, e.g., *ibid.*, 1312–1313; 1004–1007; A.D. Hérault, A.240, fols. 13–15; R. Michel, *Beaucaire, p.j.*, no. 3, pp. 376–377.

names recorded are almost all those of major prelates and northern knights.[4] There were at least a few loyal nobles in the region about Carcassonne (*barones terrarii*) who supported the crown against Trencavel's rebellion in 1240.[5] A list of *terrarii* summoned to military garrison at Carcassonne in 1269 refers to knights of the entire *sénéchaussée*. A considerable number of them were descendants of the northern followers of Simon de Montfort, a fact indicative of the transformation in the ranks of the *petite noblesse* of western Languedoc.[6] No comparable influx of foreign lords occurred in the *sénéchaussée* of Beaucaire, where heresy was much less common and the native nobility initially more submissive.[7]

Alterations in the nature of the *curia* were the consequence of basic administrative changes in the county of Toulouse and the royal *sénéchaussées*.[8] Absentee lordship necessitated the development of a civil service in Languedoc. With some qualifications, one may speak of the centralization of justice and administration in the courts of the royal and comital seneschals. This centralization was, of course, paralleled in the kingdom as a whole. Just as the *curia regis*, in one of its aspects, was becoming the high court or Parlement, so likewise the councillors, clerks, and lawyers of Alfonse's immediate entourage were the supreme jurisdiction for all of his far-flung domains.[9] However, there

[4] *H.L.*, VIII, 903–906.

[5] Guillaume de Puylaurens, *Cronica*, 160.

[6] *H.L.*, VIII, 1661–1662. Some of the names are: Philippe de Montfort, lord of Castres, Guy de Lévis de Mirepoix, Lambert de Monteil, lord of Lombers, Lambert de Limoux, Géraud de Capendu, Bérenger de la Grave, Philippe Goloinh, his nephew and brothers, and the abbot of Fontfroide; cf. Molinier, *ibid.*, VII, 552; and P. Timbal, *Coutume de Paris*, pp. 87–90.

[7] Michel, *Beaucaire*, pp. 109–161, 189–191.

[8] See generally Molinier, *H.L.*, VII, 474–475, 487–508.

[9] C. V. Langlois, "Les Origines du Parlement de Paris," *R.H.*, XLII (1890), 88–101; E. Boutaric, *Saint Louis et Alfonse*, pp. 373–421.

was little or no official connection between these highest courts and general assemblies in Languedoc in the thirteenth century. Judicial appeals had always been permitted in the area of written law, and many such cases evidently came before the king and Parlement.[10] Reports and petitions by individuals, communities, and agents of government furnished Louis and Alfonse with information about their southern lands. But this random procedure was not institutionalized at Paris. Some time after 1270, when Alfonse's *curia* disappeared, the so-called "parlement of Toulouse" came into being as temporary delegations of the royal Parlement.[11] This was in keeping with the tendency of the preceding half-century, when administrative decisions, judgments, and investigations were controlled by seneschals and investigators in the Midi.

The seneschal's court was the central executive and judicial organ in each district of Languedoc. With a judge, a standing body of jurisconsults, clerks, and other lower officials (*officiales*), it heard cases in first instance and on appeal.[12] Depending on the importance of the matter, local notables—clergy and laity—might be called in to advise and deliberate. In a criminal assize for three peace-breakers at Carcassonne in October 1270, the seneschal pronounced sentence upon "counsel and diligent deliberation" with nine knights and major officials of his district.[13] Directives

[10] É. Chénon, *Droit Français*, I, 692; Molinier, *H.L.*, VII, 522, 526–528.

[11] *H.L.*, X, *Notes*, 6, and n. 1 (Molinier). Alfonse held a parlement at Toulouse in 1270, of which an important roll survives, A.N., J.1031ᴬ, no. 11 (partly transcribed by H. G. Richardson, "The Origins of Parliament," *Trans. Royal Hist. Soc.*, 4th ser., XI [1928], 177–183). It is now definitively edited by Fournier and Guébin, *Enquêtes Administratives*, no. 128, pp. 289–354, with introductory explanation, pp. xlviii–l.

[12] See Molinier, in *H.L.*, VII, 492–495; Michel, *Beaucaire*, pp. 46–48, 101, 324. The *sénéchaussées* were Beaucaire, Carcassonne, Toulouse-Albigeois, Agenais-Quercy, and Rouergue.

[13] *H.L.*, VIII, 1705–1706.

of Alfonse often required seneschals to proceed "with the advice of good men," a phrase which apparently refers in most cases to the notables and advisers who regularly attended his southern courts.[14] In both judicial and administrative matters, local inquest was the normal procedure for obtaining the information on which decisions were based. For cases relating to important places, like Carcassonne, royal officials, ecclesiastics, and townsmen might be called upon individually to state facts and also attend the court session.[15] On the other hand, assessments of rural revenues and similar work were done by unidentified local men, sometimes acting as juries.[16]

The authority of the regular courts is a notable feature of these activities. Whether summoning litigants, witnesses, and advisers, or directing local affairs, administrative needs or convenience determined the form and function of the court process. Seneschals also convoked vassals, townsmen, and villagers for military purposes. Communities frequently sent contingents to royal armies, though before the reforms of mid-century, the king's officials sometimes made the military summons an excuse for financial exactions.[17] Judicial and administrative summonses were probably issued in epistolary form from the earliest days of royal government in Languedoc. General or military convocations were administered in two stages: first, the despatch of written or verbal instructions to local officials, who then, secondly, made public announcements of the summons in their communities.[18] Ordinances went into effect when read in public

[14] *C.A.*, I, nos. 249, 256, 273, 485, 856.

[15] B.N., Doat, LXIV, 12–14; cf. *H.L.*, VIII, 1396–1399.

[16] *Cartulaire . . . de Carcassonne*, ed. M. Mahul, II, 288–289; *H.F.*, XXIV, 622–629; *H.L.*, VIII, 1379–1380.

[17] See Michel, *Beaucaire*, pp. 27–28, 228; *H.F.*, XXIV, 352–353, 369A, 376–377; A.N., J.894, no. 9, *testes* 4, 47; *H.L.*, VIII, 1349, xxx; 1506–1509.

[18] A.N., J.894, no. 9, t. 1, *pro rege*; *H.F.*, XXIV, 428–429; Michel, *Beaucaire*, p. 68. There might, of course, be an initial directive from the king, e.g., *H.L.*, VIII, 1361,xiv.

sessions.[19] Publicity, then as now, set limits on arbitrary government, but it is only in this restricted sense that the voluntary or required association of free men in the work of the courts had any constitutional significance. The reform ordinances for county and royal domains of 1254 provided that oaths of officials, nominations of the notoriously unscrupulous sergeants, and the exposure and punishment of erring agents should occur *in assizia publica*.[20]

The royal summons in Gévaudan was derived historically from rights to the viscounty of Grèzes.[21] Aragonese and Toulousan officials are known to have acted on these rights before 1229. Whether the French crown could convoke nobles of Gévaudan in judicial assizes was a major issue in the investigations beginning in 1269, and ample testimony was given in the affirmative. There are reports of barons in royal courts held at Mende, Marvéjols, and elsewhere.[22] Occasional appeals from local feudal judgments[23] probably emboldened the seneschals in their jurisdictional claims. After 1240 or so, the range of summons for all purposes pushed beyond the royal lands in Gévaudan, to the growing discomfiture of the bishops. The first important royal assembly was that of 1233, in which the bishop publicly conceded to the seneschal an important share in the operations of the regional peace.[24] Judicial-military convocations for the peace were made thereafter by the seneschal and bishop together, or by the king's agents alone.[25] It was reported that Seneschal Oudard de Villers

[19] See, e.g., art. 33 of Alfonse's reform ordinance of 1270, *H.L.*, VIII, 1723: "Et ne aliquis se possit per ignorantiam excusare, hanc ordinationem in omnibus assisiis ter per senescallos precipimus publicari. . . ."

[20] *Ibid.*, 1347, art. 12; 1348, art. 17; 1353–1355.

[21] See generally C. Porée, *Gévaudan*, pp. 195ff, 410–415.

[22] A.N., J.894, no. 9, *testes* 40, 43, 29, 34, 38, *et alii;* A.D. Lozère, G.736.

[23] A.N., J.894, no. 9, *t.* 18.

[24] Above, pp. 119–120.

[25] A.N., J.894, no. 9, *testes* 29, 31, 40, 43, 52, *et alii;* cf. A.D. Lozère, G.736.

(1243–1253) once obtained a peace oath from the bishops of Mende and Uzès and barons of Gévaudan.[26] In addition to judgments, officials used assizes in Gévaudan to ordain in administrative matters, collect recognitions, and make announcements.[27] In 1263 the seneschal summoned nobles of Gévaudan in hopes of finding out what had transpired in the bishop's assembly of St-Chély d'Apcher and to exert political pressure in the interest of the crown.[28] Thus, caught between rival authorities, each in need of their support, the lords in Gévaudan were probably convoked more frequently than those of any other part of royal Languedoc in the reign of Louis IX.

Governmental functions were increasingly standardized in respect to time and place. Convocations of men outside the limits of their administrative districts were discouraged. Men of Gévaudan were sometimes summoned against their will to distant places like Alès, Beaucaire, or Nîmes.[29] But the ordinances of 1254, in conformity to customary and canonical rules, inveighed against arbitrary citations to unusual locations.[30] This may have enhanced the relative importance of towns like Nîmes, Béziers, Toulouse, Agen, Rodez, and Mende. Yet, while royal officials had the right to call men of Languedoc to central places, their administration remained subject to contrary influences of localism and individualism. In negotiations for crusading taxes, each

[26] A.N., J.894, no. 9, *t.* 48.

[27] *Ibid.*, *testes* 26, 27, 35, 38, 40.

[28] Porée, *Gévaudan*, pp. 448–449, 503–504,x,xi; and pp. 447–449.

[29] A.M. Montauban, AA.2, fol. 24; A.N., J.894, no. 9, *testes* 36, 39, etc.; Porée, *Gévaudan*, pp. 447, 502–503,vii–viii; and cf. privileges of Aigues-Mortes, *Layettes*, ii, no. 3522, 618B.

[30] *H.L.*, viii, 1349, art. 28; 1355. Cf. Beaumanoir, *Coutumes de Beauvaisis*, ed. A. Salmon, 2 vols. (Paris, 1899–1900), i, *Des Semonses,* cc. 80–82, 91–93; "Der Ordo Judiciarius 'Scientiam,'" ed. Wahrmund, *Quellen . . .* , ii,i, 36–37.

town and individual was dealt with as a special case. Moreover, the collection of oaths of fealty took place mainly at the local level, at least in the early years of the period. Not only regular officials but also the roving investigators commissioned by the king and count handled these and similar problems. These special officials were free to proceed as they saw fit.[31] By continuing to visit rather than summon, they helped to preserve localism. On the other hand, it is in their work that we find some of the first evidence of central negotiation in Languedoc.

OATHS AND RECOGNITIONS
IN CENTRAL ASSEMBLIES

Feudal oaths and recognitions of rights of lordship had been given and received in assemblies for a long time in the Middle Ages. A noble customarily did homage and fealty in the presence of peers and notables. Or a lord might take advantage of a feudal assemblage to receive submissions from a number of vassals at once.[32] Some occasions of this kind in Languedoc have already been noted.[33] The practice became fairly common in the thirteenth century in consequence of efforts to increase efficiency in the administration of feudal affairs and to make them a matter of orderly record. Sometimes towns and villages were included, and sometimes administrative gatherings assumed political significance. These conditions, however, were lacking, or at

---

[31] Save that, of course, they remained directly responsible to Louis and Alfonse; see Molinier, *H.L.,* vii, 464–466, 505–508.

[32] For a well-known instance see Galbert de Bruges, *Histoire du Meurtre de Charles le Bon, Comte de Flandre (1127–1128),* ed. H. Pirenne (Paris, 1891), cc. 55–56. See also A. Coville, *Les États de Normandie* (Paris, 1894), pp. 10, 15–16; and F. Olivier-Martin, *Histoire du Droit Français,* p. 260.

[33] Above, pp. 48, 116–117.

any rate, were less manifest, in the subordinate baronies.[34] The ensuing account is therefore limited to Capetian administration.

Even before Louis VIII arrived in Languedoc in June 1226, submissions were coming in from individuals and towns. They took the form of letters and deputations to the king and notices of acts made before royal commissioners. At least thirty-five major nobles and twenty communities, in all parts of Languedoc, are known to have made professions of fealty and obedience to the crown and Church in 1226 and 1227. The bishop of Béziers received the submissions of six regional knights at Aspiran, in the Hérault valley, on 14 April 1226,[35] and prelates acknowledged the king in an assembly later in the year, perhaps that of Pamiers in October;[36] but we have no other record of convocations for this purpose. Fealties and recognitions recorded "during the siege of Avignon" (summer 1226) are not dated to the day. They were undoubtedly individual and separate acts.[37]

[34] See, e.g., for Velay, *Preuves de la Maison de Polignac*, ed. A. Jacotin, IV, 130, item 12; and Cazalède, *Répertoire Général des Hommages*, pp. 137–138, 292–293, 310–311; and for Gévaudan, *Mémoire Relatif au Paréage*, pp. 443–446 (where, however, *t*. 13 is misquoted: "nobiles Gaballitani juraverunt fidelitatem dicto domino Stephano episcopo pro eo quod tenebant ab eo et fuerunt cum eo in domo sua in parlamento"; cf. A.N., J.894, no. 9: "in domo episcopi . . . in parlatorio ante fornellum veterem").

The bishop of Lodève had the right to collect fealties owed to the king in that diocese; see the privilege granted by Philip-Augustus in 1210, *Layettes*, I, no. 943. Complaints were made in the 1250's that seneschals of Carcassonne and other royal officials had summoned the bishop's men, as in Gévaudan, for administrative and judicial purposes, *H.F.*, XXIV, 539–540.

[35] *Layettes*, II, nos. 1752–1757. The three similar acts of 14 September 1226, of uncertain location, can not be accounted an assembly, nos. 1796–1798.

[36] *H.L.*, VIII, 860–861,ii; cf. VI, 615.

[37] Catalogued by C. Petit-Dutaillis, *Louis VIII*, pp. 501–503, nos. 394, 399, 400, 401, 404, 407.

The chief interest of this political settlement is that it affords early evidence of representation in procedures relating to feudal rights. The lord of Alès, for example, deputed his son to the king to perform homage and fealty and recognize fiefs in his place. For failing to appear in person, as required by custom, the elder noble pleaded infirmity as an excuse, and, in fact, his letter reads much like many a mandate-excuse for later royal assemblies in France.[38] As for the towns, Albi, Saint-Antonin, Montpellier, and other communities sent representatives or letters to the king to assure him of their good faith.[39] In some cases the king then despatched commissioners to obtain the fealties of individual townsmen in general parliaments. The consuls and councillors of Saint-Antonin, having done fealty themselves, were prepared to require the oath from all their townsmen aged fifteen or above. But on the advice of the royal agent himself, they deferred doing so until the king's arrival in western Languedoc, for fear of subjecting themselves to reprisals by Count Raymond VII. They proposed to send five or six burghers to meet the king when he arrived at Cahors or some other place in their vicinity. A new royal commission to Saint-Antonin could then expect to receive fealties from the townsmen in a public assembly.[40]

[38] *H.L.*, VIII, 851,iii: ". . . Cum propter infirmitatem & nostri corporis debilitatem ad pedes vestre celsitudinis accedere non valeamus, B. primogenitum filium & heredem nostrum vestre sublimitati duximus mittendum, ut pro nobis & loco nostri feuda, que a vestra excellentia habemus & tenemus, recognoscat, & homagium & fidelitatem, prout vestre serenitati placuerit, faciat. Quam recognitionem & fidelitatis factionem ratam & firmam habebimus. . . ." Cf. *Documents Relatifs aux États Généraux,* nos. 23–25, 27–41, 798, 802.

For the prototype in judicial procedure, see *glos. ord.* ad v. *legatum, Decretum,* dist. 18, c. 9*Episcopus*; also c. 10, and *glos. ord.* ad v. *personaliter; Rhetorica Ecclesiastica,* ed. Wahrmund, *Quellen* . . . , I, iv, 89; "*Curialis,*" *ibid.,* iii, 43.

[39] *H.L.*, VIII, 845,ii; *Layettes,* II, nos. 1788, 1790, 1787².

[40] *H.L.*, VIII, 824–825,iii.

Meanwhile, large numbers of men in Béziers and Carcassonne took dual oaths of religious orthodoxy and submission to the king before southern prelates.[41] We know of similar acts at Narbonne, Nîmes, Puylaurens, Castres, and Saint-Paul-Cap-de-Joux.[42] Several barons made engagements for vassals and men in their jurisdiction as well as themselves.[43] The commissioners sometimes utilized forms in recording acts of submission,[44] but even so, on the whole, it does not appear that this first royal settlement in Languedoc was very systematically administered.

County of Toulouse, 1243–1261

The crown made a more concentrated political demonstration in the Midi after the unsuccessful baronial revolt of 1242–1243. In the treaty of Lorris of January 1243 Raymond VII promised the king that he would actively support a royal campaign to obtain the oaths of all his barons, castellans, knights, *fideles*, and of men of his *fideles* and good towns who were aged fifteen or over. They were to swear to observe the treaty of Paris (of 1229), to support the king and Church against the count of Toulouse in the event of conflict, and to aid the work of the inquisition. A similar provision had been included in the treaty of Paris,[45] but there was no precedent in the South for so thorough an enterprise as was now undertaken. Some fifty submissions,

[41] *Ibid.*, 843–844,i; 846–847,iv.

[42] Petit-Dutaillis, *Louis VIII*, p. 506, no. 438; *Layettes*, II, nos. 1785, 1786, 1788, 1787².

[43] *H.L.*, VIII, 852–856,vii–xii.

[44] See *Layettes*, II, nos. 1788, 1787²; *H.L.*, VIII, 852–856.

[45] *Ibid.*, 1103,iv: "promisimus autem domino regi, quod juramenta omnium baronum, castellanorum & militum terre nostre & fidelium nostrorum & omnium bonarum villarum terre nostre & fidelium nostrorum, ab hominibus quindecim annorum supra, prestari faciemus domino regi coram illis, quos propter hoc destinabit, in ea forma que in pace Parisiensi plenarie continetur." Cf. *ibid.*, 890, for the relevant portions of the treaty of Paris; and 1113–1115,i.

individual and collective, are preserved in the Trésor des Chartes, recording administrative activity extending from 23 February 1243 to 30 March 1244.[46] These acts invariably indicate that oaths were taken "with the approval and express (or special) mandate" of Raymond VII.[47] The count had probably circulated a general form of permission, or instructed his agents to ask communities and notables to comply with the king's demands. Responsibility had been entrusted to Jean le Clerc and Oudard de Villers, respectively royal clerk and knight, and much of the work was actually done by the former.[48]

The campaign began at Toulouse, the largest and most important town, with a plenary parliament on 23 February 1243.[49] Count Bernard of Comminges performed fealty there on the same day.[50] The submissions of four other nobles of southern and western Toulousain also took place at Toulouse, probably in the same week.[51] Whether they came in response to a special summons, or happened to be in Toulouse at the time, is uncertain.[52] But there is no real indication here of a central assembly of nobility. In fact, relatively few other important knights swore the oath, according to the record,[53] which is what one might expect of a

---

[46] Calendared in *Layettes*, ii, 493–532. Comparison with an early inventory, B.N., MS Lat. 9988, fols. 111–112v, shows that the collection survives virtually complete.

[47] E.g., *Layettes*, ii, no. 3029. Officials of Raymond VII were often on hand, e.g., *H.L.*, viii, 1116,v; 1117,vii.

[48] Oudard de Villers was appointed seneschal of Beaucaire early in 1243, Michel, *Beaucaire*, p. 334.

[49] *Layettes*, ii, no. 3029.

[50] *Ibid.*, no. 3030.

[51] *Ibid.*, nos. 3033–3036; they are dated simply "February."

[52] Some or all of them may even have been city dwellers, particularly in the winter; cf. C. Higounet, *Comté de Comminges*, i, 114–116, for the frequent stays of Count Bernard V of Comminges at Toulouse.

[53] The one most notable of these was the count of Rodez, who swore on 27 March 1244, *Layettes*, II, no. 3170.

roving, localized procedure. On the other hand, thirty-five towns and villages took the oath, and indeed, when the documents are assembled in chronological order, they suggest an itinerary through the county lands leading from town to town. In many of these places the royal lieutenants administered the oath in local parliaments. No consulates were convoked centrally. Most of the nobles who swore the oath did so as inhabitants of these communities. For instance, Sicard de Puylaurens was among the knights, consuls, and townsmen of Saint-Paul-Cap-de-Joux who assembled on 21 March 1243.[54] At Fanjeaux the oaths of local knights and burghers were registered separately.[55] In a few cases, minor regional nobles came before the officials as the latter passed through their lands. A charter of March 1243 records the oaths of Pelfort de Rabastens, Pons-Ameil, Guillaume-Pierre de Brens, Manfred de Rabastens, Doat Alaman, and Bertrand, brother of Raymond VII.[56] Two smaller groups of Quercy knights submitted in April 1243.[57]

These facts raise the question whether the royal commissioners made any effort to summon rural nobles as they made their rounds. Certain village bayles of the county witnessed some of the recorded oaths,[58] and they could well have provided lists or information upon request. If there had been a general summons at Toulouse in February, which seems unlikely, the response was certainly poor, as suggested above. For other groups of knights, the evidence

[54] *Ibid.*, no. 3041 (cf. no. 1788, act of June 1226). For other cases of knights in the village assemblies, see Puylaurens (no. 3042), Villemur (no. 3043), Cahuzac (no. 3061), Rabastens (*H.L.*, VIII, 1115–1116,iv), Lavaur (1116,v), Laurac (*Layettes,* II, no. 3069), Mas-Saintes-Puelles (no. 3071), Saint-Circ (no. 3086).

[55] *Layettes,* II, no. 3068; *H.L.,* VIII, 1116–1117,vi. This is as far south as we can see that the commissioners went, and although the acts are dated simply March 1243, they probably belong to the same day.

[56] *Layettes,* II, no. 3057.

[57] *Ibid.*, nos. 3088, 3089; cf. no. 3085.

[58] *Ibid.*, nos. 3061, 3062, 3085, 3086, 3087.

is so slender—it even omits place names—as to make any conclusion pure conjecture.[59] In at least two instances, however, we find definite indications of some kind of effort to deal collectively with nobles comprised in an administrative district. Two acts dated March 1243, both of them probably solemnized at Montauban, record the oaths of thirty-two knights of the *baylie* of Montauban. One document lists twenty "knights and nobles" of Montalzat, Montaigu, and Cos, while the second mentions twelve others of Corbarieu and Roquefort.[60] It is hard to see why so many as twenty (if not thirty-two) regional knights should have been together at Montauban on a single day if not in response to some type of summons.

This hypothesis is supported, though not proved, by the one undoubted case of a district assembly in the oath administration of 1243–1244. On 7 April 1243 twenty-seven barons, castellans, and knights of Agenais convened in the church of Notre-Dame at Castelsarrasin and swore fidelity to the king and Church in the usual form.[61] As in some other instruments of this series, there is no mention of either royal lieutenant, though we may suppose that one of them at least, with a scribe, was on hand to receive the oaths. Raymond VII was certainly present.[62] He had evidently convoked this assembly of nobles as lord of Agenais. Since no townsmen attended, it was not, strictly speaking, a general court.[63] Oaths were recorded individually and locally for

[59] E.g., *ibid.*, nos. 3057, 3058, 3085.

[60] A.N., J.305, no. 13; J.306, no. 73 (indicated in *Layettes,* II, nos. 3056, 3059). For another possible instance see J.306, no. 78 (*Layettes,* II, no. 3087).

[61] A.N., J.306, no. 80 (*Layettes,* II, no. 3074, and see below, Appendix II, no. 1).

[62] A.N., J.306, no. 80: "nos omnes et singuli, de voluntate et mandato speciali domini nostri R., Dei gratia comitis Tholose, marchionis Provincie, et in eiusdem presentia, promittimus. . . ." Since not all those present had their personal seals with them, Raymond validated their act with his own.

[63] Cf. ch. 2, p. 79.

six towns of the region,[64] but none for nobles other than those who met at Castelsarrasin. Clearly, the plan was to deal with the baronage centrally, on a single occasion if possible, in order to avoid the trouble and expense of separate, local sessions such as were held elsewhere in the county of Toulouse for the same purpose. In fact, no comparable gathering took place in other parts of Raymond's domains. Agenais was the only district of the county with a customary assembly and it is most probable that the procedure there was determined by that local circumstance.

So while the royal commissioners were still generally inclined to visit individuals and communities one by one, their work in 1243 showed the first traces of a tendency to use regional convocations for the collecting of oaths. Turning from this settlement to the seisin of the county of Toulouse made after the death of Raymond VII, it is striking to find that what had previously been exceptional has become a regular administrative technique in 1249.

A few days after the count's death, which occurred on 27 September 1249, Queen Blanche deputed Guy and Hervé de Chevreuse, knights, and Philippe, treasurer of Saint-Hilaire-de-Poitiers, to the Midi.[65] They bore a formal commission to take possession of the Toulousan inheritance and to receive oaths of fealty there in the name of Alfonse, who was off on crusade. Arriving at Toulouse in mid-November, they called upon the townsmen to do fealty to Alfonse. This the Toulousans agreed to and duly performed early in December, but only after obtaining directly from

---

[64] Agen, Condom, Penne, Port-Sainte-Marie, Marmande, and Mézin, *Layettes,* II, nos. 3045, 3048, 3165, 3166, 3169, 3171.

[65] G. de Catel, *Histoire des Comtes de Toulouse . . .* (Toulouse, 1623), p. 378. For what follows see the remarkable letter of Philippe-le-Trésorier to Alfonse, dated 20 April 1250, printed by T. Saint Bris in *B.É.C.,* I, (1839), 394–403 (and by Boutaric, *Saint Louis et Alfonse,* pp. 69–77, but I use the earlier edition); and *H.L.,* VI, 810–812, and 812, n. 1 (Molinier).

the queen a special *forma juramenti* which included a reservation of their liberties. The appointment of Sicard Alaman as governor of Toulouse and his pledge of faithful administration were made public in a city parliament on 6 December. It is likely that the reciprocal oaths were exchanged in the same assembly.[66] Meanwhile, in the latter two weeks of November, as Philippe-le-Trésorier wrote to Alfonse, the commissioners had issued a summons "a touz les barons et aus chevaliers et aus conses de bones viles de Tholosan qu'il fussent a nos a certein jour, pour feire les feutez en vostre nom, et a ce jour vindrent li cuens de Cominges et pluseurs des autres barons et des chevaliers et des conses, et nos firent les feutez volentiers, si com nos leur requimes."[67]

The public instrument in which the oaths were registered generally confirms this report, giving the date as 1 December 1249 and the place as the Chateau Narbonnais at Toulouse. But the assembly must have been more impressive than Philippe implies. At least sixty-six nobles and notables and the consuls of fourteen communities came to discharge their obligation. Another fourteen of the leading public figures of Languedoc, including the archbishop of Narbonne, the bishops of Toulouse, Agen, and Comminges, the viscount of Narbonne, Pons Astoaud and Guillaume de Puylaurens, respectively chancellor and chaplain of the deceased Raymond VII, Guy Foucois, and the seneschal of Carcassonne, were present as witnesses to the ceremony. The proceedings opened with the reading of the queen's commission "publicly," in full session, after which the oaths were received. As the most prominent baron, the count of Comminges was the first to swear fealty, and the form of his oath was followed for the other individuals and communities. It was simply a promise of fidelity to Alfonse and

---

[66] Catel, *Comtes,* pp. 378–379; and *Layettes,* III, no. 3830.
[67] *B.É.C.,* I, 397.

Jeanne, saving royal rights guaranteed in the peace of Paris.[68]

The nobles and consuls who composed this assembly were mostly drawn from the diocese of Toulouse. The southern and central parts of the *pays* were particularly well represented by the appearance of members of the families of Montaut, Saissac, Pailhès, Montégut, Lanta, Noé, and Puylaurens. Other important nobles were Jourdain de l'Isle, Sicard Alaman, and the countess of Astarac (by deputy). The consulates of Toulousain that adhered were Fanjeaux, Laurac, and Montferrand, in Lauragais; Rieux, to the south; Lavaur and Puylaurens, to the east; and Castelsarrasin, Verdun, and Villemur, north of Toulouse. This whole group totals sixty-seven, but there follows a separate record of eight nobles and five consulates—Gaillac, l'Isle, Castelnau de Montmiral, Rabastens, and Cordes—of Albigeois. We do not know whether the summons extended to this diocese, but the number of parties appearing was significantly smaller than that of Toulousain. Possibly they had been given the option of coming to Toulouse, or later to another, closer town.

It is hard to say just what happened next, mainly because there is no documentary summons in the surviving record to guide us. Probably the assembly described above was intended to be considerably larger, and due to an overflow gathering and late arrivals, further sessions convened. Subjoined to the first instrument, complete and authentic in itself, is a second, which indicates that in the same year, month, place, and form, some sixty-six other individuals and communities came to swear the oath. This congregation is notable for its correspondence to a wider geographical scope than the first. The Toulouse area was again well represented, to be sure, but we also find among the nobles

[68] *H.L.*, viii, 1260–1263. The rights were those of the crown to assume the Toulousan inheritance in the event that Alfonse and Jeanne should die without heirs (cf. *ibid.*, 887).

the viscounts of Lautrec, Roger-Isarn of Foix, Roger d'Aspet (Comminges), Guy de Sévérac and Pons-Ato de Caylus
(Rouergue), and Guillaume-Pierre de Brens, Bérenger de
Gaillac, and Matfred de Rabastens (Albigeois). Consuls
appeared for five Lauragais communities, Avignonet, Caraman, Castelnaudary, La Becède, and Saint-Félix; for Millau, Najac, Peyrusse, and Villeneuve, in Rouergue; and for
Lauzerte, in Quercy. The oaths sworn by these parties were
authenticated collectively in the presence of a certain
knight who had not witnessed the first session. The only
other witnesses were a canon of Agen and a notary.
Although there is no indication of the month-day, the
document can certainly be assigned to the first few days of
December.[69] Towns wishing, like Toulouse, to reserve
their franchises doubtless made separate acts. Consuls and
councillors of Montauban performed fealty conditionally
on 6 December, probably in the parliament held at Toulouse that day.[70]

Still a third assembly or general session at Toulouse is
recorded on 7 December. The act is written in the same
form as that of 1 December. It likewise mentions a public
reading of the commission "before many barons and other
nobles and other persons, both clerical and lay." There
follows the oath, in the usual form, as sworn by Count
Hugo of Rodez. We should then expect to find notice of
numerous other parties who took the oath, but in fact, only
one additional name is given, that of "nobilis vir Canilha-
cus," who cannot even be identified with certainty.[71] As on
1 December, an impressive group of public figures appeared as witnesses. Nevertheless, though including some

[69] *Ibid.*, 1263–1264.

[70] Or perhaps just afterward. Sicard Alaman is mentioned in the
act as "vicar general of the county of Toulouse." A vernacular copy
is preserved in the register AA.1, fol. 108, A.M. Montauban.

[71] Cf. *Enquêtes d'Alfonse*, p. 126, n. 13; p. 143a, references in
1262 to Deodatus de Canilhaco, a brother of Guy de Sévérac.

of the same names, it was certainly a different group from
that of either of the other sessions.[72] Were it not for this
fact, it would be possible to date the large second session
7 December, and assume that the scribe had left us a confused record. As it is, we must suppose that on the 7th the
notary, with the witnesses on hand, started to write an instrument in the same form as the one of 1 December, an-
ticipating mistakenly a comparable gathering.

Another general assembly convened at Moissac, in the
abbatial hall, on 12 December 1249. The lieutenants again
read their commission publicly, and they received the oaths
of twenty-six nobles and the consuls and good men of Moissac and—again—Montauban. The record specifies in this
case that Guy, Hervé, and Philippe had been deputed to
Quercy as well as to the *partes Tolosanas*. In fact, as the
names of those in attendance reveal, the Moissac assembly
was meant to be a central meeting for the diocese of Cahors.
Members of many important families of Quercy, such as
Deurde Barasc, Fortanier de Gourdon, Amalvin de Pestillac, and lords of Mondenard and Miramont, were present and swore fealty to Alfonse. One may wonder why
Moissac and Montauban were the only towns represented.
Lauzerte and Montcuq had performed the obligation at
Toulouse; but for many communities in Quercy there is no
record of fealty at all. It may be observed, however, that
Moissac and Montauban were among the leading towns of
the district. This could be an indication of the influence of
regional custom, for we recall that by contemporary testimony only the "great towns" joined the bishop and magnates of Quercy in the levy of the peace tax.[73] In the
meeting at Moissac, as usual, various notables, including

[72] *H.L.*, VIII, 1264–1265.

[73] Above, p. 125. Other important communities were Figeac,
Gourdon, and Cahors; but the count of Toulouse had not exercized
suzerainty over the two former, while Cahors was subject to royal
lordship, *H.L.*, XII, 270.

the bishop of Toulouse and the abbots of Moissac and Montauban, testified to the proceedings.[74]

Four days later the commissioners had moved a few miles down the Garonne to Agen, where they presided over a general assembly of Agenais. It was composed of barons and knights of the diocese, consuls of Agen, and councils and burghers of regional bourgs, *castra*, and villages. Contributing to the dignity of the occasion was a distingushed array of witnesses, including the bishops of Agen and Toulouse, the abbots of Condom, Saint-Maurin, and Payrinhac, the seneschal of Agenais and other county officials, and several consuls of Toulouse. In attendance, the meeting probably resembled that which had convened for a similar purpose in 1243, with the notable addition of town deputies. But in this case we have no list of names, for the simple reason that the assembly refused to comply with the request of the commissioners to perform fealty.[75]

After the queen's mandate had been read in the customary fashion, the men of Agenais deliberated among themselves. They formulated a reply which was presented to the commissioners by a citizen of Agen.[76] He reported that the men assembled were unwilling to do fealty "at present," on grounds that such an act would be contrary to the peace of Paris, to the last will of Raymond VII, to the interests of Jeanne, wife of Alfonse, and to their liberties and customs. The rejoinder of the oath commission was that nothing was being done that would conflict with the treaty of Paris, that indeed they wished the oath to be sworn with the *reservation* of any relevant points of that

[74] *Ibid.*, VIII, 1267–1268; a different and slightly better text is printed in *Layettes*, III, no. 3832.

[75] *Layettes*, III, no. 3833.

[76] This paragraph summarizes *ibid.*, no. 3833, a remarkable but partisan notice of the contumacy of Agenais. It is partially supplemented by the letter of Philippe-le-Trésorier, in *B.É.C.*, I, 397–398. The latter is vague at this point but may mean that the citizens and diocesan nobles responded separately.

agreement. Nor would fealty run counter to Raymond's testament, which made Jeanne his heiress, because the oaths were requested for Alfonse only as her consort. As for regional liberties, the assembly was informed that the commission asked for fealty with the understanding of non-prejudice. Therefore, disallowing their "frivolous excuses," and reaffirming the queen's authority to act for her sons as well as the validity of their mandate, the commissioners once more demanded the oath of fealty, under pain of expenses or other punishments. But the men of Agenais again refused.

From an administrative point of view the assembly had been a failure. The queen's officials were obliged to go to other towns in the region to seek fealties,[77] though, to be sure, they might have done so, as a supplementary procedure, even if they had succeeded at Agen. The real interest of the incident is political. Since the status of Agenais was quite in doubt after the death of Raymond VII, the contentions of the assembly were not wholly frivolous. The people had probably heard rumors or propaganda about reversionary rights of the king of England to the district.[78] This being a matter of general regional concern, the assembled inhabitants assumed the identity of a political community. There had been no such demonstration in other areas of the county. It was a peculiar tradition of common interest and privilege in Agenais which had made possible

[77] *B.É.C.*, I, 398–399. Philippe tells us that the officials proceeded to undermine the resistance of Agenais by reaching an accord with Simon de Montfort, governor of English Gascony. The nobles and townsmen left behind had continued to seek a compromise. Some representatives of the city and barons and knights of Agenais sought out the officials while they were at Penne and offered an oath in unsatisfactory form. The men of Agen remained adamant, but some of the nobles then gave in and took the prescribed oath; cf. *Layettes*, III, no. 3845; and C. Bémont, *Simon de Montfort*, pp. 81, n. 4; 87.

[78] See Bémont, p. 81, n. 4; *H.L.*, VIII, 887, 1256; VI, 812, n. 1 (Molinier), 813.

the expression of provincial suspicion and opposition in assembly. The government might well be wary of allowing this to be institutionalized in the general court of Agenais. Even before going to Agen, the three commissioners had largely fulfilled their instructions. They relate that they had already received oaths of fealty from barons and knights of Toulousain, consuls and men of Toulouse, and barons, knights and *fideles* of the dioceses of Albi, Rodez, and Cahors.[79] The clear evidence of their use of central assemblies in Toulousain, Quercy, and Agenais has already been considered. It is tempting to assume that similar meetings convened in Albigeois and Rouergue. But we have no record of such assemblies; and, besides that, there are some definite indications of different procedures in these districts. For one thing, the sessions at Toulouse drew a considerable number of persons and consulates from both Albigeois and Rouergue, including the count of Rodez, Guy de Sévérac, the viscount of Lautrec, and consuls from no less than nine communities. By contrast, no one from Agenais and only three consulates of Quercy seem to have appeared at Toulouse; and the convocations at Moissac and Agen were apparently limited in attendance to men of those two regions.[80]

In the second place, the commissioners certainly summoned local as well as regional assemblies. There were at least two sessions at Verdun-sur-Garonne in December 1249, one for the oaths of three Gascon knights, the other for those of two nobles of Rouergue.[81] Furthermore, town parliaments for the receipt of fealties were held at this time, not only at Toulouse and in its diocese, but in Agenais, Albigeois, and Rouergue as well.[82] It seems clear that the

[79] *Layettes*, III, no. 3833. It may well be that they anticipated trouble in Agenais.
[80] Save for witnesses and notables.
[81] *H.L.*, VIII, 1264–1265.
[82] *B.É.C.*, I, 397–399; *Layettes*, III, nos. 3833, 3839, 3840; A.N., J.320, no. 58.

central assembly was not regarded as the only means of gathering oaths of fidelity; but it is hard to perceive a principle distinguishing between local and regional meetings in respect to administrative function. Philippe-le-Trésorier's account of events after the general assembly at Toulouse provides no clarification. After fortifying certain *castra* in the environs of Toulouse, he told Alfonse, "we went to other good towns of Toulousain, Albigeois, and Quercy, and received the fealties." [83] How many "good towns," and why?

This report is suggestive of a systematic procession through many communities of western Languedoc, though it is not incompatible with the more limited itinerary that can be inferred from other evidence. One should probably conclude that the queen's commissioners depended primarily on the regional assembly, but were always ready to improvise if necessary and to use supplementary local procedures. When Philippe goes on to say that they collected oaths at Marmande and Penne in Agenais,[84] it should be borne in mind that deputies of these towns were undoubtedly among those who had refused to swear in the assembly at Agen. A different explanation, however, is needed for the full-scale town meetings held in January 1250 at Peyrusse, Millau, and Puylaurens, whose consuls had already done fealty in the Toulouse sessions.[85] Probably the government was uncertain to what extent the acts made in central assemblies would be binding on individuals. Other evidence indicates that when officials received oaths centrally from consuls, they reserved the lord's right to visit the towns later and take fealty from members of the

---

[83] *B.É.C.,* I, 397.

[84] *Ibid.,* 398.

[85] *Layettes,* III, nos. 3839, 3840; A.N., J.320, no. 58. Only a single consul had represented Peyrusse, to be sure, but four appeared for Millau and two for Puylaurens, *H.L.,* VIII, 1261, 1264.

universitas.[86] From Agenais, the commission had moved to Rouergue, where its last days were devoted to recording the oaths of nobles and towns locally. Presumably they sought out those particularly who had not appeared at Toulouse. This final campaign may perhaps be described as a combination of mopping up and "good measure."[87]

The introduction of town and village representation was a most important feature of the regional assemblies of December 1249. There is no earlier evidence of this practice in the Toulouse area, though it was already known in Agenais and Quercy. In many cases, consuls alone, ex officio, were the delegates to these gatherings. From the standpoint of urban institutions, this meant simply a widening of the scope of consular activities, since it had long been customary for these officials to represent their communities in justice, treaty negotiations, petitions, and other external affairs.[88] Certain towns in 1249 also delegated

[86] Cf. *Ibid.*, 824–825,iii (1226); the principle is explicit sixty years later, "Registre des Hommages Rendus au Roi d'Angleterre dans les Sénéchaussées d'Agenais et de Condomois," ed. J. Delpit, *Arch. Gir.*, I (1859); see, e.g., the recognition by consuls of Le Mas d'Agenais, 356, no. 24: "Et si ipse dominus venerit apud Mansum potest habere de universitate dictae villae de Manso singulariter simile juramentum." Lawyers likewise debated the representative character of oaths sworn on behalf of municipalities: see *D.* xxxv, 1, 97; and the *Ordo* "Invocato Christi Nomine," ed. Wahrmund, *Quellen . . .* , v, i, 79–81.

[87] There were also local recognitions of county fiefs at Millau on 8 and 10 January 1250, *Layettes,* III, nos. 3841, 3842. If any similar activity occurred in Albigeois (see Philippe's letter, *B.É.C.*, I, 397), it must have been before the commission went to Agen, or possibly just before returning to the North late in January.

[88] See A. Dupont, *Les Relations Commerciales entre les Cités Maritimes de Languedoc et les Cités Méditerranéennes d'Espagne et d'Italie du Xeme au XIIIeme Siècle* (Nîmes, 1942), p. 10; *H.F.*, xvi, 127–128, no. 393; R. Limouzin-Lamothe, *Commune de Toulouse,* no. 60, pp. 376–378; no. 29, pp. 319–321; no. 30, pp. 321–324; etc.; A.M. Montauban, AA.1, fol. 45; P. Timbal, "Villes de Consulat dans le Midi," *Recueils Société Jean Bodin,* VI, (1954),

"good men" with their consuls. This was true of all four Quercy communities represented at Moissac and Toulouse.[89] On the other hand, only four of the twenty-five consulates of Toulousain, Albigeois, and Rouergue are reported to have delegated men other than consuls.[90] These details, while not of a kind to support conclusive generalizations, do suggest regional variations in town constitutions. Going one step further—to note the ordinary equivalence of *probi homines* and town councillors in documentary usage—[91] a certain likeness between Quercy and Agenais becomes apparent. It will be remembered that in the Agenais meeting of 16 December, while consuls represented Agen, other communities deputed "councils and burghers" (*consilia et burgenses*). By "councils," a term that may include consuls, we may understand "men of councils" or "councillors," remarking that this district affords other evidence of their prominence in civic affairs.[92] The number of deputies in the assemblies at Toulouse and Moissac,

---

355; *I.A.C., Narbonne, Annexes de la Série AA*, no. 11, pp. 13–15; and see above, pp. 90, 97–98.

[89] *H.L.*, VIII, 1263–1264, 1267–1268, Lauzerte, Montcuq, Moissac, Montauban.

[90] *Ibid.*, 1262, 1264, Gaillac, Cordes, Castelnaudary, Najac.

[91] "La Charte des Coutumes de Bioule en Quercy (1273)," ed. E. Forestié, *Bull. Soc. Archéol. Tarn-et-Garonne*, XXXIII (1905), 134, art. 6; '*Te Igitur*,' p. 152; *H.L.*, VIII, 750–751; A.M. Montauban, AA.2, fols. 43, 45; "Anciennes Coutumes de Montcuq," edited anonymously, *R.H.D.F.É.*, VII (1861), 104; C. Baradat de Lacaze, *Astafort-en-Agenais* (Paris-Agen, 1886), p. 145, art. 27; *Arch. Gir.*, XVII, 16–17, art. 3; 62–63, art. 23; P. Dognon, *Institutions*, pp. 61–62, 83–91.

[92] See *Chartes d'Agen*, nos. 16, 17, 32, 35; and ch. 2, above, pp. 97–99; Dognon, *Institutions*, pp. 61–62. These places show that "consilia" here does not mean "counsels." "Consul" was rendered "coselh" in Gascon, and *this* word also meant "counsel": the ambiguity is perfectly illustrated by *Chartes*, no. 15.

whether consuls, "good men," or (as in two cases) knights,[93] varied between one and eleven, three or four being most common. It was clearly for reasons of administrative convenience and publicity that the oath commission dealt centrally with delegates of communities. The adherence of town leaders, even if not regarded fully binding on their fellow townsmen, was good insurance against local disaffection. Should special grievances or reservations come to light, the government would know where to apply additional pressure.[94] Neither nobles nor townsmen, however, were asked to provide information in any regular way.[95]

Like his predecessors, Alfonse depended on his inherited rights after becoming count of Toulouse. He continued to communicate or negotiate with individuals and towns separately. As his administration became more specialized and efficient, he was able to exercise increased authority in Languedoc, a tendency that was already apparent by the middle 1250's. But his officials lacked detailed knowledge of feudal holdings and obligations in the county. The last Raymonds never made a comprehensive survey of their rights and their archives must have been very inadequate. In 1258 Alfonse resolved to make a record of his own.[96]

[93] Saint-Paul-Cap-de-Joux sent only knights, Castelnaudary, knights with her consuls, *H.L.*, vIII, 1264.

[94] This representation of towns, or of councils, ex officio might have been regarded as legally requisite, in view of the change of government, which touched local administrative rights. But in the circumstances, including lack of evidence, this side of the matter must be dismissed as of negligible significance.

[95] Later in the winter, various other men of the Midi came to the court at Melun to negotiate "des besongnes dou pais," including Sicard Alaman, who brought a written evaluation "de toute la terre," Philippe's letter, *B.É.C.*, I, 400.

[96] The report of Sicard Alaman (preceding note) cannot have been very thorough, and, in any case, was strictly financial. See generally Molinier's introduction to *C.A.*, II; cf. Boutaric, *Saint Louis et Alfonse*, pp. 223–278

The work began in the spring of 1259 and continued by fits and starts for several years.[97] Much of the record is preserved for Agenais, Albigeois, Quercy, and Rouergue. Recognitions were not collected in Toulousain at this time.[98] No preliminary directives have survived. The seneschals evidently gave, or passed on, orders to their subordinate judges and bayles to summon fief-holders locally to make recognitions and do fealty. There were no central convocations for the *sénéchaussées*, nor were towns represented as such in the local sessions held in the *baylies*.[99] For these reasons the operations of 1259–1261 are without significance in the history of representation in Languedoc; but they do illustrate the growing importance of the administrative subdivisions of the *sénéchaussées*. We recall the precedents of 1243 for gatherings in the *baylies*. Again in 1259 oaths of fealty were taken, apparently the only political acts in these meetings. It is clear that the local agents issued summonses of some sort, as if for assizes, in order to take account of as many men at a time as possible. But recognitions were also received separately and irreg-

[97] Recognitions were taken in Rouergue as early as 1258 and as late as 1263, but the main activity falls into the period 1259–1261. The documents are: A.N., J.315, no. 94, excerpted in *Layettes*, III, no. 4487 (Quercy, May 1259); A.N., J.314, no. 57, excerpted in *Layettes*, III, no. 4570, and printed by Tholin and Fallières in *Rec. Trav. Soc. Agen*, 2° sér., XIII (1897), 11–62 (Agenais, probably 1259); A.N., J.316, no. 112, described in *Layettes*, IV, no. 4690, and printed by E. Cabié, *Droits et Possessions du Comte de Toulouse dans l'Albigeois* (Paris, 1900), pp. 2–118 (Albigeois, 1259–1261); A.N., J.316, no. 113, described in *Layettes*, IV, no. 4667; J.316, no. 111, described *Layettes*, IV, no. 4847; J.315, no. 96, described *Layettes*, IV, no. 4665; *Inventaire des Archives du Chateau de Vezins*, ed. H. Bousquet, 3 vols. (Rodez, 1934–1942), I, 345–347 (Rouergue, 1258–1263). The rolls were copied in A.N., JJ.11, together with lists of revenues for Albigeois and Rouergue.

[98] Boutaric, *Saint Louis et Alfonse*, pp. 246–247.

[99] E.g., at Mondenard on 9 May 1259, A.N., J.315, no. 94; at Rabastens in late August 1259, *Droits et Possessions*, ed. Cabié, pp. 2–31; and at Peyrusse on 26 October 1260, A.N., J.315, no. 96.

ularly. The recording process itself was not wholly uniform, as may be seen by comparing the careful, extended, but undated recognitions of Agenais with the fragmentary roll for Quercy of May 1259, which is the only record to include information about county serfs. Nevertheless, very similar forms were used in all districts.[100] Many nobles in Rouergue acknowledged fiefs free of services.[101] In Albigeois the obligations were now sometimes defined with reference to diocesan limits, as they long had been in Agenais. The regional summons in its various aspects was envisioned in affirmations like that of Guitard de Saint-Vast: "I am obliged to follow the same count [Alfonse] in his business throughout the diocese of Albi." [102]

Royal Administration, 1270–1271

In May 1270, shortly before embarking on his last fateful crusade, King Louis IX directed men of the *sénéchaussée* of Carcassonne and neighboring western counties to make public recognition of their holdings at the seneschal's request. This was a political maneuver. It was probably suggested to the king by the experienced seneschal Guillaume de Cohardon (1266–1272; 1274–1276), who was having trouble with some independent-spirited magnates of his district. We find no comparable directive for Beaucaire. The seneschal was left to administer the project as he saw fit, though it was specified that vassals must present written evidence of their obligations.[103]

The sequel to this directive is known to us only for the *viguerie* of Béziers, and even here the record seems to be incomplete. There is a vague allusion to other convocations and recognitions, but these have left few if any traces.[104]

[100] Cf. generally *Rec. Trav. Soc. Agen,* 2ᵉ sér., XIII, 11ff. with *Droits et Possessions,* pp. 2ff.; and A.N., J.315, nos. 94, 96.

[101] A.N., J.315, no. 96.

[102] *Droits et Possessions,* p. 64; see also pp. 10, 37, 62, 104.

[103] *Ordonnances,* XI, 347–348; B.N., Doat, CLV, 49rv.

[104] For a possible one, see *Le Fonds Thésan,* p. 114.

Six months elapsed, and the king died, before the seneschal put his mandate to serious use in what was the most important subdivision of the *sénéchaussée*. On 1 December 1270 he issued a general summons to churchmen, nobles, and townsmen of Béziers and the *viguerie*. They were to present themselves in person at Béziers in ten days' time to hear the king's orders, recognize their fiefs and holdings, and do fealty to the seneschal acting for the king. The letter was probably prepared in several copies and carried through the district.[105] This is the first surviving epistolary summons for an administrative assembly of major proportions in Languedoc. It bears close affinities to letters for other royal assemblies of this period in the *sénéchaussée* of Carcassonne, and as such will be considered further in the next chapter. No representation of towns and villages was contemplated, the "burghers" being summoned as individuals having fiefs and properties. Though the *viguerie* was a larger unit than the *baylie*, the convocation of men in a subordinate district of this kind may be remarked as falling into the same pattern already observed in the Toulousan domains.

What happened on 11 December 1270 we do not know. Very likely some men appeared and did as they were told. A recognition of holdings at Conas on the twelfth is extant and may have been recorded at Béziers.[106] But the assembly cannot have been very successful from the seneschal's point

---

[105] B.N., Doat, CLV, 49v–50, following the letter of Louis IX: "Quarum literarum auctoritate praedictus senescallus [Cohardon] quasdam recognitiones invenire praedicto domino Rege recepit [*sic*], tandem ad audiendum praedictum mandatum domini Regis, et ad faciendum iuxta ipsum mandatum post aliquas vocationes praedictus senescallus vocavit praelatos, barones, terrarios, et alios de vicaria Bitterrensi per literas suas sub his verbis": (for text of the summons, see Appendix II, no. 6).

[106] *Archives de la Ville de Pézenas . . . Inventaire de F. Resseguier*, ed. J. Berthelé (Montpellier, 1907), no. 1166. I have not seen the original piece.

of view, for he is later reported arriving at Béziers on 9 February 1271 to act in accordance with the same royal instructions, as if he had not already done so. On this occasion he met with major prelates of the *viguerie,* who promptly countered with a set of propositions alleging infringements of their rights. They especially objected to recent attempts by royal officials to obtain feudal recognitions and fealties from vassals and tenants of the church. Presumably they had put pressure on laymen not to comply with the king's directive, and certainly the churchmen had avoided making any previous recognitions themselves. The seneschal was no more successful in the February meeting. The best he could get was a general acquiescence in royal rights, a delay in anticipation of further instructions from the new king, and a promise from the prelates that they would not seek new recognitions themselves in areas whose rule they disputed with the crown.[107]

The seneschal had previously directed the vicar of Béziers to obtain oaths of fealty locally from villagers of the district.[108] This may have been connected with the failure at Béziers in December 1270. On the other hand, it is clear that the collection of fealties in towns and villages presented a different administrative problem. There is little evidence of representative or token oaths in lower Languedoc in 1270–1271, and none at all that such oaths were made in central convocations. The tradition of summoning town parliaments separately to register oaths en masse was well established. Assemblies for this purpose were held at Béziers and Narbonne in May 1271.[109] The situation at Narbonne was complicated by the fact that this city was subject to lords who were none too eager themselves to

[107] B.N., Doat, CLV, 50v–54v (Appendix II, no. 6). This assembly is considered further in chapter 6.

[108] *Ibid.,* 52v. Names of those who refused to comply were to be transcribed. Cf. below p. 174.

[109] *H.L.,* VI, 926; B.N., Doat, L, 282–285; cf. LX, 65.

recognize royal suzerainty. Negotiations with the viscount Aymery and his brother Amaury continued well into the spring.[110] Finally, on 22 May at Carcassonne, they made professions of feudal subjection before judges acting for the seneschal, although Aymery refused to do fealty to anyone but the king in person. The viscount was further directed to convoke "consuls, *consilium* and *universitas* of citizens of the city and bourg of Narbonne early on the Tuesday after Pentecost [26 May], in the accustomed place, in order to swear to the lord king of France, in the hand of one of the same judges, as they have sworn to other predecessors of the lord king." [111] The assembly at Narbonne occurred on 27 May and was far less than a full parliament. Four consuls of the city, six of the bourg, a number of councillors, and some nineteen citizens appeared. They were asked to do fealty, to promise to aid the king even against the viscount, if necessary, and to cause individual fellow townsmen to make the same professions. Finally, the rights of all parties concerned having been reserved, the notables did fealty "for themselves and the entire university." [112]

To all appearances, then, local operations continued to be more important than central convocations in the administration of feudal affairs in lower Languedoc in 1270 and 1271, but it must be recognized that the evidence is not very satisfactory. Several individual recognitions by knights were recorded at Béziers in mid-January 1271.[113]

[110] B.N., Doat, CLV, 56–57v. See also L, 282–283.

[111] *H.L.*, VIII, 1735–1739. Cf. B.N., Doat L, 281–282. Aymery and Amaury were disputing the vicecomital inheritance, and this occasioned a curious performance on 22 May when the former pretended not to notice his brother's recognition of virtually the same holdings. See J. Regné, *Amauri II, Vicomte de Narbonne (1260?–1328)* . . . (Narbonne, 1910), p. 45.

[112] B.N., Doat, L, 282–284v; A.M. Narbonne, AA.99, fol. 255.

[113] "Documents Relatifs à la Seigneurie de Boussagues de la Fin du XII° au Milieu du XIV° Siècle," ed. F. Pasquier, *Bull. Soc. Archéol., Scient. et Litt. de Béziers*, 3° sér., III (1899), 257–261;

Whether a new summons had been served for that period cannot be determined.

The circumstances are clearer to us in the county of Toulouse, which passed to the crown in the summer of 1271. Significantly enough, the work was entrusted to Seneschal Guillaume de Cohardon of Carcassonne, now the ranking expert in this aspect of royal administration, and he was to be assisted again, as before in lower Languedoc, by Barthélemi de Pennautier, judge of Carcassonne.[114] They proceeded to use a combination of local and central techniques, and the latter were very important. We must examine the record of this *saisimentum* in detail so as to understand why and how the central or general assemblies were employed.[115]

H.L., VI, 926. I have been unable to check A.M. Pézenas, Arm. A, 10/6/1, homages by Raymond Vassadel and Aymery de Clermont on 17 January 1270 (1271?), noted in the 18th-century *Inventaire de F. Resseguier*, ed. J. Berthelé, no. 1165. In the *sénéchaussée* of Beaucaire, town magistrates at Alès, "nomine suo et nomine universitatis ville Alesti et successorum suorum consulum in dicta villa," did fealty to royal commissioners on 15 November 1271, Michel, *Beaucaire, p.j.*, no. 53, pp. 463–464.

[114] Also engaged was a former seneschal of Carcassonne, Jean de Cranis; see *H.L.*, IX, 1–2. On the careers of these officials see *H.F.*, XXIV, 252–253; and A. Molinier, "De Quelques Registres du Trésor des Chartes relatifs au Midi de la France," *H.L.*, VII, 260, 264–266. Pennautier was one of those important *clerici regis* who rivaled his superior seneschal in influence, a situation that had parallels elsewhere in France, e.g., J. R. Strayer, *The Administration of Normandy under Saint Louis* (Cambridge, Mass., 1932), pp. 98–99.

[115] In G. La Faille, *Annales de la Ville de Toulouse depuis la Réunion de la Comté de Toulouse à la Couronne . . .* , 2 vols. (Toulouse, 1687–1701), I, *preuves*, 1–51, to be cited hereinafter as *Sais. Tolosae*. La Faille's copy of this lost document is mediocre at best, though apparently as full as possible. Professor Yves Dossat, of Montauban, who is preparing a new critical edition, tells me that he has found no better text. La Faille was working from rolls which were themselves incomplete, but it is clear that we

The campaign began at Toulouse—this was now customary—in the middle of September 1271. For more than two weeks the commissioners busied themselves with local matters concerning Toulouse. The townsmen performed fealty in assembly on 20 September, although the seneschal was embarrassed by their demand to see an official royal mandate, which in fact he did not yet have.[116] Philip III addressed such a commission to him on the 19th, and it is only from its receipt at Toulouse on 4 October that any pattern or routine can be discerned in the government's activities.

The king's directive was brief, merely asking the seneschal to take possession of the county of Toulouse, Agenais, and whatever properties Alfonse and Jeanne may have had in the *sénéchaussée* of Carcassonne.[117] Cohardon and Pennautier decided, first, to have this commission "shown, read, and made public" to the consuls of Toulouse and to other barons, knights, and people (*populis*), and when this had been done, to take formal possession of the county and other lands which had belonged to Raymond VII. This operation was to be more comprehensive than those of 1243 and 1249, more so even than that of 1259–1261.

---

have the opening: "INCIPIT REGISTRUM DE SAISIMENTO Civitatis Tolosae & Comitatus Tolosani & Terrae Agenensis & totius Terrae quae fuit Domini Raymundi quondam Comitis Tolosani, facto. . . ."

[116] *Ibid.*, 1–3, nos. 1–3. The consuls took oath on 16 September, *H.L.* IX, 2. See generally C. Langlois, *Le Règne de Philippe III le Hardi* (Paris, 1887), pp. 169–172, for a summary of the fealty campaign of 1271. He was not concerned with the procedural aspects.

[117] *H.L.*, X, 79–80. French proceedings in Agenais in 1271 were in violation of English rights, as established in 1259; see G.P. Cuttino, *Livre d'Agenais*, pp. vii-viii*bis*. Henry III started his own enterprise for the seisin of Agenais and Quercy in October 1271, but this was already too late, *Calendar of the Patent Rolls, 1266–1272* (London, 1913), 581–582; cf. 662; *H.L.*, IX, 8–9.

The officials planned to examine and make inventory of county records, to eliminate superfluous officials and pensions, to institute other officials, and to require accounts for the preceding year. Finally, "since oaths of fidelity should be the key to the custody of the land and county," the seneschal was to ask and receive fealty on behalf of the king from cities, other good towns, *castra*, barons, knights, and others, according to a certain form. Although it was omitted from their record, perhaps inadvertently, it is nevertheless clear that this form should contain a clause of recognition of fiefs, properties, and obligations.[118] The *saisimentum* was thus intended to be a basic source of information on the king's new southern domains, as well as a comprehensive collection of fealties.

The resolutions further specified that the seneschal should go to the "good towns" in order to obtain the oaths of nobles, townsmen, and villagers in those towns *and their districts*, individually and "amicably." [119] For the central area of the county this plan was put into effect as follows. First, an immense assembly composed chiefly of nobility of Toulousain and Albigeois convened at Toulouse, apparently as an effort by the seneschal to dramatize the campaign and to accomplish a major task with one stroke. This was followed by a general tour of the *baylies,* those "districts" mentioned in the preliminary resolutions. The work in each *baylie* of Toulousain commenced with a plenary oath-taking parliament in the main town. Then, in at least two *baylies,* and perhaps in others for which we have no information, the royal officials held sessions lasting for several days to account for other men of the countryside. They received deputies from the minor outlying con-

[118] *Sais. Tolosae,* 3–5, nos. 4–6.

[119] *Ibid.,* 4, no. 6: "Item . . . quod dictus Senescallus requirat & recipiat juramenta . . . & quod eat ad ipsas bonas Villas, ut haec in singulum de se & de suis districtibus possint concordius expedire." For the local administrative units of the county *sénéchaussées,* see Boutaric, *Saint Louis et Alfonse,* pp. 175–179.

sulates of the district, who did fealty and recognized
holdings and obligations on behalf of their communities.
Knights who had not appeared at Toulouse occasionally
presented themselves at these gatherings of the *baylie*. With
significant variations, which will be noted in due course, a
similar technique was used in Agenais, and perhaps also in
Rouergue and Quercy. This procedure was thorough but
slow. So with winter coming on and only about half the
work done, the commission decided, probably late in
November, to conclude operations with a second general
assembly. Composed of consuls and notaries as well as
nobles of Toulousain, this meeting convened at Toulouse
on 20 December 1271.

The officials had evidently issued summonses for the
first assembly at Toulouse even before receiving their
mandate on 4 October, because the first session took place
just four days later. There are no letters of convocation in
the record, and it is possible that the summons was given
by word of mouth. Most of the oaths were administered to
knights grouped by *baylies*, which indicates a collective or
individual summons by the bayles.[120]

The total of separate oaths of fealty is 423, but the
initial assemblage, in the Dominican cloister on the morning of 8 October, was even larger. Barthélemi de Pennautier began by reading the king's commission to a
gathering made up of Sicard Alaman, the veteran county
lieutenant, many other "good men" of the city of Toulouse,
the counts of Astarac and Comminges, Jourdain and Isarn-
Jourdain de l'Isle, Jourdain de Saissac, Arnaud de Marquefave, and "very many other barons, knights, and nobles
summoned to swear fealty to the lord king for the fiefs they
hold of him in the county of Toulouse." The judge also
communicated the substance of the treaty of Corbeil, by
which the king of Aragon in 1258 had abandoned all his
rights in Toulousan lands. The seneschal then took over

[120] *Sais. Tolosae,* 5–12, nos. 7–12.

and, perhaps in some symbolic gesture, in the name of the king, assumed possession of the "whole county of Toulouse," including the *civitas*, the district of Agenais, and "all other territory" that had belonged to Raymond VII. Finally, he ordered that all those present should be obedient to the king and his officials, and that they should swear fealty to those officials acting for the king, as required. Such elaborate preliminaries are the mark of a thoroughly ceremonial assembly, intended to serve notice publicly to all men of the county, whether they were present or not, that regal lordship was now in force.[121]

At this point, the barons and knights responded by recognizing the king as their immediate lord, but asking the reservation of their liberties. Furthermore, on behalf of the men of the county, they put in a plea for good and faithful administration, without abuses. The session ended with a request that they be allowed to deliberate among themselves, though the nobles also left the impression that they were ready to comply with the royal injunction.[122] There is

[121] *Ibid.*, 5, no. 7. These were less a juridical formality than the enrolled oaths. The king had technically become lord in August, when Alfonse died. The provision that fealty should be sworn before any official anticipates later sessions handled by subordinates of the seneschals, or others. Though by no means representative of all men of the county, the assembly was evidently intended to *inform* them. Delegates of Agenais were not on hand, but that district was "received" by the king at this meeting; no oaths were taken there for another month.

[122] *Ibid.*, 5, no. 7: "Qui Barones & Milites responderunt quod praedictum Dominum Regem Francorum suum esse Dominum immediate recognoscebant, & quod habita deliberatione, post prandium plenius responderent & facerent quod deberent; protestantes quod ipsis omnibus sit salvum jus suum in libertatibus & suis bonis consuetudinibus approbatis, praecipiens Administratoribus ibi praesentibus, quod Comitatum Tolosanum, Barones, & Milites, & Populos bene & fideliter pro Domino Rege Francorum regant, secundum jura & secundum consuetudines locorum bonas & approbatas, & quod ab omni abusu desistant, & ab omni indebite novitate."

no record of any further discussion. Brief as it is, this notice of a common front presented to the government at the accession of Philip III by the nobility of the Toulousan heartland is of considerable interest. It was without precedent in this part of the county. The pressure of energetic administration, little felt under the preoccupied Raymonds, had become a force to reckon with in the time of Alfonse, yet more so with respect to the towns than nobles.[123] Probably the regional knights felt an identity of interest with the men of Toulouse, who were engaged with the crown in a serious struggle over their privileges, which was to last until 1286.[124] The reservations of the assembled nobles were perhaps influenced by the similar resistance of the Agenais community in 1249–1250. Ironically, this first manifestation of collective political consciousness in Toulousain was a consequence of the government's decision to convoke the assembly. Whatever the legal rights involved, there could have been no spontaneous gathering of nobility at the time in this area.

Having made their point, on the afternoon of 8 October the nobles began to file individually past the royal officials, each one swearing a simple oath of fidelity. The jurors are listed under rubrics which indicate the presence of both urban and rural knights.[125] The twenty-three administrative units mentioned include seventeen *baylies* of Toulousain, four of Albigeois, one town, and the *viguerie* of Toulouse. Recognitions of fiefs were not given,[126] probably in order to save time, but even so the proceedings lasted on into a second day.

---

[123] See generally Boutaric, *Saint Louis et Alfonse*, pp. 494–528.

[124] Molinier, "La Commune de Toulouse & Philippe III," *H.L.*, x, 153–162.

[125] E.g., "DE CASTRO DE FANO JOVIS, & Bajulia ejus," *Sais. Tolosae*, 6, no. 8; the distinction has no great importance, since many of the *chefs-lieux* were little more than villages.

[126] With two exceptions, Viscount Bertrand of Lautrec, and the bishop of Couserans, *ibid.*, 10–12, nos. 9–12.

From 9 October to 2 November we lose track of the fealty commissioners. It is quite possible that they spent these three weeks in Rouergue and Quercy, for whose inhabitants there is no record of oaths.[127] Since men of these districts had not appeared at Toulouse, we may further surmise that operations began in those areas with general assemblies.

Early in November, the seneschal and the judge of Carcassonne were again in Toulousain, at Verdun-sur-Garonne. On the 2nd they convoked the town parliament, read their commission, and took possession of the *castrum* "with all its rights and appurtenances, and with the whole *baylie* and district, with villages of that *baylie*, and with all properties and rights of those places." [128] This suggests that the parliament was thought representative of the entire district, which was not in fact the case. The gathering which heard the commission and then did fealty collectively was limited to consuls and individuals of the *universitas castri*.[129] On the other hand, the officials and scribe were evidently thinking loosely in terms of the larger gathering of the *baylie*, which, while doubtless never assembled at once in any one place, was nevertheless an actual state of affairs during the next few days. Notice had already been served to the consulates of this populous district, and we have the record of oaths received from the consuls and *meliores* of no less than forty-two villages between 3 and 7 November. Eleven nobles, none of whom had appeared at Toulouse, but using the same form as in that assembly, also promised fidelity at Verdun.[130] The villagers, in addition to fealty, recognized the direct or indirect suzerainty of the

---

[127] Cf. Langlois, *Philippe III*, p. 171; and Lacoste, *Quercy*, II, 327–328 (the work in Quercy may have followed the Agenais campaign in November).

[128] *Sais. Tolosae*, 12–13. no. 13.

[129] *Ibid.*, 12–13, no. 13; cf. Appendix I, pp. 302–305, 309–310.

[130] *Sais. Tolosae*, 19, no. 31.

king and specified royal rights to military service, hospitality, and other dues.[131]

It is not clear whether mediate lords of the twenty-six consulates not directly subject to the king were notified of the summons. The date that was set must have been 3 November, but there was possibly some option as to the place of appearance. Delegates of fourteen places discharged their obligations at Verdun on the third, and nine of these were royal villages.[132] That same day, or more probably the next, the commission moved a few miles north to the abbey town of Belleperche, where five more communities—three of them all or partly royal—were accounted for.[133] At this point the scribe intended to close his record for the *baylie* of Verdun, for we find this illuminating notation: "other villages of the *baylie* of Verdun have neither appeared nor sworn, wherefore the remedies of law should be exercised against them." [134] The king's officials went to Castelsarrasin on 5 November, and proceeded to collect oaths in that *baylie* as they had in Verdun.[135] The disadvantages of their method must have become apparent when deputies of numerous other villages of the Verdun district now appeared at Castelsarrasin and Moissac.[136] These delegations totaled twenty-three, of which twenty were seigneurial villages and only one directly subordinate to the king.[137] These statistics suggest that the

[131] The officials were apparently working from some kind of record previously drawn up. There is a preliminary list of 26 towns expected to swear, *ibid.*, 13, no. 14, of which the roll accounts for all but six.

[132] *Ibid.*, 13–19, nos. 15–17, 19–30.

[133] *Ibid.*, 19–21, nos. 32–36. The first act bears no date; nos. 32–35 are dated "as above"; no. 36 is dated 5 November.

[134] *Ibid.*, 21.

[135] *Ibid.*, 21–25, nos. 37–49.

[136] Not to mention the *universitas* of one little place whose consuls had already done fealty at Verdun, *ibid.*, 14, no. 16.

[137] *Ibid.*, 26–35, nos. 50–73.

delay was connected with problems arising from the summons of non-royal communities.

The ordinary delegation from the villages of the *baylies* of Verdun and Castelsarrasin consisted of two or three consuls, accompanied by one or several local notables. The consuls invariably acted "for themselves and the university," while the notables swore as individuals.[138] In some cases, however, the latter were included with the consuls *before* the formula "pro se et universitate," which seems to indicate that the royal commission generally regarded the whole deputation as fully representative of the village.[139] There was certainly no intention of taking the oath of every individual in village parliaments, for which we find no record at all. Two variations in the usual practice may be mentioned for their illustration of the application of corporate principles in representation. The consuls of two villages, Raissac and Montbéqui, appeared at Verdun as delegates of the "communitas dictarum villarum," which they acknowledged to be the king's "property." [140] And we find a link between the passing, pre-consular rural regime and newer administrative conceptions in the appearance of Arnaud de Lavilledieu, who performed fealty as lord and delegate of the "university of manses of Mausac," in the *baylie* of Castelsarrasin.[141]

From Castelsarrasin the royal oath commissioners passed into Agenais, where they spent about a week. Unfortunately there survives only a fragment of their record for this

[138] E.g., Cordes-Tolosanes, *ibid.*, 21, no. 36. As in this instance the notables were often styled *meliores*; in some cases the village bayle appeared, e.g., 17, nos. 23, 25.

[139] *Ibid.*, 30, no. 60; 31, nos. 63–64; 34, no. 73.

[140] *Ibid.*, 17, no. 24. Cf. the English *villa integra*, discussed by B. Lees, *Eng. Hist. Review*, XLI (1926), 98–103.

[141] *Sais. Tolosae*, 24, no. 44; cf. J. H. Mundy, *Toulouse*, p. 135. Cf. too, the canon law specifying the summons to diocesan synods of only those abbots "populum habentes," e.g., *glos. ord.* ad v. *dioecesana, Extra*, I, 33, *9Quod super*.

region.[142] But what we have is enough to indicate certain changes in procedure in the direction of further centralization, no doubt as a means of saving time and energy.

If this was their intention, as we may suppose, then it would seem most appropriate in Agenais, with its tradition of regional assemblies, to begin operations there by summoning such a meeting in a central town, and obtaining as many fealties as possible at the outset. And so it happened. At Agen on 12 November the seneschal Guillaume de Cohardon met with nobles of Agenais and consuls of Agen and other "good towns" in a "parliament or general court, according to the usage of the said land." [143] Theoretically this enabled the officials to receive the oaths of all the most important knights of Agenais, and from the list of jurors we know that at least ninety-two nobles attended the meeting.[144]

Unfortunately, no such list is available for the consulates represented there. Individual acts of fealty serve to identify four communities, but there is no reason to think that the record is complete at this point. This evidence does suggest, however, that the seneschal was trying to carry out the seisin of entire *baylies* of Agenais in the central assembly, without actually visiting them. Consuls of the bastide of Villeneuve-sur-Lot appeared "for themselves and the *universitas* . . . of Villeneuve . . . and for the parishes of the honor and district of the same [community]." Having heard

---

[142] A.N., Q. no. 254 (presently 606), a 17th-century copy published by Tholin and Fallières in *Rec. Trav. Soc. Agen.*, 2° sér., XIII (1897), 63–88, previously cited as *Sais(imentum). Agen(ense).* This copy seems to be dependable and is indeed far superior to that of La Faille in the matter of proper names. But the omission of certain words regarded as superfluous by the editors, sometimes renders its interpretation difficult, as in the document for Puymirol, below, p. 181. Langlois, *Philippe III,* overlooked the material for Agenais.

[143] *Sais. Agen.*, 72, 85.

[144] *Ibid.*, 85–87.

the royal mandate in full session, the deputies, including town notables, swore fealty and made recognition of the king's rights in the town and *baylie* of Villeneuve. They enumerated twenty-eight parishes, two *castra*, and two villages (*villae*). The latter four communities, they asserted, even if subject to mediate lords, owed the king fealty, military service, and *lods et ventes*. They concluded by reserving their liberties.[145]

The opening formula of their act indicates that the consuls and notables of Villeneuve were representative of the parishes of the *baylie*; but it omits mention of the villages.[146] Probably this was because the district of Villeneuve included certain consulates important in their own right, places which, moreover, were accustomed to sending delegates to the general court of Agenais. The consuls and notables of at least two such communities, Sainte-Livrade and Eysses, appeared at Agen on this occasion, performed fealty as village representatives, and recognized holdings and obligations in the usual way.[147]

We know of the deputation of one other *baylie* town, Port-Sainte-Marie. The consuls and notables swore fealty and made their recognition and reservation in a form like that of Villeneuve. But although the roll includes the fealty and homage of one of the local lords,[148] there is no mention of delegates or oaths of any of the twenty-one *castra* and villages in the *baylie* of Port. Again, the opening clause of the document provides an explanation. It states explicitly that the consuls of Port-Sainte-Marie had been convoked as

[145] *Ibid.*, 75–76. The official term "bajulia" is always at least loosely equivalent in this document to the more common local words "honor" and "districtus."

[146] *Ibid.*, 75: "Noverint universi quod, vocatis consulibus pro se et universitate bastide de Villanove . . . et pro parrochiis de honore et districtu ipsius. . . ."

[147] *Ibid.*, 77–78.

[148] *Ibid.*, 80.

deputies of the *castra,* as well as of the university of the town and parishes of the district.[149]

The work in this assembly at Agen took several days. There were at least two plenary sessions, on 12 and 14 November. The royal commission was made public at the start, whereupon the men of Agenais, in a move reminiscent of their resistance in 1249, refused to do fealty until some royal official of the district had first sworn to maintain their liberties and customs. Accordingly, though ignoring certain other protests, Cohardon announced the appointment of a seneschal for Agenais, who took the required oath publicly on the 14th.[150] Only then could the commissioners obtain the fealties. Consistent with their practice at Toulouse, they took special pains with the *civitas.* The consuls and leading men of Agen swore fidelity to the king on behalf of the "university of citizens" in the assembly of 14 November. We are reminded of the similar representative act in the meeting at Narbonne in the preceding May; it is no accident that the same royal officials were involved.[151] Then on 17 November the judge Barthélemi de Pennautier presided over a parliament of Agen in which crown rights in the city were officially recognized with the reservation of local seigneurial privileges and liberties. Though the multitude of townsmen probably did not perform fealty as individuals, some sort of common oath seems

[149] *Ibid.,* 78: "Noverint universi quod convocatis consulibus ville de Portu Sancte Marie . . . pro se et universitate dicte ville et pro parrochiis et castris de honore et districtu bajulie dicte ville. . . ."

[150] *Ibid.,* 85. The appointment had been made on the twelfth or before, because we find the new official, Jean de Mortery, styled "senescallus Agenensis," 67, in an act at Penne of that date. The public notice of the oath of the nobility, dated 14 November, indicates that the first full meeting occurred on the twelfth. But the notice preceding the fealty sworn by the consuls of Agen, 72, refers to a plenary session on the thirteenth, which asked—and was granted—overnight postponement. See also n. 154.

[151] Above, p. 166.

to have been made.[152] Nevertheless, the assembly formally ratified the oath previously sworn by the consuls and notables on their behalf.[153] This was an explicit affirmation of the principle of representation, doubtless solicited by the officials. It is the only hint in the available *saisimentum* that oath-taking consuls were empowered proctors, or were regarded as such.

Not all *baylies* of Agenais were handled in the meeting at Agen, for we know of two other fealty assemblies elsewhere in the region. Much the most remarkable one of these was convoked by the commissioners on 12 November at Penne d'Agenais.[154] It was three-fold in composition: it was a public parliament of consuls and burghers of Penne; also present were individuals and nobles from outlying parts of the *baylie* of Penne; and the assembly included the consuls and delegates of at least three other *baylie* towns and their districts, Monflanquin, Tournon, and Castillonès. The seneschal of Carcassonne read his commission to the

[152] Probably like the collective oath clearly described at Penne on 12 November, *Sais. Agen.*, 65, text quoted below, n. 155.

[153] *Ibid.*, 72–75 (also A.D. Lot-et-Garonne, MS d'Argenton, III, no. 94, 58–59); note esp. (*Sais. Agen.*) 75: "eam [the recognition] facientes pro se et tota universitate predicte civitatis, ratum et gratum habentes juramentum fidelitatis quod nuper consules et alii, pro ipsa universitate et singulis de ipsa, domino Regi prestiterunt in manu predicti senescalli Carcassone." The omission of men of the bourg of Agen is probably without significance. Possibly a second act was drawn for them, or, more likely, they were understood as included in the *civitas*; cf. *Layettes*, III, no. 3833; *Sais. Tolosae*, 2–3, no. 2.

[154] *Sais. Agen.*, 63–72. This date presents a problem unless we suppose that summonses had been issued for the twelfth, and that the royal party arrived from Agen only late in the day, or on the next. Otherwise, one should prefer to suspect an error in this date ("pridie idus Novembris," 67) rather than in that of Agen ("ad crastinum Beati Martini Hiemalis," 85), for it seems unlikely that the commission would visit a smaller (and probably more distant) town before going to Agen.

whole gathering and received fealties and recognitions in various forms according to the groups involved.

The notables of the *baylie* joined the men of Penne in the collective oath which was customary in the towns. Their appearance in the parliament distinguishes this procedure from that followed at Verdun, where, it will be recalled, deputies of the consulates appeared only on the day following the town assembly. Technically, these outsiders acted as individuals, not as deputies of the sixty-odd parishes and *castra* in the *baylie*, but they seem to have been regarded as collectively representative of the district.[155] Their knowledge probably facilitated the delimitation of jurisdictions, boundaries, territories, and rights included in the recognition. Eleven nobles of the town and *baylie* did fealty individually. With one possible exception, none of these repeated the oath at Agen; and more than half of the group was made up of *juniores* and *domicelli*.[156]

The summons of delegates from other *baylies* is the most interesting aspect of this assembly at Penne. The representation of Monflanquin, Tournon, and probably Castillonès [157] as well, resembled that of Penne, except that

---

[155] *Ibid.*, 64–65: "convocata universitate proborum hominum dicti castri, per vocem preconis, ut moris est, necnon et plurimis de honore et districtu dicti castri . . . requisivit [the seneschal] consules et universitatem predicti castri de Penna et plurimos de bajulia et honore et districtu ipsius castri, quod jurarent fidelitatem . . . ; ad hec predicti consules . . . et ipsa universitas et singuli de ipsa, qui ibi erant presentes, et plurimi de honore et districtu et de dicta bajulia videlicet [many names given] . . . et alii quorum nomina scribi singulariter, propter nimiam multitudinem, multum esset tediosum, ad requisitionem predicti senescalli Carcassone, perlectis eis litteris domini Regis, quorum tenor inferius continetur, promiserunt et, elevatis manibus ad sancta Dei evangelia, juraverunt quod. . . ."

[156] *Ibid.*, 67. The "dominus Arnaudus Pagani, miles," at Penne, may be the same as "Arnaldus Pagani, miles," at Agen, 86.

[157] For this place there is only an 18th-century summary, which leaves us in doubt on certain details, *ibid.*, 89–90.

men of the *baylie* towns did not accompany their consuls en masse. Notables of *chef-lieu* and countryside appeared together in each case, but Tournon presents the additional feature of special deputations from villages of the *baylie*.[158] Included in the record are the fealties and recognitions made at Penne by representative consuls of Cuzorn, and "good men" of Blanquefort and Lastreilles.[159] Two nobles of this *baylie* also presented themselves to swear fealty, one "for himself and his vassals," and the other "for the *castrum* of Le Pech de Lestele."[160] This variety in response indicates that the summons was given in general rather than specific terms and was left to be interpreted and carried out as the different localities saw fit.

The other *baylie*-town assembly noted in the record convened at Puymirol on 18 November 1271. This was a parliament of consuls, notables, and university, but, unlike that of Penne, it did not include men of the neighboring countryside. It reminds us of the deputation from Port-Sainte-Marie to Agen several days before, because the Puymirol notables professed to act for themselves, their fellow burghers, and men of the villages, *castra*, and parishes.[161] Puymirol was a particularly extensive *baylie* of eastern Agenais.[162] However, we do not know whether any effort was made to summon or visit its villagers. Very likely the representative oath was thought sufficient.

Though lost to our sight between 14 November at Agen

---

[158] *Ibid.*, 67–70, 89–90.

[159] *Ibid.*, 71. The two non-consular communities are indicative of the relatively undeveloped condition of the rural constitution in northern Agenais.

[160] *Ibid.*, 72.

[161] *Ibid.*, 82–84, to be supplemented by the fuller copy in A.D. Lot-et-Garonne, E. Suppl. 691 (Laroque-Timbaut, AA.2), no. 1.

[162] Listed in its *ressortum, Sais. Agen.*, 83–84, are 12 parishes and 14 *castra*. The extension of Auvillar into Agenais, of which Puymirol made recognition, was some 10 miles up the Garonne; cf. *H.L.*, VIII, 1286, an account of 1257.

and 18 November at Puymirol, the oath commissioners were probably busy during those days.[163] Whether or not they completed the seisin of Agenais, it seems clear that their summons of central and compound district assemblies expedited this work. In view of the presence and submission of town representatives in the general assembly at Agen, one may even regard the *baylie* campaign as secondary and supplementary, which was certainly not the case in Toulousain. Administrative practices peculiar to Agenais may well have contributed to changing the crown's procedures in this region. We do not, in fact, know how the summonses were distributed. Quite conceivably the seneschal of Agenais and local bayles negotiated general directives sent by the commissioners before their arrival. It should be emphasized that the general assembly at Agen was not a strictly *ad hoc* convocation, but rather a meeting, for a specified purpose, of the customary *curia generalis* of Agenais.

Relative success in Agenais may have influenced the decision of the government to conclude operations in the Toulouse area with a comprehensive assembly like that of Agen. The seneschal and judge of Carcassonne were again in Toulousain on 22 November, when they read their commission and received fealties in town parliaments at Villemur and Buzet. The burghers of these places made recognitions that included lists of villages in their respective *baylies,* but there is no evidence of delegations from outlying communities.[164] The oath parliament at Castelnaudary three days later was also limited to townsmen.[165] At this point the record becomes miscellaneous and fragmentary, giving the impression that the commission had

---

[163] The seneschal may have been elsewhere in the diocese receiving oaths when his subordinate, Barthélemi de Pennautier, met the parliament at Agen on the seventeenth, above, p. 178.

[164] *Sais. Tolosae,* 35–38, nos. 74, 75.

[165] *Ibid.,* 39–40, no. 77.

abandoned any regular routine before the general assembly at Toulouse on 20 December.[166]

This final gathering was directed by Florence de Varennes and Guillaume de Neuville, special lieutenants who had recently come to Languedoc to relieve the seneschal and judge of Carcassonne of their extra duties.[167] Again in this case we are reduced to conjecture about the summons. A certain regularity in the village deputations—invariably two, three, or four consuls, unaccompanied—suggests that a form-summons of some kind had been circulated.

The government registered the fealties of 414 individuals and communities in five daily sessions lasting until 24 December. The grand total of 809 nobles, consuls, and notaries who are listed were surely never all together in one place. Not only were the oaths sworn separately,[168] but there is no mention of a preliminary address by the commissioners. Possibly they had embodied their publicity in a more than usually explicit convocation form; but in any case, the campaign, now three months old, was certainly common knowledge. There is no evidence that recognitions of holdings and obligations were received at this meeting. The king's officials had decided that their initial prospectus

---

[166] B.N., Doat, CLV, 71v–72v, recognition by a noble at Toulouse on 25 November; *Sais. Tolosae*, 40–42, nos. 78–81, fealties of two knights at Carcassonne on the twenty-ninth, two knights and a lawyer at Castelnaudary on 17 December, as well as two men "dicentes se esse consules de Fanojove."

[167] *Sais. Tolosae*, 43–50, no. 84; Langlois, *Philippe III*, p. 171. Cohardon was among the witnesses. Cf. Michel, *Beaucaire, p.j.,* no. 53, pp. 463–464.

[168] *Sais. Tolosae*, 43, no. 84: "Barones, Milites, Nobiles, & etiam Consules Villarum & Castrorum infra scriptorum nomine ipsorum, & illorum quorum sunt Consules, juraverunt in manibus praedicti Domini Guillelmi de Novavilla. . . ."

was too ambitious.[169] The notaries present subscribed a separate oath of honest service.[170]

This attendance at Toulouse was limited to the diocese, though it appears that not even that district was fully represented. The absence of contingents from the *baylies* of Verdun and Castelsarrasin could be accounted for by the local campaigns conducted there in November, but this does not explain why Buzet and Villemur are missing. Actually there is no way of knowing whether the jurors were fully listed, and it is possible that men of unreported districts also performed fealty at this time.

The consuls of 109 communities, including Toulouse, presented themselves as representative jurors in these sessions. We have no record that any of these consulates, except for Toulouse, had yet sworn fealty to the king. Here evidently is the principal reason for this second general assembly at Toulouse. But it also appears that the crown was trying on this occasion to do a more thorough job with the nobility. Although fewer in number by some 100, nevertheless more than half of the nobles in the December gathering (a total of 164) had not sworn the oath in the first assembly at Toulouse. The fullest adhesions came from the populous Lauragais *baylies* of Laurac, Saint-Félix, and Avignonet, with an aggregate of 126 nobles and 69 consulates. Even without certain *baylies,* as noted above, the royal commissioners must have felt at the conclusion of these sessions that the submission and fidelity of the *sénéchaussée* of Toulouse had been thoroughly guaranteed. By stating explicitly that the consuls swore in the

[169] A survey of dues and obligations in the *sénéchaussées* of Toulouse and Albigeois was made about a year later, A.N., JJ.25. Bayles were asked to make inventory of royal domain in their districts, and their written reports were incorporated in this register; see fol. 307, and cf. above, p. 161. See also *H.L.,* x, 88.

[170] *Sais. Tolosae,* 50–51, no. 85. A few of them are listed under the oath of fealty, no. 84, 46–47.

name of their communities,[171] the officials indicated that they had no intention of continuing their work in village parliaments.

The general convocation of men from the secular orders for explaining policy and for establishing a tangible, legal rapport between government and governed had become a familiar event in Languedoc as the age of Saint Louis and Alfonse closed. Use of this device was determined by the circumstances and requirements of the newly established foreign rule in the Midi. It did not replace, nor would it in the future, the roving, localized negotiations that were less dependent on the power to summon. But it had become a viable, sometimes preferable, alternative. Extension of the summons to towns and villages marked a tightening of control over men of the third estate, while, at the same time, it sharpened the awareness in burghers and villagers of their communal interests at both the local and regional levels. The informal and ex officio representation of towns was spreading from the hills and dales of upper Languedoc toward the coast through the practices of royal government. This tendency was confirmed in a series of special assemblies held in the *sénéchaussées* of Beaucaire and Carcassonne.

[171] See n. 168.

V · Assemblies in the Sénéchaussées of Beaucaire and Carcassonne (1254-1275)

The king's officials were not solely dependent on their court personnel in forming administrative policy. During the later years of Louis IX, they occasionally received instructions to confer with other faithful or prudent men for one reason or another. In 1255 the king of Aragon sought permission to cross royal lands in order to deal with his resistant subject town of Montpellier. Louis IX directed the seneschal of Carcassonne to allow the passage only upon examination of securities that the Spanish soldiers would cause no damage. To decide this question the seneschal was to summon the marshal of Mirepoix, Pierre de Voisins, other *fideles*, and prelates, and to act with their counsel.[1] Some time afterward, when it appeared that the mandate had not been carried out, the king wrote a similar order for "counsel . . . with our faithful men of the land." [2] Finally, a directive dated 23 June 1255 indicates that such a meeting had taken place, or soon would do so; [3] but there is no more information about it.

Long-standing territorial disputes between the kings of Aragon and France were settled by the treaty of Corbeil in 1258.[4] Several years later, probably in 1263, new troubles arose over hostilities by the princes of Aragon in the *sénéchaussée* of Carcassonne.[5] Royal commissioners ordered the

---

[1] *H.L.*, VIII, 1393–1394,i; VI, 848–849.
[2] *Ibid.*, VIII, 1394,iii.
[3] *Ibid.*, 1394–1395,iv.
[4] *Ibid.*, VI, 858–861.
[5] *Ibid.*, 853–854. Vaissete believed the undated document in

seneschal to lose no time in calling Olivier de Termes and three or four others among the king's more trustworthy vassals to a meeting at Narbonne, or Béziers, or Carcassonne, whichever should seem more convenient, "so that we may have your counsel and theirs about this matter." [6] Both of the assemblies just mentioned were connected with a potential military levy of the district, and they serve again to suggest the close administrative tie between convocations for military service and those for advisory purposes. The principle that a question of common regional concern should be the subject of common discussion emerges quite clearly.[7] These were *ad hoc* meetings, called by the government for its own practical purposes.

It was in the same period that the most remarkable consultative assemblies of thirteenth-century Languedoc began to meet. They were convoked by royal seneschals on several occasions after 1254 to deliberate on the regional grain supply.[8] The immediate origin for these assemblies can be

---

question was of about 1257. Molinier showed that it postdated the treaty of Corbeil and supposed that this invasion was one otherwise attested for 1263 by the *infants d'Aragon*, 853, n. 4; his conjecture is confirmed by *I.A.C., Narbonne, Annexes de la Série AA*, no. 51, p. 91, dated 15 September 1263.

[6] *H.L.*, VIII, 1411–1412: "vos rogamus & requirimus modis omnibus, quatenus visis litteris convocetis sine dilatione quacumque Oliverium de Terminis et alios tres vel quatuor de fidelioribus domini regis apud Narbonam vel Bedier [*sic*] aut Carcassonam, seu ubi dictorum locorum eos competentius habere poteritis, ut vestri & ipsorum super hoc possimus habere consilium. . . ."

[7] For a comparable though more restricted issue in the *sénéchaussée* of Beaucaire in 1256, see R. Michel, *Beaucaire, p.j.*, no. 23, pp. 415–416.

[8] While there is no adequate study, see generally *H.L.*, VI, 912, n. 3 (Molinier); the same writer's "Administration de Louis IX & d'Alfonse," *ibid.*, VII, 508–511; P. Dognon, *Institutions*, pp. 198–199 (who criticizes Molinier, but errs himself, notably in asserting

found in an article of certain reform ordinances published by Louis IX in 1254, requiring the seneschals to take counsel with prelates, nobles, and townsmen when legislating on exports from Languedoc.

The trade in provisions was of paramount importance in a medieval society. Basic foodstuffs, notably grain, or wheat, and wine, were subject to regulations of all sorts. The licensing and control of markets were attributes of political power. Both in law and fact, such public authorities as lords, consuls, and even the pope, had regulated the commerce of grain and other provisions in various localities of Languedoc.[9] Correspondingly, few privileges were more coveted than that of self-regulation, or at least a voice in the matter. Of special concern was the control of prices

---

that only four such assemblies met); Michel, *Beaucaire,* pp. 49–51; and most recently, A. Dupont, "Les Ordonnances Royales de 1254 et les Origines des Conseils de Sénéchaussées dans le Languedoc Méditerranéen," *Fédération Historique du Languedoc Méditerranéen et du Roussillon: XXXme et XXXIme Congrès: Sète-Beaucaire (1956–1957),* pp. 227–235.

The word in the documents is "bladum," which can mean either "wheat," specifically, or "grain." The latter meaning is given in the following discussion, since it is more inclusive, and I do not know certainly that wheat was meant in any case. Cf. P. Wolff, *Commerces et Marchands de Toulouse . . .* (Paris, 1954), pp. 170–171.

[9] See Dognon, *Institutions,* p. 99; *Layettes,* I, 280, art. 90; III, no. 3937, 128a. The latter, an agreement of May 1251 between Charles of Anjou and Alfonse, lords of Avignon, is probably related in some way to the ordinances of 1254. The brothers gave up arbitrary regulation of prices and exports, and the act continues: "set nec interdicere poterunt dictis civibus [of Avignon] bladum suum, vel vinum, vel alias res, de civitate extrahere, vel exportare vendendas, vel exportare volentibus vendere, nisi sint hostes manifesti dominorum comitum . . . quibus dicti cives vendere poterunt prohiberi." Also *H.L.,* VIII, 475–476; *Gallia Christiana,* VI, *inst.,* 153; A.M. Narbonne, AA.103, fol. 12v; "Statuts . . . de l'Université de Toulouse," ed. Molinier, *H.L.,* VII, 435, no. 2; *Layettes,* II, no. 3522, 621b; etc.

and exports, and in this connection we sometimes hear echoes of outraged common opinion. A bad harvest in a given area might cause short-run conditions of hardship, while encouraging profiteering and hoarding. Merchants of southern French port towns were often able to sell their provisions abroad at higher prices than in the local market.

Mercantile interests were undoubtedly influencing legislation on the grain trade in the first half of the thirteenth century. An undated ruling at Narbonne prescribed the obligation of the sovereign courts there to consult the consuls of city and bourg before imposing a ban on the export of grain.[10] And in 1248, in a petition to the king's investigators, the men of Beaucaire claimed that it had been the custom of the early seneschals to take counsel with the local inhabitants when prohibiting the export of grain or wine from the town, and to take such a step "only for the evident necessity of the land or lord." [11] No other evidence

[10] *I.A.C., Narbonne, Annexes de la Série* AA, no. 114, p. 195: "Can vet de blat se fa, las Corts nol podon far ses volentat e ses autrejament de consols, e pus que autrejas seria per las Corts e per los consols de la Ciutat e del Borc nol podon alargar ni penre deniers ses volentat e d'autrejament de consols entro al temps de que seria faig lo vet." On internal evidence the piece can be dated 1238–1270. Dognon, *Institutions*, p. 318, supposed that it antedated the 1254 statutes, but this is quite uncertain. An example of regulation as described above, dated 5 April 1270, is preserved, A.M. Narbonne, AA.109, fol. 37; cf. HH. (uninventoried), document of 30 March 1270, wherein it is claimed that such a privilege had belonged to the authorities in Narbonne "tempore cuius non extat memoria."

[11] *H.L.,* VII, *Enquêteurs,* 114 (*H.F.,* XXIV, 478gh): "consuetudo fuit antiquissima in castro Belliquadri & rupta a quinque annis citra, quod quando senescallus Belliquadri vel alius pro eo faciebat interdictum in castro Belliquadri, ne bladus vel vinum extraheretur de castro predicto, faciebat hoc cum consilio habitancium dicti castri & hoc faciebat tantum pro evidenti necessitate terre vel domini." See Michel, *Beaucaire*, pp. 23–26, on the origin of the seneschalship. Legally, this plea implied that the superior right linked to necessity can only be acted upon in consultation with those whose (inferior) rights are involved; cf. G. Post, *Traditio*, I, 372.

in support of this contention survives.[12] It should be emphasized that the burghers of Beaucaire were referring to consultation limited to one town.

Yet, as Molinier pointed out, this petition helps to explain why Louis IX included the article relating to grain export in his legislation several years later.[13] These ordinances were three in number, dating from July, August, and December 1254.[14] The first two were issued in response to complaints by the men of Beaucaire and Nîmes, respectively, while the latter was a detailed directive for general administrative reforms in both royal *sénéchaussées* of Languedoc.

An extract from the July laws for Beaucaire will serve to indicate the salient points: "Indeed, in order that the same men [of Beaucaire] may have freer use of their possessions, we firmly prohibit our seneschals from banning, for reasons of their own, the sale of grain or wine or other marketable products to people wishing to export those things, with the addition of this qualification, however, that at no time should it be permitted to export arms or provisions to the Saracens, as long as they are at war with Christians, nor indeed to any persons whatsoever at war with us. Never-

---

[12] Cf. Michel, *Beaucaire, p.j.*, no. 20, pp. 410–411, complaint by Sommières in 1254 that the royal vicar had banned wine (export) in a manner contrary to local custom.

[13] *H.L.*, VII, 510; and see also Dupont, "Ordonnances Royales de 1254," pp. 227–228. Cf. act for Avignon, 1251, partly quoted above, n. 9; also *Layettes*, III, 205b, petition of Montpellier in 1248, granted by Louis IX before embarking on crusade: "quod de cetero non fiat in terra sua interdictum aliquod vel prohibitio de non portandis et introducendis victualibus de terra sua [that of king of France] ad Montempessulanum, nisi forte ex magna causa et urgenti necessitate." But in these cases there was no mention of counsel. It is worth noting that Montpellier felt obliged to seek new assurances to the same effect before 1254, A. Germain, *Histoire du Commerce de Montpellier . . . ,* 2 vols. (Montpellier, 1861), I, *p.j.*, no. 25, 221; see also *p.j.*, no. 20, 213.

[14] *H.L.*, VIII, 1337–1340, 1345–1352.

theless, should there be urgent cause, on account of which it may seem that such a prohibition ought to be made, let the seneschal convoke a dependable council comprising some of the prelates, barons, knights, and men of the good towns [*consilium non suspectum, in quo sint aliqui de prelatis, baronibus, militibus & hominibus bonarum villarum*], with whose counsel he should make the said prohibition, and [which] once made he should not abrogate without a council similarly composed; nor should he grant special grace to anyone, for prayer or price, while the prohibition is in effect." [15] The statute goes on to say explicitly that the same practice shall also be observed in the *sénéchaussée* of Carcassonne.

It is clearly implied here, in the first place, that seneschals had forbidden certain exports in order to profit by the sale of licenses. The same grievance lay behind the Beaucaire petition of 1248.[16] Secondly, the ordinance mentions the ban on sales for export of grain, wine, and "other marketable products," although in the actual assemblies, except that of Beaucaire in 1258, grain alone was in question. The "urgent cause" justifying such prohibitions is not stated, but later references identify it as regional shortages in supply, resulting in high prices. As for the assembly, the ordinance for Beaucaire refers explicitly to a convention of men from the well recognized juridical orders of clergy, nobles, and townsmen. The allusion to the latter as men of "good towns" indicates that the meeting should include persons residing outside the limits of Beaucaire and Nîmes, without, however, specifying *viguerie*, *sénéchaussée*, or other administrative units. The consultation has outgrown the urban confines of earlier regional custom. The repre-

[15] *Ibid.*, 1338. For corresponding passages in the other ordinances, see 1340 (Nîmes, August), where the reference to assembly reads: "cum celebri & maturo consilio"; and 1349–1350, art. 31 (December).

[16] *Ibid.*, VII, *Enquêteurs*, 114; Molinier, "Administration," 510.

sentative character of such an assembly is suggested, though not exactly defined, by the phrase, "some of the prelates, barons, knights, and townsmen." Perhaps the most interesting thing about the ordinances of 1254 is that they establish the principle, and associate it with a prescribed assembly, that an interested community has the right to be consulted on a particular matter. The legislators may have had in mind the Roman-canonical theory of *quod omnes tangit . . .* , which was involved in the summons for counsel as well as that for consent. In either case, the authority who summons, faced with "urgent cause," would have the final right to decide.[17] In practice, as will be shown, the consultative voice regarding grain export in Languedoc was to be very restricted; it was hardly "une attribution d'États" in the later sense of the term.

Other points may be noted briefly. Once a prohibition has been agreed upon, its termination (prior to a predetermined date) must be approved by a similar assembly. During an interdict no special favor may be accorded. Finally, the reservation that in no circumstance should supplies be sent to the Saracens during the holy war reminds us of the Mediterranean orientation of commercial Languedoc. The ordinance of August for Nîmes condenses these various provisions without essentially changing them. Its additional requirement that the ban against devastators of cultivated lands may not be dissolved "sine magno consilio" suggests the influence of the provision relating to grain exports.[18] Article 31 of the great December ordinance is an inclusive summary of the points already discussed. As Molinier observes, the reference it makes to the as-

---

[17] "No. quod omnes tangit, ab omnibus debet tractari," *glos. ord.* to *Extra,* III, 10, 10; also Innocent IV, *Apparatus*, and Hostiensis, *Commentaria*, ad v. *consilio, Extra,* III, 10, 4; cf. Post, *Traditio,* IV, 204–205; and I, 371–374.

[18] *H.L.,* VIII, 1339–1340,ii. Could it also be related to the old peace institutions?

sembly as *consilium* would be obscure if the other texts were not available to explain what it means.[19]

The first known assembly of the kind envisioned in these statutes convened in the *sénéchaussée* of Beaucaire at an uncertain date, probably early in 1258. We learn of it indirectly through an order which Louis IX sent to his seneschal in October 1259, requiring that he lift an embargo on provisions and other products destined for Montpellier and adjacent lands. This regulation was unnecessary, Louis implied, in view of the peace he had made with Aragon, an apparent reference to the treaty of Corbeil concluded in May 1258. So in November 1259 the seneschal addressed to the men of his district a patent letter announcing the complete removal of the ban and expressly permitting exports to Montpellier and other territories belonging to Aragon.[20]

The interdict had been established "de consilio vestro," according to this letter. Doubtless the recipients included the very persons who had previously assembled. Closely

[19] *Ibid.*, 1349: "Defensum autem bladi vel vini vel mercium aliarum non extrahendarum de terra sine causa urgente non faciant, & tunc cum bono & maturo consilio non suspecto, & factum cum consilio, sine consilio non dissolvant, nec eo durante cuiquam faciant graciam specialem." Two other clauses place a general embargo on export to the Saracens and other enemies in time of war. Cf. vii, 510. The August ordinance is likewise imprecise about the composition of the "council," but I doubt that this is significant. Future events showed that the seneschals normally interpreted the law as stated in the Beaucaire statute, and there is no record of strictly local bans and consultations at Nîmes. See viii, 1664, 1666. Cf. Dupont, "Ordonnances Royales de 1254," p. 229.

[20] *H.L.*, viii, 1449–1450,iv. The seneschal, Geoffroi de Roncherolles, took office some time between January and June 1258 (Michel, *Beaucaire*, p. 334). It is unlikely that the ban described here was passed after the end of hostilities in May. Vaissete's idea, *H.L.*, vi, 862, of a resumption of hostilities in 1259 would permit us to date the assembly in that year, but is unsupported and improbable.

resembling in form those letters of convocation available
for later meetings, it is quite possible that the document
was patterned on the earlier summons. This has led
modern writers astray in their accounts of the assembly:
R. Michel and A. Dupont both mistakenly refer to the
seneschal's extant patent letter as a general summons.[21]
But it is clear that no further meeting was planned or needed. The king's decision to suspend the law on this point
was announced, and that was the end of it. Those addressed, in this order, were the bishops of Nîmes, Uzès,
and Maguelonne, the abbots of Saint-Gilles, Psalmody, and
Cendras, the lords of Lunel, Uzès, and Aimargues, and the
consuls and *universitates* of Beaucaire, Nîmes, Uzès, Alès,
Anduze, Sauve, and Sommières, and generally all prelates,
nobles and other men, and government officials. With due
allowance, then, we may suppose that the assembly mentioned in the letter had been composed of the bishops, the
leading abbots and nobles, and delegates from the important towns of the district. Probably it convened in one or
another of these towns.

Another interdict in the *sénéchaussée* of Beaucaire is
reported in a case that came before Parlement in 1261. The
export of grain had been prohibited this time because of its
high price (*caristia bladi*).[22] The bishop of Mende had allowed some grain to pass out of his own domains and into
royal territory, where it was confiscated by the king's officials, "on account of the ban." Presumably the royal area
in question lay outside the *sénéchaussée*, because the bishop

[21] Michel, *Beaucaire*, p. 49, n. 3; Dupont, "Ordonnances Royales
de 1254," pp. 231–232. Dognon, *Institutions*, p. 198, n. 4, and
Molinier, *H.L.*, VII, 510 (cf. VI, 862, n. 3) merely mention the assembly and place it in 1259 without giving reasons. Vaissete read
the document carefully (VI, 862), but in his curtailed account
said nothing about the assembly that did meet.

[22] This is the usual expression for a situation that could otherwise be described as a shortage, or poor harvest; cf. *H.L.*, VIII,
1739.

apparently did not deny that the grain had been exported. This ban was manifestly different from the one terminated in 1259. There is no reason to doubt that it had likewise been agreed upon in assembly in accordance with the royal statutes. We find an interesting hint of its proceedings in the report of the bishop's plea in Parlement: "Episcopus peciit sibi reddi bladum suum, dicens quod senescallus, *ipsum non vocatum*, non potuit ita ligare . . ." (italics mine). This probably alludes to the procedural rule of canon law that nothing should be done in prejudice of rights without a proper summons of the parties involved.[23] The bishop is unwilling to be bound by a ruling he had not been invited to discuss or approve. Indeed, the bishop of Mende seems to have been absent from both of the assemblies so far considered, for besides this evidence, he is not listed with the prelates of the *sénéchaussée* addressed by the seneschal in 1259.[24] Of course, the campaign to extend royal authority into Gévaudan was now in full swing, and the church of Mende was at odds with the crown on many counts. The bishop lost his case in 1261, on the grounds that the grain had been seized not in his own domains, but in those of the king.[25] No other export assemblies in the district of Beaucaire are mentioned, though the grain shortages attested in the *sénéchaussée* of Carcassonne in later years must have been felt in some degree in eastern Languedoc too.[26]

[23] Legal sources cited by Post, " 'Quod Omnes Tangit,' in Bracton," 202–205.

[24] To be sure, Gévaudan had been administered for some time by bayles dependent on the seneschals, who may have thought of it as a separate district; see Michel, *Beaucaire*, p. 10; above, ch. 3, p. 120.

[25] *Olim*, I, 522, no. 11.

[26] In October 1271 men of the *sénéchaussée* of Carcassonne argued that they could not depend on neighboring regions for grain supply, since the *caristia bladi* was being felt, and had necessitated anti-export legislation, in those other areas too, A.M. Narbonne,

Not until 1269 did a similar assembly convene in the *sénéchaussée* of Carcassonne. In July of that year some consuls of Narbonne came before the seneschal, Guillaume de Cohardon, and petitioned for an embargo on grain from the district. Their motives are not made clear, though they can perhaps be reconstructed from evidence of the proceedings. And for the first time, that evidence is extensive. We know that in response to their request the seneschal summoned clergy, nobility, and townsmen of the *sénéchaussée* to an assembly scheduled to meet at Carcassonne on 4 August.[27] This act was based directly on the royal ordinance of December 1254, which was mentioned explicitly and even quoted.[28]

The full text of the letter of convocation is given in the statute subsequently enacted at Carcassonne. It is the earliest surviving epistolary summons for a royal assembly in Languedoc.[29] Dated 26 July 1269, and general in form, it was probably prepared in several copies and circulated

---

HH. (uninventoried), 14 October 1271; cf. A.M. Toulouse, layette 62, undated letter of Alfonse relating to shortage in the Toulouse area.

[27] The convocation was set for the Sunday after the feast of St-Nazaire (28 July), which in 1269 fell on 4 August. The summons refers to this date as 2 August, *H.L.*, VIII, 1666: "die dominica post festum beati Nazarii, videlicet IIa [not XIa] mensis augusti." Vaissete, *ibid.*, VI, 912, gave the date as 11 August, which was a Sunday, to be sure, but is otherwise inaccurate. I follow the weekday reckoning, supposing a local variation in the calendar date, or a slip in the month-day figure.

[28] *Ibid.*, VIII, 1664: "sed cum juxta statutum domini Regis juratum hujusmodi deffensum fieri sit prohibitum sine causa urgente, & tunc etiam cum bono & maturo consilio nec suspecto sit faciendum, & factum cum consilio sine consilio non sit dissolvendum, nec eo durante, cuiquam sit facienda gratia specialis." Cf. 1349, quoted above, n. 19.

[29] Not counting the military summons to Carcassonne written by Cohardon on 5 February 1269, *ibid.*, 1661–1662, mentioned above, p. 138; see also p. 164, and below, p. 212.

through the *sénéchaussée*.[30] Heading the list of addressees was the archbishop of Narbonne, followed by the bishops of Béziers, Agde, Lodève, Maguelonne, Albi, and the bishop-elect of Carcassonne; their chapters were also summoned. For the regular clergy, notice was sent to the abbots of twenty-two monasteries and fourteen directors of other religious houses, notably the Hospitallers and Templars. Almost as large as the ecclesiastical contingent was the group of nobles, a total of twenty-seven. These men are styled *terrarii* and *barones*.[31] Some thirteen of them figure also in the list of *terrarii* summoned to Carcassonne earlier in 1269 for military reasons, notably those who, like Philippe de Montfort, Guy de Lévis, and Lambert de Limoux, were descended from the French lords of the post-conquest settlement.[32] The viscounts of Narbonne and Lautrec, who were also included, probably ranked as barons.

Finally, the summons went out to the consuls of twenty-six towns and villages, termed "good towns,"[33] including Carcassonne, Béziers, Agde, Pézenas, and Albi. Though not listed in the letter, Narbonne, having made the original petition, was undoubtedly expected to appear. The total of individuals and communities convoked thus amounts to 104. Except for the possibility of informal invitations, this was the entire summons, for the letter as we have it is complete and explicit. It explains the reason for the assembly,

---

[30] The last words are: "Reddite litteras portitori," as in so many such documents, *ibid.*, 1666; cf. 1740; B.N., Doat, CLV, 50. For the list that follows, *H.L.*, VIII, 1664–1665.

[31] *H.L.*, VIII, 1666; cf. 1664: "senescallus . . . convocavit . . . terrarios, barones, milites. . . ."

[32] *Ibid.*, 1661–1663; cf. above, ch. 4, p. 138.

[33] *H.L.*, VIII, 1666; cf. again 1664: "convocavit . . . consules & majores communitatum. . . ." "Major" here evidently does not mean "mayor": there was no such office in towns of the Carcassonne area. It probably refers to notables of towns other than consuls who might serve as delegates.

referring to both the Narbonne petition and the king's regulation of 1254.[34]

[34] *Ibid.*, 1665–1666.

Assembly of the Sénéchaussée of Carcassonne, at Carcassonne, August 1269

PARTIES KNOWN TO HAVE BEEN SUMMONED

Asterisks (*) indicate summoned parties known to have attended. Geographical range of clergy and nobles corresponds roughly to that of towns, indicated on map, p. 199.

CLERGY: Archbishop of Narbonne*; bishops of Béziers*, Agde*, Lodève, Maguelonne, Albi, elect of Carcassonne*; chapters of Narbonne, Béziers, Agde, Lodève, Maguelonne, Albi, Carcassonne; abbots of Lagrasse*, Montolieu*, Villelongue*, Alet*, St-Polycarpe*, St-Hilaire, Jocou*, Caunes*, Quarante, Fontfroide, St-Paul, St-Aphrodise, St-Jacques*, Fontcaude, St-Thibéry, Aniane, St-Guilhem-du-Désert, Valmagne, St-Pons-de-Thomières*, Castres, Ardorel, Candeil; prior of Cassan; *prévôt* of St-Salvi; preceptors of (Hospitallers) Magrie, Rustiques, Douzens, Homps, Périeis, Pézenas, Capestang, Campagnoles, Narbonne, Albigeois; (Templars) Narbonne, Albigeois.

NOBLES: Philippe de Montfort*, Guy de Lévis de Mirepoix*, Jean de Bruyères*, Amaury, viscount of Narbonne, Lambert de Limoux, Simon de Limoux, Géraud de Capendu*, Guillaume de Voisins*, Raymond d'Aban, Guillaume d'Aban, Gaufrid de Caldairon, Philippe Goloinh*, Étienne de Dardé, Philippe de Bosc-Arcambaud, Guillaume Acurat, Rainfrid-Ermengaud, Jourdain de Cabaret, Lambert de Monteil (Lombers), Isarn, viscount of Lautrec*, Amaury de Lautrec, Bertrand de Lautrec*, Jourdain de Saissac, Bérenger de Puisserguier*, Aymery de Boussagues*, Bérenger-Guillaume, lord of Clermont*, Guillaume de Lodève, Pierre de Clermont. Gaufrid de Voisins attended, though not known to have been summoned.

DISTRIBUTION OF TOWNS SUMMONED AND ATTENDING

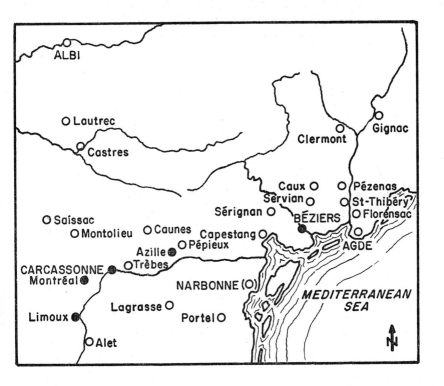

O SUMMONED

● SUMMONED AND
REPORTED PRESENT

On 4 August 1269 these prelates, barons, and consuls appeared "pro majori parte" at Carcassonne. Our list of them numbers only thirty names, but it is evidently incomplete. It includes the archbishop of Narbonne and three bishops, nine abbots, and twelve nobles, but no chapters, priors, *prévôts,* or preceptors. The consuls of Carcassonne, Béziers, Montréal, Limoux, and Azille are reported, followed by the phrase "and many others from the afore-said towns and other places."[35] Probably most of the towns summoned sent delegates, while the prelates and nobles, presumably less concerned economically, took less interest. In any case, the gathering was of sufficiently moderate size that it could meet in the house of the "lord-marshal," that is, the town dwelling of Guy de Lévis de Mirepoix.[36] Between the extraordinary convocation and the ordinary royal *curia* the connection is manifest. The former was grafted on to the latter, so to speak. The decisions in the assembly were made in the presence of the king's judges for the *sénéchaussée* and city of Carcassonne, the vicar of Carcassonne, the receiver of revenues, notaries, and others, including two commissioners who were in charge of negotiations for the crusade subsidy in the Midi.[37]

The seneschal communicated the Narbonne petition in the first session. Deliberation followed. The procedure probably took the form of discussion, led by the notables in the different groups, resulting in recommendations which were placed before the whole gathering for consideration. At a second session on 5 August, the archbishop of Narbonne and Philippe de Montfort spoke for the prelates and nobles. They reported that in view of the great abundance of grain in the *sénéchaussée* and its moderate price in the

---

[35] *Ibid.,* 1666.

[36] *Ibid.,* 1668: "Actum Carcassone, in domo domini marescalli." On the family de Lévis and its hereditary title, see *ibid.,* vi, 656, and n. 3 (Molinier).

[37] *Ibid.,* viii, 1666, 1668; cf. Molinier, in *B.É.C.,* xxxiv (1873), 164.

markets, they did not feel the need for, nor did they advise, a general interdict on grain export.[38] This causes us to wonder about the original petition. Even allowing for improvement in the harvest, the statement by the clergy and nobles makes it seem unlikely that Narbonne could realistically have pleaded scarcity and high price just a few days before.

The probable explanation is to be found in the consensus of the assembly. After the advice against a general and inclusive embargo, the whole meeting (*Consulunt tamen omnes*) recommended a limited interdict on exports by land or sea to the Saracens or Pisans or other enemies of the Church or of Charles of Anjou, king of Sicily. It proposed to allow the free transport of grain to Christians and cities held by Christians—an evident reference to Levantine holdings of the crusaders—and to the cities and ports of Angevin domains in the Mediterranean.[39] This, or something like it, must have been the substance of Narbonne's initial petition. The preliminary discussions may well have evoked a proposal for an all-inclusive ban, to which the opinion of the prelates and nobles, referring to the "great abundance of grain," could be explained as an effective reply.

The assembly further recommended provisions for administrative machinery to ensure observance of the limited embargo. A commission was to be established to check the securities of out-bound merchants and examine the testimonies which they brought back from authorities at their legitimate destinations. The seneschal accepted the program in this form, and with the counsel of "many other good men," that is, his advisers, he enacted and published it in the assembly. He appointed the bishop of Béziers, the lord Philippe de Montfort, and a royal judge to serve as export commissioners. No time limit on the interdict was set.[40]

[38] *H.L.*, VIII, 1666–1667.
[39] *Ibid.*, 1667.
[40] *Ibid.*, 1667–1668.

The next assembly for which we have extensive evidence occurred two years later, in August 1271. In the meantime, however, there had been at least one other meeting of the same type, and perhaps more than one. In March 1270 the seneschal of Carcassonne launched proceedings against the consuls of Narbonne, accusing them, and also the archbishop and viscount, of violating various prohibitions (*deffensa*) enacted by royal officials. First, it was alleged, they had given license to certain persons who wanted to export grain from Narbonne by sea. This was in violation of the "general prohibition made by the same seneschal, according to the statutes of the lord king, of the export of grain from the *sénéchaussée* of Carcassonne, by sea or by land"; it was also "contrary to the second prohibition made in similar fashion by his lieutenant, the lord knight Gaufrid de Colletrio, vicar of Béziers." Apparently the consuls could do no right, for the court even laid against them the infringement of a third edict which was quite the reverse in import. Relaxing the *generalia deffensa*, this had permitted the export of grain to Aigues-Mortes and certain other places; the consuls were said to have restricted such commerce illegally.[41]

The problems presented by this information may be summarized in two questions: (1) how many regulations were issued between August 1269 and the next March? (2) how many assemblies convened? To begin with the latter, it will be observed that the second prohibition, that of the vicar, was enacted in a "fashion similar" to the promulgation of the seneschal's earlier edict. This first ruling, moreover, was made "according to the statutes of the lord king" concerning the export of grain. Since this must mean that

---

[41] A.M. Narbonne, HH. (uninventoried), 30 March 1270 (also in B.N., Doat, L, 255–257v; see Appendix II, no. 5); *I.A.C., Narbonne, Annexes de la Série AA*, no. 64, pp. 98–99, an *ordinatio* of the seneschal which was produced along with the *deffensa* and other instruments in the trial in September 1270.

the seneschal had convoked an assembly, we must conclude that the vicar had done likewise. This latter meeting probably occurred late in 1269 or early in 1270. Presumably it modified the earlier general embargo in the direction of tighter control.[42]

We are then led to inquire whether the seneschal's "general prohibition" alluded to here is the same regulation which was issued in the assembly of 4-5 August 1269 at Carcassonne. One consideration would seem to weigh against this possibility. As has been noticed already, the August meeting abandoned the idea of a general prohibition in favor of a limited embargo, which would not prevent exports to the Holy Land or supporters of the Church. On the other hand, we cannot be sure that the latter ruling itself would not have been regarded as a *generale deffensum*.[43] Furthermore, it seems likely that the seneschal would have mentioned the August ruling in citing Narbonne for violations; and indeed, it is improbable that so many as four different regulations were passed on this matter between August and March.[44] There were at least three, however, the last one providing for some easing of restrictions introduced by

[42] Molinier, *H.L.*, VI, 913, n. 1, using another version of the same document, A.N., J.308, no. 79, mentions this assembly, but confuses its decisions (which we know only by inference) with those of the royal commissioners who advised the *relaxatio* established by the third edict mentioned above. See also the passage partially quoted below, n. 45.

[43] In 1271 a prohibition of all grain export except to Acre was termed a *generale deffensum*, *H.L.*, VIII, 1742.

[44] But in a defense of their stand, dated 30 March 1270, A.M. Narbonne, HH. (uninventoried), the consuls tried to create the impression of a wearisome succession of edicts and counter-edicts: "quod, facto deffenso bladi in Narbona et in senescallia Carcassone per dominum senescallum Carcassone et Biterris et postmodum per dominum Arnulfum de Choardono, militem domini regis, restricto seu iterum facto, et postea etiam per eundem dominum Arnulfum relaxato. . . ."

the vicar's edict. One finds no clear indication of an assembly on this occasion.[45]

The story of Narbonne's involvement in this situation can be partly reconstructed. It concerns us here only as it serves to illuminate the political and economic circumstances surrounding the grain-export assemblies. The consuls' first reaction to their citation to court in 1270 was a rather garbled set of propositions [46] setting forth their position and appealing against the relaxation of the embargo. They admitted that they had recently prohibited the export of grain from Narbonne by sea, but claimed to have done so "for legitimate and necessary reasons." They were now prepared to ease their ban in the interests of the king and the crusade and to permit the transport of grain to Montpellier, Aigues-Mortes, Acre, or elsewhere, as might be necessary.[47] The consuls denied any intent to give offense to the crown. Their proposals were such as to suggest that the main reason for imposing a local embargo was their desire to assert and defend the town's right to do so. Narbonne's fundamental claim, one not given up even when the case was terminated some months later, was that consuls, archbishop, and viscount had, by prescriptive right, the authority to impose local regulations on the trade in grain, as long as these

---

[45] Cf., however, *I.A.C., Narbonne, Annexes de la Série AA*, no. 64, p. 99a: ". . . credant [consuls of Narbonne] quod generale deffensum de blado et de aliis rebus de senescallia Carcassone non extrahendis, per mare vel per terram, urgente necessitate et cum bono et maturo consilio nec suspecto faciendum, et ipsum relaxandi, mutandi, vel minuendi, cum consimili concilio . . . ad solum dominum regem Francie pertineat et ad suum senescallum. . . ."

[46] See n. 44. By Arnulfus de Choardono, who is otherwise unknown, they evidently mean Arnulfus de Curia Feraudi, who ordered the seneschal to make the "relaxation" edict. This document is printed in Appendix II, no. 5.

[47] A ruling to this effect was in fact issued a few days later, on 5 April, at Narbonne, A.M. Narbonne, AA.109, fol. 37.

were not in conflict with those of the *sénéchaussée*.[48]

The making of statutes that were to be binding on the whole *sénéchaussée* thus proved to be an exercise of power that grated on the traditional and jealously guarded independence at Narbonne. In fact, resistance to royal authority was general in this area. One recalls that other problems came to light late in 1270 when the seneschal tried to collect feudal recognitions from prelates. The grain-export assemblies also became involved in crusading politics. Worth noting in this respect are some appeals made by representative consuls of Narbonne and Béziers in the autumn of 1271. At that time the force of a new general embargo was being weakened by the grant of special licenses to export grain to Acre. To emphasize the relative scarcity of grain in the *sénéchaussée* of Carcassonne, the consuls asserted that in October the market price was higher there than in Acre. Moreover, they represented it as a notorious scandal that concessions were made to Genoese merchants at a time when Genoa was at war with Acre. They implied that the Genoese and others, under pretext of transporting to Acre, were actually selling in Genoa itself, where the price of grain was extremely high.[49] Three weeks later, the consuls of Narbonne added to these charges a story of bribery and smuggling by two individuals who had obtained special licenses.[50] Even allowing for exaggeration, there is a ring of truth in these reports of war profiteering and graft.

The general embargo then in effect had been instituted by an assembly of the *sénéchaussée* of Carcassonne in August 1271. In this case the motivation is not in doubt. The official minute states explicitly that the petitioners, "persons

[48] A.M. Narbonne, HH. (uninventoried), 30 March 1270; cf. *I.A.C., Narbonne, Annexes de la Série AA*, no. 64, p. 99. There is evidence of a local ban in AA.99, fols. 364v–365, 7 September 1272.

[49] A.M. Narbonne, HH. (uninventoried), 14 October 1271.

[50] *Ibid.*, 4 November 1271 (also in B.N., Doat, L, 304–308).

of certain good towns of the *sénéchaussée*," had reported
the likelihood of high priced grain due to a bad harvest.
They requested a "general prohibition" according to the
royal statute. Thereupon the vicar of Béziers, acting as the
seneschal's lieutenant, convoked "prelates, barons, consuls
and communities of the cities and other good towns" to an
assembly at Béziers on 13 August.[51]

The summons differed in certain respects from those on
previous occasions. A single letter of general address had
been prepared for the meeting at Carcassonne two summers
before; and the same method was followed in December
1270 when the same seneschal convoked an assembly in
the *viguerie* of Béziers to obtain recognitions.[52] In form,
the second of these letters differed from the first only in the
fact that the addressees were not specifically named. But in
1271, instead of a single letter, a number of forms (at least
fifteen) were produced. Drafted probably on 5 August,
they varied only in the clause of address.[53] Twelve of them
are indicated in the text of the statute: eight for the clergy;
three for the nobles; and one for the towns, a summons to
Narbonne, Carcassonne, Béziers, Agde, and Lodève. The
scribe notes that others were convoked whose letters were
not at hand when he wrote the document.[54] Of this group,
one prior, two nobles, and the consuls of Pézenas actually
appeared. Three forms would have sufficed for their summons. All counted, it appears that at least sixty-three persons and communities were addressed. Though the actual

[51] *H.L.*, VIII, 1739–1740.

[52] See above, p. 164; below, p. 212.

[53] The form given in the minute is dated merely "mense augusti,"
but a registral copy of the letter sent to the towns, preserved in the
archives of Narbonne, AA.109, fol. 38 (Appendix II, no. 7), is
dated "nonis Augusti"; a misreading in the first instance is possible.
There are a few inconsequential variations in the text.

[54] *H.L.*, VIII, 1742: "Item multi alii fuerunt vocati, quorum lit-
tere pre manibus non habentur, de quibus venerunt infrascripti,
videlicet. . . ."

total was probably slightly greater, it must have remained considerably less than the number called to Carcassonne in August 1269. The letters of 1271 again set forth clearly the reasons for the assembly.[55] The changed procedure of summons is not easily explained. Possibly it had something to do with the abbeys. For the first time we observe the convocation of certain monastic *communities*, along with, yet distinct from, their abbots. Seven of them were conveniently notified in a single form letter. While the omission of the words "and their convents" in the indicated summonses to other abbots could conceivably be accidental, one must presume that it was intentional. The implication is that two spheres of rights, pertaining to the abbot as head and the monks as members,[56] were recognized in some monastic corporations but not in others. Yet it seems impossible to establish that interests in the grain supply were thus differentiated in the abbeys of lower Languedoc. Nor can the summons of abbots and convents, in some cases, and abbots alone, in others, be laid to constitutional differences between the orders; Benedictine houses were included in both kinds of summons. Whatever the reason for not fully recognizing the corporate rights of some abbeys, it may have been thought that separate forms would help to veil the discrimination. Otherwise, it is hard to see any administrative advantage in the arrangement of the summons of 1271. Whether letters of convocation were general or particular, several agents must have been needed to circulate them in the various localities of the *sénéchaussée*.[57]

[55] *Ibid.*, 1739–1742.

[56] On the canonist theory of corporations, see P. Gillet, *La Personnalité Juridique en Droit Ecclésiastique* . . . (Malines, 1927), esp. pp. 160–162; B. Tierney, *Foundations of the Conciliar Theory* (Cambridge, 1955), pp. 110–127.

[57] As a whole the lists yield to no very meaningful pattern, but it might be remarked that the three monastic letters were to (1) abbots and convents of lower Languedoc (2) abbots of lower Languedoc (3) the three major abbeys of southern Albigeois.

The gathering at Béziers on the appointed day numbered only twenty-three. There is no indication that any other unspecified individuals or communities might have been present. The list is of particular interest on two counts. First, it confirms the impression we have of the earlier assembly that the clergy and nobility were not greatly concerned by such proceedings; and it further suggests that attendance at the king's convocation was regarded as a wearisome obligation. Secondly, the list provides the first clear evidence of proctorial representation in royal assemblies of Languedoc. The nature and function of this representation will be considered later. Here it will suffice to describe the attendance in general terms.

Assembly of the Sénéchaussée of Carcassonne,
at Béziers, August 1271

PARTIES KNOWN TO HAVE BEEN SUMMONED

Asterisks indicate summoned parties known to have attended; double asterisks indicate formal representation; triple asterisks indicate excuses and/or letters of adherence.

CLERGY: Archbishop of Narbonne***; bishops of Béziers, Agde*, Lodève**; elect of Carcassonne; chapters of Narbonne, Béziers, Agde, Lodève, Carcassonne**; abbots of Montolieu**, Lagrasse, Caunes**, Villelongue, Alet, St-Polycarpe, St-Hilaire; convents of Montolieu, Lagrasse**, Caunes, Villelongue, Alet, St-Polycarpe, St-Hilaire; abbots of Fontfroide, St-Paul*, St-Aphrodise*, St-Jacques*, St-Thibéry**, St-Pons-de-Thomières***, Valmagne, Jaucels, Aniane, Castres, Candeil, Ardorel; chapter of Albi; preceptors of Douzens, Magrie, Rustiques, Périeis, Pézenas; prior of Cassan*.

NOBLES: Aymery, viscount of Narbonne*, Amaury de Narbonne*, Isarn, Bertrand, and Amaury, viscounts of Lautrec***,

Lambert de Monteil, Étienne de Dardé, Guy de Lévis, Lambert de Thurey*, Gaufrid de Faugères, Aymery de Boussagues*, Bérenger-Guillaume, lord of Clermont*, Bérenger de Puisserguier*, Jean de l'Isle*.

DISTRIBUTION OF TOWNS SUMMONED AND ATTENDING

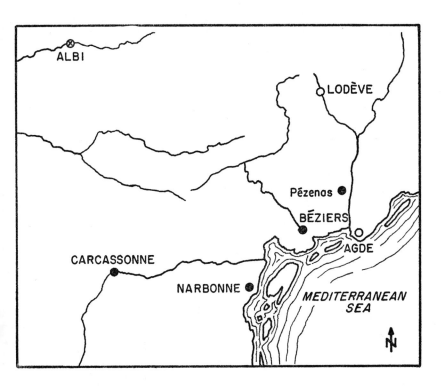

O SUMMONED

⊙ SUMMONED AND
REPORTED PRESENT

⊗ ATTENDED BY PROXY;
NO MENTION OF SUMMONS

Of the greater prelates, only the bishop of Agde and the abbots of Saint-Paul of Narbonne, and Saint-Jacques and Saint-Aphrodise of Béziers appeared in person. The church court of Narbonne excused the archbishop "by letter," saying that he was on a trip to northern France. A letter of excuse sent by the abbot of Saint-Pons-de-Thomières announced his approval of any decisions reached in the assembly. Representatives, most of them proctors, appeared for the bishop of Lodève, the chapter of Carcassonne, and the abbots of Montolieu, Caunes, and Saint-Thibéry. The houses of the Hospitallers were conspicuously absent, and it should be noticed that of thirteen abbeys and chapters especially summoned as communities, only one chapter is said to have responded. Seven nobles appeared, namely Aymery, the viscount, and Amaury of Narbonne, Lambert de Thurey, Aymery de Boussagues, Bérenger-Guillaume, lord of Clermont, Bérenger de Puisserguier, and Jean de l'Isle. Viscount Isarn of Lautrec forwarded his advance ratification in writing. The towns did better: consuls of four of the six places that we know were summoned actually attended, with Lodève and Agde missing. Albi, though we have no record of her summons, sent a proctor. Just as in August 1269, this assembly convened with high royal and curial officials and advisers. The meeting place was the king's *palatium*.[58]

The proceedings may be treated briefly. A minor problem arises about the date. Though the minute indicates the arrival of those summoned on the thirteenth, the statute is dated 16 August. Probably allowance was made for latecomers, particularly in view of the small attendance; and in any case, there could have been several sessions. The royal lieutenant enacted a "general interdict" which, in form and substance, was what the assembly had approved and unanimously recommended. It prohibited all exports of grain from the *sénéchaussée*, by land or sea, except to Acre,

[58] *H.L.*, VIII, 1741–1744.

for a period extending to 24 June 1272. Again as in 1269, a three-man export commission was set up to administer the law. Certain new details are indicative of experience with grain embargoes and their enforcement. It was now made explicit that, in order to transport grain to Acre, one must obtain a license from the export officials. In an effort to counteract smuggling and complicity in illegal transport, the main anti-export provision made it unlawful even to load outbound vessels with grain. The smouldering conflict between royal government and seigneurial privilege again erupted when the abbot of Saint-Paul of Narbonne tried to reserve local and individual rights in the administration of securities and penalties. But the presiding lieutenant disallowed any such qualification of the king's full and unrestricted authority.[59]

Later in 1271, as we have seen, the consuls of Narbonne reported the abuse of permission to export to Acre. On 14 October they requested the convocation of another assembly of the *sénéchaussée*, if this should be necessary, for the repeal of the provision in question.[60] But there is no evidence of further meetings for about three years. The prohibition of 1271 probably terminated, as planned, with the early harvest of the next year. A local decree for the Narbonne coastal area is reported in September 1272.[61] Then in December 1274 new proceedings began on the petition of the consuls of Béziers and men of certain "good towns" of the *sénéchaussée* of Carcassonne. They pointed to an unusual inflation in the price of grain, whereupon the veteran seneschal, Guillaume de Cohardon, in order "to have counsel on these matters, convoked prelates, barons, *ter-*

---

[59] *Ibid.*

[60] A.M. Narbonne, HH. (uninventoried).

[61] A.M. Narbonne, AA.99, fol. 364v; and printed from the original by A. Blanc, *Le Livre de Comptes de Jacme Olivier . . .* (Paris, 1899), *p.j.*, no. 19, pp. 379–380; cf. A.N., J.1029, p. 3.

rarii, and consuls of the cities of the *sénéchaussée*" to an assembly at Carcassonne.[62]

This summons numbered some eighty-five individuals and communities, a total smaller than that of the first reported assembly but probably larger than the Béziers convocation of 1271. Further administrative variation is in evidence. This time forms were prepared for each of the several *vigueries,* the letters being directed to clergy, nobility, and towns of a given district. We have in full the patent summons, dated 13 December 1274, for the *viguerie* of Béziers. It corresponds in some respects to the convocation letter of 1 December 1270 for the same district. It differs, however, in specifying the addressees: the archbishop of Narbonne, the bishops of Béziers, Agde, Lodève, and Maguelonne, fifteen abbots, and the leaders of several other religious houses; the viscount of Narbonne and his brother, sixteen other nobles, and two seigneurial vicars; finally, the consuls of Narbonne, Béziers, Agde, Pézenas, and Lodève. "In the same way," the seneschal wrote to men of other *vigueries*: the bishops of Toulouse and Carcassonne and proctors of the bishopric of Albi, ten abbots and proctors of the monastery of Lagrasse, directors of five other churches or religious houses, some thirteen nobles, including Jourdain de l'Isle, and the consuls of Carcassonne and Albi. The meeting date was set for 3 January 1275.[63]

The summons of the bishop of Toulouse and Jourdain de l'Isle may occasion surprise, but it can probably be explained by their interests and holdings within the *sénéchaussée.*[64] The standing proctors at Albi and Lagrasse are

[62] *H.L.,* x, *preuves,* 125–126.

[63] *Ibid.,* 126–128; A.M. Pézenas, Arm. A, 2/3/1 (wrongly dated 6 December 1274 in the *Inventaire de F. Resseguier,* no. 167). The convocation date was also mistaken in *H.L.,* x, 128 and B.N., Doat, CLV, 123–131. See Appendix II, no. 8.

[64] Toulouse-Albigeois was now a royal district in close relations with the *sénéchaussée* of Carcassonne, which, however, still included southern Albigeois. The bishop, who was Bertrand de l'Isle,

indicative of vacancies in those ecclesiastical positions.[65] We can only speculate why chapters and monastic convents were not convoked as individuals on this occasion. The poor response of these communities to previous summonses may have had something to do with it. Again the question arises whether we have here a full list of those summoned. Nearly five-eighths of the names occur in the form for the *viguerie* of Béziers, which is given *in extenso*. A comparable number for other *vigueries* would have resulted in a much larger summons than eighty-five. Absolute certainly about the total is impossible without the texts of the other letters. Yet it is very conceivable that in summarizing their contents the scribe included all, or almost all, of the names. There is no general phrase to cover some who were not designated, nor any other indication that the list is incomplete. Furthermore, of those who appeared, only two are missing from the summons as we have it.[66] Also it should be taken into account that the Béziers district, which included Narbonnais, was more densely populated than the other *vigueries* and included all the seacoast towns of the *sénéchaussée*. Presumably this region was more directly concerned with an embargo than the others. Finally, the seven towns summoned included all six *civitates* of the *sénéchaussée*, which accords with the statement in the preamble that "cities" were convoked. Except

---

was in touch with the political situation in lower Languedoc; and Jourdain de l'Isle had just been called to military duty there, *H.L.*, VI, 613; X, 124–125, 127; B.N., Doat, CLV, 50v–54v.

[65] See L. de Lacger, "L'Albigeois au Siècle de Saint Louis: Les Évêques Durand de Beaucaire et Bernard de Combret, 1228–1271," *Rev. d'Hist. Ecclés.*, LII (1957), 48–49; cf. *Gallia Christiana*, VI, 953.

[66] These were Philippe Goloinh and Raymond d'Aban. Guillaume de Thurey came in place of the deceased Simon de Thurey, whose summons is not recorded; while Gaufrid de Varennes attended probably as Jean de Montfort's deputy.

for Pézenas, an important place on the lower Hérault,[67] it is likely that only episcopal towns received the summons.

[67] Pézenas was the scene of another regional assembly, discussed in the next chapter.

Assembly of the Sénéchaussée of Carcassonne, at Carcassonne, January 1275

PARTIES KNOWN TO HAVE BEEN SUMMONED

Asterisks indicate summoned parties known to have attended; double asterisks indicate representation.

CLERGY: Archbishop of Narbonne*; bishops of Béziers*, Agde*, Lodève**, Maguelonne, Toulouse, Carcassonne*; proctors of church of Albi**; abbots of St-Paul*, Fontfroide, St-Aphrodise*, St-Jacques, St-Thibéry*, Valmagne, Aniane, St-Guilhem-du-Désert, Villemagne, Jaucels*, St-Chignan*, Lodève, St-Pons-de-Thomières**, Fontcaude**, Quarante*, Montolieu**, Villelongue*, Alet, Jocou, St-Polycarpe*, St-Hilaire*, Castres, Candeil**, Ardorel, Caunes; proctors of Lagrasse**; preceptors of Pézenas, Nébian, Périeis, Homps, Rustiques, Douzens, Magrie*; hospital of Narbonne; prior of Cassan.

NOBLES: Aymery, viscount of Narbonne*, Amaury de Narbonne, Guillaume de Durban, Bernard de Durban, Gaubert de Leucate, Bérenger de Boutenac, Pierre de Clermont, Bérenger-Guillaume, lord of Clermont, Gaufrid de Faugères, Aymery de Clermont, Bérenger de Puisserguier, Aymery de Boussagues, Déodat Armand, Guillaume d'Anduze, lord of Olargues, Sicard de Murviel, Guillaume de Lodève, Guiraud de Lodève, Jean de l'Isle, Pons de Thézan, Pierre de Villeneuve, lord of Caux, the seigneurial vicars of Florensac, Vias, the marshal of Mirepoix, Jean de Montfort** (?, see n.66), the lords of Lombers**, Jourdain de l'Isle, Isarn, Bertrand, Amaury, Sicardet, viscounts of Lautrec, Lambert de Thurey*, Géraud de Capendu, Jean de Bruyères, Guillaume de Voisins*.

Raymond d'Aban, Philippe Goloinh, Guillaume de Thurey, and Gaufrid de Varennes attended, though record of their personal summons is lacking. See note 66.

DISTRIBUTION OF TOWNS SUMMONED AND ATTENDING

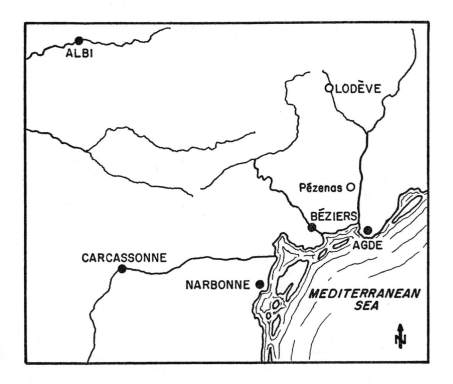

O SUMMONED

● SUMMONED AND
REPORTED PRESENT

Theoretically, therefore, the seneschal, in compliance with the ordinance of 1254, had convoked an assembly of the *sénéchaussée*. In fact, however, it was a gathering of men in the *viguerie* of Béziers, supplemented by elements from neighboring districts.

Thirty-four individuals and communities honored the summons personally or by deputy. These were the archbishop of Narbonne, the bishops of Béziers, Agde, Carcassonne, and Lodève (by representative), nine abbots themselves and four others through deputies, and one Hospital preceptor. The proctors of Albi and Lagrasse sent delegates. The nobles who attended were the viscount of Narbonne, Lambert de Thurey, Gaufrid de Varennes, Raymond d'Aban, Philippe Goloinh, Guillaume de Thurey, Guillaume de Voisins, and a deputy for the lord of Lombers. Finally, coming from the towns, the consuls of Narbonne, Béziers, Carcassonne, Albi, and Agde. Robert de Cohardon, the seneschal's son and lieutenant, presided over the assembly, assisted by the chief judge of the *sénéchaussée* and the judge of Carcassonne. As usual, royal court personnel and others attended the meeting, which on this occasion took place in the bishop's palace in Carcassonne city.[68]

So far as they can be reconstructed, these proceedings reflect more clearly than those of the previous assemblies the continuing seigneurial particularity and distrust of royal motives. The gathering itself, apparently led by the prelates and nobles,[69] seems to have taken the initiative in the sessions. This was partly, no doubt, because of the youth and

----

[68] *H.L.*, x, 128–131.

[69] It is they who are most pointedly mentioned, *ibid.*, 129: "Et tunc predicti domini prelati, barones, terrarii & alii comparentes suprascripti, consuluerunt . . ."; cf. *infra*: "protestationes factas a dictis consiliariis, prelatis, baronibus & aliis. . . ." The lords, too, rather than consuls, claimed jurisdictional rights in the ban, as explained below.

inexperience of the lieutenant, and partly, perhaps, because some of the barons had recently been alerted for military service to the crown.[70] The magnates drafted a seven-point program, most of which accorded with previous royal statutes, but which the lieutenant objected to as "conditiones seu protestationes." His reservation that the king alone had the authority to make such a ban indicates that he thought the assembly's activity was something more than *consilium*. Though he seems to have opposed the entire program, at least in its form, he probably found the substance of the second and third provisions especially unsatisfactory. These sought the recognition of possible local exemptions or privileges by assurance of non-prejudice, and specified that the ban should have effect only among persons and in places subject to the seneschal, where he has the right so to rule.[71]

Nevertheless, in view of the "urgent necessity" and after careful consideration, the lieutenant enacted legislation in virtually the same terms proposed by the assembly. It provided for a general embargo on grain, prohibiting its export from the *sénéchaussée* by land or sea. There was no mention of an exception to be made for Acre. Securities and penalties were to be administered by a sworn commission, as in previous years. The law should remain in force until the next 24 June, during which period no special favor could be granted. Short of this term, the ban could not be ended without another assembly.[72]

Following this enactment, the archbishop and viscount of Narbonne, the bishops of Béziers and Agde, and Lambert de Thurey and Gaufrid de Varennes—who said that he

---

[70] *Ibid.*, 124–125.

[71] *Ibid.*, 129: "2. Item quod dictum deffensum faciat inter personas, & in locis ubi poterit & debebit de jure per senescallum.— 3. Item dixerunt quod per hujusmodi consilium non intendunt sibi vel aliis aliquod prejudicium generari."

[72] *Ibid.*, 129–130.

was acting for Jean de Montfort—all claimed rights to confiscations and amends for the violation of the grain embargo. The chief judge rejected their demands, though not without indicating the possibility of an investigation. He took this opportunity to admonish the whole assembly against any infringement of the king's complete and unqualified right to administer the interdict and its penalties. It was perhaps at this point that certain royal statutes, to which attention had been directed in the letters of summons, were communicated.[73]

There is no need to recapitulate the various points that show the direct filiation of the grain statutes from the royal ordinances of 1254. Reference to the latter is both explicit and implicit in all of the documentation for the assemblies of 1258, 1269, 1271, and 1275. Necessarily some implementation was required to meet special situations, for example in the matter of limited embargoes which would permit transport to the Holy Land. But it is clear that the king's officials and scribes had the texts of 1254 before them when they wrote provisions prohibiting special favors during an interdict, and disallowing suspension of the law "without counsel." The best testimony to the continuity of the principles laid down in 1254 is the written form of the grain-export statutes. Inclusion of the letters of summons and description of the convocations are by no means extraneous features—they are fundamental to the substance of the law. If the seneschal must call an assembly in order to enact an embargo, then the written statute must furnish evidence of such a gathering.

In function these assemblies mark no very radical departure from the past. Like many earlier meetings in Languedoc, their activities could be described as consultative, deliberative, and political (or propagandistic). But within

---

[73] *Ibid.*, 131. There need be no surprise that these statutes are not mentioned in the minute, which is itself simply the full text of the grain-export ordinance. Cf. below, p. 220.

limits that are not easy to determine precisely, they also had a certain authority. As we have seen, Louis IX legislated in 1254 in response to petitions and protests received by the investigators. With allegations of the irresponsible exercise of power in the background, the royal ordinances convey unmistakably the sense of a constitutional limitation on the seneschal's administrative authority. In the one matter of prohibiting the export of grain, at least, the men of the *sénéchaussée* had the right to advise, or in effect, to approve legislation.

In practice this meant that they also had the initiative. In 1269, 1271, and 1275, the only occasions for which we have information, proceedings commenced with petitions. But, save possibly in the last of these assemblies, the king's officials seem to have controlled the deliberations. They made preliminary explanations based on the petitions, and asked for the opinion and counsel of the gathering. They were mindful to reserve for themselves the formal right of enactment: all the extant statutes were *issued* by the presiding officer alone, with the counsel of the assemblies. It is true that the act of 1271 speaks of counsel *and consent (de unanimi consilio & consensu),* but the context makes it clear that *consensus* here simply means common agreement. The three statutes all use the word "consulere" ("to give counsel") in reference to the work of the gatherings, with the indication that this followed preliminary requests for *consilium.*[74] Thus, if the seneschal was unable to act without an assembly, neither could the latter act without the seneschal. Nor did the convocation exceed its limits. The difficulties with Narbonne and certain individuals in 1271 and 1275, conflicts over bounds of authority, were not constitutional but political. Narbonne was concerned to preserve rights to her local ban, not to help extend or further institutionalize the restricted power of the

---

[74] For these points of usage, see *H.L.,* VIII, 1664, 1666–1667; 1739–1740, 1742; X, 125–127, 129–130.

assembled men of the *sénéchaussée*. One suspects that the expression of individual rights and jealousies was usually more pronounced than corporate solidarity in these meetings. Moreover, the relatively mediocre response to the summonses suggests that the right to advise which was guaranteed by the king became in effect the obligation to advise in actual practice.

In these circumstances the seneschals were not likely to find the assemblies a serious limitation or burden. To avoid trouble they had only to observe the letter of the law of 1254 and obtain the consensus of the *sénéchaussée*. In matters which, like the state of the harvest, were beyond the cognizance of one or a few persons, the association of regional men in administration was a useful way of obtaining information and opinion. And since the enactment of a ban on export was bound to cause some dissatisfaction, royal officials were probably glad to attribute responsibility to the advice of an assembly. Finally, the assembly of the *sénéchaussée* served the government as an instrument of publicity. According to the ruling of August 1269, the seneschal "approved, accepted, and published" the *consilium*, and "solemnly proclaimed the edict to be set forth"; the other statutes contain comparable declarations.[75] The convocation letters of 1274 explain as an additional reason for the forthcoming meeting the need "to hear certain new statutes of the lord king and directives which concern you."[76]

Closely related to the question of function is that of the composition of these assemblies of the *sénéchaussée*. We should like to know what principles governed the selection of persons and communities to be summoned, and in what sense the convocations may be regarded as representative. The imprecision of contemporary terminology is a stumbling block. But it seems clear that the assembly of the

[75] *Ibid.*, VIII, 1667; cf. 1743; X, 130–131.
[76] *Ibid.*, X, 127.

sénéchaussée envisaged by Louis IX and his officials was never intended to include all freemen of the district. The oft-repeated phrase *bonum et maturum consilium*, derived from the ordinance of December 1254,[77] partly implies that select assemblage of notables which, as we have seen, was the usual gathering. Only in the Nîmes statute of 1254 can there be found any elucidation of a principle of limitation: "consilium non suspectum, in quo sint *aliqui* de prelatis, baronibus, militibus & hominibus bonarum villarum" (italics mine). The statutes of 1269, 1271, and 1275 speak of the convocation of clergy, knights, and townsmen without qualification, but in all three instances the term *aliqui* was certainly understood. To be sure, it was feasible, and perhaps sometimes intended, to summon all bishops and abbots of the *sénéchaussée*, but there is no instance of an integral convocation of nobles or consulates. Therefore, if the grain-export assemblies were composed of important men and communities of the district, one may regard the binding of other, unsummoned elements to observance of the statutes as a kind of virtual representation. Such was the case with the bishop of Mende in 1261. But we must avoid ascribing modern political conceptions to this medieval situation. While in theory the right to be consulted meant a right to be summoned, there is nothing in the regulations and records to indicate that any particular parties could think of themselves as entitled to the summons or to the vote in royal assemblies. Finally, both in theory and practice, one observes in the grain-export meetings the convocation of *men* of estates, but not *representatives* of estates. Once again the traditional juridical classification of clergy, nobility, and townsmen is invoked, but without any connotation of corporate delegations of the orders. Those

---

[77] *Ibid.*, VIII, 1349, art. 31; 1664, 1666; cf. A.M. Narbonne, HH. (uninventoried), 14 October 1271: "vicarius Biterris . . . statuit cum maturo consilio iuxta statutum domini Regis ne bladum . . . extraheretur."

convoked, including the towns, came only as individuals.[78]

But to say that orders were not represented does not mean that there was no representation in these assemblies. The grain statutes provide some of the best early evidence on delegations from persons and communities. In general, it is true, we find ex officio representation of religious and lay communities and an expectation that individuals should appear in person. Bishops usually represented their churches and, even more often, abbots and preceptors their conventual communities. The summonses of 1269 and 1271, however, indicate special recognition of cathedral chapters. It is quite uncertain whether the failure to address them in 1274 indicates a feeling that the bishops were adequately representative of chapters. But as was noted, neither chapters nor abbeys seem to have responded well to separate summonses when issued in 1269 and 1271, and there is no evidence of their attendance in 1275. As for the towns, it was generally recognized that consuls should be the delegates. In 1269 and 1274 the consuls alone were addressed, while the minute of 1271 indicates the convocation of "consuls and communities" and goes on to say that the consuls who appeared spoke for themselves and their co-consuls (if not all consuls were delegated) and communities.[79] The only exceptions to this rule were the summons of "lords and consuls" of Gignac in 1269,[80] and Albi's

[78] Nor do we find such terms as *status, gradus,* or *ordo* in the documentation. These belong to a later day. Note, in this regard, the characteristically brilliant but misleading generalization by Molinier, *H.L.,* vii, 510: "Ce qu'on appela plus tard les trois ordres était représenté, dans cette assemblée [that of 1269]: le clergé par les évêques . . ."; cf. Dognon, *Institutions,* pp. 219–220; and É. Lousse, *Société d'Ancien Régime,* i, 244ff.

[79] *H.L.,* viii, 1741: "Item sub eodem modo & forma scripsit [the vicar] consulibus et communitatibus Narbone, . . ." *Infra,* regarding attendance: "item consules Narbone, videlicet Johannes Benedicti, Petrus Abbati, pro se & aliis conconsulibus & pro communitate urbis & burgi Narbone; item consules Biterris, scilicet

delegation of a proctor in 1271. The so-called "Articles of the Citizens" of 1270 show that Narbonne was then well accustomed to the practice of deputing consuls to central locations like Béziers, Paris, and even the Roman Curia, as administrative agents. They seem to have received formal mandates, however, only when they represented the town in financial negotiation and litigation; they were evidently not empowered in the export assemblies.[81]

The introduction of proctorial representation is an especially notable feature of these convocations of the *sénéchaussée*. How new it was may be suggested by the fact that the letters of summons make no provision for it.[82] There is no evidence of agency, formal or otherwise, in the meeting of 1269, and one suspects that the appearance of proctors at Béziers in August 1271 came as something of a surprise. The letters of 1269 and 1271 request simply that those addressed should attend the forthcoming assemblies,[83]

Guillelmus de Rivosicco . . . [and six others], pro se & pro communitate civitatis Biterris; . . . [etc.]."

[80] I have no information about Gignac (upper Hérault) to account for this variation. Perhaps the nobles were unusually prominent in this place, controlling, or well represented in, the consulate. See Dognon, *Institutions*, pp. 68–69; and *H.L.*, x, 534–535.

[81] *I.A.C., Narbonne, Annexes de la Série BB*, ii, no. 1, 3: "Secundum capitulum. Quod dicti consules, pro negotio sive causa universitatis, non possint aliquem vel aliquos destinare, sine consensu consilii preconizati vel majoris partis, scilicet Parisius vel in Franciam, vel ad curiam Romanam, nec alibi ultra duas dietas computandas a civitate Narbone." Cf. articles 3 and 4; also *ibid., Annexes de la Série AA*, no. 64, pp. 99–100; A.M. Narbonne, HH. (uninventoried), 14 October, 4 November, 1271; and AA.105, fols. 80v–81. I plan a special study of these questions.

[82] Cf. letters of 1302 (Paris) and 1303 (Montpellier), *Documents Relatifs aux États Généraux*, nos. 1, 74, 75.

[83] See *H.L.*, viii, 1666: "requirimus vos & mandamus, quatinus . . . ad nos apud Carcassonam veniatis . . ."; nor is it implied that empowered agents should respond. Cf. 1740.

but the summons of December 1274 explicitly requires *personal* appearance.[84]

Proctors came to these assemblies chiefly as delegates of the clergy. This may be regarded as support for the contention that proctorial representation in assemblies originated in ecclesiastical practices. It is probable that chapters of Languedoc sent proctors to the council of Bourges in 1225,[85] and possible that Dominican friaries of the Midi sometimes delegated empowered agents to provincial chapters in the subsequent period.[86] Despite a scanty documentation, there are at least two instances of proctorial representation in provincial councils before 1269. In April 1243 the chapter of Carcassonne deputed proctors to a council at Béziers which heard an appeal by Count Raymond VII against the authority of certain Dominican in-

[84] *Ibid.*, x, 127: "mandamus, quatenus . . . ad nos apud Carcassonam personaliter veniatis. . . ." This must have been a usual requirement in summonses to do homage and the like; and we find it in the royal convocation form for the administrative assembly at Béziers in December 1270, B.N., Doat, CLV, 50.

[85] Matthew Paris, *Chronica Majora*, ed. H. Luard, III, 105–109; *Register of S. Osmund*, ed. W. H. Rich Jones, II, 51–54; etc. Cf. *H.L.*, VIII, 866. This evidence proves the presence of proctors, and from the special importance of southern affairs on the agenda, I infer that some of the proctors must have been from Languedoc.

[86] But these agents are not termed "proctors" or "syndics" in the Dominican records of southern France, nor is there evidence of formal grants of *plena potestas, Acta Capitulorum Provincialium Ordinis Fratrum Praedicatorum; Première Province de Provence—Province Romaine—Province d'Espagne (1239–1302)*, ed. C. Douais (Toulouse, 1894). On the other hand, the Dominican general chapter often delegated its *potestas* to *visitatores*, priors, or other friars, for various administrative purposes, e.g., *Acta Capitulorum Generalium Ordinis Praedicatorum ab Anno 1220 usque ad Annum 1303*, ed. B. Reichert (Rome, 1898), pp. 11, 23, 25, 27, 35, 41, etc. The provincial chapters granted *potestas plenaria* to priors and *diffinitores* who convened in the *generalissimum* chapter of Paris in 1228 (cited by Post, "Plena Potestas and Consent," *Traditio*, I, 369).

quisitors in his lands.[87] Again at Béziers, in May 1255, proctors represented two bishops and three abbots in a provincial council which deliberated on the king's claim to the services of ecclesiastical contingents in the siege of a stronghold of heretics in that area.[88] There is precedent even for the lone town known to have employed proctors in the assemblies of the *sénéchaussée*. Albi had been thus represented before the seneschal of Carcassonne in 1259 during royal proceedings against the bishop and town for their private war against Gaillac.[89]

It is not always clear that this procuration was employed for its judicial utility—that is, as a device to ensure complete procedural consent to decisions *in absentia*.[90] On the other hand, we know certainly that royal courts in Languedoc had sometimes required full powers—the Roman-canonical *plena potestas*—for just that purpose during the reign of Louis IX.[91] Procuration may have been new in assemblies, but it was not so in courts. The silence of the summonses regarding procuration in 1269–1274 would suffice to assure us that the government was not imposing it on the *sénéchaussée*. But there was no need of it, in any case, for as we have seen, legal consent was not essential in the grain-export assemblies. Even a handful of clergy, nobles, and townsmen, like the twenty-three who appeared in 1271, was enough to satisfy the requirement of "good and mature counsel," and one observes no impulse to secure the formal adhesion of every person or community summoned. Plainly the seneschals did not regard these convocations as primarily or strictly judicial in character. It is true that the institutional focus of the extraordinary as-

[87] *Gallia Christiana*, VI, *inst.*, 155.

[88] Mahul, *Cartulaire . . . de Carcassonne*, IV, 535–536.

[89] *H.L.*, VIII, 1456–1457.

[90] Cf. generally Post, "Roman Law and Early Representation in Spain and Italy, 1150–1250," *Speculum*, XVIII (1943), 211–232; "Plena Potestas and Consent."

[91] *H.L.*, VIII, 1307, 1456–1457, 1477–1478.

sembly was the ordinary royal court of the *sénéchaussée*. But it is the court as an administrative organ, with power to summon for service in person, whose character carries over into the export assemblies. And the personal attendance of individuals and administrators has analogies with the preferred procedure in councils and synods.[92]

Since the government had no motive, the summoned parties themselves must have taken the initiative in delegating proctors. The officials had not expressly *prohibited* procuration—at least not until 1274; the legal formulas for *plena potestas* in mandates were by this time readily available; why not use those formulas? The record suggests that some parties did and others did not, and that the practice was voluntary with those summoned. It also appears that constituents thought of the mandate as a sort of written excuse for failing to attend an assembly. Apart from those who sent proctors in 1271,[93] three other individuals merely sent letters of excuse (so they are termed in the statute); but at least two of those letters included the clause of *ratihabitio*, signifying the advance ratification of any decisions to be reached in the meeting.[94]

[92] *Decretum*, dist. 18, cc. 5, 9, 10, etc.; *glos. ord.* ad v. *personaliter*, *Extra*, I, 33, 17*Humilis doctrina*; and for the synodal custom of Rodez in the 13th century, see *Thes. Anecdotorum*, IV, 673–674.

[93] At least four principals provided their deputies with formal mandates, *H.L.*, VIII, 1741–1742. E.g. (description of attendance): "Item, Raimundus Vaireti, canonicus Lodovensis, cum mandato procuratorio domini episcopi Lodovensis; . . ." The reference to the Albi mandate is the one certain indication of corporate procuration: "item Guillelmus Grava, pro consulibus & communitate Albie, cum mandato procuratorio sigillato cum sigillo pendenti consulum civitatis Albie."

[94] *Ibid.*, 1741–1742: "item pro vicecomitibus Lautricensibus littera approbationis de hoc quod fiet, per vicarium sigillata cum sigillo domini Isarni, vicecomitis Lautricensis . . . curia domini archiepiscopi Narbonensis excusavit litteratorie ipsum dominum archiepiscopum, quod iter arripuerat eundi in Franciam. Item abbas

All this rested on a misunderstanding of the summons. Those who deputed proctors would have done better to save themselves the notary's fee. There is no evidence that mandates were even inspected, much less rejected, either in 1271 or 1275. No mandates for these assemblies have survived, as they have for later convocations in which royal officials took care to include or copy them in their records.[95] Moreover, the practice of informal delegation continued. In 1271 the abbot of Saint-Aphrodise appeared for both himself and the abbot of Saint-Thibéry, having been "constituted by the latter in his presence"; and two clerics came "for the chapter of Carcassonne church."[96] In the assembly of 1275 the character of the deputations is still less clear. Eight parties were represented, but there is no indication of formal procuration. In four cases the minute reports that delegates merely claimed to represent their principals, from which we might infer that the other deputies were in fact proctors, although not so styled.[97] The seneschal, however, was evidently not much concerned with the form of delegation, which is not surprising in view of his preference for personal appearance on this occasion. The individuals represented, for their part, should have been better able to understand that it was pointless to empower their agents in formal, Roman-canonical style. In the case of communities, however, it is not impossible that procuration was some-

---

Sancti Poncii Thomeriarum excusavit se per suam litteram, approbans quidquid ordinaretur cum consilio aliorum prelatorum." Cf., for canon law and procedure, *Decretum*, dist. 18, c. 10, and *glos. ord.* ad vv. *litteratorie, rationem*; "*Curialis*," ed. Wahrmund, *Quellen* . . . , I, iii, 43; *Rhetorica Ecclesiastica, ibid.*, I, iv, 89.

[95] See, e.g., *Documents Relatifs aux États Généraux*, nos. 77–122.

[96] *H.L.*, VIII, 1741.

[97] *Ibid.*, x, 128–129. To take but one example: ". . . prior de Lavineria pro domino abbate Sancti Pontii ut dicebat. . . ." Three of the other four deputies were ecclesiastical.

times regarded as a way of impressing the government and assembly with a sense of local autonomy and corporate rights. Nevertheless, the earliest use of the new representation in royal assemblies of Languedoc was very limited. It was voluntary with the parties involved and not dependent on requirements for procedural consent by central authorities.

The later history of the legislation on grain export will be taken up again in due course. The assembly of January 1275 was the last of its kind for some time. Meanwhile, officials of Philip III were beginning to employ meetings of similar composition for other purposes in Languedoc; and the range of uses for provincial assemblies continued to expand in the later thirteenth century. A new generation of rulers was building on the initiative and experience of those able administrators who first resorted to the central summons of regional men during the reign of Louis IX.

᎒VI᎒ *The Later Thirteenth Century* (1271-1302)

Languedoc was a royal province after 1271. Strong government there was one common feature of the two dissimilar reigns of Philip III (1270–1285) and Philip IV (1285–1314). The former pursued his father's papal-Angevin policy to a disastrous end. He campaigned several times in southern France and became heavily dependent on its men and resources, far more so than Louis IX had been. Philip the Fair, though embroiled with Gascony, gave up the old Mediterranean designs in favor of an aggressive new politics in the east and north of France. But he continued his predecessor's reliance on the South, and Languedoc paid heavily for his program. Many of his officials were natives of the Midi. He entrusted great authority to the seneschals who governed Languedoc in his name.[1]

FEUDAL AND DIOCESAN ASSEMBLIES

There remained, however, some important baronial enclaves, such as Foix, Narbonne, Rouergue, Lunel, and Montpellier. Major prelates and lesser nobles likewise retained vassals and domains. Feudal courts continued to meet in these principalities somewhat as they had done in the past. As late as 1297, the old obligation to service "of plea and of war" turns up in a record of homage by several nobles who declare themselves to be "faithful and lawful

---

[1] See generally C. V. Langlois, *Philippe III*, esp. pp. 44–46, 59–63, 96–116, 150–166, 304–375; J. R. Strayer, "The Crusade against Aragon," *Speculum*, XXVIII (1953), 102–113; Strayer and Taylor, *Early French Taxation*, pp. 4–7, 27–29, 32–40, 43–55, 63, 66–69, 73–82, 85–93; and A. Luchaire, *Manuel des Institutions*, pp. 551–552.

feudatories and vassals" of the count of Rodez.[2] Some years earlier, the bishop and count of Rodez together had summoned nobles to the city for consultation.[3] Yet we hear little of feudal judgments by vassals. Doubtless many that occurred were left unwritten, but such evidence as is available suggests that they were unusual. A criminal assize at Lautrec in 1299 was attended by vassals and notables of the viscounty, syndics of the community of Lautregais, as well as a crowd of vengeful local people. Though the viscount had summoned the court, he evidently lost control over it. It pronounced a harsh sentence to which he objected and from which he, the viscount himself, promptly appealed to the king—the most revealing fact of all.[4] Other documents of Lautrec and Narbonne show that knights and notables were present when the viscounts transacted important feudal business.[5] The men convened as witnesses, or in order to lend weight to decisions, but not to advise. Of counsel and consent, indeed, very little is said, and we are left with the impression that consultation with vassals in Languedoc had declined in importance during the century. This impression is confirmed by the findings of Professor Higounet, whose study of Comminges is still the only thorough investigation of a feudal principality in Languedoc. While the vassals of Comminges were *consiliarii* of the count in the middle of the thirteenth century, a hundred years later they were being summoned as witnesses.[6]

---

[2] B.N., Doat, CLXXVI, 240v. See also J. Regné *Amauri II, p.j.*, nos. 4, 5, pp. 357–360, homages to Amaury of Narbonne in 1298 according to the old formulas.

[3] A.D. Aveyron, C.1840, fol. 314v, an old inventory of archives at Montauban, item dated 1278: "Mandement faict par raimond Evesque de Rodez et Henry comte a plusieurs gentilshommes de venir a rodez pour des affaires inportants." I owe this reference to M.J. Bousquet, archivist of the Aveyron.

[4] *H.L.*, x, 353–354.

[5] *Ibid.*, 206–207, 122–124; Regné, *Amauri II*, p. 351.

[6] C. Higounet, *Comminges*, I, 206.

This does not mean that feudal lords were giving up all control of vassals. Written acts of homage and recognition abound in the later thirteenth century, and many of them were registered in traditional courtly ceremonies.[7] What is more, after mid-century major barons sometimes used the summons, like their Capetian superiors, to make comprehensive records of their suzerainty.[8] One of the largest convocations of this kind occurred at Narbonne in the third week of March 1272, when Viscount Aymery received no fewer than twenty-seven homages.[9] On the other hand, in Languedoc as elsewhere, the possession of vassals was losing its importance; it would eventually be little more than a mark of prestige. Private warfare was much reduced, and most fighting was done for the king. Moreover, the counsel of untrained knights was decreasing in value in an age of improving government. Though lords remained jealous of their right to summon, they exercised it less often than in the past.[10] Instead of courts of vassals, they now relied more on courts of officials, professionalized groups of skilled advisers and lawyers. Thus, in 1292 the viscount of Narbonne deferred a decision that touched the archbishop until he had a chance to confer with the latter or his *curiales*; and it is clear that these "court men" were a stand-

[7] *H.L.*, x, 122–124; Regné, *Amauri II*, p.j., nos. 4–6, pp. 357–361; A. Philippe, *Tournel*, no. 10; C. Porée, *Gévaudan*, pp. 382–383, n. 3; A.D. Lozère, G. 143.

[8] See, e.g., *Documents Historiques Relatifs à la Vicomté de Carlat*, eds. G. Saige, Comte de Dienne, 2 vols. (Monaco, 1900), I, nos. 14–105; Cazalède, *Hommages de l'Évêché du Puy*, pp. 137–138, *et passim*, though this evidence is not explicit on the point in question. Cf. A.D. Aveyron, C.1840, fol. 91v.

[9] B.N., Doat, XLVII, fols. 27–130, catalogued analytically by Regné, *Amauri II*, pp. 16–19. *H.L.*, x, 122–124, is merely one of this series. See also Regné's catalogue, nos. 74–82, pp. 23–24, Amaury's even larger assembly at the time of his accession to the viscounty in 1298.

[10] See A.D. Aveyron, C.1840, fol. 314v; and B.N., Doat, XLVIII, 248; cf. A.D. Haute-Garonne, 1G.346, pp. 15–16.

ing body with institutionalized authority to act for the archbishop in his absence.[11] The viscount's own court had long since acquired a specialized identity, although vassals still sometimes appeared in it.[12] Central administrative organs developed in the county of Comminges in the time of Bernard VI (1241–1295), and this tendency was probably paralleled in other major baronies of Languedoc.[13] Townsmen figure prominently in convocations by feudal lords in the later thirteenth century, more so, indeed, than in previous decades.[14] The good men of Narbonne had a considerable share in local seigneurial authority. When the archbishop and viscount sometimes acted without consulting them, passing measures relating to the coinage and fairs, for example, minor constitutional crises arose.[15] Consuls or officials might act for townsmen in such matters in a quasi-representative capacity. But nowhere does it ap-

---

[11] *Livre de Comptes de Jacme Olivier*, p.j., no. 32, pp. 450–451; see also *H.L.*, VIII, 1742.

[12] *H.L.*, X, 122–124; and above, p. 55; Regné, *Amauri II*, pp. 300–301, 350–352; *p.j.*, no. 6, p. 361; and B.N., Doat, L, mention of viscount's *consilium* in 1287. Cf. Doat, XLVIII, 248v, where in a royal document of 1301 the word "curiales" is used in reference to vassals of the viscount of Narbonne.

[13] Higounet, *Comminges*, I, 206. P. Dognon, *Institutions*, pp. 49–54, says very little on this point.

[14] Philippe, *Tournel*, nos. 4, 5, and cf. no. 1, act of 1219, with Porée, *Gévaudan*, pp. 382–383, n. 3, similar act of 1292; also *H.L.*, X, 124, and Regné, *Amauri II*, pp. 351–353.

[15] *Livre de Comptes de Jacme Olivier*, p.j., no. 46, pp. 509–510 (act of 1301): "preconizationem . . . super facto nundinarum Narbone factam esse in prejudicium et lesionem jurium et libertatum ville Narbone, in eo quia in dicta preconizatione non dicebatur: "De consilio proborum hominum Civitatis et Burgi Narbone," prout dixerunt hactenus fuisse in similibus factum et observatum et tantis temporibus de quibus in contrarium memoria non existit." See also document of 1310, p.j., no. 64, pp. 654ff; also B.N., Doat, LI, 247–249 (coinage, 1305); and Regné, *Amauri II*, pp. 102, 177–180, 304–305.

pear that they or other burghers were summoned as representatives.

The institutions of the diocesan peace virtually disappeared in the later thirteenth century. This fact is set in the clearest possible light by the struggle in Gévaudan. In the *paréage* of 1307 the bishop finally gained the king's recognition of limited rights in the maintenance of the peace.[16] But this concession came too late. Decades of police work by royal agents had effectively altered the balance of power. There could be no question of reviving the old associative life in Gévaudan on its original basis of militant vigilance subject to the bishop. Of the episcopal peace in Quercy, much the same story may be told. It is true that sessions continued to be held occasionally, at Cahors, for "swearing the peace." But the bishop was obliged to share receipt of the peace oaths with the royal seneschal, according to agreements of 1306.[17] And by that time the right they shared must have seemed archaic. The significant fact is that nothing more is heard about taxation or campaigns for the peace in Quercy.[18] The *pezade* continued to be levied in Albigeois and Rouergue, but its character had changed completely; its original purpose was ignored or forgotten.[19] Everywhere in Languedoc, in fact if not yet always in law, breaches of the peace were falling under royal jurisdiction. The insistent opposition to private war was being felt even in baronial lands.[20]

---

[16] *Ordonnances*, XI, 396–403; cf. A.D. Lozère, G.25.

[17] See A.N., J.341, no. 5; "Memorandum des Consuls de la Ville de Martel," ed. H. Teulié, *Revue de Philol. Franç.*, VII (1893), 259; A.M. Martel, CC.2, fols. 9v, 12v, 17, 45, 60, 62. References to Martel's deputations to swear the peace cease after 1302.

[18] Cf. Albe, *Cahors: Inventaire*, no. 120, pp. 122ff.

[19] See ch. 3, pp. 105–110.

[20] *H.L.*, X, 83–84,v; 131–132; *Livre de Comptes de Jacme Olivier, p.j.*, no. 24, pp. 391–392; A.M. Montpellier, Arm. H, cass. 3, no. 3678; *Lettres Inédites de Philippe le Bel*, ed. A. Baudouin (Paris, 1887), *annexes*, no. 19; *Olim*, III[1], 105–106, no. 60; B.N., Doat, CLXXV, 313v.

THE GENERAL COURT OF AGENAIS IN DECLINE

The lone territory of feudal Languedoc whose custom provided for a central assembly was Agenais. Its general court survived Alfonse of Poitiers, but not without a considerable metamorphosis. Royal and ducal governors tended to overlook the assembly's customary function of deliberating on military problems. On the other hand, they were ready to use it for their own political and administrative purposes, as in the French seisin campaign of 1271. The need to register fealties and recognitions of obligations was to be the main reason for summoning the men of Agenais in the later thirteenth century.

The traditional attendance was modified by the appearance of clergy in the general court. There is an indefinite and somewhat vague allusion to their presence in the assembly of November 1271.[21] But it is certain that prelates and chapters were summoned in 1279 to sit with nobles and town delegates in a large political gathering. In 1286 Edward I directed his officials to secure feudal recognitions from churchmen as well as other tenants; and three years later, he prescribed a general court that was to include men of all three estates.[22] Clerical attendance in these assemblies, like that of the other orders, was individual; we find no evidence of the representation of an ecclesiastical estate. Deputations from religious houses were probably more common than the one surviving reference of 1286 would indicate,[23] but the parish clergy were undoubtedly

[21] *Sais. Agen.*, 85: prelates are mentioned only after "barons and knights and other nobles"; the other surviving document, p. 72, has no reference to clergy. This assembly is discussed above, pp. 176–179. On the absence of clergy in the early general court, see pp. 91–92.

[22] *Chartes d'Agen*, no. 60; P.R.O., Ancient Correspondence (SC 1), xiv, no. 136; *Arch. Gir.*, I, no. 181; *R.G.*, II, no. 1428.

[23] *Arch. Gir.*, I, 362, no. 51, Condom the only house represented by a proctor-syndic; cf. the king's directive, 348–349; and for 1279, *Chartes d'Agen*, no. 60, references to chapters.

ignored. The prelates were becoming identified with the nobility, and those having seigneurial jurisdiction may have been counted as barons for administrative purposes.[24] A collective procuration and petition by clergy and nobles of Agenais in 1289 may have been drawn up in an assembly.[25] Even in this period, however, the clergy did not always attend regional meetings.[26]

The seisin of Agenais by Philip III was not to have permanent results, for it was in violation of English rights to the district. Arrangements for the restoration of English suzerainty were completed in the summer of 1279, following the treaty of Amiens.[27] The final formalities received publicity in what was probably the largest and most impressive assembly of the century in Agenais. The bishop, three abbots, "other prelates and chapters," barons, knights and nobles, in numbers considerably greater than the twenty-two who are known by name, the deputies of ten specified towns and villages [28] and of others not named, and a "great multitude of other persons": such was the crowd that convened in the Dominican cloister at Agen on 9 August in response to a summons by French officials; and among twenty-five witnesses to the transactions were important men from outside the diocese, including major Gascon lords, two abbots, and a bishop.[29] The French agents officially transferred the direct lordship of Agenais to King Edward's uncle, William of Valence, who had been

[24] See next note; also *Gascon Calendar*, nos. 1269, 1702; P.R.O., Ancient Petitions (SC 8), 262/13092.

[25] *R.G.*, II, nos. 992, 1056, 1062.

[26] *Livre d'Agenais*, no. 17, p. 37; *Chartes d'Agen*, no. 141.

[27] See p. 168, n. 117; and Cuttino, *Livre d'Agenais*, pp. ix–xiv.

[28] Listed above, ch. 2, p. 90.

[29] *Chartes d'Agen*, no. 60; *Livre d'Agenais*, no. 2, pp. 8–9. Lists of reliefs, homages, and military obligations were drawn up at about this time; they name more than 100 fief-holders and 32 towns, but this cannot be taken as evidence of attendance; cf. below, p. 238, and n. 36.

empowered to serve as recipient. They charged the men assembled and all other regional subjects to be obedient to the king of England and to perform fealty, homage, and their other obligations for him. The inhabitants of Agenais were absolved from their allegiance to the king of France, with the reservation of "superiority and supreme jurisdiction." Finally, the French seneschal was removed from office and ordered to render account. A notary of Agen, by request of the royal agents, the bishop, and the whole assembly, recorded and authenticated these acts in a public instrument.[30]

The difficult task of obtaining fealties now fell to the English commissioner. But certain details had been disputed at tiresome length before the agreements just mentioned. There may well have been some other discussion and speechmaking in this session.[31] Moreover, the word had previously circulated through Agenais that the new seneschal might be the lord of Bergerac, a disreputable man who was said to be unable even to govern himself.[32] This report was not unfounded, and the commissioner himself probably favored the feared Gascon noble.[33] Uneasiness was doubtless discernible in the assembly on 9 August. The people of Agenais could be expected to make an issue of the seneschal, as in the past, when asked to do fealty. For these various reasons the commissioner decided to postpone the work overnight.

Agen must have been an excited city that evening. The next day, clergy, nobles, and consuls reassembled in the town hall. It is possible that matters threatened immediately

[30] *Chartes d'Agen*, no. 60 (an original, of which *Livre d'Agenais*, no. 1 is a copy), pp. 84–85, 89.

[31] *Livre d'Agenais*, p. xi; no. 2, pp. 7–8; P.R.O., Anc. Corresp. (SC 1), xiv, nos. 136, 137 (in *Livre d'Agenais*, pp. xix-xx). Jurisdictional questions about two bastides and the matter of Queen Eleanor's pension in Agenais were left unsettled.

[32] P.R.O., Anc. Corresp., xiv, no. 136.

[33] King Edward certainly did, *Livre d'Agenais*, pp. xxi-xxii.

to get out of control, for the commissioner's first act was a concession. Taking counsel "in full court" with his advisers, he announced the temporary appointment of Jean de Grilly, seneschal of Gascony, to the seneschalcy of Agenais; and Grilly was directed to swear to maintain the customs faithfully. But the men of Agenais were still dissatisfied. They now argued that it was customary for the lord to make oath in person, upon his first entry into Agenais; only after he had done so should he receive their oaths. They even had a general *protestacio* drawn up in legal form. At this point a compromise was approved and put into effect. The new seneschal, facing the assembly, and with gospel and cross at hand, swore an oath of protection and loyalty twice, once in place of the king, and a second time as seneschal. When this had been done, the men of Agenais in turn swore fealty to the commissioner and seneschal acting for King Edward.[34]

In a letter to the king soon afterward, the bishop of Agen wrote that he himself had been the first to take the oath, and that the other clergy, nobles, and consuls had followed suit with great zeal and affection. But this account has little to say about the community's stand for its privileges, a stand with which the bishop evidently had little sympathy. The bishop had, in fact, profited from the occasion to gain confirmation of his lordship in Agenais. He joined the commissioner and seneschal in ordaining that the administrative organization of Agenais should remain unchanged.[35] In this

---

[34] *Ibid.*, no. 2, pp. 8–9. Professor Cuttino kindly answered a question about this text for me. My account attributes more importance to it than do those of Cuttino, pp. x–xi, and F. M. Powicke, *The Thirteenth Century, 1216–1307*, 2nd ed. (Oxford, 1962), pp. 292–293. The compromise in question may not have been new in 1279; it is implied in undated forms for oaths of Le Mas, A.D. Lot-et-Garonne, E. Suppl. 1824, p. 6.

[35] P.R.O., Anc. Corresp., xiv, no. 136, and cf. no. 73, both in *Livre d'Agenais*, pp. xix–xxii. Also *ibid.*, no. 2, p. 8, reference to

act and in the earlier turn of events, the assemblage had cause for relief, so that the bishop's report of its favorable disposition in doing fealty is not implausible. There is no clear evidence of further proceedings. At some time in the period of the transfer of Agenais, officials recorded the names of fief holders who owed reliefs and of nobles and towns obligated to do homage and military service; but these lists are not precisely dated, and they cannot be assigned with certainty to the assembly of 1279.[36]

A full inquiry into feudal holdings was undertaken seven years later when Edward I personally visited Gascony. On 12 November 1286 the king commissioned the seneschal and judges of Agenais to receive recognitions of fiefs and obligations from prelates, nobles, and towns. The commissioners began to record recognitions at Agen on the fourteenth, and in the next five days they collected 136 depositions from individuals and representatives. Between 18 November and the following 26 January, when they closed the record, only eight more recognitions were listed.[37] It is therefore clear that the officials had issued a summons of some kind which required appearance at Agen on or soon after 14 November. Whether so advertised or not, these proceedings were administered as an assembly.[38] The king himself was in Agen between 15 and 27 Novem-

---

the summons of *bishop,* clergy, nobles, and towns, followed by mention of the protest made "per los autres prelatz, religios, baros, cavalers, cosselhs . . . ," without naming the bishop.

[36] *Livre d'Agenais.*, nos. 4–10, pp. 13–20.

[37] *Arch. Gir.*, I, nos. 181, 182 (348–387).

[38] The analogous summons in early spring 1274 of Gascon tenants to Lectoure, *Rec. Feod.*, no. 174, provides strong support for this view. In that case, too, the delay was very brief: "veniat [each tenant] hodie vel cras per totam diem ad dominum regem, in aula episcopi Lectorensis, facturus sibi homagium et fidelitatem, et alia deveria. . . ." Other tenants were summoned to the court towns of Bordeaux and St-Sever; and cf. above, p. 84, n. 241.

ber 1286,[39] and he may well have addressed the gathering at some point.

It would be interesting to know whether contemporaries thought of these gatherings as general courts. The assembly of 1279 is only once termed "court" in several pertinent documents, and there is no such reference for that of 1286. Yet both these meetings resembled the undoubted general courts of 1249 and 1271. The new uses and changing composition of the old institution might alone account for neglect of the original terminology. Anyway, the employment of general assemblies for the exchange of oaths had become customary in Agenais. In 1299 it was said to be well known that the newly appointed seneschal should swear protection and loyalty "to communities and barons and nobles of Agenais and they [should do the same] to him." [40] That this implied the summons of a regional assembly is clear from the precedents of 1271 and 1279 and from other evidence as well.[41]

Along with this late development, however, there was an older and continuing tradition of fealty proceedings in local meetings.[42] Men of the city and suburban jurisdiction of Agen were accustomed to assembling when the overlord first appeared there to exchange oaths with him. And when a seneschal was appointed, the consuls were to receive his

[39] J.P. Trabut-Cussac, "Itinéraire d'Edouard Iᵉʳ en France, 1286–1289," *Bull. Inst. Hist. Research,* xxv (1952), 171–172.

[40] *Chartes d'Agen,* no. 92 (p. 157): "nam notum et certum est in Agennesio quod senescallus, in sui novitate, communitatibus et baronibus et nobilibus de Agennesio et ipsi vice versa tenentur jurare eidem domino senescallo. . . ."

[41] *Arch. Gir.,* I, 384, no. 135, consuls of Lagruère are obligated to swear a representative oath of fealty *at Agen* when the lord first comes to Agenais; also, for Le Mas, A.D. Lot-et-Garonne, E.Suppl. 1824, p. 6; and *Chartes d'Agen,* no. 141.

[42] On the *baylie* sessions of 1259, see above, pp. 161–163. Local assizes were evidently used for similar purposes under Edward I, n. 44 below.

oath and make their own as representatives.[43] These were local privileges, which had the effect of defining the responsibilities of lord and seneschal toward people of the seigneury of Agen. The new usage, as enunciated in 1299, constituted a similar privilege for the community of all Agenais. Now there may have been some confusion late in the century between the oath assembly of Agen and that of Agenais.[44] But it appears from a curious case a few years later that the two customs remained distinct, and that the strong consulate of Agen, then at odds with its lordly neighbors, was unwilling to give up its privileged individuality in Agenais. In 1311 a newly appointed seneschal, with the later custom in mind, summoned barons and consuls of Agenais to meet at Agen. We do not know certainly that these parties exchanged oaths, but quite possibly they did. Our only record of this occasion reveals the seneschal acting under the influence of the consuls of Agen. He read to the assembly from the "Book of the Consuls," that is, he publicly recognized the old obligation recorded in the charter of Agen. Accordingly, he took oath to the consuls of Agen and they reciprocated. Presumably the latter rep-

---

[43] H. Tropamer, *Coutume d'Agen*, p. 26. The representative oath is described thus: "E si lo senher volia metre senescalc en Agenes, aquel senescalc deu jurar prumerament al coselh d'Agen per lor e per tota la universitat de la meissa ciutat e dels borcs d'environ; el coselh deu jurar apres al senescalc per lor e per tota la universitat del meiss loc."

[44] *Livre d'Agenais*, no. 21, p. 50, and *Arch. Gir.*, I, 375, no. 97, references in 1280's to seneschal's oath to clerical tenants either separately or *in plena assizia Agenni*; the former document was also copied on the Gascon Rolls, *R.G.*, II, no. 938, where the reading is "Agennensi" for "Agenni." Strictly speaking, "assize" means a periodic local court held in various assize towns; see esp. King Edward's administrative ordinance for Agenais of 1289, Brit. Mus., Cotton. MS Julius E. 1, fols. 158v–159. Professor Cuttino generously placed a transcript of this document at my disposal.

resented the suburban villagers, but surely not the diocesan barons and consuls present.[45]

Thus by the later thirteenth century the assembled men of Agenais had added limited political rights to their limited financial rights. The tax to secure the episcopal coinage against arbitrary mutation was still sometimes made in the general court, though it is doubtful whether any other impositions in Agenais were granted in regional assemblies after 1271.[46]

Yet financiers were certainly aware of the general court. In April 1289 Edward I directed his seneschal to convoke a "general court of the whole Agenais," including men of all three estates, in order to obtain a ten-year *fouage* of six pennies for the rebuilding of a bridge over the Garonne at Agen.[47] The theory alone concerns us here, for we have no evidence that this projected assembly actually convened, or that a six-penny tax was imposed.[48] Recourse to the general court in the "business of the bridge" seems to have been a new idea, but it might well have been argued that a body which customarily approved *fouage* for one purpose could be convoked to grant the same kind of tax for another. The royal directive was in accord with the interests of the men of Agen. They had taken the initiative in this project for the "common utility of the whole land," and

[45] *Chartes d'Agen*, no. 141; cf. G. Tholin, *Ville Libre et Barons: Essai sur les Limites de la Juridiction d'Agen* . . . (Paris, 1886), pp. 16–45, 73ff. (unclear, p. 18, about the meeting of 1311); Rymer, *Foedera*, II¹, 281; and M. Gouron, *Les Chartes de Franchises de Guienne et Gascogne* (Paris, 1935), no. 127.

[46] See above, pp. 95–96; *Chartes d'Agen*, no. 59; and below, p. 275.

[47] *R.G.*, II, no. 1428.

[48] For later documents, see *Chartes d'Agen*, nos. 104, 111 (*corr.* 110), 120, etc. The *opus pontis* on the Garonne was perennial: see Labrunie, "Les Ponts sur la Garonne," ed. G. Tholin, *Rev. de l'Agenais*, V (1878), 441–444; C. Higounet in *Annales du Midi*, LXII (1950), 351.

they may have petitioned the king to impose a general tax.[49] Some sort of financial campaign had been under way for several years.[50] In 1287 the seneschal had asked inhabitants with seigneurial jurisdiction to convoke their men in local meetings "to hear our mandate and complete the work of building the said bridge." [51] We lack details about this particular scheme, but there is no indication that it was successful. The king's request for a general court should be understood as a drastic measure, substituting central publicity and negotiation for ineffective local procedures.

Whatever the interest of these precedents, the general court was not destined to become a constitutional body. In 1325 Charles IV, in circumstances exactly like those of 1289, ordered a ten-year *fouage* in Agenais for bridge repair, but nothing was said of an assembly, and the seneschal was left free to proceed as he saw fit.[52] A few years earlier, Edward II had apparently dealt individually with magnates and towns of Agenais in efforts to raise a war subsidy.[53] Administrative legislation may sometimes have received publicity in general assemblies but was not issued or ratified by them.[54] It is possible, however, that the community had some continuing influence in restraint of the bishop's monetary prerogatives. In 1316 men of Agen had control of operations in the episcopal mint; and it was the practice at that time for coins to be struck on the request of consuls of the city and towns of Agenais.[55] But there is no mention

[49] As they did in 1325, *Chartes d'Agen*, no. 156; see also nos. 70, 77–79.

[50] At least since 1286, *ibid.*, no. 70; also nos. 77–79.

[51] *Ibid.*, no. 78; cf. A. Ducom, *Agen*, p. 75, similar activity in 1282.

[52] *Chartes d'Agen*, no. 156.

[53] Rymer, *Foedera*, II^1, 467, 475.

[54] *H.L.*, VII, *documents*, 419–426; *Livre d'Agenais*, p. xx; Brit. Mus., Cotton. MS Julius E. 1, fols. 158–159v.

[55] A.D. Lot-et-Garonne, new G.2, no. 11 (*Rec. Trav. Soc. Agen*, VII, *preuves*, no. 5, 615–616); no. 6, 616–617; Ducom, *Agen*, p. 148; and cf. "Chartes d'Agen," *Arch. Gir.*, XXXIII, no. 44.

of the general court in this matter, nor do we hear of the *fouage* for the coinage after 1292. The bishops were losing their coinage rights in the fourteenth century, and they probably fared quite as badly with the territorial lord as with the community.[56]

As a matter of fact, the general court was in full decline. We do not find the term "curia generalis" (or its Gascon equivalent) in reference to any session in Agenais after 1289. Moreover, few plenary assemblies to the middle of the fourteenth century, even counting administrative gatherings, bear much resemblance to those previously described. There are several allusions to the general court in charters and confirmations, but these are not *de novo*, and the articles in question may be regarded as anachronistic.[57] Though the general army survives, we no longer see it in its old connection with the court.[58] As a judicial body the general court was certainly in abeyance, and perhaps had long been so, by the early fourteenth century. It appears from undated petitions of the time of Edward II that the barons wished to institute—or to revive—a high court of justice composed of nobles and town consuls of Agenais.[59] Their efforts were not successful.

[56] See Ducom, pp. 150–151; and no. 1, pp. 271–274; D. Nony, "La Monnaie Arnaudine: Essai de Numismatique," *Annales du Midi*, LXXI (1959), 10–12.

[57] Customs of Fumel, confirmed in 1297, *Arch. Gir.*, VII, 18, art. 12; A. Lagarde, *Tonneins*, p. 118, art. 25 (this charter contains new articles, but the one cited and many others correspond to articles in the customs of Marmande); A.N., JJ.72, fol. 150v; "Coutumes d'Agen," ed. Moullié, *Rec. Trav. Soc. Agen*, V (1850), 241–244, *vidimus* of 1370.

[58] C. Baradat de Lacaze, *Astafort en Agenais*, p. 200, charter of 1304; *Chartes d'Agen*, no. 145 (p. 281); "Chartes d'Agen," *Arch. Gir.*, XXXIII, no. 48; cf. P.R.O., Chancery Miscellanea (C 47), 26/13, art. 1, and *Chartes d'Agen*, no. 74, art. 1; no mention of lord's *ost* in the article, repeated from the Marmande charter, which speaks of the court, Lagarde, *Tonneins*, p. 118.

[59] P.R.O., Anc. Pet. (SC 8), 262/13092 (also C 47, 25/2/31), townsmen of Agenais concerning intentions of the nobles: "Item

The governors had given up the general court as a customary institution. They were usually able to cope with breaches of the peace without calling on their subjects, and, just as elsewhere in Languedoc, the peace was now less disturbed than it had been a century before. With the development of bureaucratic administration, it no longer seemed practical to retain an ungainly feudal tribunal. The summons of regional men was useful, to be sure, and officials felt free to widen it to include clergy and to employ convocations for new purposes. By doing so, however, they undermined what little institutional identity the general court had ever possessed. Possibly the lords and seneschals recognized that a customary assembly was potentially a privileged one. They were careful to preserve their prerogative unlimited. They may have noticed how the license they had allowed to the men of Agenais had enabled the latter to gain a measure of control over the bishop's authority.

Another reason for the decline of the general court was that the interests of nobles and townsmen diverged in the later thirteenth century. We still find expressions of an undivided community of Agenais on occasion;[60] but it

---

intendunt inpetrare quod judicia que fient in Agenesio fiant de consilio et acordo baronum, militum et consulum villarum Agennesii et id in quo maior pars conveniret teneretur, quod esset contra jus et in preiudicium domini nostri Regis et terre Agennesii, pro eo quia difficiliter convenirentur et cause non possent expediri et ille qui plures haberet amicos tam ratione nobilitatis quam pecunie et alias culpabilis evaderet qui deberet forsitan condempnari et condempnaretur eciam qui deberet absolvi." Cf. Chanc. Misc. (C 47), 30/1/27–28; Anc. Pet. (SC 8), 276/13776, 13783, wherein the prelates, nobles, and others with jurisdiction request a high court composed of prelates and nobles, as, they say, "observatum fuit diutissime in patria Agenesii." Art. 7 (30/1/28) again fails to mention towns in claiming that it was an old custom that the regional lord should swear to clergy and nobles of Agenais.

[60] *The War of Saint-Sardos (1323–1325): Gascon Correspondence and Diplomatic Documents*, ed. P. Chaplais (London, 1954),

became common for the different estates to deliberate separately on matters that concerned them individually. Some of the surviving petitions from men of one or more of the orders probably originated in assemblies of corresponding composition.[61] On certain questions there was outright hostility between the estates. Nobles and prelates accused townsmen of usurping their jurisdictions; townsmen accused nobles, and especially churchmen, of evading responsibility for public works and local expenses.[62] In major issues between government and nobility, such as the building of bastides and the limits of jurisdiction, the burghers were inclined to side with the government. Towns of Agenais seem to have supported Edward II faithfully, and they appreciated the advantages of efficient, nonfeudal justice. They opposed the desire of the lords to recover the jurisdiction of the general court.[63] This helped to seal the fate of the old assembly.

Changes in the realities of political geography were contributing to the same result. Agenais continued to have its own administration and its own assemblies in the later

---

no. 30, a deputation from prelates, nobles, and townsmen of Agenais in 1324; P.R.O., Chanc. Misc. (C 47), 29/8/2, a memorial of complaints against the French by nobles and towns in 1318; also 24/3/3; cf. entries in *Gascon Calendar*, nos. 1681, 2028, complaints "communitatis tocius Agennesii de injuriis eis [*sic*] factis per nobiles patrie illius," but the references are to a community of towns.

[61] See, e.g., *R.G.* II, no. 992; P.R.O., Chanc. Misc. (C 47), 25/4/5 (cf. *Chartes d'Agen*, no. 73, to be dated 1320, not 1286). As we have seen, the towns discussed their special problems at least as early as the 1220's. This matter is examined further below.

[62] *H.L.*, VII, *docs*, 419–426; *Chartes d'Agen*, nos. 58, 74 (p. 122), 101, 102; *R.G.*, II, no. 1056; III, no. 2129; P.R.O., Chanc. Misc. (C 47), 26/13.

[63] See *R.G.*, II, no. 992; Rymer, *Foedera*, II¹, 361, 475; P.R.O., Chanc. Misc., 25/2/31; and see n. 59 above.

thirteenth and fourteenth centuries; [64] but in some respects its old diocesan individuality was being compromised in the circumstances of general Aquitainian policy. We begin to hear of the association of men from several districts together, or from the whole duchy. In 1285, for instance, prelates, nobles, and towns of Gascony and Agenais, possibly in assembly, joined in submitting to the king an advisement concerning the "liberty" of those lands.[65] Assemblies of the duchy took place in the fourteenth century.[66] Meanwhile, the administrative subdivisions of Agenais gained more importance. Many new *baylies* were formed in the time of Edward I, and periodic judicial sessions were instituted in various assize towns. The district of Agen, set apart by older custom, retained its pre-eminence in the fourteenth century. There and elsewhere the government used local assemblies for proclamations and political purposes.[67]

[64] See Brit. Mus., Cotton. MS Julius E. 1, fols. 158–159v; "Chartes d'Agen se rapportant aux Règnes de Jean le Bon et de Charles V," *Arch. Gir.*, xxxiv (1899), no. 78, assembly of three estates of Agenais in 1363; the distinction between Gascony and Agenais is evident in *R.G.*, e.g., ii, no. 901; iii, no. 3265.

[65] P.R.O., Chanc. Misc. (C 47), 30/1/5, quoted by P. Chaplais, "Le Duché-Pairie de Guyenne: l'Hommage et les Services Féodaux de 1259 à 1303," *Annales du Midi*, lxix (1957), 23, n. 83. See also F.M. Powicke, *Thirteenth Century*, 2nd. ed., pp. 300–304, on the administrative unity of the duchy, and on ways in which the ordinance of 1289 for Agenais required officials there to administer holdings in neighboring dioceses; see also "Chartes d'Agen," *Arch. Gir.*, xxxiii, no. 65.

[66] P.R.O., Chanc. Misc. (C 47), 29/8/17; "Chartes d'Agen," *Arch. Gir.*, xxxiv, no. 81; B.N., Doat, cxvii, fols. 140ff.; cf. 129ff.

[67] *Chartes d'Agen*, no. 82; *Olim*, ii, 8, 13; A.N., JJ.36, fol. 9v; G.P. Cuttino, "The Process of Agen," *Speculum*, xix (1944), 171, no. 1. Also P.R.O., Chanc. Misc. (C 47), 29/8/17, seneschal of Gascony in 1318 directs the consuls of Agen to summon consuls of villages of the *assisiatus* of Agen for the purpose of electing proctors, along with other places in the duchy, to protest against French usurpations in the English domains; and cf. *War of Saint-*

ROYAL ASSEMBLIES IN THE SÉNÉCHAUSSÉES

Enough has been said already of the routine work done by judges, clerks, and other officials of the royal courts in Languedoc.[68] Local judicial and administrative activity under Philips III and IV no doubt increased in volume but did not change in character. Nobles, notables, and townsmen were often called on for assistance. The regular court sessions, or assizes, had special importance, for in addition to hearing suits, they provided an opportunity for discussion, for making announcements, and even for passing local laws.[69] The central government of Philip the Fair came to rely heavily on the assizes for giving publicity to legislation.[70] One suspects that these sessions sometimes turned into political assemblies.

Yet it is not so much the court as the seneschal, with his power to summon *ad hoc*, that must interest us. The court in its usual form was a local body, meeting at Béziers or Toulouse or Nîmes, but the seneschals' responsibilities comprised whole districts, even provinces. On important problems they sometimes felt it necessary to convoke distant men to court to give information, deliberate, or furnish counsel. The grain-export assemblies initiated under Louis IX were a special instance of this sort of work. The con-

---

Sardos, ed. Chaplais, no. 68 (p. 85), reference to general assemblies at Bordeaux, Marmande, and Agen.

[68] Ch. 4, pp. 138–140.

[69] *H.L.*, x, 174–177, 370–375, 389–392; L. Ménard, *Histoire Civile, Ecclésiastique, et Littéraire de la Ville de Nismes*, 7 vols. (Paris, 1750–1758), I, *pr.* no. 75, 105; no. 77, 106–107; no. 108, 135–136; B.N., MS Lat. 11017, p. 49; Doat, xlix, 325–327v; A. Baudouin, *Lettres*, no. 132; A.D. Aveyron, 2E178, no. 5, fol. 3.

[70] *H.L.*, x, 209,i; 230; 256–257,i; 270,vi; 272–273; *Ordonnances*, I, 316, 347, 360; B.M. Toulouse, MS 640, fols. 297–304; E. Roschach, *Inventaire des Archives Communales de la Ville de Toulouse . . .*, I (Toulouse, 1891), 40–41; B.N., Doat, xlix, 332–338v; li, 48v–50; A.N., JJ.36, fol. 9v; A.M. Montpellier, Arm. H, cass. 3, no. 3684; Baudouin, *Lettres*, nos. 133–134.

sultations after 1275 were usually less striking, though quite various. They show how the royal government continued to depend on feudal habits and obligations. In October 1275 the king directed the seneschal of Carcassonne to take counsel with "well-informed" men of the *sénéchaussée* about some long-standing, difficult questions relating to breaches of the peace.[71] From another case that we know more about, it is clear that deliberation and military service were still closely linked in administrative practice. On 18 September 1278 the seneschal of Carcassonne wrote out a summons for the seigneurial seneschal of Montfort to appear at Carcassonne on the following 8 October with his complement of knight service, in order to give *consilium* and *auxilium*. Additional letters according to the same form were sent to twenty-eight other knights of the region. The proceedings are reminiscent of the summons to garrison duty at Carcassonne in 1269, but the document was provided with a rubric that indicates a different explanation. The lord Sicard de Puylaurens had requested permission to fight a duel against the viscount of Lautrec, so it looks as though the seneschal were summoning his knights as peers on a point of French law.[72] If all the nobles brought their "service due" as requested,[73] this court must have had the identity of a feudal army. The same confusion—or conflation—of obligations shows up very

[71] *H.L.*, x, 131–132: ". . . mandamus vobis, quatinus habito consilio cum sapientibus senescallie vestre. . . ."

[72] *Ibid.*, 151–152: "DE CONVOCATIONE TERRARIORUM ET ALIORUM MILITUM, FACTA OCCASIONE APPELLATIONIS DUELLI, QUAM FECIT SICARDUS DE PODIO-LAURENTIO CONTRA D. AMALRICUM VICECOMITEM LAUTRICENSEM." I follow Molinier's explanation of the *appellatio duelli*, IX, 58, n. 4, 59. The seneschal had been directed to proceed "juxta consuetudines Francie" in cases concerning the king and the *terrarii*, Ménard, *Histoire de Nismes*, I, *pr.* no. 75, 104b. P. Timbal, *Coutume de Paris*, does not discuss this event, though it bears on his discussion at pp. 86–90.

[73] See ch. 2, p. 23, for this custom in earlier feudal practice.

clearly in a recognition made by a knight of Albigeois in 1286: "If it should happen," he avowed, "that the said lord king has business or war in the county of Toulouse and therefore convokes the armies [*sic*] or community of knights and nobles in the bishopric of Albi, I am obliged to follow him under arms through the whole county of Toulouse and serve him faithfully. . . ." [74]

There are some notable cases of legislative consultation in the *sénéchaussée* of Beaucaire. Early in 1281 the seneschal decided to take action in response to an angry volume of complaints against lords and "strong men" who had been troubling inhabitants and travelers by imposing new tolls and *péages* for their own profit. In an assembly at Nîmes he ordained that henceforth no one in the *sénéchaussée* should levy such tolls and that all impositions inaugurated in the past thirty years should be held null and void. The enactment was made with the advice of ten royal officials, including the major judge and eight local judges. Among the witnesses were the lords of Uzès and Alès, two nobles, a castellan, and three lawyers, but "many others" were not named. The judges and officers received pointed injunctions to take notice and enforce the law; this is why their counsel was required and recorded, and it may be the only reason why. [75] Then in June 1302 another seneschal convoked a large assembly in the assizes at Alès. Objections had been voiced in the courts against secret and fraudulent donations. This practice was now declared illegal and the gifts were nullified. The seneschal enacted the ordinance, with

[74] A.M. Cordes, CC.27: "si contingeret quod dictus dominus Rex haberet negocia seu guerram in comitatu Tholosano et propter hoc congregaret excercitus sive comunitatem militum et nobilium in episcopatu Albiensi, debeo ipsum sequi cum armis per totum comitatum Tholosanum et servire ei fideliter. . . ." Cf. *H.F.*, XXIII, 781–783, some statements of military obligations in 1272.

[75] *H.L.*, x, 174–175; Langlois, *Philippe III*, p. 327. Unusual precautions were taken to ensure that the ordinance would be written publicly just as it was passed, *H.L.*, x, 175–177.

the special advice of the major judge, "according to the counsel of barons, informed men,[76] judges, nobles, and burghers." As usual, the names are not all given, but the list does specify seven lords and nobles, two clerics and a lawyer, ten royal officials, including four judges, the seigneurial vicar of Alès, and a consul of Alès.[77] Again, as in 1281, the witnesses were a group distinct from those who gave approval. Again too, though the seneschal took advice, it does not follow that he felt constitutionally obliged to do so. In 1302 the consultation probably had considerable value for publicizing the law, a law which itself made publicity a requisite for legality. The clause indicating counsel was cited when the ordinance was confirmed three decades later.[78] It would be instructive to know how such assemblies were planned. The seneschals could probably rely to some extent on the normal attendance at assizes. Yet some of the notables must have received summonses. In both courts described above, men from distant parts of the *sénéchaussée* were on hand; and in 1302 came individuals from Gévaudan and Aigues-Mortes, a hundred miles apart. On the latter occasion the consul of Alès was an informal deputy ex officio, without a mandate.[79] It is unlikely that towns were asked to send delegates to either meeting.[80]

A remarkable case of legislation in the *sénéchaussée* of

[76] But the word I so translate, "peritorum," may be a contraction of "jurisperitorum."

[77] *H.L.*, x, 390–392.

[78] B.N., MS Lat. 11016, fol. 10rv: "Cum olim per dictum Johannem de Arreblayo militem senescallum tunc dicte senescallie, de consilio baronum, peritorum, iudicum, nobilium et plurium aliorum in assiziis Alesti tunc existentium, statuerit quod donationes. . . ."

[79] He is twice mentioned as "consul ut dicebatur Alesti," *H.L.*, x, 391; cf. 392.

[80] For a somewhat comparable instance of counsel in a royal court, held at Tarascon (Ariège) in 1272, see *ibid.*, 103–107; but these proceedings were more strictly judicial.

Carcassonne may now be considered. In the later 1260's a conflict arose between the lord of Clermont and his villagers. The trouble was that the community wanted the privileges of a corporation, according to the principles of Roman law, and the lord was resisting this move toward independence. The same problem was developing in many places of southern and eastern Languedoc as legal knowledge spread through the unprivileged hinterlands. The men of Clermont especially wished to appoint their own syndics or administrators free of their lord's control.[81] Brought before the seneschal's court at Béziers, the case dragged on for more than two years. Finally, in 1270 or early in 1271, Guillaume de Cohardon announced a decision against the villagers. They were not to have their own officials, who might be used to "raise horns" against the lord. They could only have temporary syndics for judicial needs, and these representatives were to be chosen by a method entirely under the lord's control.[82]

Thus far the proceedings were judicial, but the case had political implications that did not escape the seneschal. Many a lord in the vicinity of Béziers had restive villagers to whom he would like to see this decision applied. Especially firm in their opposition to municipal privileges were the prelates. The celebrated archbishop of Narbonne who

[81] A study of this subject is much needed. See meanwhile P. Viollet, *Institutions*, III, 14–15, 18, 22, 59–69; Beaumanoir, *Coutumes de Beauvaisis*, ed. A. Salmon, I, cc. 154–173; *Layettes*, II, 620a; R. Grand, *Les Paix d'Aurillac* (Paris, 1945), pp. 52–53; *Olim*, I, 933, no. 24; *Cartulaire de la Ville de Lodève*, ed. E. Martin (Montpellier, 1900), no. 58; G. de Burdin, *Documents Historiques sur la Province de Gévaudan*, II, 183–193; *C.A.*, II, no. 1820; A.D. Gard, E.Suppl. 530 (Aimargues, FF.1); *H.L.*, X, 449–452; *Ordonnances*, XII, 454.

[82] A.M. Aniane, AA.3, 14th-century copy of a statute dated 13 February 1271. It has not been generally known that this important text is preserved. Dognon, *Institutions*, pp. 131–132, cited it from late and faulty references and was unable to date the assembly accurately or precisely.

later became Pope Clement IV (1265–1268) had served as arbiter in a number of these disputes in past years, and his decisions invariably had been favorable to the lords. In fact, the Clermont case was settled in the very terms of one of those earlier decisions.[83] Approval of a general ordinance to the same effect could be obtained easily in an assembly properly composed.

The opportunity presented itself in February 1271 in a meeting at Béziers. In attendance were the bishops of Toulouse, Béziers, and Lodève, and the bishop-elect of Carcassonne; the abbots of Saint-Paul of Narbonne, Saint-Pons-de-Thomières, Saint-Guilhem-du-Désert, Lodève, Saint-Hilaire, Quarante, Saint-Jacques, and Saint-Aphrodise of Béziers, and "many other men" skilled in both laws. The abbot of Saint-Aphrodise, a local knight, three royal judges, and three lawyers are identified as special consultants to the seneschal; and still other names, mostly ecclesiastical officials, figure in the list of those who advised or approved. The seneschal acted with their "common counsel" and that "of many other wise men congregated in common council at Béziers." He ordained that the verdict on Clermont should now be the law throughout the *viguerie* of Béziers. Lords were authorized to take action against any of their villagers who ventured to organize general syndicates.[84]

[83] A.M. Aniane, AA.3: ". . . Tandem predictus senescallus, volens utrique parti super hiis utiliter providere, domini Guidonis Fulcodii quondam archiepiscopi Narbonensis vestigiis inherendo, qui in casu consimili tam apud Caunas quam in multis aliis locis salubriter modo consimili ordinavit, vocatis . . . ordinavit. . . ." See also *Cartulaire de Lodève*, nos. 56, 58; A.M. Agde, AA.1: important cases at Lodève and Agde around 1260.

[84] A.M. Aniane, AA.3: ". . . assidentibus predicto domino senescallo domino Petro . . . [follow names of consultants and guarantors] et multis aliis bonis viris quibus recitatis a predictis prelatis plurimum comendatis, predictus senescallus, de comuni consilio ipsorum et domini Rayambaudi, sui judicis, et magistri Bartholo-

This statute remained in effect for a long time. Early in the fourteenth century it was cited in royal regulations, which do not fail to remark that the law was made by the seneschal in consultation with men of the *sénéchaussée*. "With the counsel of prelates *and barons*": so the phrase recurs,[85] and, indeed, it is likely enough that the "many other wise men" mentioned in the statute as we have it included some lay nobles. Nevertheless, the scribes who wrote these later documents had evidently not read the statute carefully. This impression is supported by the fact that the law was often mistaken as a prohibition of con-

---

mei de Podio, domini regis Francie clerici, judicis Carcassone, magistri Symonis de Carcassona, judicis Biterris, magistri Bernardi de Porciano, officialis Carcassone, magistri Raymundi Crassensis, canonici Sancti Pauli Narbone, et multorum aliorum sapientium congregatorum in comuni consilio Biterrensi, ordinavit, statuit et edixit de creatione sindicorum in dicto castro Clarismontis et in omnibus aliis villis et castris, que sunt in juridictione domini regis Francie in vicaria Biterrensi, ita perpetuo, ut superius statuit, edixit et mandavit inviolabiliter observari, ne ipsis universitatibus cum opus fuerit sindicorum comoditas subtrahatur, et ne occasione perpetuorum sindicorum et generalium eis detur materia adversus dominos malignandi, et si que universitates castrorum vel villarum predictas vel aliqui de ipsis adversus predicta aliquid presumpserint atemptare, a dominis quibus subsunt vel suberunt debite puniantur et per juris remedia disistere compellantur vel per superiorem propter eorum negligantiam vel deffectum. Actum Biterris, anno dominice incarnationis millesimo ducentesimo septuagesimo, idus Febroarii, in presentia et testimonio magistri Raymundi Vayreti, canonici Lodovensis, magistri Hugonis, officialis Lodovensis, domini Poncii, archidiaconi Carcassone, domini Petri de Sancto Justo, archidiaconi Biterris, magistri Amelii Mercati, domini Guirardi Ermengaudi de Biterris, domini Guillelmi Aymardi, domini Petri Siguarii, militis, et mei, Petri de Parisius de Podio Nauterio, notarii publici domini regis Francie, qui hec scripsi, . . . et signavi. Hoc est transcriptum . . . [written in 1328 by royal order]."

[85] Italics mine. See *Ordonnances*, XII, 436, 453, 454; *H.L.*, X, 449 (also in *Les Archives de la Cour des Comptes . . . de Montpellier*, ed. E. Martin-Chabot [Paris, 1907], pp. 196–197, but misdated and poorly edited).

sulates.[86] These later references may have some value, however, as an indication of the prevailing constitutional theory of the fourteenth century. A law designed to be generally applicable ought to have the approval of clergy and nobles.[87]

Let us now consider how it happened that the prelates and magnates who counseled the seneschal in 1271 were assembled at Béziers. The text makes it clear that they were there for other reasons.[88] The statute was dated 13 February, and luckily we have further information about the doings of the same prelates in Béziers on that day.

It will be recalled that the seneschal had been trying for some time to collect fealties and recognitions of fiefs in the *viguerie* of Béziers. At least one assembly had already been called for that purpose. Then, in a convocation at Béziers on 9 February, prelates of the region presented Cohardon with a set of articles alleging encroachments on their jurisdictional and political rights.[89] The first of these articles is of special interest from our point of view. In it the churchmen claimed that the seneschal, or officials of his court, had attempted to summon them in an unprecedented and improper way, namely, by means of a public crier [90]— the usual method of summoning townsfolk to the public parliament.[91] The prelates probably resented its implications. If their charge had any truth, then they must already

---

[86] See *Ordonnances,* XII, 453, 454; Dognon, *Institutions,* pp. 131–132; cf. *H.L.,* x, 449, 534–535,ii.

[87] Cf. note above.

[88] A.M. Aniane, AA.3: "Noverint universi quod, cum venerabiles patres . . . [bishops, abbots, lawyers] et . . . senescallus Carcassone et Biterris in domo domini episcopi Biterrensis apud Biterrem convenissent pro quibusdam negociis pertractandis. . . ." The historians of councils do not mention a synod at Béziers at this time.

[89] See above, pp. 164–165.

[90] B.N., Doat, CLV, 50v–51 (Appendix II, no. 6, pp. 319–320).

[91] See Appendix I, p. 301.

have been in Béziers for their own reasons, and the seneschal had tried to take advantage of that circumstance. The seneschal denied the accusation, saying that the summons of prelates to acknowledge feudal holdings had been made "decently and honorably through his patent letter." He referred them to the text of the letter of 1 December 1270, which they seem to have ignored. He protested that he had not caused them to be summoned by crier, and expressed his disapproval of such a procedure "if it was done." [92] Thus at the very start of Philip III's reign, the royal summons is assuming a legal, even privileged, character. It was not a question of the right to be summoned, which existed only in the judicial sense that the touching of interests entitled their possessors to a hearing. But it was becoming clear that the summons must be administered according to recognized and formal precedent.

This assembly at Béziers on 9 February 1271 had the composition of a large provincial council. It numbered five bishops, including Bertrand of Toulouse, acting for himself and the absent archbishop of Narbonne, as well as the abbots of nine monasteries, and "many other priors and the proctors of other abbots and . . . many other ecclesiastical persons." This is a fuller list than the one already recited for the legislative meeting four days later, but so far as the names are given, there is considerable correspondence. It is clear enough that we are dealing with two sessions of the same general assembly; and, like that of the thirteenth, the gathering of 9 February is described in one place as a "common council." [93] The seneschal's counter-

[92] B.N., Doat, CLV, 51v (Appendix II, p. 320). The prelates may well have had the canon law on summonses in mind. This required a formal citation, specifying time, reasonable place, and legitimate cause. See *Decretum*, dist. 18, c. 13*Si episcopus*, and *glos. ord.*; Innocent IV, *Apparatus* to *Extra*, I, 33, 9*Quod super*; cf. *Rhetorica Ecclesiastica*, ed. Wahrmund, *Quellen* . . . , I, iv, 88–89; "Der Ordo Judiciarius 'Scientiam,' " *ibid.*, II, i, 36–37.

[93] B.N., Doat, CLV, 50v–51v (Appendix II, pp. 319–320). Cf. n. 84 above.

proposals were presented in the earlier session, followed by another appeal for compliance with the royal mandate. We then hear of a postponement until the next Friday, which was 13 February, when Guillaume de Cohardon again convened with the prelates [94] in the episcopal hall at Béziers. It was in this session that the seneschal, though conceding nothing and reserving the king's rights, announced a delay in the fealty proceedings pending further instructions from the king. The statute on syndicates then came up for consideration and approval. Clearly, the seneschal had not succeeded in his objectives with the free-spirited prelates of his district. But he had placed them in such a position that further resistance would be difficult; and there were soon to be more serious encounters. He had passed a law that would apply in their own domains, a serviceable precedent, and implicated them in a measure that was likely to be unpopular with many people.

Clergy and laity were associated in other assemblies at the close of the thirteenth century when Philip the Fair came into conflict with the Inquisition. These can best be described as ceremonial bodies, for it is doubtful that they resulted from any very organized summons. In April 1299, on the instance of the seneschal's lieutenant, many lords of the Carcassonne area convened in the city with the bishops of Albi and Béziers, the abbots of Lagrasse, Saint-Papoul, Saint-Pons, and Fontfroide, and the inquisitors Nicholas d'Abbeville and Bertrand de Clermont. Their object was to effect a reconciliation with the men of Carcassonne, who had been holding out, under religious censures, against the excesses of the local inquisition. Despite conciliatory overtures, the townsmen decided to continue their resistance.[95]

[94] However, the bishops alone are mentioned in an abbreviated phrase, Doat, CLV, 53v (Appendix II, p. 321); cf. A.M. Aniane, AA.3, *loc. cit.* above, n. 84.

[95] *H.L.*, X, 278–281; H. C. Lea, *History of the Inquisition*, II, 69–70; G. W. Davis, *The Inquisition at Albi, 1299–1300* (N.Y., 1948), pp. 57–58.

But in a second, somewhat similar assembly the next fall, the Church succeeded in bringing Carcassonne to terms.[96] The king was now actively regulating inquisitorial procedure. The notorious Albi trials of 1299–1300 further inflamed a smouldering discontent among the laity of western Languedoc.[97] Finally Philip IV personally visited the Midi, and encountered a flood of complaints. He held a major assembly at Toulouse in January 1304 which was composed of prelates, barons, lawyers, and counselors. Nothing is said of towns, though we know that they presented complaints through deputies. In fact, there is no detailed attendance list, which suggests that the assembly was not systematically administered. Any gathering of influential notables to sound out and consult would satisfy the king's purposes. On 13 January he issued a conciliatory ordinance which hardly went beyond his earlier pronouncements on the Inquisition. The text is in the form of a royal patent letter, but the specific provisions are worded impersonally. Careful deliberation with the assembly is noted, and it looks as if that body were indeed legislating.[98] Its constitutive role, however, was probably more apparent than real, the consequence of another of those difficult situations in which Philip the Fair often found himself.[99]

The assemblies held by officials of Philip III to collect fealties and recognitions of fiefs have already been treated at length.[100] Less is known about the administration of Philip IV in this regard, which is perhaps not surprising in view of the fact that Languedoc was a settled royal territory when he came to the throne in 1285. Yet it is clear that

[96] Lea, II, 70; J. Guiraud, *Histoire de l'Inquisition au Moyen Age*, 2 vols. (Paris, 1935–1938), II, 373–376.

[97] *H.L.*, x, 273–278,i–vii; Davis, *Albi*, pp. 35–71; Lea, II, 71–72, 76–77.

[98] *H.L.*, x, 428–431.

[99] Cf. J. R. Strayer, "Philip the Fair—a 'Constitutional' King," *A.H.R.*, LXII (1956), 25–31.

[100] Ch. 4, pp. 163–185.

the young king lost no time in arranging to secure his southern inheritance. At Carcassonne on 18 October 1285, a scant two weeks after his father's death, Philip notified the nobles, townsmen, and clergy of Languedoc that he had commissioned the archbishop of Narbonne and lord of Mirepoix to receive their oaths of fidelity. They were to travel on circuit, visiting towns.[101] Nothing was said in the directive to indicate how the commissioners might use the summons.

Some scraps of evidence for their proceedings in Rouergue and Albigeois have come to light. On 3 December they were in the *baylie* of Najac, probably at the royal castle, where they received the submissions of nobles and town consuls.[102] We may be sure that a summons had been issued and that most of the work was done in a *baylie*-assembly. The consuls of Najac, Saint-Antonin, Verfeil, Cadoulette, La Salvetat, and La Bastide are listed. They undoubtedly made personal and representative oaths like those tendered in 1249 and 1271. At the request of the seneschal of Rouergue, the curial notary of Najac began to record fealties and recognitions of fiefs on 25 January 1286.[103] His register showed activity in the *baylie* of Peyrusse as well as Najac;[104] and other *baylies* of Rouergue may have been accounted for in like manner. As for Albigeois, a noble's recognition at Cordes on 8 March 1286 shows that the seneschal of Toulouse-Albigeois had sub-delegated authority to receive such acts locally.[105] But we

[101] *H.L.*, x, 198: "[commissioners are sent] . . . ut fidelitatis juramenta nobis prestanda vice nostra recipiant a vobis & vestrum quibuslibet dictaque loca visitent. . . ."

[102] A.D. Aveyron, 2E178, no. 26.

[103] *Ibid.*, no. 27; *H.F.*, xxiv, "Chronologie des Baillis . . . ," 225.

[104] L. Delisle, who found this document in a bookstore, printed excerpts in *H.F.*, xxiv, 225. Professor Strayer kindly referred me to B.N., MS Lat. 17734, evidently the same manuscript, and his notes show that the Peyrusse work was done in a general assembly too.

[105] A.M. Cordes, CC.27.

do not know whether an assembly met for this reason in the *baylie* of Cordes. Apparently, therefore, the royal officials commenced by convoking men of the *baylies* to do fealty and then left it to the seneschals to obtain and record recognitions of fiefs and revenues as they saw fit.[106] This procedure resembled that followed in 1271 in Toulousain and Agenais. But in the earlier campaign, the *baylie*-assemblies had been accompanied by general convocations; and we may further recall that Edward I ordered a central assembly of Agenais for the same purpose in 1286. So it is a fact worth remarking that French officials in Languedoc did not convoke major assemblies for political administration in 1285–1286 at the accession of Philip the Fair.[107]

The large convocation continued to be thought of as a device for the special circumstances of taking first seisin. Such an occasion presented itself in 1293, when the first important assembly at Montpellier in the name of a king of France was held. By an exchange agreement with the bishop of Maguelonne, Philip had assumed direct control over parts of the Montpellier barony, and suzerainty over the king of Majorca for the rest. The seneschal of Beaucaire had responsibility for making the transaction known and putting it into effect. On 16 April 1293, in the Minorite cloister, he convened with some barons of the *sénéchaussée*, royal officials, the Majorcan lieutenant, and citizens of Montpellier. He read the act of exchange to them and ac-

---

[106] The method was probably somewhat different in the *sénéchaussées* of lower Languedoc, with their larger *vigueries*. See B.N., Doat, LX, 64v–65, royal directive of 4 February 1286 that the seneschal and bishop should receive fealties from the men of Béziers in common (*vidimus* by archbishop of Narbonne, bishops of Agde and Elne, 25 March 1286). Cf. *H.L.*, v, 1582, nos. 227, 228, fealties to archbishop by bishops of Toulouse and Uzès in spring 1286.

[107] Cf. B.N., Doat, VII, 230–231, notification of a royal commission to investigate the feudal holdings of clergy, townsmen and nobles in the *sénéchaussée* of Carcassonne, 18 December 1291.

cordingly took formal possession of the former episcopal
rights for the king. He received oaths of fealty from the
inhabitants, and appointed a temporary lieutenant, who
swore, in turn, to uphold the local customs; and, finally, he
undertook some regulatory negotiations with the official for
Majorca.[108] We are reminded of the strikingly similar situation and ceremonial in the great convocation of August
1279, when Agenais passed under English lordship.[109] But
the two assemblies differed markedly, and significantly, in
composition.

Consultation on Grain Export

Only one type of royal assembly in French Languedoc
can be said to have had a legal existence, like that of the
general court of Agenais, in the later thirteenth century.
The laws of 1254 requiring the seneschals to consult men of
the three orders when regulating the export of provisions
long remained in effect; indeed, though revised in their application, they were never repealed under the *ancien
régime*.[110] However, they were not immediately extended
to the *sénéchaussées* aquired by the crown in 1271. The
relatively fertile uplands of Languedoc were less subject to
grain shortages than the coastal plain and their merchants
less attracted to the markets of overseas enemies than those
of Beaucaire, Montpellier, and Narbonne.[111] We hear occasionally of consultation about the grain supply in Tou-

[108] A.M. Montpellier, Arm. C, cass. 18, no. 1490; *H.L.*, IX, 168–
169; A. Germain, *Commune de Montpellier*, II, 96–120, 286–297,
304–308.

[109] Above, pp. 235–238.

[110] A. Dupont, "Ordonnances Royales de 1254," pp. 234–235.
Seigneurial regulation of exportation continued at Narbonne in the
later 13th century, B.N., Doat, XLVIII, 188v; L, 439–440; LI, 89v–
92; cf. A.N., J.320, no. 78.

[111] See *Livre de Comptes de Jacme Olivier*, p. 851. Cf., for a
later period, P. Wolff, *Commerces et Marchands*, pp. 172ff., esp.
179.

lousain and Rouergue during the reign of Philip IV. But the assemblies mentioned were not composed in accordance with the royal statutes for lower Languedoc.[112]

In the districts of Beaucaire and Carcassonne the trade in provisions was much regulated after 1275.[113] The seneschals, when ruling on the transport of grain, may sometimes have convoked assemblies in the prescribed way. Yet it is not certain that they did in any instance, and quite clear that some pronouncements were issued on their own authority alone.[114] A new factor bearing on the situation was that the kings were taking a more direct interest in the coastal trade. From the 1270's on, there seems to have been a kind of standing interdict on the export of provisions from the kingdom of France.[115] This put the city of Montpellier in a precarious position; and it sufficiently explains a long series of royal privileges granted to the inhabitants. They were to be supplied without hindrance, despite bans on export, provided that Montpellier would not serve as a port for further trade overseas.[116]

Moreover, the crown could legislate on the local grain

[112] A.M. Toulouse, layette 87 (also AA.5, no. 208, 25 March 1305); cf. A.M. Cordes, HH.5; A.D. Aveyron, 2E178, no. 2, fols. 8b, 106va.

[113] A.M. Montpellier, Arm. B, cass. 20, nos. 1040, 1080; A. Germain, *Commerce de Montpellier*, I, *p.j.*, no. 51, 284; *H.L.*, x, 249,iv; 427–428.

[114] See *H.L.*, x, 249,iv; A.M. Montpellier, Arm. B, cass. 20, nos. 1078, 1079, 1083; Baudouin, *Lettres*, no. 53; *H.L.*, x, 427–428; *Livre de Comptes de Jacme Olivier*, *p.j.*, no. 68A, 671–672.

[115] A.M. Millau, c.1 (2nd inv., no. 145); Langlois, *Philippe III*, p. 347; Germain, *Commerce*, *p.j.*, no. 51, 284; A.M. Montpellier, Arm. B, cass. 20, nos. 1077, 1080; *Ordonnances*, I, 351–352; etc.

[116] Germain, *p.j.*, no. 51, 284; A.M. Montpellier, Arm. B, cass. 20, nos. 1041, 1076–1078, 1081, 1083. The men of Montpellier were sometimes freed from the restrictions of the general embargo, B.N., MS Lat. 11017, p. 10v; MS Lat. 9192, fol. 69; A.M. Montpellier, Arm. B, cass. 20, nos. 1079, 1081, 1085; *H.L.*, x, 518,vi.

trade over the seneschal's head, as had happened in 1259. Thus in 1290 the king suspended a regulation against transport from one *sénéchaussée* to another, and the seneschals were overruled on other occasions too.[117] In these circumstances, and in view of the constant changes in short-run market conditions, the seneschals often must have been tempted to dispense with the cumbersome procedure of convoking general assemblies whenever the situation required it. Yet however convenient, this neglect constituted a transgression in the one small area of administrative authority in which the seneschal happened to be most restricted—subject to the king and obligated to the men of the *sénéchaussée*. By the later 1290's discontent had been aroused, the constitutional dimension of the statutes of 1254 was recalled, and the clergy of Languedoc protested to the king. They charged that the seneschals had placed interdicts on the export of grain from their districts without royal mandate or consultation with prelates and barons. Accordingly, in March 1300 Philip IV ordered the seneschals of Beaucaire and Carcassonne to make no further rulings of this sort, unless by special royal license, or in case of necessity, in which instance they should enact, or revoke, prohibitions only upon "diligent deliberation" with those prelates and barons "who can conveniently be present."[118] This pronouncement manifestly recalls the legislation of Louis IX, save that townsmen are granted no place in the assembly prescribed. Apparently the clerical petition had neglected to mention the right of towns to participate in the decision on grain export. In like manner, it may be remarked, certain petitions from Agenais magnates a few years later passed over in silence the accus-

---

[117] *H.L.*, x, 249,iv; also A.M. Millau, c.1 (2nd inv., no. 145); Baudouin, *Lettres*, no. 53; A.M. Montpellier, Arm. B, cass. 20, nos. 1079, 1083.

[118] Baudouin, *Lettres*, no. 53.

tomed attendance of town consuls in the general court of Agenais.[119]

There are some indications that the officials attended better to their obligations after 1300. Royal policy against the export of provisions from the kingdom was confirmed, and the seneschals were even more frequently supervised by the king in the matter.[120] A case of 1304 illustrates these points and shows, moreover, just how Philip the Fair conceived that an assembly of the *sénéchaussée* might function. The men of the Carcassonne district had petitioned the king that, in the general embargo on foodstuffs, an exception be allowed for wine, of which there was a local oversupply. The king informed the seneschal that he had granted the petition. But he requested that an assembly of "faithful men" and town consuls, such as appear useful in the matter, be summoned anyway, so that, "with speedy deliberation," the administrative arrangements could be worked out.[121] Whether this assembly met we do not know. Another local ban in 1308 was probably made in the approved way.[122]

The amendment seems to have been enough to satisfy the political sensitivities of Languedoc. Consultation on the supply of provisions figured among the remonstrances presented by southern towns to Louis X at his accession in 1315. But it was not so much the recognized right to be consulted as the freedom to export that they sought. In other words, while conceding that temporary interdicts

[119] P.R.O., Chanc. Misc. (C 47), 30/1/27–28; Anc. Pet. (SC 8), 276/13776, 13783.

[120] *Ordonnances*, I, 351–352, 381, 424–425; A.M. Montpellier, Arm. B, cass. 20, nos. 1080, 1081, 1085; *H.L.*, x, 518,vi. A major department of administration was enforcing the ban, *Comptes Royaux (1285–1314)*, eds. R. Fawtier, F. Maillard, 3 vols. (Paris, 1953–1956), I, 617–618.

[121] *H.L.*, x, 427–428. The wording suggests that the king intended no concession to the procedural principle *quod omnes tangit . . .* in relation to administrative rights.

[122] A.M. Montpellier, Arm. B, cass. 20, no. 1083.

might sometimes be necessary, the towns wished to abandon the standing embargo of the previous reign. The king granted their petition in a provision of a major reform ordinance for Languedoc promulgated on 1 April 1315. This was a confirmation of the statute of 1254, and indeed something more than that. For the first time, the requirement that the seneschal deliberate with men of the three estates when it is a question of banning the export of foodstuffs was extended to and made generally applicable in all districts of the Midi.[123]

The history of the legislation on grain export after 1315 lies beyond the scope of this book. Suffice it to say that the seneschals did summon general assemblies in conformity with the statutes.[124] In the fourteenth century the community was becoming increasingly conscious of its right to be consulted. The concept of a regional council was evolving; and it may be that the "whole council" of the *séné-chaussée* of Beaucaire mentioned in 1321 in connection with certain statutes was thought of as analogous to the sort of assembly that customarily deliberated on the supply of provisions.[125] If so, one could say that there was developing an institutionalized general assembly in the *séné-*

[123] *Ordonnances,* I, 553. The ordinance was despatched separately, under appropriate address, to seneschals and towns of Languedoc. See generally A. Artonne, *Le Mouvement de 1314 et les Chartes Provinciales de 1315* (Paris, 1912), pp. 46–48, 152–153; and cf. A.M. Toulouse, AA.3, no. 172, with A.M. Montauban, AA.2, fol. 67; etc. Louis X had previously confirmed his father's policy, B.N., Doat, VIII, 81–82v.

[124] A.M. Montpellier, Arm. B, cass. 20, no. 1048; cf. nos. 1045, 1047; Arm. A, cass. 18, no. 359 (references to regional statutes, and consultation in seneschal's *curia,* all dating from 1333–1341); other instances could probably be found.

[125] B.N., MS Lat. 11016, fol. 214: "In statutis senescallie Bellicadri factis cum toto consilio ipsius senescallie . . ."; see also *Archives de la Cour des Comptes . . . de Montpellier,* ed. Martin-Chabot, *documents,* no. 70, p. 141; and cf. *H.L.,* x, 610, and Dognon, *Institutions,* p. 199.

chaussée. But these are questions for the historians of Estates in Languedoc.

Military Obligation and Taxation

Most of the assemblies thus far considered in this chapter conformed to pre-existent patterns of seigneurial or royal administration, or custom, or statute. Some changes occurred, to be sure; but little was obliterated in practice—and nothing at all in theory—after the passing of Louis IX and Alfonse. Yet there were also some novel developments of great importance in this period. Philip III was hardly settled on the throne when a private war broke out in defiance of royal authority. The resulting campaign of Foix proved to be but the first of a series of conflicts involving the king of France that were to weigh on the men of Languedoc for generations to come. Successive military crises, breaking the peace of the thirteenth century, provided occasions for diverse and unusual assemblies and negotiations. Many of these had little or no precedent in the earlier experience of Languedoc. Martial convocations increased in size and were more systematically administered. Under royal pressure, the nature and extent of military obligations became the subject of a continuing discussion between crown and community. And finally, for the first time, taxation by the king became a cause for the summons of assemblies in Languedoc.

The count of Foix was the last independent magnate of Languedoc. His resistance in 1272 resulted in a massive demonstration of royal power. In addition to summoning the feudal levies of the entire kingdom to duty, Philip III called out the militia of townsmen and villagers. Men of the South were to join the expedition at Toulouse a month after Easter (24 May), and the king arrived there with the bulk of the army on 25 May.[126] General summonses had been published in the *sénéchaussées.* The vicars and bayles

---

[126] Langlois, *Philippe III*, pp. 59–61; *H.L.*, IX, 11–16; X, 116, 119, and *Notes*, 9–11.

probably administered the convocations locally and headed the contingents from their districts. Barons led their own knights, as was customary.[127] During the march southward from Toulouse, the king of Aragon appeared. He took up the rebel's cause in a conference with the military leaders at Boulbonne. But when the count of Foix rejected the terms there agreed upon, the army proceeded to besiege the stronghold of Foix. On 5 June the count capitulated; he was imprisoned at Carcassonne, and a royal seneschal was installed in his domains.[128]

Subsequent military convocations were administered in similar fashion. In the summer of 1276, when uprisings threatened the French government in Navarre, royal commissioners ordered general levies in all the *sénéchaussées* of Languedoc.[129] Almost simultaneously a turn of events contrary to French interests in Castille drew another large army to the Midi, but it is unlikely that many men of Languedoc participated in this expedition, which broke up ignominiously in the Gascon Pyrenees.[130] Not until 1282 do we find much detailed information about the procedure of local summons. Military preparations by the king of Aragon occasioned a defensive muster in the border lands. The decision this time was made, or announced, in an assembly at Carcassonne composed of royal officials and lords of the *sénéchaussée*. The seneschal's convocation letter spoke of "important affairs" concerning the king. News of

[127] *H.F.*, xxiii, 782–783.

[128] Chron. de Berdoues, *H.L.*, viii, 215; Langlois, p. 61.

[129] *Histoire de la Guerre de Navarre en 1276 et 1277 par Guillaume Anelier de Toulouse*, ed. F. Michel (Paris, 1856), cc. 91, 97; Guillaume de Nangis, *H.F.*, xx, 504–507; Primat, tr. J. Vignay, *H.F.*, xxiii, 94; *H.L.*, ix, 51–54. Castellans were responsible for calling out the local populace to service in the *sénéchaussée* of Carcassonne, A.D. Aude, B.1219, no. 2. The *terrarii* had been called to preparedness by the seneschal in December 1274, *H.L.*, x, 124–125; cf. Langlois, p. 98.

[130] Langlois, pp. 99, 104–107; *H.L.*, ix, 54.

the Sicilian Vespers (30 March 1282) apparently had not yet reached Carcassonne when the assembly met on 25 May. It was agreed that the seneschal should summon the knights and nobles of his district "in horses and in arms" to service at Carcassonne on 16 June; castellans and vicars were to convoke and lead the local contingents.[131] New plans were probably made when news of the Sicilian disaster arrived. In mid-July the vicar of Béziers directed his subordinate bayles to muster the knights in nine different localities. They were to appear at Béziers ready to serve on 8 August 1282. Messengers carried these orders from town to town where they were made public.[132]

The great vassals of the *sénéchaussée* of Carcassonne received another summons in the spring of 1283 on the occasion of the famous duel between Peter of Aragon and Charles of Anjou.[133] Clearly the Carcassonne lords who held their fiefs according to French custom were bearing the brunt of the military load in Languedoc. They were again convoked as a group for service in the crusade against Aragon in 1285; then twice recalled in the year following the French retreat; and summoned yet again in 1289, in company with "other men at arms," to meet new threats on the Spanish border.[134] The seneschals of Toulouse, Beaucaire, and Carcassonne are said to have led contingents of nobles and militia in the expedition to Aragon.[135] Most

---

[131] *H.L.*, IX, 80–81. Philip III received word of the revolt at the end of May, Langlois, pp. 139–140.

[132] B.N., Doat, CLV, 156–159v; 154–155 evidently relates to the same summons, not that of 1283 as Molinier states, *H.L.*, IX, 89, n. 1.

[133] *Ibid.*, 89.

[134] *Ibid.*, 103, 123–125, 140, and n. 2; X, 236–238,ii,vi; B.M. Toulouse, MS 640, fol. 302. The viscount of Narbonne contributed his feudal levy to the campaign of summer 1286.

[135] Desclot, *Cronica*, ed. Coll i Alentorn, 5 vols. (Barcelona, 1949–1951), IV, c. 137; *H.L.*, IX, 103; see also X, 195–196,ii; and J. Petit, *Essai de Restitution des Plus Anciens Mémoriaux de la*

likely the convocations were carried out as in previous campaigns.

Under Philip the Fair, procedures of the military summons come into clearer focus. Numerous armies were proclaimed for duty in Aquitaine and the North between 1294 and 1314. Precedent and experience were serving to establish a standard practice and routine. It is striking to find that in numbers and function the militia levies of Narbonne in 1285 correspond precisely to those of Agen for the Gascon war in 1296.[136] The towns now invariably received summonses, even for local campaigns, thus opening the way to financial compositions if the service were not rendered.[137] The crown tended to survey local operations closely. The king or special deputies would order levies in the *sénéchaussées,* and the men of Languedoc were reluctant to respond to summonses not so authorized.[138] Moreover, the use of central lists made possible a better regulation of the southern contribution to national armies. Such lists must have been convenient for the administration of the central assemblies of the kingdom that began to meet in this period. Few lords of Languedoc are named in general convocation surveys of 1296 and 1302–1303; but for the Flemish muster of 1304 we have long lists of southern

---

Chambre des Comptes de Paris (Paris, 1899), *documents,* no. 32, p. 179.

[136] *H.L.,* x, 195–196,ii; *Chartes d'Agen,* no. 98, showing contingents of 200 sergeants, "centum cum balistis et centum cum lanceis et telis"; cf. Baudouin, *Lettres,* no. 175.

[137] *H.L.,* ix, 180; x, 292; 320, xxix; 400–403; *Comptes Royaux (1285–1314),* ii, nos. 17875, 17877; and pp. 679ff.; Ménard, *Histoire de Nismes,* i, *pr.* no. 118, 141–142; ii, *pr.* no. 3, 11; A.M. Cajarc, EE.53; A.M. Montpellier, Arm. H, cass. 3, nos. 3683, 3685; Arm. A, cass. 16, no. 315; B.N., MS Lat. 9192, fol. 55v; Doat, li, 47v–48v; and preceding note.

[138] See Ménard, i, *pr.* no. 107, 134–135; no. 113, 138; no. 118, 141–142; *H.L.,* x, 400–403; Ménard, ii, *pr.* no. 3, 11; *Monuments Historiques: Cartons des Rois,* ed. J. Tardif (Paris, 1866), no. 1024; and cf. *H.L.,* ix, 140, and n. 2.

nobles, many of whom are accounted "with a certain number of armed men and foot." The king wrote directly to these nobles in form letters classified according to the several *sénéchaussées*.[139] It was usual for the contingents to assemble with seneschal or commissioner in Languedoc before setting off for a distant rendezvous with the main army. This was the "show of arms," the intermediate stage of the military process in which royal letters could be read and additional explanations made.[140] The practice had its disadvantages. In 1313 the seneschal of Beaucaire summoned men of Gévaudan to a show of arms at Nîmes, preparatory to a new campaign against Flanders. The bishop of Mende protested, reasonably enough, that this meant a long journey in the wrong direction; and the king thereupon ordered the seneschal to make some equitable adjustment in favor of Gévaudan.[141] Vicars and bayles proclaimed the summons publicly in their localities, although the barons probably received their citations individually from messengers.[142] The greater lords continued to insist on the right to administer the convocation for themselves in their own lands.[143] The record of such a sub-summons in Narbonnais

[139] *H.F.*, XXIII, 786–788, 791–794, 799–801; *H.L.*, X, 439–445; and cf. the valuable findings of C. H. Taylor, "The Composition of Baronial Assemblies in France, 1315–1320," *Speculum*, XXIX (1954), esp. 452–453.

[140] Ménard, I, *pr.* no. 107, 134–135; II, *pr.* no. 3, 11; *Lettres de Philippe-le-Bel Relatives au Pays de Gévaudan*, ed. J. Roucaute, M. Saché (Mende, 1897), no. 79. Townsmen could be arrayed in arms locally, A.M. Montpellier, Arm. G, cass. 2, nos. 3136–3137; Arm. C, cass. 2, no. 1121; B.N., Doat, LI, 48; XLIX, 309; CXLVI, 160–163v.

[141] Roucaute, *Lettres*, no. 79.

[142] *Comptes Royaux (1285–1314)*, I, nos. 9987, 10005, 10011, 12044; II, nos. 17875, 17877; B.N., Doat, LI, 48v–50; MS Lat. 9192, fol. 69v; *H.L.*, X, 292; *Chartes d'Agen*, no. 98; Ménard, I, *pr.* no. 121, 144–145; II, *pr.* no. 3, 11.

[143] *H.L.*, IX, 125; B.N., Doat, XLIX, 325–327v; LI, 48; A.D. Lozère, G.27.

in 1302 is preserved.[144] The viscount presented his vicar
with a patent letter containing the king's order to appear in
arms at Arras on 5 August. The vicar then wrote to groups
of vassals residing in several districts of the viscounty.
Sworn messengers carried the letters to the *castra*. The
vassals were directed to appear personally before the vicar
at Narbonne on 10 July to discuss certain urgent matters
touching the king and viscount. Forty or more persons were
thus addressed and about that number appeared at Narbonne. But not all those cited attended. There were some
deputies and proctors, and excuses on account of infirmity
and absence. Credentials were examined and apparently not
in all cases accepted. The vicar then caused the viscount's
letter, containing the royal summons, to be read to the
gathering, in both dialect and Latin. But when asked to
signify their obedience to the summons, the vassals apparently refused. Instead, with unconscious subservience to
the needs of history, they asked to have an instrument made
of all the proceedings so far. The vicar repeated his demands, but without much success; only two parties changed
their minds. Thus the military array had turned into a political assembly, and we may plausibly suppose that similar
things sometimes happened in the seneschals' convocations.[145]

[144] B.N., Doat, xlix, 260–269.

[145] The rest of this Narbonne story is curious and instructive,
though no full recitation can be given here. The local summons
had evidently become a matter of record because it was a matter
of jurisdictional dispute. The day after his setback, the faithful
vicar set out on a tour of the viscounty, renewing the summons
publicly before witnesses in the various *castra*, and putting it in
writing, B.N., Doat, xlix, 281v–288. Meanwhile some of the vassals appealed to the king's court at Béziers against the military
obligation but doubtless met little sympathy; the appeals were soon
renounced, and the viscount's authority recognized, Doat, xlix,
296–303, 310, 320–324. See also 288, a vicecomital vassal is ordered to accompany the seneschal to the royal host; and 289–293,

The principles underlying military obligations in Languedoc came under discussion early in the reign of Philip III. The unprecedented comprehensiveness of the royal summons for Foix, reaching beyond immediate tenants to rear-vassals and free men, was remarked bitterly in the Agenais-Quercy area.[146] Bishops in the province of Narbonne argued that they and their subjects were prescriptively exempt from duty in the king's army. Any previous service had been rendered by grace alone, save in the case of the bishop of Agde, who admitted having a legal obligation. The seneschal of Carcassonne, Guillaume de Cohardon, countered by shifting the grounds. He appealed to the theoretical right of state. Privilege is suspended, he said in effect, when the king acts, as he had done in Foix, "to defend and preserve the kingdom in peace for the common utility of all." Arguments such as these, derived from Roman principles, were creating a public law that would incontrovertibly justify national military service and taxation.[147]

The proceedings of this dispute between crown and clergy are of some interest. The seneschal had opened a suit against the bishops of Agde and Béziers and inhabitants of their jurisdiction, who had failed to provide the service required of them in the war of Foix. Other prelates of the Narbonne province then took up the cause of the prose-

---

dispute between crown and viscount on the summons in Narbonne. On 18 July 1302 the viscount ordered a public summons in city, bourg, and suburbs of Narbonne. Late in August, when continued delays were doing the king no good, royal officials not surprisingly tried to effect another summons without the viscount; but this only created a new issue in September, Doat, XLIX, 309–311.

[146] *H.F.*, XXIII, 782.

[147] *H.L.*, X, 111–113; cf. Molinier, IX, 22, nn. 1, 2. For a fine discussion of the legal development, see G. Post, "Two Notes on Nationalism in the Middle Ages," *Traditio*, IX (1953), 280–296, esp. 295, citing the poet Geoffroi de Nés, on royal defense of the *status regni* even against internal enemies.

cuted bishops. The elect of Carcassonne was appointed deputy for the episcopate. He and the bishops of Toulouse, Agde, and Béziers, and proctors for the church of Narbonne appeared before the seneschal at Carcassonne on 13 September 1272. They presented him with a general protestation, the chief point of which has already been stated. The seneschal took no interest in the ecclesiastical representation. He pointed out that his present suit did not concern Toulouse, Carcassonne, or Narbonne. On the other hand, the case did concern the villages subject to the bishops of Agde and Béziers; and syndics of these places did in fact attend this session.[148] Not consuls ex officio, as in the grain-export assemblies of this very period, let it be noted. Guillaume de Cohardon is distinguishing clearly between deliberative and judicial assemblies. Yet it was a curious court session that comprised deputies sent by the men of two estates. And undeniably this gathering of 1272 had a political dimension.

Taxation was not ostensibly at issue in the bishops' case. But the seneschal sought an amend for default of service, and his suit was upheld by Parlement.[149] Other men who had not marched to Foix later felt pressure for obviously financial reasons.[150] This first great royal campaign in the Midi had been extremely costly, even though it ended within the time limits set on unpaid feudal duty. Many soldiers must have been in the king's pay throughout.[151] Nevertheless, the financial drive began only after the war, and it took the form of compositions in commutation of military service,[152] despite continued resistance to the royal

[148] *H.L.*, x, 111–115: ". . . . comparuerunt etiam comunitates villarum & castrorum, scilicet per sindicos, coram predicto senescallo."

[149] *Olim.*, I, 899–900, no. 45.

[150] *H.L.*, x, 116–119; Baudouin, *Lettres*, Annexes, no. 7.

[151] See *H.L.*, IX, 21; Langlois, *Philippe III*, pp. 363–365.

[152] A.M. Montauban, AA.2, new fol. 25v; Albe *Cahors: Inventaire*, no. 90; cf. *H.L.*, IX, 23, n. 1.

principle of common liability. Negotiation was required not for consent but to obtain payment. In the fall of 1272 royal officials approached men in the domains of the count of Rodez. The proceedings were probably judicial, as in the case of Agde and Béziers. Numerous villages and the town of Rodez established syndics to negotiate the fine or tax. There may have been an assembly of these representatives, comparable to the session at Carcassonne in September, but this is not certain. The surviving procurations were made in local parliaments according to a standard form, and by order of the comital judge.[153] Evidently the count had been contacted, and perhaps cited. But the crown was encroaching on his lordship by dealing directly with his tenants.

Payments in place of military service continued to be asked by Philip III and by his son after him. Since each noble, barony, and town was a special case, it was usual to deal with them individually and locally. Individual negotiations, in fact, had been the rule in all royal taxation in thirteenth-century Languedoc. The practice persisted, not only for impositions, in their various forms, but also for feudal aids and loans.[154] After 1276 one or another of these subsidies was being collected almost incessantly in the South. Even when new grants were not requested, the accounts of old ones remained in arrears.[155] The procedures varied according to circumstances and the type of levy.

[153] The procurations of Maleville, Cassagnes, and Estaing can be found in B.N., Doat, CLXXIII, 157–166 (cf. Molinier, *H.L.*, IX, 23, n. 1). That of Cassagnes is mentioned in an old inventory, A.D. Aveyron, C.1840, fol. 137, which lists other mandates for Rodez (fol. 109v), Marcilhac (139), Prades (153), and Peyrebrune (246v).

[154] *H.L.*, VIII, 1668–1671; X, 214,vi; 248,ii; IX, 174; A.M. Montpellier, Arm. H, cass. 3, nos. 3681–3683; A.M. Millau, CC.516 (no. 7); A.M. Toulouse, layette 62 (9 December 1285); *Chartes d'Agen*, no. 90, to cite only a few examples.

[155] *Comptes Royaux (1285–1314)*, I, nos. 8986, 9955–9980, 10244; II, nos. 14349, 14600, 14617, 14633, 14670, 14873, 15075.

The only aspect of these individual negotiations that concerns us is representation. Though royal agents sometimes confronted the mass of townsmen in a given place, it was usual to meet with notables, consuls, or appointed deputies. Cities like Toulouse, Narbonne, Albi, Montpellier, and Nîmes were in almost constant communication with the government, making payments, promises, petitions, and protests, and obtaining assurances and receipts.[156] So small a town as Najac in Rouergue sent deputies again and again to discuss taxation with the seneschal, not always on the latter's summons.[157] Procuration was commonly employed, especially when, as often happened, the negotiations passed into a stage of litigation.[158] But there is little evidence that royal officials were requiring full powers to expedite individual decisions on taxation. The principle seems to have been understood even in the time of Louis IX,[159] but was infrequently invoked in the later thirteenth century. While prelates and barons generally acted for themselves, they too appointed proctors when making protests and petitions. Sometimes barons appeared to be, or claimed to be, acting for their inhabitants. This was the case notably in Foix and

---

[156] See, e.g., *H.L.*, VIII, 1669,ii; *Archives de la Cour des Comptes de Montpellier*, ed. Martin-Chabot, no. 415; A.M. Narbonne, AA.107, fol. 71; B.N., Doat, XLVIII, 222–223v; CXLV, 87–91v; A.M. Toulouse, layette 61 (6 November 1297); A.M. Nîmes, NN.1, no. 2; A.M. Alès, 1S XII, no. 1; A.M. Montpellier, Arm. G, cass. 6, no. 3383; Arm. H, cass. 3, nos. 3681–3683; etc.

[157] A.D. Aveyron, 2E178, no. 2, fol. 22v, *et passim*.

[158] A.M. Narbonne, AA.103, fol. 63v; A.M. Millau, CC.510 (19 November 1295); A.M. Montpellier, Arm. H, cass. 3, nos. 3681–3683; Arm. E, cass. 1, no. 1986, and many other pieces relating to an amend levied on Montpellier for failing to respond to a military summons in 1282 (cf. Molinier, *H.L.*, IX, 132, n. 5); etc.

[159] A.M. Narbonne, AA.105, fols. 80v–81r, royal agents in 1269 report an offer of money for crusade made by deputies of Narbonne who had appeared "cum sufficienti mandato syndicatus."

Rouergue, where the crown was trying to obtain grants from sub-tenants in the 1290's.[160] Some of the documentation on finance might be interpreted to mean either local or central activity. Accountants recorded names and sums, but not procedures. Their lists—like that of nobles in Toulousain making payments on old war loans in 1293, or that of towns in the *sénéchaussée* of Beaucaire paying subsidy in 1302—may point to previous convocations.[161] Otherwise well-attested summonses of towns seem to have left traces in the royal accounts.[162] In a remarkable case of a somewhat different kind, Philip III expressed himself in very ambiguous terms. Using a common form, he wrote collective letters of non-prejudice in May 1276 to men of the three orders of Agenais, Quercy, and Toulousain. The king noted that they had granted an aid for crusade, but did not say how or when.[163] The crusade plan soon had to be given up; the subsidy left no record in surviving accounts, and it may be that the letters were issued mistakenly and that no negotiations occurred. Yet even if this were so, it is possible that the crown contemplated general regional assemblies in Languedoc.

Of important southern convocations dealing with taxation that certainly took place, only one is known in the reign of Philip III after 1272. In 1285 a royal agent sum-

[160] *Documents Historiques . . . de Carlat*, ed. Saige, I, nos. 141, 142; *H.L.*, X, 328–338, 340–343; B.N., Doat, CLXXV, 311–314; CLXXVI, 101–107; CLXXVII, 260–268. See Post in *Speculum*, XXIX (1954), 429, n. 44, on the continued representation of French rural elements by lords in the early 14th century.

[161] *Comptes Royaux (1285–1314)*, I, nos. 8986, 10244–10266, 13560–13566; see also Ménard, I, *pr.* no. 75, 105.

[162] *Comptes Royaux (1285–1314)*, I, nos. 11053–11179, and A.N., J.1032B, no. 17; C. Langlois in *R.H.*, XCV (1907), 29, 37–45, 48–49. Also *Comptes Royaux*, II, nos. 21401–21433, and Ménard, *Histoire de Nismes*, I, *pr.* no. 125, 148–149.

[163] *Chartes d'Agen*, no. 59; A.M. Montauban, AA.3, fols. 29v–30 (cf. AA.1, fol. 64, variant reading); A.M. Toulouse, AA.54, no. 4, pp. 37–38. See Langlois, *Philippe III*, pp. 96–101, 350.

moned rear-vassals and sub-tenants in Rouergue and demanded money from them as an aid for the knighting of the king's eldest son. The assembly may have included deputies from seigneurial villages. Legally, the official was seeking consent, for the men convoked were not obligated to pay feudal aids to the king, their overlord. Moreover, their immediate lords had not been notified.[164] This was probably a tactical error. The crown could normally have expected to collect the aid from its own vassals, but we do not know that it succeeded even in this in Rouergue.[165] The attempt to collect from rear-vassals certainly had to be abandoned. The magnates, in fact, took up the cause of their own men in a spontaneous manifestation of collective resistance to the crown, one of the earliest of its kind in Languedoc. Early in October 1285 the bishop and count of Rodez, and some twenty other lords of Rouergue, appeared at Rodez before the same royal official and registered a protest. Some of them were acting for individual persons and communities as well as for themselves, and all of them claimed to be representing their own men. They laid more stress on their subjects' rights than their own.[166]

Heavy taxation under Philip the Fair began in 1294, when war broke out in Gascony. For the first time the government tried to collect money from the French clergy without consulting the pope. But it could not do this without obtaining the consent of those asked to pay. Provincial councils were held for this purpose, in Languedoc as elsewhere in France.[167] The royal directives for these councils have a place of some importance in the history of French representation. Although a national assembly had at first

---

[164] *H.L.*, x, 193.

[165] See B.N., Doat, CLXXVI, 243–244, 250, 253, negotiations continued with prelates and barons of Rouergue, for themselves and their subjects, for some years; cf. Strayer, *Early French Taxation*, p. 43.

[166] *H.L.*, x, 192–194.

[167] Strayer, *op. cit.*, pp. 25–28, 44–45.

been planned, the king explained that provincial meetings would occasion less trouble and expense for the clergymen.[168] Probably the object was to weaken the anticipated opposition by dividing it, as Professor Strayer has suggested.[169] Nevertheless, this is the first theoretical statement about the use of regional assemblies by a secular authority in Languedoc. It is amplified by instructions for the use of procuration in these councils. While bishops, abbots, and other prelates were to convene in person, religious corporations were directed to send "suitable proctors with full and sufficient mandates for discussing, agreeing, and ordaining" on the matter of the tax.[170] Here at last it is clear that procuration will be used procedurally in an assembly. We are a long way from the unsolicited powers of attorney of Carcassonne and Agenais in previous years. The actual councils, the conditional grants made in them, and later councils for similar purposes are of no further concern in this study.[171]

Laymen of Languedoc were doubly burdened in 1294. Besides being summoned to military duty and required to fine for default or exemption, they were subjected to a *fouage* to meet expenses of the southern army.[172] The latter tax was an innovation. But the government thought of it as linked to the military obligation, not wishing to go to the trouble of obtaining consent. There is no evidence that the hearth tax was justified in assemblies, although town deputies of Foix were convoked to help with the assessment.[173] On the other hand, a special royal commission at Toulouse

---

[168] *H.L.*, x, 302–303,ix, letter of 3 August 1294 to the bishop of Uzès.

[169] See *Early French Taxation*, p. 26.

[170] *H.L.*, x, 303; Ménard, *Histoire de Nismes*, I, pr. no. 98, 129.

[171] See Strayer, *op. cit.*, pp. 26–28, 32, 38; also *Comptes Royaux (1285–1314)*, I, no. 13899, mention of a "general convocation of prelates of Languedoc" at Nîmes in accounts of 1302–1303.

[172] Strayer, pp. 44–45.

[173] B.N., Doat, CLXXVI, 1–5v; cf. *H.L.*, IX, 173.

negotiated the financial compositions with prelates, barons, and towns. Probably they confronted the army when it assembled there and excused the men and towns willing to make financial terms.[174]

The drive for men and money continued in 1295. When the king called on the district of Beaucaire for support, the seneschal summoned barons and knights to Viviers, probably early in April. He presented an argument of defense of the realm and "especially" of the *sénéchaussée* in order to justify a general tallage. With the approval of the nobles, he ordained that a contribution of one and a half per cent be levied on real estate for maintenance of the army. Local assessors were to be appointed.[175] This must have occasioned administrative convocations in baronies like Montpellier, as it certainly did in Foix the year before. The assembly of Viviers was politic without being very representative. It was not even thought necessary to list names of those present. Towns were not called, presumably, because they were not to be taxed as collectivities.[176]

Early in 1296 the consuls of Montpellier received a sum-

[174] *Comptes Royaux*, I, nos. 10471, 10491; *H.L.*, x, 292. There may have been an assembly of Quercy towns for compositions, *Comptes*, I, nos. 8906–8926.

[175] Strayer, *Early French Taxation*, p. 46; B.N., MS Lat. 9192, fol. 61. Besides invoking the legal sanction of "defense," implying the superior right of state, the seneschal drew on the Roman-canonical notions of corporate and procedural consent: "de consilio et providencia baronum et nobilium dicte senescallie seu maioris partis . . . eorum ad hoc specialiter vocatorum"; but the ordinance itself speaks only of defense of the realm and counsel of the barons and nobles summoned to Viviers. See Gierke, *Genossenschaftsrecht*, III, 220–223, 321ff.; Post, " 'Quod Omnes Tangit,' in Bracton," *Traditio*, IV, esp. 200–209.

That this decision took the form of an ordinance is noteworthy in view of the other ordinances of the same region known to have been passed in assemblies, pp. 249–250 above.

[176] But cf. A.M. Alès, 1S III, no. 1, a damaged roll, relating to this or another imposition at Alès in 1295.

mons to appear in person or by proxy at Nîmes on Easter Sunday. They were to hear certain ordinances brought by royal commissioners, almost certainly the new directives for the levy of a fiftieth. This tax had been approved by northern magnates in January, but it still had to be publicized and its collection arranged locally.[177] Evidently an assembly at Nîmes was contemplated. The consuls of Montpellier appointed a proctor and gave him general powers in what is one of the few surviving mandates for a thirteenth-century convocation.[178] Nothing else is known of this meeting at Nîmes, which prompts the reflection that we should likewise be ignorant of the Viviers assembly the year before were it not for the preservation of a written protest *post facto*. Assemblies dealing with finance must have been common in Languedoc after 1294 even though relatively few of them can be traced today.

The local negotiation of taxes centrally imposed continued after the turn of the century. The government was hard pressed and the people more resistant in 1303–1304 when urgent demands were again put before general assemblies in Languedoc.[179] At least two kinds of provincial convocation, corresponding to distinct stages in the procedure, can now be discerned. The king came to the Midi in the winter of 1304 prepared to compromise on heavy

---

[177] B.N., MS Lat. 9192, fol. 64v, cf. 66; Strayer, pp. 48–49.

[178] B.N., MS Lat. 9192, 64v: ". . . [consuls] facimus, ordinamus et constituimus certum et indubitatum procuratorem nostrum te Johannem de Foissaco, notarium Montispessulani, presentem et recipientem, videlicet ad comparendum pro nobis et nostro nomine coram dictis magistris dicta die dominica de Passione et ad audiendum ordinationes predictas et alia dicenda a dictis dominis magistris et ad alia faciendum que facienda fuerint in premissis et occasione premissorum, ratum et firmum habituri perpetuo quicquid per te dictum procuratorem nostrum aut tecum in et super premissis actum fuerit sive gestum. . . ."

[179] *H.L.*, x, 413,ii, order for general explanatory assembly in Beaucaire, May 1303; see Strayer, *Early French Taxation*, pp. 61–62.

subsidies already announced for that year, and some men of Languedoc probably had a say in approving that compromise. This might be called a central assembly of Languedoc, but it is unlikely that any general summons was issued. Nothing is said of such a convocation in subsequent documents relating to the taxation of 1304; moreover, the king's own announcement of the "subsidy granted" in Languedoc was very vague.[180]

Then came well-attested stages. Orders for administration of the aid went out to Gévaudan and to the barony of Montpellier, and perhaps elsewhere. In Gévaudan, assemblies composed of notables and pairs of deputies from localities were to meet at Marvéjols and La Canourgue to do the assessments; and the rector of Montpellier received instructions to similar effect.[181] But for most of Languedoc the real bargaining was yet to come. In early spring, royal commissioners set out to tour those *sénéchaussées* in which compliance still seemed doubtful. They convoked nobles and probably towns at Toulouse on 3 April 1304; nobles and towns at Carcassonne three days later, at Beaucaire on 16 April, at Rodez on 18 April, and in Albigeois on an uncertain date.[182] Subsidies were approved separately by men of the two orders, in forms that varied somewhat from one

---

[180] Strayer, pp. 66–67; *H.L.*, IX, 255–259; X, 431–432, i, ii; A.N., J.384, no. 1; and cf. above, p. 257, for the general assembly at Toulouse in January 1304. Proctors of Rouergue consulates appeared before the king in this period, A.D. Aveyron, 2E178, no. 2, fol. 70v.

[181] A.D. Aveyron, C.1519; Ménard, *Histoire de Nismes*, I, *pr.* no. 125, 147.

[182] *H.L.*, X, 432–435 (there had been petitions from towns of Toulousain in February, B.N., Doat, VII, 340; cf. *Ordonnances*, I, 399); Ménard, I, *pr.* no. 125, 148–149; A.D. Aveyron, 2E178, no. 2, fol. 71 (four deputies of Najac go to Rodez to meet the commissioners; and they return for further discussions on 30 April); A.M. Cordes, CC.27.

area to another but were subject to searching conditions.[183] Little is heard of general assemblies in Languedoc for purposes of taxation during the remaining years of Philip the Fair.[184] The local resistance encountered in 1304 may have contributed to the decision to experiment with central negotiations for the new taxes of 1310 and 1314.[185]

THE TOWNS: ASSEMBLIES AND REPRESENTATION

Besides convening with men of the other orders, townsmen or their deputies assembled by themselves. They had been convoked alone at least as early as the 1220's in Agenais and the practice was conceivably of equal antiquity in other areas. But we are poorly informed about such assemblies before the reign of Philip III.[186] Royal officials summoned townsmen more and more often in the later thirteenth century, for various purposes. In 1274 the judge of Pézenas convoked communities of the *sénéchaussée* of Carcassonne in order to raise money for the building of a bridge over the river at Pézenas.[187] Early in 1278 the seneschal of Beaucaire and notables of the coastal area near Aigues-Mortes consulted representative men from six towns concerning a private violation of the right of way. They

[183] See preceding note, and Strayer, *Early French Taxation*, pp. 67–68.

[184] For collection procedures centralized at Toulouse in July 1313, see *Comptes Royaux (1285–1314)*, II, 750–751; cf. Strayer, pp. 81–82.

[185] See Strayer and Taylor, *Early French Taxation*, pp. 78–79, 82–85, 150–153.

[186] On Agenais see ch. 2, pp. 97–99. Records of consular expenses show deputations from towns to central places in Quercy and Rouergue after mid-century, *Enquêtes d'Alfonse*, p. 241, no. 95; A.M. Millau, CC.342, *sub anno* 1267; "Memorandum des Consuls de la Ville de Martel," ed. H. Teulié, *Revue de Philol. Franç.*, VII (1893), 257–260; VIII (1894), 17, 19, 23. But it is not certain that these were assemblies.

[187] A.M. Pézenas, Arm. B, 1/1/11; cf. A. Delouvrier, *Histoire de Pézenas et de ses Environs . . .* (Montpellier, 1900), p. 83.

acted as inspectors, but their opinion was adopted as an ordinance in the assizes.[188] Overflows of the river Vidourle occasioned a major assembly in December 1299. Acting on the king's orders to summon those whom the matter "touches," a phrasing indicative of a legal procedure according to the principle *quod omnes tangit* . . . , the seneschal conferred with officials, notables, and deputies of numerous towns at Marsillargues, and with their counsel enacted an appropriate administrative ordinance.[189]

With the redoubled military and financial needs after 1290, conventions of towns became very common. Zealous officials in Lauragais convoked consuls of places subject to the bishop of Toulouse in 1294 to account for arms-bearing men and provisions in the localities.[190] Similar assemblies were held in the county of Foix a few weeks later, the county of Valentinois in 1297, and undoubtedly in other baronies in the same period.[191] Royal agents responsible for negotiating war subsidy in Toulousain summoned village notables to Toulouse for that purpose in 1298.[192]

A remarkable assembly was ordered in Quercy in June 1295. French commissioners summoned twenty-six consulates [193] of the region to meet at Cahors and consent to a loan. The convocation letter was unusually full. It requested

[188] A.D. Gard, G.760 (marked "Pescheries N, 38").

[189] A.D. Hérault, E.Suppl. (Marsillargues, AA.1, no. 13); copies in A.D. Gard, E.Suppl. 498 (Aimargues, DD.2) and A.D. Hérault, AA.4, fols. 22–26.

[190] A.D. Haute-Garonne, 1G346, pp. 7v-8v, 15–16. They were countermanded by the seneschal of Toulouse.

[191] Above, p. 277; Regné, *Histoire du Vivarais*, II, 125; cf. 355. Cf. *Archives de la Cour des Comptes de Montpellier*, no. 484; B.N., MS Lat. 9173, fol. 140; *Comptes Royaux (1285–1314)*, I, no. 12076.

[192] A.N., J.1032B, no. 17; C. Langlois, "Les Doléances des Communautés du Toulousain . . . (1297–1298)," *R.H.*, xcv (1907), 29, 31, 37–48.

[193] At least: the officials who carried the letter were free to notify other places not specified.

bayles and consuls to attend in person and to be on hand a day in advance of the "parliament," to ensure full attendance and a prompt start. It invoked the legal notion of "right of state" to justify the loan and other matters to be discussed and ordained. And it set a procedural, or proctorial, requirement on the representation. The deputies were to take steps to facilitate ready compliance with requests that would be made of them and obviate reference back to their communities.[194] Unfortunately, nothing further is known about this assembly.

Very few convocations of towns, in fact, left any direct record. Many are known only through references in financial accounts. A book of municipal expenses for Najac shows that the consulates of Rouergue were convening fairly frequently after 1290. They met on the seneschal's summons, regularly at the abbey of Loc-Dieu, sometimes at Villefranche or Rodez. They discussed taxes and loans, demands for military service, and other matters of regional concern.[195] If the case of Najac was typical, the deputies

[194] A.M. Gourdon, CC.41, no. 3, and published by Albe, *Cahors: Inventaire*, pp. 187–189. This document seems to have been misread badly by J. Baudel, "Notes Pour Servir à l'Histoire des États . . . du Quercy," *Annuaire . . . du Lot* (1881), pt. 3, p. 12. He wrote that Bishop Barthélemi de Roux convoked the consuls of Quercy towns at Cahors on 11 June 1270, and gave a list of the towns that corresponds almost exactly, and in order, with the list given in the summons of (13) June 1295. Now, it is true that a parchment attached to the latter describes a convention between a bishop and certain "comunas dejos nominadas." But I do not see that this second document is dated, nor is it clear that it refers, or how it could refer, to the consulates listed in the royal summons. Baudel certainly invented the date and the bishop's name, besides speaking of the assembly as "États" and assuming that "représentants du clergé et de la noblesse" were probably summoned too! Cf. Albe, p. 186, n. 1.

[195] A.D. Aveyron, 2E178, no. 2, fols. 28vb, 40va, 66b, 66v, 71, 78v, 79a, 85rv, 106va, 115b, etc. I am much obliged to the learned archivist of Aveyron, M. Jacques Bousquet, for calling my attention to this document.

were normally consuls or notables. The same men tended to serve repeatedly as representatives.[196]

Expense accounts of upper Languedoc often mention individual deputations to neighboring places to confer with royal officials. These were usually voluntary on the part of the towns represented, but in some references summonses or convocations may be implied.[197] A number of undoubted assemblies seem to have been held on the initiative of the towns alone.[198] In the face of rising governmental demands, a sense of community was developing among the towns of various regions. Yet the voluntary assemblies, however interesting from a constitutional point of view, are very obscure. In many cases it can only be inferred that they took place from the collective petitions and procurations that proliferate in the later thirteenth century and after. Commercial towns of the Garonne valley had probably assembled before their proctors undertook litigation against the king of England in 1285 over the "great custom" of wine.[199] Conventions of Agenais consulates may be more certainly deduced from procurations of 1280–1281 relating

[196] A.D. Aveyron, 2E178, no. 2, fols. 11a, 28rv, 40va, 79a, 85v, etc.; and some of the same men served as deputies for other purposes, e.g., fols. 22vb, 29va, 34b, 49vb, mostly discussions relating to war subsidy, 1295–1300. Cf. B.N., Doat, cxlvi, 62–63v; *Documents Relatifs aux États Généraux*, ed. Picot, no. 102. See also (Aveyron) 2E178, no. 4, fol. 11, regulations of Najac in 1299 concerning consular deputations and expenses (transcribed by C. Laroche in an unprinted study of Najac, ii, *p.j.*, 50–51; again my acknowledgments to M. Bousquet).

[197] See above, n. 186, and A.D. Aveyron, 2E178, no. 2, fols. 11, 22vb, 34rv, 49vb; A.M. Millau, CC.344, fol. lv; CC.346, fols. 4v, 5. For Quercy in the period 1294–1309, cf. A.M. Martel, CC.2, fols. 14, 46, 50, 66, 68v, 69v, 86.

[198] A.D. Aveyron, 2E178, no. 2, fols. 11a (1292, reference to an assembly possibly summoned by the count of Rodez), 49vb, 28vb, 40va, 71b, etc. For instances in Quercy, see A.M. Martel, CC.2, fols. 7v, 68v.

[199] See Wolff, *Commerces et Marchands de Toulouse*, pp. 123–124, and n. 40; *R.G.*, ii, no. 921.

to arbitration over rights in the local salt trade.[200] Other instances are doubtful. A "procuraire per los cossolatz de Rozergue" who was deputed to the royal court in 1304 might have been chosen in assembly, but we do not know surely that he was.[201] And what is to be said of the intense associative activity in Quercy beginning in 1307? In June of that year thirty-one regional towns and villages addressed a procuration to the king on the subject of taxation; [202] in 1309 the towns of Quercy divided into groups to prepare mandates for negotiating the aid *pro filia maritanda;*[203] and in 1311 no less than forty-eight communities joined in a procuration by which they appealed to the pope against a decision of the bishop of Cahors relating to usury.[204] These acts could have resulted from various procedures other than conventions, but the latter course must have seemed the most expeditious in Quercy, with its tradition of diocesan assemblies. Some if not all of these procurations were probably drafted in assemblies of towns on the instance of the leading communities. It should be remarked that the many towns and villages in 1311 chose notables from only

[200] P.R.O., Exchequer T.R., Misc. Books, vol. 275, 256v–257v, mandate made at Condom on 15 March 1281 by the consuls of five localities, acting for themselves and the men of 22 other places; cf. *R.G.*, II, no. 455. Another clear instance turns up among the procurations made in 1303 for an assembly at Montpellier, *Documents Relatifs aux États Généraux*, no. 112.

[201] A.D. Aveyron, 2E178, no. 2, fol. 73b; cf. B.N., Doat, CLXXVI, 218, consuls of Millau, Saint-Antonin, Villeneuve, and Peyrusse have a proctor before the seneschal of Rouergue in June 1297. Cf. also A.M. Martel, CC.2, fol. 73.

[202] A.M. Cahors, BB.6.

[203] A.N., J.356, nos. 5, 14; *Registres du Trésor des Chartes*, I, ed. R. Fawtier (Paris, 1958), no. 819; A.M. Cahors, "Livre Nouveau," I, 186; D.320. Cf. Strayer, *Early French Taxation*, pp. 77–80.

[204] A.M. Cahors, FF.15 (copy in B.N., Doat, CXIX, 23v–26).

six great towns—Cahors, Montauban, Gourdon, Lauzerte, Figeac, and Rocamadour—to be their proctors.[205]

The instances just cited take on added interest when read with other evidence for collective and representative action by the towns. The form of deputations from individual towns to assemblies had not really changed since the middle of the thirteenth century. Procuration was still exceptional, the representatives usually being consuls or notables without mandates. Although our information is not very satisfactory on this point, it seems likely that the royal officials requested full powers or the equivalent only when summoning towns for judicial or financial reasons.[206] But when two or more towns acted in common, they often appointed proctors or syndics.[207] A voluntary assembly of towns was only an extension of bilateral or multilateral activity.[208] It might sometimes approximate the totality of towns or consulates in a given area. Yet, as far as we know, the meeting of this kind was never explicitly identical with that totality, so that, while undoubtedly a collectivity, it fell short of being a corporate estate. The "consulates of Rouergue" represented in 1304 were not described as the "university of consulates."

On the other hand, the principle of a regional estate of towns was implied in the dawning practice of what may perhaps best be called virtual representation. Let us recall that in Quercy the consuls of the city had occasionally acted for all men of the diocese in negotiations with the bishop over the coinage.[209] This usage seems to have con-

[205] A.M. Cahors, FF.15.

[206] *Regeste Dauphinois*, ed. U. Chevalier, 7 vols. (Valence, 1912–1926), III, no. 14907; A.M. Gourdon, CC.41, no. 3. Many of the deputies mentioned in consular accounts were doubtless furnished with proctorial powers.

[207] *Gascon Calendar of 1322*, nos. 1012, 1345; *Chartes d'Agen*, no. 88; instances in Quercy cited above, nn. 202–204.

[208] See A.D. Aveyron, 2E178, no. 2, fols. 49vb, 50va, 124b.

[209] Above, ch. 3, p. 129.

tinued in the later thirteenth century, although, to be sure, the towns of Quercy did not always leave it to the city to represent them in their monetary rights.[210] It is possible that the "great towns" customarily consulted when the peace tax was levied [211] were vaguely understood to be representative of the other towns in Quercy. If so, the representation of those forty-eight communities in 1311 by proctors chosen from a few of the larger towns assumes considerable significance. Quercy seems to have led Languedoc in evolving its own practice of representation of the diocese. But Agenais cannot have been far behind. Many if not all of its nobles had been represented in 1253.[212] Consuls of *baylie* towns acted for rural men of their districts in 1271,[213] and a decade later we find five consulates of Agenais appointing deputies not only for themselves but also for the men of twenty-three other places with interests in a sub-regional issue.[214] Then, in 1294 the principle of the virtual representation of townsmen was invoked on a scale approximating the whole of Agenais. To help pay for a mission previously made to England "for the common utility of the city and diocese" of Agen, the consuls of Condom and Agen agreed to seek recompense from other towns that had not contributed.[215] This device had

---

[210] B.N., Doat, cxviii, 183v–189, and '*Te Igitur,*' no. 384, agreements between bishop and consuls of Cahors in 1282. But Cahors had had the support of proctors of other towns in Quercy the year before in a protest in Parlement against the bishop's practice of nullifying his old coinage when he issued a new one. Later, probably in the 1290's, a bishop convened with the towns and arrived at agreements stressing the towns' collective interest in the diocesan coinage, A.M. Gourdon, CC.41, no. 3 (cf. above, n.194).

For the early 14th century, see A.M. Martel, CC.2, fols. 69v, 73.

[211] Ch. 3, pp. 125–126.

[212] Ch. 2, pp. 100–101.

[213] Ch. 4, pp. 177–178, 181.

[214] P.R.O., Exchequer T.R., Misc. Books, vol. 275, 256v–257.

[215] *Chartes d'Agen*, no. 88.

wider possibilities. In 1312, as Professor Taylor has shown, the French government sought to finance a national assembly of towns on the basis of a virtual representation of dioceses. At that time appeal to the principle was made in various parts of Languedoc, including Albigeois and Toulousain as well as Quercy.[216] Native institutional development has reached an important confluence with royal institutional experiment.[217]

[216] C.H. Taylor, "The Assembly of 1312 at Lyons-Vienne," *Études d'Histoire Dédiées à la Mémoire de Henri Pirenne* . . . (Bruxelles, 1937), p. 338, n. 8; pp. 341–345, 347–348. Pamiers can be added to his account of Languedoc dioceses summoned, *Comptes Royaux (1285–1314)*, II, no. 17243[2]. Something like virtual representation had probably been implied in the royal directive for the convocation of cities at Paris, February 1302, *Documents Relatifs aux États Généraux*, no. 1.

[217] Fuller accounts of provincial representation are possible. It is much to be hoped that Professor Taylor will publish the results of his studies on Quercy. Rouergue, Gascony, and other areas are deserving of similar treatment.

❦VII❧ Conclusion

In 1302 Philip the Fair decided to place his anti-papal politics before the mass of Frenchmen. Early in the year, cities of Languedoc were summoned to Paris, though it is uncertain whether their deputies attended the general assembly in April.[1] Then in 1303, meetings of men from the three orders of Languedoc were held at Montpellier and Nîmes.[2] These assemblies are well known, having been commonly regarded as a new venture in the history of French institutions. The belief that they were "assemblies of estates" dies hard.[3] Those of Languedoc certainly were not, at least not in the sense preferred by the stricter French institutionalists.[4] Yet they were new in some other respects which can perhaps only be appreciated by those who approach them from the earlier history of assemblies in the South. There was little or no precedent for the convocation of men from all or most of Languedoc in one place, as happened at Montpellier in July 1303. The special elections held by townsmen in parliaments at Lunel, Lodève, Viviers, and elsewhere in response to royal requests for empowered

[1] *Documents Relatifs aux États Généraux*, ed. G. Picot, nos. 1–6; C.H. Taylor, "Some New Texts on the Assembly of 1302," *Speculum*, XI (1936), 38–42; cf. H. Hervieu, *Recherches sur les Premiers États Généraux*, pp. 71–74; R. Fawtier, *L'Europe Occidentale de 1270 à 1380*, part 1, p. 254.

[2] *Documents Relatifs aux États Généraux*, nos. 74–176; the meeting scheduled for Carcassonne, nos. 177–188, was very restricted; cf. pp. xxxv–xxxvi.

[3] C. H. McIlwain, "Medieval Estates," *Camb. Med. Hist.*, VII, 684–687; cf. Fawtier, *L'Europe Occidentale de 1270 à 1380*, part 1, pp. 253–256.

[4] See Introduction, p. 7.

deputies,[5] if not entirely novel, were certainly a departure from the general practice of allowing the consuls to represent the towns in assemblies as they saw fit. The crown had rarely if ever made it so clear that it wanted a representation of burghers as well as municipal officers in assembly.[6] Finally, the articulation of the notions of majority and representation in some of the mandates suggests a more mature awareness of procedural niceties than had previously been in evidence.[7]

In other respects, however, and indeed in most respects, the royal assemblies of 1303 resembled earlier general assemblies in Languedoc. The conveyance of letters of summons locally through *vigueries* of the *sénéchaussée* must have seemed a familiar procedure to the people thus notified.[8] These communications were no more welcome than they had been in the past. Attendance was still commonly regarded as an obligation rather than a right, although, to be sure, there had already been occasions when their own legal interests entitled parties to be summoned. Moreover, despite the fact that procuration was requested

[5] *Documents Relatifs aux États Généraux*, nos. 116, 117, 122, 100, 121, etc; and for the Paris assembly of 1302, see Taylor, "New Texts," 41–42, election in assembly at Pézenas.

[6] *Documents Relatifs aux États Généraux*, no. 74, directive for summons dated 5 July 1303: "mandamus quatinus omnes prelatos et barones, capitula, collegia, conventus et priores ecclesiarum kathedralium, collegiatarum et conventualium insignium, nec non et consules, syndicos et universitates civitatum et castrorum aliarumque villarum insignium vicarie vestre [Béziers] citetis sive citari faciatis et perhemptorie, ut dicti prelati et barones, priores et consules personaliter, ceteri vero per procuratores, sindicos vel yconomos ydoneos cum sufficienti mandato et potestate . . . compareant." Cf. *H.L.*, VIII, 1741.

[7] *Documents Relatifs aux États*, e.g., nos. 100, 117; see also Taylor, "New Texts," 41. But England was probably in advance of France in most of these respects; cf. M. McKisack, *The Parliamentary Representation of the English Boroughs during the Middle Ages* (Oxford, 1932), ch. 1, esp. pp. 14–17.

[8] *Documents Relatifs aux États*, nos. 74, 75.

only from corporations, numerous individuals also presented mandates, chiefly as excuses.[9] The idea that men not summoned, like those in many rural parishes, were virtually represented may have been vaguely in the air, but this is no more explicit in 1303 than it had been in the statutory assemblies of 1269–1275.

The conclusion emerges clearly that Languedoc had acquired considerable experience with assemblies and representation by the close of the thirteenth century. General assemblies had assumed a place in tradition even if they were not in most cases established institutions. Some of the practices connected with assemblies had attained a formal or legal status. Men had convened on numerous occasions in consequence of orderly procedures of summons. These persons had frequently functioned or been treated as members of recognized social estates. Towns and religious communities had been represented in assemblies, often indirectly and informally, but sometimes directly and in accordance with the Roman-canonical formulas for judicial representation. Assemblies had been put to a wide variety of uses, including some that were one day to be institutionalized.

These results accumulated through the thirteenth century, though not all periods were equally fruitful. In view of the important assemblies of 1302–1303, it is remarkable to discover that the preceding quarter-century had been an unprogressive age for general assemblies comprising men of the two or three orders. Regional custom in Agenais and royal statute in the coastal *sénéchaussées* continued to prescribe such assemblies, but in practice they met less frequently than before 1275. On the other hand, convocations of nobles or townsmen alone became more common under Philip III and Philip the Fair. These kings for the first time made use of assemblies to explain military necessities and negotiate financial subsidies. Other kinds of meetings in

[9] *Ibid.*, nos. 74, 75, 92, 96, 98, 99.

the same period are impressive for their variety and their testimony to a vigorous associative life, but few of them are important from an institutional standpoint.

It is the preceding generation, that of Louis IX and Alfonse of Poitiers, which stands out in the early history of assemblies in Languedoc. Faced with the problem of securing the loyalty of newly acquired territories, Capetian governors began to convoke men in central places for political and administrative reasons. They summoned townsmen as well as nobles, and town deputies and clergy also participated in advisory sessions in lower Languedoc to deliberate on the grain supply. Royal officials learned the advantages and disadvantages of plenary sessions for their various tasks. Two of these men emerge as pioneers in this branch of administration, the capable seneschal Guillaume de Cohardon, and his lieutenant Barthélemi de Pennautier. Some result of their experience may perhaps be discerned in the apparent preference of their successors for more localized procedures and limited assemblies in the last quarter of the thirteenth century.

The pre-Capetian period has a lesser, yet not negligible, significance. Representation of towns and villages originated in feudal assemblies. It dates back to the twelfth century in Agenais and possibly Quercy too, though we know next to nothing about the actual assemblies. Consular deputations ex officio were customary in the general court of Agenais. This practice was adopted elsewhere in the Midi, prevailed in the thirteenth century, and survived even in the later age of Estates. Perhaps it is best explained by the Roman law, which attributed a representative character to municipal officials whether they had proctorial powers or not.[10] Late in the thirteenth century, Toulousan law professors spoke of consuls as "representing" their city.

---

[10] P. Gillet, *Personnalité Juridique*, pp. 7–9; cf. also pp. 75–76; Bernard of Pavia, *Summa Decretalium*, ed. E. A. T. Laspeyres (Ratisbon, 1860), p. 31 (I, 34, 4).

They also regarded townsmen as legally responsible for acts of their officials.[11] The feudal obligations of counsel and suit remained theoretically in effect when the Capetians succeeded to southern baronies. Otherwise there was little institutional continuity between the older bodies native to Languedoc and royal assemblies after the conquest.[12] The new government was impersonal and professionally oriented, and its assemblies were typically non-feudal. In any case, baronial assemblies had not developed significantly under the counts of Toulouse, nor much more so in the smaller lordships. Only in Agenais could the new governors find a well-established body to use as they saw fit. The diocesan convocations for the peace, which likewise had a recognized existence in upper Languedoc, lost their *raison d'être* when royal administration began. But we know that the epistolary summons, indicative of planned assemblies, was known in Gévaudan before the Capetian officials arrived; and it was widely used thereafter.

Representation, considered in all its forms, progressed throughout the thirteenth century. Roman-canonical procuration by individuals and local corporations, having been used in the judicial practice of Languedoc since 1200 or so,[13] and in church councils by mid-century, was introduced in secular assemblies during the quarter-century after 1250. The religious precedents may have been influential, but this cannot be demonstrated with certainty. Procuration

[11] *Responsa Doctorum Tholosanorum*, ed. E. Meijers (Haarlem, 1938), pp. 213; 226: "consules predicti, qui universitatem dicte civitatis [not specified] representant, ut est supra ostensum, domum comunem habere possunt." In the 14th century the legist Jean Faure says that in cases involving the legal rights of many members of communities it suffices to summon the consuls or administrators, *Commentaria in Quatuor Libros Institutionum* (Lyon, 1593), p. 621.

[12] Cf. P. Dognon, *Institutions*, pp. 195–201.

[13] Studied in my doctoral thesis (1958; Princeton University Library; University Microfilms, Ann Arbor, Michigan), ch. 2.

was not at first a device for procedural expediency, and was only rarely so employed in convocations before 1300. Communities wider than towns and religious corporations also began to assume the character of constituencies. In Agenais something resembling an estate of nobility was represented around mid-century. A generation later, nobles and towns were acting separately in groups to appoint deputies, though it is doubtful that they were yet being summoned to assemblies as collectivities. In 1304 the king received a petition, probably one of the first of its kind in Languedoc, from (the?) men of the three estates of Béziers-Carcassonne.[14] The custom of Quercy had long attributed to its leading towns some sort of responsibility for the diocese. Virtual representation does not otherwise come clearly into view until the last decade of the thirteenth century, though it is possible that royal officials already had some sense of it in their rather experimental administration of the grain-export assemblies down to 1275.

Most assemblies in Languedoc served the purposes and convenience of the rulers who convoked them. Their history corresponds to the course of public events in the thirteenth century: war and peace, political settlement, economic regulation, and finance. Military circumstances were very important. They not only account for the origins of the general court of Agenais and much of importance in the associative work of other northern dioceses, but were paramount in the royal politics of the later thirteenth century. As late as 1300 the administration of assemblies and armies—the form of letters and procedures of summons—ran closely parallel. Whatever the subject at hand, princes, or more commonly their officers, initiated and controlled proceedings in assembly. They collected the spoken and written evidence of allegiance, gave publicity to decisions (already reached), or issued in their own names acts advised by those who attended. Counsel had limited constitu-

14 *H.L.*, x, 427–428.

tional significance, though it seems to have been legally requisite in many situations during the thirteenth century. It sometimes served as a device for implicating communities in difficult decisions.

About consent in assemblies relatively little is heard, but that little is remarkable. The general court of Agenais, in another manifestation of its adaptability, became the instrument by which the towns and magnates acted on their newly gained rights in the episcopal coinage. The bishops of Cahors suffered a comparable restriction of their monetary prerogatives. In Quercy, too, the finance of peace armies was negotiated in general assemblies, including delegated townsmen. Elsewhere, peace movements had been instituted in conventions, but without constitutional sequel. Royal officials did not convoke assemblies for financial purposes until the reign of Philip III, and rarely did so before the 1290's. Even then they avoided procedures that might attribute authority to assemblies.

More important than consent for the development of constitutionalism in Languedoc was the linking of privilege with assemblies in various ways. Royal agents encountered resistance from the men of Agenais when using the general court of that district to obtain fealties. Reciprocal oaths of good government and fidelity were commonly made in assemblies by the later thirteenth century. Moreover, the general summons had become sufficiently institutionalized that magnates might grumble if it were administered in an unprecedented and undignified manner. Traditions such as these were not likely to be effaced. They undoubtedly survived the institution with which they had at first been associated in Agenais; and they probably subsisted in the custom of Languedoc to find a place in the privileged bodies of a much later day. It is especially in this sense —this recognition of developing collective privilege—in accord with the views of Professor Lousse and the corporatist historians, that the experience of thirteenth-century

Languedoc has significance in the larger history of representation. Yet this is not to deny that the actual assemblies, whether prescribed by law or contrived *ad hoc*, could have been memorable precedents. The conciliar summons had come into general use and had been extended to include townsmen; and experiments with representation had been undertaken.

Something more needs to be said of these various developments in their relation to the two laws, which afforded a wealth of analogies, precedents, and models. The institutionalized summons, particularly in its epistolary form, owed much to canon law and procedure. Grants of full powers to representatives were commonly patterned on the forms of written law. The Roman-canonical principle "what touches all should be approved—or discussed—by all" explicitly or implicitly underlies many a summons for counsel or consent. Canon law relating to laymen in councils or synods helps explain some of the mixed assemblies of the crusading period. References to corporate or majoritarian decisions, though very rare in general convocations, unmistakably betray their legal origin.

Yet it is by no means clear that principles always influenced practice in Languedoc. Canon law was directly pertinent to but few important assemblies studied in this book, and Roman law to none at all. Even if probable, it is not certain, that the canonist argument for popular consent to monetary mutations had bearing on developments in upper Languedoc. The recognized distinction between counsel and consent very likely derives as fully from customary practice as from written law. Perhaps not surprisingly, Roman-canonical influence seems most evident in those meetings where legal rights were, or presumably were, involved. But the ubiquitous relevance of *quod omnes tangit* . . . should not lead us to conclude that much stress was laid on the authority of assemblies in the thirteenth century. People were motivated by practical realities at least as much as by legal theories, and most people seem to have been more conscious of their obligations than their rights. In any case, even those obligations had their sanction—or analogy—in the two laws. We begin to find references to "urgent cause," "necessity," and the like, implying the superior right of authorities to obtain the approval that they were obliged to seek. In view of this it is remarkable how slowly procuration came to be used as a way of getting judicial-conciliar consent. Canon law required bishops to attend councils or synods, and in person, when justly summoned.[15] It prescribed a procedure of excuse that was sometimes followed in secular assemblies. Even the use of assemblies to explain laws or policies could find support in canon law. But this takes us beyond the range of demonstrable influences. Independent parallels and experiment have a role in history that can easily be underestimated.

Whatever the point of view, the thirteenth century must be regarded as a time of origins, a formative age, in the development of French parliamentary institutions. For, of course, Languedoc became a part of France in that period. The expansion of Capetian authority is the predominant fact of this history. The appeals to "right of state," heard in Languedoc at least as early as 1272, must have been repeated in many a later assembly where the exigencies of alleged emergencies brought national designs into conflict with local rights. The rise of procuration among communities may have had some significance in this connection. It is understandable that increasing royal authority should sometimes have encountered unsolicited representative procedures that were indicative of a growing consciousness of local and corporate privileges.

Localism persisted, indeed, despite royal inclinations toward governmental unity. Languedoc was bound to

---

[15] This point not having been documented above, reference may be made to *Decretum*, dist. 18, cc. 5, 9, 10; Innocent IV, *Apparatus*, to *Extra*, I, 33, 9, ad v. *statuendum*.

France, but only through the king and bureaucracy.[16] Otherwise it remained more like a collection of provinces than one province. The term "Lingua de Hoc" did not enter the administrative vocabulary until the close of the thirteenth century.[17] It is significant that an assembly for the whole territory summoned in 1303 should have broken down into sessions held in three different places.[18] Previously the basic unit for general assemblies had been the city and surrounding countryside. Within that compass the most nearly national issues—the crusade, or wars of Philip the Fair—had been presented to the people. And such localized problems as the coastal trade or the taking of seisin, district by district, had occasioned some of the very remarkable assemblies of thirteenth-century France. The study of early French representation cannot be divorced from the local environment.

The place of Languedoc in the national picture is not yet wholly clear. As the most distant of royal districts from the king's northern base of operations, it may have served in some ways as a testing-ground for Capetian bureaucratic government. Southern officials of the later thirteenth century were certainly discreet and empirical in their use of assemblies. They continued to employ alternative administrative procedures. Yet no other royal provinces of France seem to have had so much experience with convocations in

[16] See J. R. Strayer, *Early French Taxation*, p. 93.

[17] See, e.g., *H.L.*, x, 247,iii.

[18] *Documents Relatifs aux États Généraux*, pp. xxi–xxxvii; no. 137. Moreover, administrative practices varied from one district to another in conformity with different circumstances. Seneschals of Carcassonne were accustomed to summoning and dealing with more towns and villages in their *sénéchaussée* than the seneschals of Beaucaire were in theirs (see pp. 194, 197ff., 281). Probably this is why the seneschal of Carcassonne seems to have been given more latitude than the seneschal of Beaucaire in citing towns for the assembly of Paris in 1302 (Taylor, "New Texts," 39–40). If so, it is significant that the central chancery should be aware of these variations.

bailliage or *sénéchaussée* as Languedoc. This may help to explain the fact that in the summer of 1303, when the king sought political commitments all around the nation, general assemblies were held only in Languedoc. The full significance of early assemblies and representation in Languedoc will become evident when comparable studies of other areas are made. Meanwhile let us no longer prejudice the subject or deny it a place in historical research by seeking a proto-constitutionalism in the twelfth and thirteenth centuries. Something of this may indeed turn up, but only as a by-product of investigations more realistically conceived. Medieval assemblies and representation can best be understood in the perspective of administrative history.

APPENDIX I

۞ Aspects of Town Assemblies in the Thirteenth Century

Urban parliaments and assemblies have no place in this study in their own right. But it would be misleading to ignore them entirely, for they were the most common and characteristic local assemblies of medieval Languedoc. The fact that they could be summoned by lords as well as consuls helps to explain why the former could often do without central convocations of town deputies. Moreover, some feudal courts included parliaments, or were confused with them; and in other instances, where the primal identity of the town seems to be that of a seigneurial unit, local assemblies must have been more like aristocratic courts than parliaments. In certain functions, too, the town assemblies bear some relation to provincial bodies. What follows is a summary of various points about town meetings that may contribute to our understanding of regional convocations.[1]

Most urban assemblies fall into well-recognized medieval categories, and they had the character of established institutions. First there was the general town meeting, most often referred to as the *parlamentum* or *colloquium generale*. Theoretically the whole town, or its aggregate of freemen, the parliament was contemporaneous with the ori-

[1] There are no detailed studies of southern French town assemblies, but see generally P. Dognon, *Institutions*, pp. 72–91; P. Timbal, "Villes de Consulat dans le Midi . . . ," *Recueils Société Jean Bodin*, vi (1954), 360–369; and for Toulouse, J. H. Mundy, *Toulouse*, ch. 12.

ginal seigneurial community.[2] Unquestionably it antedated the organization of consulates or specialized local governments. The consuls only gradually came to share the lords' right to convoke it. The parliament convened at irregular intervals on a general, public summons, issued usually through the shouts or horn blasts of a town crier.[3] The gathering might occasionally include several hundred townsmen —and thus be bigger than a general regional assembly— but, except in villages, it must have been uncommon for any large proportion of the populace to assemble. While patricians and notables usually dominated the parliaments, the "little people," or *populares*, were by no means excluded.[4] Quite distinct were the appointed or elected municipal councils. They were instituted together with or after the consulates, and were usually, but not always, organs of consular government.[5] Though varying greatly in size, the councils tended to be relatively small, often comparable in

[2] Dognon, p. 87; cf. J. Ramière de Fortanier, *Chartes de Franchises du Lauragais* (Paris, 1939), pp. 39–40; R. Grand, *Les "Paix" d'Aurillac*, ch. 1.

[3] A. M. Toulouse, AA.3, fols. 230–231; *Coutumes et Privilèges du Rouergue*, eds. E. Baillaud, P. Verlaguet, 2 vols. (Toulouse, 1910), II, 14; *I.A.C., Narbonne, Annexes de la Série AA*, no. 42, p. 70. An undated Narbonne custumal, *ibid.*, no. 111, p. 187, probably of the late 13th century, required the consuls to convoke parliaments at least once a month. The phrase *ut moris est* was commonly added to formulas, e.g., *H.L.*, VIII, 1669,ii; *Chartes du Lauragais*, p. 293; *Layettes*, IV, no. 5399.

[4] Dognon, *Institutions*, pp. 69, 86, discussing a period running considerably beyond the 13th century, found that 300 to 400 was the maximum number designated when documents give names. But lists of jurors sometimes indicate larger gatherings, e.g., *Layettes*, II, no. 2429. See also C. Compayré, *Études Historiques et Documents Inédits sur l'Albigeois* . . . (Albi, 1841), pp. 149–150; *Chartes d'Agen*, no. 44.

[5] Dognon, pp. 87–88, suggests that they were strictly subject to the consuls. But lords also acted with them, R. Limouzin-Lamothe, *Commune de Toulouse*, pp. 274–275; *I.A.C., Narbonne, Annexes de la Série AA*, no. 8, pp. 9–11.

numbers to the consular bodies. A large but indefinite *commune consilium* appears at Toulouse in the mid-twelfth century, becoming smaller in the following years, and again enlarging as the *commune ac generale consilium* during the crusade period.[6] The latter body may at times have included a hundred or more leading citizens, but this was exceptional for Toulouse as well as for the Midi in general.[7] Councillors can usually be identified socially with the ubiquitous *probi homines*, townsmen, including knights, who had attained prominence through birth and wealth. There was no hard and fast line between "councils" and otherwise unqualified gatherings of "good men" which were similar in composition and function.[8] Councils and consular bodies were composed according to representative principles in many towns of Languedoc in the thirteenth century.[9] But this practice had no significant bearing on representation in assemblies. Besides parliaments and councils, mixed bodies of knights, consuls, burghers, even clergy, convened on occasion.[10] It is not always clear to what territorial scope such gatherings correspond.

Attendance in town parliaments was restricted as a rule to men living within the town limits. For practical purposes these limits, at least among the cities and *castra*, were the walls and fortifications. Even in these places, however, scattered tenements and small farms could be found outside

[6] Limouzin-Lamothe, pp. 152–154; Mundy, *Toulouse*, pp. 149–151.

[7] In some large communities, including Béziers, the bourgs of Narbonne and Carcassonne, and Millau, there were two bodies of *consiliarii*, the "privy" and general councils, Dognon, *Institutions*, pp. 88–89.

[8] *H.L.*, VIII, 391–392; *Layettes*, I, no. 743, art. 3; A.D. Tarn-et-Garonne, A.297, fols. 181v–183v; "Statutes on Clothmaking: Toulouse, 1227," ed. Sister Mary Ambrose Mulholland, *Essays . . . in Honor of Austin Patterson Evans*, p. 172.

[9] That is, in correspondence to social groups and corporations; see Dognon, *Institutions*, pp. 69, 90–91.

[10] See, e.g., *Privilèges du Rouergue*, I, 100; *H.L.*, VIII, 1547.

the walls. Many suburban inhabitants were included politically in the urban unit. They were enfranchised, sharing in their town's liberties and its obligations. But there is no reason to think that they were very regularly included in the public summons.

In larger communities, such as Agen, Toulouse, and Narbonne, rural appurtenances sometimes extended far beyond the boundaries of jurisdiction (often called the *dex*).[11] Like so many seigneurs, the towns came to control outlying villages and parishes. In 1263 several consuls of Narbonne made a certain protest to the viscount, speaking "for themselves and the whole *universitas* of the city of Narbonne and for the men of the villages who belong to their community [i.e., of Narbonne] and are, and are known to be, citizens of the aforesaid city."[12] The men of outer suburbs, like those of nearby ones, were welcome in the *universitas* of obligations, particularly town taxes, but were otherwise left out; and the parliamentary summons rarely, if ever, reached them. Agen may have been exceptional in this respect. The local custom provided that men of the "city and bourgs of Agen" should congregate when the lord first appeared there to receive his oath and to offer theirs in turn. And when a seneschal was appointed, the consuls were to act as representative recipients and jurors for the association of "city and surrounding bourgs."[13] The

[11] On jurisdictional limits at Toulouse see Mundy, *Toulouse*, pp. 125–128; Limouzin-Lamothe, *Commune de Toulouse*, pp. 222–223. Also Dognon, *Institutions*, pp. 150–151; *C.A.*, I, no. 341; A.M. Narbonne, AA.109, fol. 36; for mention of *dex*, "Coutumes de Clermont-Dessus," ed. H. Rébouis, *N.R.H.D.F.É.*, V (1881), 75; *C.A.*, I, no. 486; II, no. 1647.

[12] A.M. Narbonne, AA.24. Cf. A.M. Nîmes, 00.82, similar situation at Nîmes early in 14th century.

[13] H. Tropamer, *Coutume d'Agen*, p. 26; cf. *Layettes*, II, no. 177; *Chartes d'Agen*, no. 44. One of these bourgs, Lamothe-Bézat, received a charter in 1252 from two citizen-lords in Agen, M. Gouron, *Chartes de Franchises de Guienne*, no. 1131. Cf. also Sabatier, "Les Bourgs de Béziers," *Bull. Soc. . . . de Béziers*, 2ᵉ sér., IX (1877), 129–148.

seigneury of Agen, so specified, doubtless extended beyond the central city and bourg; how far beyond is uncertain.

In the barony of Lunel, which encompassed numerous "small villages" (*villete*), the notables of the central town sometimes spoke for, or assumed, a kind of community of "the land of Lunel" in their campaign for municipal rights.[14] In western Languedoc there were a few places with political institutions clearly representative of districts extending considerably beyond the immediate town limits. An explanation for this may be found in the fact that certain rural consulates evolved directly from small viscounties and seigneuries. By the middle of the twelfth century, there were consuls "d'Ambilet e d'Ambialadès," a little Tarn valley viscounty. And in 1232 Sicard-Bertrand of Lautrec granted a charter of liberties to the "universitat de Lautrec et de Lautreguès."[15] This corporate union of town and countryside long remained in effect. A memorandum of southern towns summoned to an assembly in 1316 lists "Lautrico" and "Lautergisio";[16] and a subsequent fourteenth-century charter indicates that members of the "one single consulate" were chosen equally from the town and from three other places of Lautregais.[17] For lack of evidence we cannot say how plenary parliaments in these areas

[14] A.D. Gard, C.66; A.N., J.302, no. 6; cf. B.N., MS Lat. 9173, fol. 140.

[15] Charters edited (badly) by Compayré, *Albigeois*, pp. 335, 494. The Ambialet document seems to date from the 12th century, but M. Greslé-Bouignol, archivist of the Tarn, believes that the text is almost hopelessly corrupt.

[16] Mention of "Ambialadès," *ibid.*, pp. 342–344; "Lautreguès," e.g., A.D. Tarn, E.2196, no. 2; E.12, no. 8; C. H. Taylor, "Assemblies of French Towns in 1316," *Speculum*, XIV, 281.

[17] Compayré, *Albigeois*, p. 449, art. 1 (1338): "Quod in dicta villa seu Castro et toto vicecomitatu est unus solus consulatus in quo sunt sex consules annuales quorum tres sunt ville predicte et alii de locis Lautriguesii . . ."; this was surely true earlier. The 12th-century charter of Ambialet refers to "seix homes d'Ambilet d'Ambialadès [*sic*]," as composing the consulate, p. 333.

might have been constituted. But there seems to have been a kind of local seigneurial assembly, probably a carry-over from earlier feudal practices. Gatherings of knights and "good men" are attested both at Lautrec and Paulin just before the institution of consular government, an apparent indication that there was as yet no clear differentiation between courts and parliaments.[18] In 1270 men of numerous manses in the valley of Cèze (Gévaudan) received from their lord a corporate charter, which guaranteed their right to assemble freely as a university.[19] The establishment of administrative townships, or *baylies*, tended to broaden the local community in the course of the thirteenth century. It has been shown that assemblies began to be held in *baylies* and *vigueries*.[20]

Town parliaments embodied such residual powers as townsmen possessed, but their rights were usually very limited. It is true that in some places they were electoral organs. They chose consuls at Albi and Rabastens,[21] and sometimes at Toulouse.[22] We hear of proctors or syndics being elected

[18] *H.L.*, VIII, 582–583 (Lautrec, 1209), an enfranchisement approved by the viscount, "ab coisseil & ab voluntat d'aquests cavaders sobredigs [6 names] & ab cosseil & ab voluntat dels barrias del castel de Lautrec [15 names]"; these *barrias* were evidently the more prominent townsmen living in the agglomerated dwellings below the castle or fortifications (cf. DuCange, ad.v. *barriani*, and *H.L.*, VIII, 1295); Compayré, *Albigeois*, p. 340 (Paulin, 1253), customs granted to the men "de Paulinh e de la terra de Paulinhès," by viscount of Lautrec, with approval "dels cavaziers e dels donzels e dels prohomes de Paulinh."

[19] A. Philippe, *Tournel*, no. 42, pp. 154–161.

[20] But I know of no legal statement in Languedoc quite like that of the Gascon custumal of 1275 which authorized the consuls of Sainte-Gemme to convoke their councillors "and other good men of the said *baylie*" to deal with town business, J. Monlézun, *Histoire de Gascogne . . .*, 6 vols. (Auch, 1846–1867), VI, 275.

[21] Compayré, *Albigeois*, pp. 160, 168–169, 449; cf. pp. 471–472.

[22] See Mundy, *Toulouse*, pp. 156–157, and references; A. Molinier, "Commune de Toulouse & Philippe III," *H.L.*, X, 150–151;

in assemblies at Montpellier, Pamiers, and elsewhere; and as early as 1207 the customs of Saint-Bertrand-de-Comminges provide for the choice of town syndics by consuls, councillors, and other "good men" of the city.[23] If deputies to regional assemblies were not so elected, it was not for lack of precedent in other activities.

In legislative matters, the councils generally advised, while the parliaments approved. In towns where the base of political power was unusually wide, as at Albi and Agen, the general assembly may have had some control of legislation.[24] The record is usually too discontinuous to indicate whether, at a given period, lords and consuls were obliged to consult assemblies,[25] though individual documents have a certain interest. An important statute of December 1258 regulated the proportion of wealth to be paid as annual *taille* respectively by citizens of Narbonne resident in the town or *pays*, and those resident elsewhere. Its opening—

see also Limouzin-Lamothe, *Commune de Toulouse*, no. 103, p. 460; and cf. A.M. Toulouse, AA.3, no. 129, fols. 197–200.

[23] A.M. Montpellier, Arm. E, cass. 1, nos. 1979, 1986, 1987; Arm. G, cass. 6, no. 3388; A.M. Villeneuve-les-Maguelonne, AA.1, fols. 30v–31; *Layettes*, IV, no. 5299; A. D. Aude, H.153, no. 1. Syndics of Tourbes in 1247 were "constituti a com[m]unitate tocius populi castri de Turvibus," a phrase very suggestive of a plenary assembly, *H.F.*, XXIV, 352, no. 153*bis*; and a mandate for Agen of 1262, drafted in the name of *consules et universitas*, may likewise have been the work of a town meeting, *Chartes d'Agen*, no. 54; "tota" precedes the word "universitas" in an accompanying letter of the same date, no. 53. *I.A.D., Haute-Garonne, Série E. Supplément*, p. 6, art. 49.

[24] B.N., Doat, CV, 197; Compayré, *Albigeois*, p. 163; *Chartes d'Agen*, nos. 2, 44.

[25] Toulouse, with its rich cartulary, is exceptional in this respect and it seems significant that most enactments of the years just before and after 1200 were made with the consent of the common council; and these legislative bodies tended to increase in size and importance: see Mundy, *Toulouse*, p. 364, n. 15; A.M. Toulouse, AA.5, no. 139. See also, for an unusual law, at Narbonne, above, p. 301, n. 3.

"the *universitas* of city and bourg of Narbonne consenting, the consuls and general council, having consulted many wise men, have ordained that . . ."—indicates plainly the approval of an assembly, but contrasts its passivity with the active initiative of consuls and council.[26] The urban *taille* replaced the declining seigneurial *taille*, but on a different basis. It was not an arbitrary tax, even when, as was often the case, it lay within the consuls' administrative prerogative. And when princes demanded money, as they did increasingly, the right of the inhabitants to approve such taxes, written into many charters, was sometimes exercised in assemblies.[27] In the first extensive financial negotiations, during the decade or so before the crusade of 1270, towns were consulted individually.[28]

The constitutional function of town assemblies has not yet been made fully clear. Historians have long believed that, in general, southern French townsmen had greater powers in government than their northern counterparts.[29] If so, this must have resulted in some measure from the growing recognition of legal rights within the communities. The revived Roman law was available to contribute to the proc-

[26] A.M. Narbonne, AA.109, fol. 36. This act is mentioned in a memorandum, fol. 31, as one of "duo statuta facta a communitate Narbone."

[27] C. Stephenson, *Mediaeval Institutions*, pp. 12–13; *I.A.D., Haute-Garonne, Série E. Supplément*, p. 4, art. 25; Limouzin-Lamothe, *Commune de Toulouse*, no. 81, pp. 419–420; B.N., Doat, LXXXVII, 30–31; M.A.F. de Gaujal, *Rouergue*, I, 328; *Ordonnances*, XII, 482; etc.; and for assemblies, *H.L.*, VIII, 1669–1671,ii,iii (these documents present difficulties of interpretation which cannot be dealt with here); A.M. Narbonne, AA.105, fols. 80v–81 (cf. *I.A.C., Narbonne, Annexes de la Série BB*, II, no. 4, 7–9; and no. 1, 4).

[28] See Stephenson, *Mediaeval Institutions*, pp. 20–24, on Alfonse of Poitiers' *fouages*; and for royal impositions, *H.L.*, VIII, 1669,ii; A.M. Narbonne, AA.105, fols. 80v–81.

[29] See P. Viollet, *Institutions*, III, 70; É. Chénon, *Droit Français*, I, 647.

ess, though just how far it did will require detailed study beyond the limits of this appendix. All that can be said here is that theoretically any assembly was bound to hear matters touching popular interests, thus, according to procedural rules, justifying the summons. Nevertheless, *quod omnes tangit* . . . was not explicit in the written custom of Languedoc. And in practice it appears that town assemblies were more important in their political-administrative role than their constitutional role. Townsmen usually meet because consuls and lords find it expedient to summon them. It was the part of practical wisdom, whether in accord with a law of rights or not, to explain policies and laws and justify taxes. This is especially evident in local assemblies convoked to "approve" charters of customs.[30] Other important acts are passed "in the presence of" townspeople.[31] Publicity of this sort had a juridical aspect, to be sure. What occurred in assemblies was recorded in legal documents, official records whose certification was somewhat dependent on the number and character of those present. That this could be put to a test is shown by a decision of royal *enquêteurs* in 1262, which upheld certain seigneurial rights in a village near Béziers partly because they had received public recognition in an assembly there.[32] But attendance

[30] Ramière de Fortanier, *Lauragais*, p. 656, promulgation of a charter for St-Michel-de-Lanès in 1266 with consent of *universitas*; but the enactment cannot have been invalid without such consent, for the consuls had petitioned in the first place for clarification of the local constitution. It was expedient that the villagers should know their law, and what was understood was thereby regarded as approved. Cf. *Arch. Gir.*, vii, 13–14; *I.A.C., Narbonne, Annexes de la Série AA*, no. 50, p. 89.

[31] A.M. Pézenas, no. 1190 (11,11,7); A.M. Narbonne, AA.107, fol. 78v; *H.L.*, v, 40; Limouzin-Lamothe, *Commune de Toulouse*, no. 103, pp. 460–463; and cf. *Layettes*, ii, nos. 3350, 3351; iii, nos. 3588, 3599.

[32] *H.F.*, xxiv, 664jk. Usually the assembly was legal evidence of publicity rather than validity (cf. A. Giry, *Manuel de Diplomatique*, p. 614); but in some cases its designation forms part of the

and approval do not necessarily, or even normally, mean initiative or consent.

There are many examples of municipal assemblies that were called to hear explanations of policies or to rally support. This was especially needful in time of war, and it is not by chance that the viscount of Narbonne insisted on his rights to *parlamentum* and *exercitus* in the same context in certain articles of about 1260.[33] The *Chanson* describes efforts by the bishop of Béziers to swing a plenary assembly over to submission to the crusaders in 1209; and the situation was similar at Toulouse in 1216, when the abbot of Saint-Sernin urged the cause of Simon de Montfort before "cavaler e borzes e la cominaltatz."[34] Loyalty in time of peace was also important. Public oaths of all kinds were administered in town assemblies. This activity was thoroughly political and propagandistic, designed to reinforce seigneurial authority. Charters commonly specify that the community should swear fidelity and obedience to the overlord or consuls.[35] It is not always clear that this had to be done in assembly, but the records show that it often was.[36] The progress of urban rights against lords and crown can be measured in the oaths increasingly required of officials.

witness list proper, which thus has its extreme extension, and imparts to the document a technically unimpeachable character: e.g., Limouzin-Lamothe, *Commune de Toulouse*, no. 103, pp. 460–463.

[33] *H.L.*, VIII, 1464: "Item habet generale parlamentum & exercitum & cavalcatam in hominibus antedictis commorantibus in Narbona & preconisationes exercitus." Cf. pp. 82, 85–89 on the administrative connection between armies and assemblies in Agenais.

[34] Ed. E. Martin-Chabot, I, 48; II, 218, 220. See also *Layettes*, V, no. 527; *H.L.*, VIII, 2402–2403.

[35] E.g., *H.L.*, VIII, 1168; Gaujal, *Rouergue*, I, 327; "Les Coutumes de l'Agenais: Monclar . . . ," *N.R.H.D.F.É.*, XIV (1890), 405; "Charte de Coutumes de Gimont," ed. A. Thomas, *An. du Midi*, VIII (1896), 10, art. 15; and see also Compayré, *Albigeois*, pp. 379–382.

[36] A.M. Cahors, DD.12*bis*; B.M. Alès, 1S IV, no. 4; and see ch. 4, pp. 162ff.

At Agen the oaths were mutual and reciprocal; and by mid-century, public oaths of faithful administration had a recognized place in the customs of Languedoc.[37] Though most of the evidence of oaths in town assemblies dates from the period of royal administration, it is evident that this practice, like other activities in parliaments, had been inherited from the older feudal Languedoc.

[37] Above, p. 303 and n. 13; *H.L.*, VIII, 1168; *N.R.H.D.F.É.*, XIV, 405; Gaujal, *Rouergue*, I, 327; A.M. Narbonne, AA.109, fol. 34; *Cartulaire de . . . Lodève*, ed. E. Martin, no. 57, p. 65; *H.L.*, X, p. 168, art. 6; VIII, 1345–1347, and art. 12; *Enquêtes d'Alfonse*, no. 9, p. 70 (11); no. 10, p. 71.

APPENDIX II

Select Documents

1. 7 April 1243, Castelsarrasin. Oath of fealty to king and Church sworn by twenty-seven assembled barons, castellans, and knights of Agenais.
Original, A.N., J.306, no. 80.
Indicated in *Layettes*, II, no. 3074; *H.L.*, VIII, 1119.

Noverint universi quod nos barones, castellani, et milites Agennensis diocesis, videlicet Arnaldus Oto, vicecomes de Lomania et de Alto Vilar, Amaneus de Lebret, Bernardus de Roviniano, Arnaldus de Monte Acuto, Bego de Calvo Monte, Ugo de Roviniano, Nopars de Caumont, Esquiu de Fumel, Aimericus de Roviniano, Bernardus de Duroforte, Gausbertus de Thesaco, Raimundus de Planels, Arnaldus de Duroforte, Arnaldus Araman de Aspero Monte, Raimundus de Poiols, Arnaldus de Duroforte, Pontius Amaneus de Madeliano, Gasto de Gontaut, Arnaldus de Monte Pesat, Arnaldus de Yspania, Aimericus de Roviniano, Vitalis de Gontaut, Galterus de Fossato, Raimundus Bernardus de Balencs, Guillelmus Aramun de Pis, Arnaldus Garsias de Fossato, Guillelmus Aramun Lorc, nos omnes et singuli, de voluntate et mandato speciali domini nostri R., Dei gratia comitis Tholose, marchionis Provincie, et in eiusdem presentia, promittimus bona fide domino Ludovico, Dei gratia regi Francie, et tactis sacrosanctis evangeliis manibus propriis iuramus, quod si comes Tholose vel alius nobiscum habuerit consilium de pace facta Parisius, consulemus eis, quod eam servent, et nos servabimus eam quantum ad nos pertinet posse nostro, et dabimus operam efficacem quod comes Tholose servet eam. Et si comes Tholose veniret contra, nos adherebimus ecclesie et domino regi Francie contra ipsum, nisi infra .xl. dies postquam monitus fuerit hoc emendaverit vel iuri steterit coram ecclesia de hiis que ad ecclesiam pertinent, et iuri coram domino rege Francie de hiis que ad dominum regem Francie pertinent. Promittimus etiam et iuramus quod nos iuvabimus ecclesiam contra hereticos credentes, receptatores hereticorum, et omnes alios, qui ecclesie contrarii existent, occasione heresis vel contemptus excomunicationis in terra, et dominum regem Francie iuvabimus contra omnes, et quod eis faciemus vivam guerram donec ad mandatum ecclesie et domini regis revertantur. Et si comes Tholose moveret guerram domino regi Francie vel heredibus eiusdem, quod absit, nos adhereremus domino regi Francie et heredibus eius contra eundem comitem Tholose. In cuius rei testimonium nos omnes supradicti et singuli, quia propria sigilla nobiscum non habebamus, presentem paginam sigillo domini nostri R., Dei gratia comitis Tholose, marchionis Provincie, supradicti, facimus communiri. Actum est in ecclesia Beate Marie extra Castrum Sarraceni, anno Domini .m°. cc°. x1°. iii°, vii° ydus Aprilis.

2. November 1251. Monetary convention between the bishop and consuls of Cahors, the latter representing city and diocese.

    Copy, B.N., Doat, cxviii, 124–125v.

Bartholomaeus, Dei gratia episcopus Caturcensis, universis et singulis ad quos litterae istae pervenerint, salutem in Domino. Noverit universitas vestra quod cum nos mutaverimus et innovaverimus monetam Caturci et ipsam fecerimus operari in lege trium denariorum boni argenti ac legitimi tenentis duos denarios et obolum sterlingorum tantummodo et non plus usque ad finum argentum in qualibet marcha argenti et in pondere viginti solidorum et quatuor denariorum pro qualibet marcha, et debent fieri sex denarii tantum in libra qualibet obolorum ad tres denarios minus pogeza legis talis argenti sicut de denariis superius est expressum et viginti solidorum ponderis pro qualibet marcha, ipsam monetam praedictam mutatam et innovatam duximus consulibus Caturcensibus nomine suo ac totius universitatis Caturci et totius terrae Caturcini [*sic*] recipientibus confirmandam, promittentes et firmiter convenientes consulibus supradictis, nomine suo ac totius universitatis Caturci et totius terrae Caturcini recipientibus, quod monetam praedictam Caturcensem quam mutavimus et innovavimus bonam et legittimam servabimus et custodiemus toto tempore vitae nostrae tali lege et pondere, sicut superius est expressum, promittentes insuper et firmiter convenientes consulibus supradictis recipientibus nomine suo ac totius universitatis Caturci et totius terrae Caturcini quod dictam monetam factam et faciendam non mutavimus nec innovavimus, imo ipsam bonam et firmam et legitimam tali lege et pondere sicut superius est expressum servabimus, tenebimus, et custodiemus toto tempore vitae nostrae et ad vitam nostram firmiter confirmamus et ita ut superius dictum est et expressum nos Bartholomaeus episcopus antedictus promisimus et promittimus consulibus supradictis recipientibus nomine suo ac totius universitatis Caturci et totius terrae Caturcini quod nos omnia supradicta et singula in hac praesenti carta contenta rata habebimus, tenebimus toto tempore vitae nostrae atque firma. In cuius rei testimonium praesenti cartae sigillum nostrum duximus apponendum. Actum et datum anno Domini millesimo ducentesimo quinquagesimo primo mense Novembris.

3. 22 November 1265, Narbonne. The viscount of Narbonne confirms his coinage before a public parliament of the town, meeting in his court.
    Contemporary copy, A.M. Narbonne, AA.109, fol. 34. Indicated in *I.A.C., Narbonne, Série AA*, ed. Mouynès, p. 140.

Anno nativitatis Christi m.cc.lx quinto et x kalendas Decembris, dominus Amalricus, Dei gratia vicecomes et dominus Narbone, vocato parlamento generali in curia sua, et ibi, ad preces et instanciam Guillelmi Ramundi de Montepessullano, Poncii Alarosii, Bertrandi Stephani et Ramundi Lumbardi, consulum civitatis Narbone, Petri Arnaldi de Naissa, Boneti Contastini, Guillelmi Arnaldi de Trularibus, Bernardi Faidia, Bernardi Revelli et Ramundi Andorra, consulum burgi Narbone, et tocius populi Narbone tam civitatis quam burgi, juravit monetam Narbonesam quam de novo faciebat, in manu dicti Poncii Alarosii, et eam manutenere et conservare in omni vita sua, et eciam confirmavit monetam Narbonesam per dominum Aimericum, patrem suum condam, nuper factam.

4. 5 December 1265, Cahors. Monetary convention between the bishop and consuls of Cahors, the latter representing city and diocese.

    Original, A.M. Cahors, DD.5.
    Partially printed in G. de Lacroix, *Series & Acta Episcoporum Cadurcensium*, pp. 134–135; indicated in Albe, *Cahors: Inventaire*, no. 68, p. 64.

Bartholomeus, Dei gracia episcopus Caturcensis, universis presentes litteras inspecturis, salutem in Domino. Noveritis quod cum nos fecissemus operari monetam in lege trium denariorum argenti et in pondere viginti solidorum et quatuor denariorum pro qualibet marcha, et predecessor noster bone memorie G., episcopus Caturcensis, fecisset operari monetam in minori pondere atque lege, quia moneta quam operari feceramus nimis grossa erat et toti terre per consequens honerosa videbatur, consules Caturci pro se ipsis et universitate Caturci et pro consulatibus et villis nec non et pro tota terra Caturcinii, ipsis consulatibus seu maiori parte ipsorum consencientibus, nos requisiverunt et cum instancia rogaverunt quod pro communi utilitate et evidenti tocius Caturcinii necessitate, a dicte monete fabrica cessaremus et operari monetam faceremus in lege duorum denariorum et oboli et unius grani argenti, ad argentum Montispessulani, et in pondere viginti trium solidorum minus duobus denariis pro qualibet marcha. Nos vero utilitatem communem nostre proprie preferre volentes ac dictis consulibus Caturci facere gratiam specialem, dictorum consulum de Caturco et consulatuum de Caturcinio precibus annuentes, eis annuimus et concessimus quod monetam faceremus in lege duorum denariorum et unius oboli et unius grani argenti, ad argentum Montispessulani, et in pondere viginti trium solidorum minus duobus denariis pro marcha, que equaliter currat cum moneta facta a predecessore nostro G., episcopo Caturcense, et quod isto modo et sub ista forma faceremus operari dictam monetam, quod propter hoc, nec ratione dicte factionis seu innovationis dicte monete, nullum ius adquiratur nobis seu nostris successoribus innovandi vel mutandi monetam, et quod dictis consulibus et universitati et aliis villis nullum propter hoc preiudicium generetur. Promittimus etiam dictis consulibus Caturci

pro se et universitate Caturci et tota terra Caturcinii recipientibus quod ratione dicte mutationis facte a nobis de dicta moneta
non possit eis aliquod fieri preiudicium in futurum nec nobis
vel successoribus nostris aliquod ius adquiri mutandi vel innovandi monetam. Et recognoscimus eis quod postquam semel
monetam mutaverimus, aliam facere sine eorum voluntate non
possumus nec debemus nec etiam aliquis successorum nostrorum potest, postquam semel monetam innovaverit vel mutaverit,
aliam facere nec mutare seu innovare. Et nos consules civitatis
Caturci recognoscimus vobis domino Bartholomeo, Dei gracia
episcopo Caturcensi, et ecclesie Caturcensi quod quilibet successorum vestrorum qui pro tempore fuerit episcopus Caturcensis poterit mutare vel innovare monetam Caturcensem semel
tantum modo et non amplius. Preterea nos dictus episcopus
promittimus et firmiter convenimus dictis consulibus Caturci
recipientibus pro se et universitate Caturci et pro tota terra
Caturcinii pro nobis et successoribus nostris, de concensu et
voluntate capituli nostri cathedralis ecclesie Sancti Stephani
Caturcensis, quod a nobis et successoribus nostris non oppona-
tur eis in posterum seu dicatur quod ratione dicte mutationis
nos et successores nostri ius habeamus aliquod immutandi vel
innovandi monetam. Insuper nos dictus episcopus promittimus
eisdem consulibus Caturci pro se et universitate Caturci et pro
tota terra Caturcinii recipientibus quod monetam predictam
quam innovamus vel mutamus de voluntate et de concensu
eorumdem in lege predicta duorum denariorum et oboli et unius
grani argenti, ad argentum de Montepessulano, et in pondere
viginti trium solidorum minus duobus denariis pro qualibet
marcha bonam et legittimam servabimus toto tempore vite
nostre et in tali lege et in tali pondere, prout supra proximo est
expressum, ipsam tenebimus et fideliter custodiemus et decetero
ipsam non mutabimus nec innovabimus nec aliam operari
faciemus et ipsam ad totam vitam nostram firmiter confirmamus. Et nos episcopus antedictus promittimus eis quod omnia
predicta et singula firma et illibata servabimus et quod contra
non veniemus aliquo jure vel aliqua ratione. Et nos capitulum
predictum voluntatem nostram et concensum omnibus predictis
prestamus et recognoscimus eisdem consulibus Caturci pro se
et universitate Caturci et pro tota terra Caturcinii recipientibus

omnia predicta et singula de concensu et voluntate nostra fuisse facta et promittimus eis omnia predicta et singula nos firma et illibata servare et contra non venire aliquo iure vel aliqua ratione. Et nos episcopus predictus in fidem et testimonium predictorum sigillum nostrum presentibus litteris duximus apponendum; et nos capitulum predictum in fidem et testimonium predictorum sigillum nostrum presentibus litteris duximus apponendum; et nos consules Caturci predicti sigillum nostrum presentibus litteris duximus apponendum in fidem et testimonium predictorum. Datum Caturci, anno Domini m° cc° lx° quinto, mense Decembris, die sabbati post festum Beati Andree apostoli.

5. 30 March 1270, probably at Narbonne. The consuls of Narbonne, having been cited by the seneschal of Carcassonne for violations of the grain-export statutes, set forth their position.
   Original or contemporary minute, A.M. Narbonne, HH. (uninventoried).
   Copy, B.N., Doat, L, 255–257v.

Noverint universi quod cum dominus Berengarius Peltrici, Arnaldo de Narbona, Johanni Benedicti, Bernardo Geraldi, Guillelmo de Fulano, Petro Ramundi de Ripparia, Beringario Alamberti, Ramundo Andree Ferre, Johanni Taloni et Petro de Gauderiis, consulibus Narbone, qui erant coram eo constituti in domo fratrum minorum Narbone, retulisset seu exposuisset quod, facto deffenso bladi in Narbona et in senescallia Carcassone per dominum senescallum Carcassone et Biterris, et postmodum per dominum Arnulfum de Choardono, militem domini regis, restricto seu iterum facto, et postea etiam per eundem dominum Arnulfum relaxato, consules predicti dictum deffensum seu ordinationem super eo factam minime servaverunt et fecerant contra eam et ob hoc assignasset eis diem mercurii proximam ad comparendum Carcassone coram dicto domino senescallo, mandans eis nichilominus ex parte eiusdem domini senescalli, ut mandatum super relaxamento dicti deffensi ab ipso domino Arnulfo factum, tenerent et servarent. Consules predicti responderunt et proposuerunt in hunc modum: proponunt consules Narbone quod ipsi et villa seu universitas Narbone, una cum domino archiepiscopo et domino Amalrico, habent deffensum bladi in Narbona de Capite Laucate usque ad Gradum Veneris, et sunt in possessione vel quasi huiusmodi deffensi, illudque deffensum habuerunt cum dominis predictis tanto tempore cuius non extat memoria. Item quod habent consules predicti et sunt in possessione vel quasi cum dictis dominis penarum exigendarum et cautionum recipiendarum et omnium que possunt sequi ratione vel occasione huiusmodi deffensi. Item proponunt quod ipsi consules hoc anno fecerunt deffensum bladi non extrahendi de Narbona per aquam ex causis legitimis et necessariis. Item proponunt quod ipsi consules, ad honorem domini regis et utilitatem passagii ultramarini et necessitatem omnium volentium transfretare seu subsidium aliquod prestare terre sancte et alia negotia dicti domini regis, parati sunt relaxare dictum deffensum quod fecerunt, dum tamen bladum portetur apud Montempessulanum vel ad Aquas Mortuas vel ad civitatem Aconensem vel alibi etiam quocumque dicto domino regi placuerit pro dicto negotio ultramarino et dicti domini regis dum illi qui bladum extrahent de Narbona prefatis dominis Narbone et eisdem consulibus in prestanda cautione et aliis faciant, prout est actenus consuetum. Item proponunt quod, si ipsi bladum de Narbona extraxerunt vel extrahi promiserunt, non fecerunt hoc ad offensam domini regis vel suorum, set pro iure suo et ville Narbone conservando, et pro iure suo et dicte ville, quod habent in dicto deffenso utendo. Item proponunt quod ipsi, ratione dicti mandati a dicto domino Arnulfo facti super relaxamento predicto, quod dicunt esse factum in preiudicium sui et ville Narbone, appellarunt ad dominum senescallum et dominum regem supradictos, si idem dominus senescallus eam admittere recusaret. Et non recedentes ab huiusmodi appellatione seu appellationibus, set eam vel eas pocius innovantes, a dicto mandato nunc per dictum dominum Berengarium Peltrici facto de servando relaxamento dicti deffensi, et a gravaminibus inde illatis ipsis consulibus et ville Narbone, et ab ipso domino Berengario Peltrici in quantum factum est in preiudicium ipsorum et ville Narbone pro se et aliis consulibus Narbone et pro universitate Narbone et omnibus et singulis eiusdem universitatis, ad dictum dominum senescallum in presenti appellant, et si ipse appellationem huiusmodi admittere recusaverit, ad dictum dominum Arnulfum appellant, et si ipse huic appellationi similiter non detulerit vel ad eos appellare non potuerit, ad dictum dominum regem Francie appellant apostolos qua convenit instantia postulando licet extra iudicium constituti, subponentes se et villam et universitatem Narbone et omnes et singulos eiusdem universitatis et bona sua, consiliarios et fautores et coadiutores suos, protectioni et deffensioni domini B[erengarii Peltrici sup]radicti, inhibentes ei nichilominus ex parte dicti domini regis ne super hiis contra eos vel villam Narbone vel aliquem de ipsa villa procedere pr[esumat], protestantes etiam dicti con[sules] se [esse] pro[mp]tos et paratos stare et parere per omnia super premissis cognitioni et omnimode voluntati domini regis supradicti. Acta sunt hec anno Domini .m. cc. septuagesimo et .iii. kalendas Aprilis, in presentia et testimonio Guillelmi Fabri, Bernardi de Monteolivo, Bertrandi de Capitolio, Johannis Vairani, Guillelmi Arnaldi de Trularibus, et plurium aliorum, et mei Raimundi de Catalani, scriptoris Narbone publici, qui predictis interfui, et hec rogatus scripsi et in formam publicam redegi.

6. 1 December 1270; 9, 13 February 1271; Béziers. The seneschal of Carcassonne summons clergy, nobles, and townsmen of the *viguerie* of Béziers to do fealty and recognize fiefs. Proceedings at Béziers.

Copy, B.N., Doat, CLV, 49v–54v.

Venerabilibus in Christo patribus episcopis, capitulis, abbatibus, conventibus, praeceptoribus, prioribus quorumlibet ordinum, et aliis personis ecclesiasticis, et nobilibus viris baronibus, terrariis, militibus, et burgensibus, et omnibus aliis personis apud Bitterrim et in tota vicaria Bitterrensi constitutis, Guillelmus de Cohardono, miles, senescallus Carcassonae et Bitterris, salutem et sinceram dilectionem. Mandamus vobis quathinus die jovis post octabas Beati Andreae apostoli apud Bitterrim compareatis personaliter coram nobis ad audiendum mandatum excellentissimi domini regis Franciae et ad faciendum nobis pro ipso recognitiones feudorum quae tenetis ab ipso et redeventias et servicia quae pro ipsis sibi facere debetis et ad praestandum iuramenta fidelitatis et ad faciendum alia quae pro his facere debetis et ad recognoscendum domino regi et nobis pro ipso castra, villas, res, et bona quae tenetis sub eius custodia praeter feuda. Datum apud Bitterrim in crastino sancti Andreae apostoli, anno Domini millesimo ducentesimo septuagesimo. Reddite literas portitori earumdem.

Et cum praedictus senescallus apud Bitterrim accessisset in octabas Beatae Mariae Candelosae anno dominicae incarnationis millesimo ducentesimo septuagesimo ad recipiendum pro domino rege iuxta mandatum ipsius [i.e., the king's order of 23 May 1270 (Doat, CLV, 49rv; *Ordonnances*, XI, 347–348), which was the basis for the seneschal's summons of December 1270] recognitiones supradictas, venerabiles patres dominus B., Dei gratia Tholosanus episcopus, pro se et in locum domini archiepiscopi Narbonensis, cuius vices gerit, et dominus Pontius Bitterrensis et dominus R. Lodovensis, dominus B. Magalonensis, eadem gratia episcopi, et dominus B., eadem gratia electus Carcassonae, tradiderunt eidem domino senescallo quaedam capitula sub his verbis:

Haec sunt novitates seu gravamina quae dominus senescallus Carcassonae vel curiae ipsius officiales faciunt seu facere attemptarunt in praeiudicium praelatorum et ecclesiasticae libertatis.

In primis quia fecerunt apud Bitterrim eos vocari publice per praeconem, quod nunquam alias extitit attemptatum, nec congruit rationi ad recognoscendum feuda quae tenebant ipsi domino senescallo.

Item quia compellunt seu compellere nituntur aliquos ad recognoscendum domino regi feuda praelatis recognita temporibus retroactis.

Item quia compellunt praelatorum et ecclesiarum subditos recognoscere domino regi alodia et feuda quae in territoriis vel districtu castrorum, villarum, seu aliorum locorum ipsorum praelatorum et ecclesiarum possident de quibus domino regi vel suis nunquam recognitio aliqua fuit facta et aliquando sine causae cognitione occupant indebite et iniuste.

Item quia contra debitum iuris et consuetudinem ab hominibus castrorum, villarum, caeterorumque locorum pertinentium ad ecclesias et praelatos fidelitatis exigunt iuramenta.

Item quia in negociis seu causis secularibus appellationes ad se factas admitunt a judicibus seu curiis praelatorum cum ad ipsos praelatos pertineat cognitio earumdem.

Super quibus capitulis praedictus senescallus, habito consilio multorum sapientum virorum peritorum, conveniens cum praedictis praelatis in domo domini episcopi Bitterrensis, et cum abbatibus Sancti Guillelmi Anianensis, Sancti Tiberii, Sancti Jacobi Bitterrensis, Sancti Pontii de Thomeriis, de Quadraginta, Sancti Pauli Narbonensis, Sancti Aniani, de Fontecalido, Sancti Ilarii, et cum multis aliis prioribus et procuratoribus aliorum abbatum et cum multis aliis personis ecclesiasticis ibi in communi consilio congregatis, de praedictis contulit amicabiliter reddendo singula singulis hunc modum:

Ad primum capitulum dicit senescallus quod vocationem praelatorum quam fecit ad faciendum recognitiones iuxta praedictum mandatum domini regis fecit per suas literas patentes decenter et honorabiliter, ut patet per tenorem suarum litterarum superius contentarum, nec fecit eos vocari per praeconem, nec sibi placet si factum fuit.

Ad secundum capitulum dicit quod ad huc neminem compulit ad recognoscendum feuda praelatis recognita, sed bene concessit immunitatem commissi feudorum illis qui indebitas recognitiones olim fecerunt aliis, dum modo infra tempus statutum ab ipso senescallo veniant ad ipsum ad faciendum veras et debitas recognitiones et ad recognoscendum suum errorem cum veritate, nec feuda diu est, scilicet antequam ipse fuisset senescallus, praelatis recognita vult recipere praedicto modo praelatis non vocatis nec auditis.

Ad tertium capitulum dicit quod neminem ad huc ad hoc compulit, et addit ut in praecedenti capitulo. Addit etiam quod omnes recognitiones quae factae sunt recepit salvo in omnibus iure domini regis, et etiam alieno et quandocumque ei fiet fides de plano quod aliqua receperit indebite ut in capitulo continetur paratus est in locis in quibus habent merum imperium ad statum debitum reducere de plano et sine dificultate et in dubiis supersedebit donec fuerit declaratum vel aliud sibi fuerit mandatum a domino rege vel a tenentibus locum eius, ita tamen quod ipsi praelati de his interim non recipiant recognitiones.

Ad quartum capitulum dicit quod ipse vel alius pro ipso non

exegit indebite juramentum fidelitatis a subditis praelatorum sed
bene mandavit vicario Bitterrensi quod de castris et villis suae
vicariae recipiat pro domino rege fidelitatis iuramenta pro iure
quod dominus rex in hominibus vel castris vel villis habet, et si
aliqua castra vel villae iurare noluerint non faciat aliquam
compulsionem sed eorum nomina scribat, ut inde possit facere
relationem domino regi, nec per hoc intendit ius in aliquo di-
minuere dominorum, sed ius domini regis requirere et salvare
cum alias tota terra ista praedecessoribus domini regis iuraverit
et cum dominus rex habeat exercitum et cavalcatam in omnibus
hominibus huius terrae et propter hoc domino regi debeant
esse fideles; verumtamen propter gratiam et praeces venerabilis
patris domini Bertrandi, Dei gratia episcopi Tholosani, vult
supercedere a receptione iuramentorum de castris et villis praelatorum donec dominus rex vel tenentes locum eius sibi suam
mandent voluntatem.

Ad quintum capitulum dicit quod nullas appellationes indebite recipit a judicibus secularibus praelatorum, imo appellantes
ad ipsos praelatos remitit donec secundo appelletur in quibus
secundis appellationibus recipiendis quae de iure communi ad
curiam domini regis fieri debent in nullo eis iniuriatur et cum
ressortum ad dominum regem pertineat in causis secularibus
tanquam ad superiorem principem secularem.

Qua collatione habita et recitata de mandato domini senescalli per magistrum Bartholomeum de Podio, domini regis Franciae clericum, iudicem Carcassonae, in praesentia omnium praelatorum praedictorum, idem judex, de mandato praedicti senescalli et ipso praesente, praedictas literas domini regis cum sigillo pendenti ipsius domini regis sigillatas eis ostendit et perlegit
nec non et praedictas literas sigillatas cum sigillo ipsius senescalli, requirens eos nomine et mandato ipsius senescalli, praeter
dominum episcopum Tholosanum, quem nescit aliquid tenere
in dicta senescallia, quod ipsi universi et singuli recognitiones
debitas domino regi faciant et praedicto senescallo nomine
ipsius iuxta continentiam literarum domini regis praedictarum,
taliter facientes quod fidelitas, devotio, et dilectio quam ad
dominum regem habent commendari debeat apud ipsum cum
honoris multiplicibus incrementis. Post haec die veneris sequenti
praedictus senescallus conveniens cum praedictis dominis epis-

copis in domo domini episcopi Bitterris, praedictis omnibus re-
petitis, dixit eis quod ob honorem et gratiam praedicti domini
episcopi Tholosani et ad preces ipsius de praedicta requisitione
supercedere volebat donec a domino rege vel a tenentibus locum
eius aliud receperit in mandatis; addens super tertio capitulo ad
preces et ob gratiam praedicti domini episcopi Tholozani quod
de recipiendis recognitionibus alodiorum et feudorum olim non
recognitorum in castris vel villis et earum territoriis in quibus
praelati habent minores iusticias mitit in suferentia donec a
domino rege vel a tenentibus locum eius aliud receperit in mandatis, dum modo ipsi praelati nullas interim de his recipiant
recognitiones.

Quae universa et singula praedictus senescallus dixit se facere
salvo in omnibus iure domini regis et alieno; dicti vero praelati
et gerentes vices domini archiepiscopi dixerunt quod supradictas responsiones et prorogationes ob reverentiam et gratiam
domini regis Franciae illustris sustinent absque suo suarumque
ecclesiarum et subditorum praeiudicio protestantes nihilominus
quod per supradicta vel aliquod praemissorum nullum sibi praeiudicium generetur et salvo in omnibus iure suo et etiam super
responsione tertii et quinti capitulorum quod dixerunt se non
consentire nec aprobare in quantum faciunt contra se nec dominus senescallus de praedictis responsionibus in quantum faciunt
pro iure domini regis conservando intendit in aliquo resilire
vel mutare intendens ius domini regis esse ut in eis
continetur.

Dixerunt etiam domini praelati supradicti super tertio capitulo et eius responsione quod de alodiis vel feudis praedictis
interim non recipient aliquas novas recognitiones in locis in
quibus habent tantum iusticias minores nec in locis in quibus
dubium erit inter dominum regem et ipsos.

Et ego Petrus de Parisius de Podio Nauterio, notarius publi-
cus domini regis, haec acta publica in his duobus rotulis parga-
mens conscita scripsi et praedictis interfui et signum meum ap-
posui anno et diebus quibus supra regnante Philippo rege
Francorum.

7. 5 August 1271, Carcassonne. Royal letter of summons
to towns of the *sénéchaussée* of Carcassonne for an assembly at Béziers on 13 August to consider whether to
prohibit the export of grain.

Contemporary copy, A.M. Narbonne, AA.109, fol.
38. Indicated in *I.A.C., Narbonne, Série AA.,* p.
141; and *H.L.,* VIII, 1741.

Viris venerabilibus providis et discretis et karissimis amicis
suis consulibus et comunitatibus Narbone, Carcassone, Biterris,
Agathe, et Ludove [*sic*], Gauffridus de Avesia, vicarius Biterris, tenens locum domini senescalli Carcassone et Biterris, salutem et dilectionem scinceram. Cum propter messes steriles et
bladi caristiam iminentem a quibusdam fuerimus cum instancia
requisiti de deffenso generali faciendo ne bladum extrahatur
per mare vel terram de senescallia Carcassone et Biterris et ob
hoc ad diem iovis post festum Beati Laurencii apud Biterrim
consilium prelatorum et aliorum bonorum virorum, prout in
institutis regalibus continetur, duxerimus convocandum, requirimus vos, rogamus, et mandamus, quatinus ad dictum consilium die et loco predictis veniatis, ad prestandum nobis bonum consilium quid super hiis agere debeamus. Datum Carcassone nonis Augusti, anno Domini m. cc. lxx. primo. Reddite
litteras.

8. 13 December 1274, Homps (Aude, canton Lézignan).
Royal letter of summons to clergy, nobles, and towns
of the *viguerie* of Béziers for an assembly at Carcassonne on 3 January 1275, to deliberate about grain
export and hear certain statutes. In essentials this text
is identical with that included in the export statute, but
is slightly fuller and better. Only the more significant
variants are noted.

Copy, A.M. Pézenas, Arm. A, lay. 2, liasse 3, ch. 1.
Indicated in *Pézenas: Inventaire de F. Resseguier,*
ed. Berthelé, no. 167; and included in royal statute
of 3 January 1275, B.N., MS Lat. 9996, fol. 87

(another copy in Doat, CLV, 123–131), printed in
H.L., X, 125–131.

Venerabilibus in Christo patribus et amicis suis karissimis
domino P., Dei gratia Narbonensi archiepiscopo, domino Pon-
cio Bitterensi, domino P. Agathensi, domino R. Lodovensi,
domino Magalonensi,[1] eadem gratia episcopis, et viris venerabilibus et discretis dominis abbatibus infrascriptis, videlicet[2] domino abbati Sancti Pauli Narbonensis, domino abbati Fontis-
frigidi, domino abbati Sancti Afrodisii Bitterensis, domino abbati Sancti Jacobi Bitterensis, domino abbati Sancti Tyberii,
domino abbati Vallismagne, domino abbati Aniane, domino abbati Sancti Guillelmi de Deserto, domino abbati Ville Magne,
domino abbati Jucellensis, domino abbati de Sancto Aniano,
domino abbati Lodove, domino abbati Sancti Pontii de Thomeriis, domino abbati Fontis Calidi, domino abbati de Quadraginta, et nobilibus viris de viccaria Bitterrensi, videlicet domino
Aymerico, vicecomiti Narbone, Amalrico de Narbona fratri
eius, domino Guillelmo de Durbanno, domino Bernardo de
Durbanno, domino Guausberto [*sic*] de Leucata, Berengario de
Boutenaco, domino P. de Claromonte, Berengario Guillelmi
domino Clarimontis, domino Guialfredo de Felgariis, Aymerico
de Claromonte, domino Berengario de Podio Soragorio, Aymerico de Bociacis,[3] Deodato[4] Armandi, Guillelmo de Andusia
domino Olargii, Sycardo de Muroveteri, domino Guillelmo de
Lodeva,[5] domino Guiraudo fratri eius,[6] Johanni de Insula, Pon-
cio de Thesano, Petro de Villa Nova domino de Caucio,[7] pre-

---

[1] Both texts omit the name or initial of this bishop (Bérenger
Frédol, *Gallia Christiana*, VI, 771–776).

[2] Omitted, *H.L.*, X, 126.

[3] I.e., Aymery de Boussagues. This is given, *ibid.*, 126, as "Aymerico de Benatis," but since there is no record of such a place or
person, the Pézenas reading must be accepted as correct.

[4] Preceded by "domino," *ibid.*, 126.

[5] Follows list of consuls, *ibid.*

[6] Follows list of consuls, *ibid.*

[7] Follows list of consuls, *ibid.* Notes 5–7 suggest that the copyist
of MS Lat. 9996 inadvertently omitted these names and inserted
them when he caught his error.

ceptori de Pedenacio, preceptori de Nebiano, preceptori de Petrosiis, preceptori hospitalis Jherusalem de Narbona, domino priori de Cassiano, consulibus Narbone, consulibus Biterris, consulibus Agathensibus, consulibus de Pedenacio, consulibus Lodove, vicario de Florentiaco, vicario de Aviaco, Guillelmus de Cohardono, miles domini regis Francie, senescallus Carcassone et Bitterris, salutem et sincere dilectionis affectum. Cum imminens bladi caristia, ab olim tali tempore inaudita, et clamor et fames populi huius terre nos compulerint ad mandandum quod deffensum olim factum cum consilio de blado non extrahendo per terram vel per aquam de senescallia Carcassone et Bitterris observetur donec didiscerimus an dictum deffensum fuerit cum conscilio [*sic*] dissolutum, ut in statutis regalibus continetur, donec etiam vobiscum et cum domino episcopo Tholosano et cum aliis prelatis et baronibus et bonis viris de aliis vicariis nostre senescallie, quibus eodem modo scripsimus, habuerimus consilium de novo deffenso faciendo ad provisionem et sucursum omnium gentium huius terre, cum non solum in hac terra sed etiam in multis aliis longe et prope caristia invalescat, et sit tempus non modicum hinc ad messes, ex parte domini regis et nostra rogamus et requirimus vos dominos prelatos supradictos et vobis omnibus[8] aliis mandamus quatenus die jovis post octavum diem natalem Domini ad nos apud Carcassonam personaliter veniatis ad conferendum super hiis et ad dandum nobis concilium[9] ad honorem et comodum domini regis et vestrum omnium et cunctorum populorum huius terre et ad audiendum quedam nova statuta domini regis et mandata que vos tangunt. Et quia sigillum proprium pre manibus non habemus, cum sigillo dilecti nostri magistri Bartholomei de Podio, clerici domini regis, judicis Carcassone, presentes fecimus litteras sigillari. Datum apud Ulmos, die jovis post festum Beati Nycholai, anno Domini m° .cc° .lxx iiii^{to}. Reddite litteras in continenti portitori.

---

[8] Omitted, *H.L.*, x, 127.
[9] *Consilium, ibid.*

Select Bibliography of Works Cited

SOURCES IN MANUSCRIPT

I. Archives Nationales (Paris)
    J.302, 305, 306, 308, 315, 320, 341, 356, 384, 890, 894, 896, 1029, 1031, 1032.
    JJ.13, 19, 25, 36, 72.
    Q. no. 254 (606).

II. Bibliothèque Nationale (Paris)
    Collections de Baluze, Doat, Périgord.
    MSS Lat. 6009, 9173, 9192, 9988, 11016, 11017, 15393, 17734
    MSS n. a. franç. 3391, 3404.

III. Archives Départementales
    Aude (Carcassonne)
        B.1219
        H.153
    Aveyron (Rodez)
        C.1590, 1840
        2E.178
        G.10
    Gard (Nîmes)
        C.66
        E.Supplément 530 (Aimargues, FF.1)
        G.245, 300, 760
    Haute-Garonne (Toulouse)
        1G.346
        4G.230, 233, 239
    Hérault (Montpellier)
        E.Supplément (Marsillargues, AA.1, no. 13)
    Lot (Cahors)
        F.136

Lot-et-Garonne (Agen)
  E.Supplément 691 (Laroque-Timbaut, AA.2)
  E.Supplément 1824
  New G.2
  2J.54 (MS d'Argenton)
Lozère (Mende)
  G.25, 27, 71, 143, 735, 736
Tarn (Albi)
  E.12, 2196
  H.7
Tarn-et-Garonne (Montauban)
  A.297

IV. Archives Municipales
  Agde
    AA.1
  Agen
    AA.2
  Albi
    FF.14
  Alès
    1S III, IV, XII
  Aniane
    AA.3
  Cahors
    AA.1
    BB.6
    DD.1, 5, 12*bis*
    FF.4, 15
    "Livre Nouveau"; D.320
  Cajarc
    EE.53
  Cordes
    CC.27
  Gourdon
    CC.41
  Martel
    CC.2
  Millau
    CC.342, 344, 346, 510, 516

Montauban
   AA.1, 2, 3
Montpellier
   Armoire A, cassettes 16, 18, 20
   Armoire C, cassettes 2, 18
   Armoire E, cassette 1
   Armoire G, cassettes 2, 6
   Armoire H, cassette 3
Narbonne
   AA.24, 99, 103, 105, 107, 109
   HH. (uninventoried)
Nîmes
   NN.1
   00.82
Pézenas
   Armoire A, 2/3/1; 11/1/7
Toulouse
   AA.3, 5, 54
   Layettes 61, 62, 87
Villeneuve-les-Maguelonne
   AA.1

V. Bibliothèques Municipales
   Cahors
      MS 79
   Toulouse
      MS 640

VI. British Museum (London)
      Cottonian MS Julius E.1
      MS Royal 11C. vii

VII. Public Record Office (London)
      Ancient Correspondence (SC 1)
      Ancient Petitions (SC 8)
      Chancery Miscellanea (C 47)
      Miscellaneous Books, Exchequer Treasury of Receipt
         (E.36), vol. 275

VIII. Biblioteca Apostolica (Rome)
      MS Vat. Lat. 1377

SOURCES IN PRINT

Acta Capitulorum Generalium Ordinis Praedicatorum ab Anno 1220 usque ad Annum 1303, ed. B. Reichert. Rome, 1898.

Acta Capitulorum Provincialium Ordinis Fratrum Praedicatorum; Première Province de Provence—Province Romaine— Province d'Espagne (1239–1302), ed. C. Douais. Toulouse, 1894.

(Anelier). *Histoire de la Guerre de Navarre en 1276 et 1277 par Guillaume Anelier de Toulouse*, ed. F. Michel. Paris, 1856.

Les Archives de la Cour des Comptes, Aides et Finances de Montpellier, ed. E. Martin-Chabot. Paris, 1907.

Archives Historiques du Département de la Gironde. Paris-Bordeaux, 1859–.

Archives Municipales d'Agen, Chartes, Première Série (1189–1328), eds. A. Magen, G. Tholin. Villeneuve-sur-Lot, 1876.

La Baronnie du Tournel . . . Documents Publiés avec une Introduction et des Notes, ed. A. Philippe. Mende, 1903.

(Beaumanoir). *Livre des Coutumes et des Usages de Beauvaisis*, ed. A. Salmon. 2 vols. Paris, 1899–1900.

Bernardi Papiensis Faventini Episcopi Summa Decretalium . . ., ed. E. A. T. Laspeyres. Ratisbon, 1860.

Cahors: Inventaire Raisonné & Analytique des Archives Municipales: Première Partie, XIIIᵉ Siècle (1200–1300), ed. E. Albe. Cahors, n.d.

Calendar of the Patent Rolls, 1247–1258. London, 1908.

Calendar of the Patent Rolls, 1266–1272. London, 1913.

Cartulaire de Béziers: Livre Noire de Béziers, ed. J. Rouquette. Paris-Montpellier, 1918.

Cartulaire de la Ville de Lodève, ed. E. Martin. Montpellier, 1900.

Cartulaire et Archives des Communes de l'Ancien Diocèse et de l'Arrondissement Administrative de Carcassonne, ed. M. Mahul. 6 vols. in 7. Paris, 1857–1882.

La Chanson de la Croisade Albigeoise, ed. E. Martin-Chabot. 3 vols. Paris, 1931–1961.

"Chartes d'Agen se Rapportant au Règne de Philippe de Valois," ed. G. Tholin, *Arch. Gir.*, XXXIII (1898), 75–177.

"Chartes d'Agen se Rapportant aux Règnes de Jean le Bon et de Charles V," Arch. Gir., xxxiv (1899), 147–210.

Chartes de Franchises du Lauragais, ed. J. Ramière de Fortanier. Paris, 1939.

Comptes Royaux (1285–1314), eds. R. Fawtier, F. Maillard. 3 vols. Paris, 1953–1956.

Corpus Juris Civilis, 6 vols. Paris, 1548–1550. Includes *glossa ordinaria.*

Correspondence Administrative d'Alfonse de Poitiers, ed. A. Molinier. 2 vols. Paris, 1894–1900.

"Les Coutumes de l'Agenais: Monclar, Monflanquin (1256–70), Saint-Maurin (1358)," ed. H. Rébouis, *N.R.H.D.F.É.,* xiv (1890), 387–432.

Coutumes et Privilèges du Rouergue, eds. E. Baillaud, P. Verlaguet. 2 vols. Toulouse, 1910.

Desclot, *Cronica,* ed. Coll i Alentorn. 5 vols. Barcelona, 1949–1951.

Documents Historiques Inédits . . . , ed. J. Champollion-Figeac. 4 vols. Paris, 1841–1848.

Documents Historiques Relatifs à la Vicomté de Carlat, eds. G. Saige, Comte de Dienne. 2 vols. Monaco, 1900.

"Documents Linguistiques du Gévaudan," ed. C. Brunel, *B.É.C.,* lxxvii (1916), 5–57, 241–285.

Documents Relatifs aux États Généraux et Assemblées Réunis sous Philippe le Bel, ed. G. Picot. Paris, 1901.

"Documents Relatifs à la Seigneurie de Boussagues (Hérault) de la Fin du XII⁰ au Milieu du XIV⁰ Siècle," ed. F. Pasquier, *Bull. Soc. Archéol., Scient. et Litt. de Béziers,* 3⁰ sér., iii (1899), 243–311.

Droits et Possessions du Comte de Toulouse dans l'Albigeois, ed E. Cabié. Paris, 1900.

Enquêtes Administratives d'Alfonse de Poitiers, Arrêts de son Parlement Tenu à Toulouse et Textes Annexes, 1249–1271, eds. P. Fournier, P. Guébin. Paris, 1959.

Foedera, Conventiones, Litterae, et Cujuscunque Generis Acta Publica . . . , ed. T. Rymer. Rec. Comm. Ed. 4 vols. London, 1816–1869.

Le Fonds Thésan aux Archives du Chateau de Léran (Ariège): Documents Concernant Diverses Localités du Département de l'Hérault, eds. F. Pasquier, S. Olive. Montpellier, 1913.

Gallia Christiana . . . 16 vols. Paris, 1715–1865.

The Gascon Calendar of 1322, ed. G. P. Cuttino. London, 1949.

"La Grande Charte de Saint-Gaudens (1203)," ed. S. Mondon, *Revue de Comminges,* xxv (1910), 1–250.

Gratian, *Decretum.* Venice, 1600. Includes *glossa ordinaria.*

Gregory IX, *Decretales* . . . Venice, 1600. Includes *glossa ordinaria.*

(Haute-Garonne). *I.A.D., Haute-Garonne, Série E. Supplément,* ed. F. Pasquier. Toulouse, 1913.

"Hommages des Seigneurs de l'Agenais au Comte de Toulouse en 1259," *Rec. des Travaux Soc. d'Agriculture, Sciences et Arts d'Agen,* 2ᵉ sér., xiii (1897), 11–62.

Hostiensis. *In Quinque Libros Decretalium Commentaria.* 4 vols. Venice, 1581.

Innocent IV. *Apparatus super Libros Decretalium.* Venice, 1481.

Layettes du Trésor des Chartes, eds. A. Teulet, J. de Laborde, É. Berger, H. F. Delaborde. Paris, 1863–1909.

"Lettre Adressée en Égypte à Alphonse, Comte de Poitiers, Frère de Saint Louis," ed. T. Saint Bris, *B.É.C.,* i (1839), 389–403.

Lettres Inédites de Philippe le Bel, ed. A. Baudouin. Paris, 1887.

Lettres de Philippe-le-Bel Relatives au Pays de Gévaudan, eds. J. Roucaute, M. Saché. Mende, 1897.

Le Livre d'Agenais, ed. G. P. Cuttino. Toulouse, 1956.

Le Livre de Comptes de Jacme Olivier, Marchand Narbonnais du XIVᵉ Siècle, ed. A. Blanc. Paris, 1899.

Mansi, J. (ed.). *Sacrorum Conciliorum Nova et Amplissima Collectio.* Florence, 1759–1798; new series, Paris, 1901–.

(Matthew Paris). *Matthaei Parisiensis Monachi Sancti Albani Chronica Majora,* ed. H. Luard, R.S. 7 vols. London, 1872–1883.

(Médicis, É.). *Le Livre de Podio, ou Chroniques d'Étienne Médicis, Bourgeois du Puy* . . . , ed. A. Chassaing. 2 vols. Le Puy, 1869–1874.

"Memorandum des Consuls de la Ville de Martel," ed. H.

Teulié, *Revue de Philologie Française,* VII (1893), 253–264; VIII (1894), 17–34, 279–295.

(Mende). *Mémoire Relatif au Paréage de 1307 Conclu entre l'Évêque Guillaume Durand II et le Roi Philippe-le-Bel,* Société d'Agriculture, Sciences & Arts de la Lozère. Mende, 1896.

Les Miracles de Saint Privat suivis des Opuscules d'Aldebert III, Évêque de Mende, ed. C. Brunel. Paris, 1912.

(Narbonne). *Ville de Narbonne; I.A.C., Annexes de la Série AA . . . BB,* ed. G. Mouynès. Narbonne, 1871–1879.

Nepos de Montauban. *De Exceptionibus Liber, Qui Fugitiuus Vulgo Dicitur,* in Masuer, *Iurisconsvlti Galli Longe Celeberrimi Practica Forensis.* . . . Lyon, 1577.

Les Olim, ou Registres des Arrêts Rendus par la Cour du Roi . . . , ed. A. Beugnot. 4 vols. Paris, 1839–1848.

Ordonnances des Roys de France de la Troisième Race. 22 vols. Paris, 1723–1849.

Patrologiae Cursus Completus . . . Patres . . . Latinae, ed. J. Migne. 221 vols. Paris, 1844–1864.

(Pézenas). *Archives de la Ville de Pézenas, Inventaires et Documents,* I, *Inventaire de F. Resseguier,* ed. J. Berthelé. Montpellier, 1907.

(Pierre des Vaux-de-Cernay). *Petri Vallium Sarnaii Monachi Hystoria Albigensis,* eds. P. Guébin, E. Lyon. 3 vols. Paris, 1926–1930.

Preuves de la Maison de Polignac . . . , ed. A. Jacotin. 5 vols. Paris, 1898–1906.

"Prise de Possession de l'Agenais, au Nom du Roi de France, en 1271," *Rec. Trav. Soc. Agen,* 2ᵉ sér., XIII (1897), 63–90.

(Puylaurens). "Guillaume de Puylaurens et sa Chronique," ed. Beyssier, *Bibliothèque de la Faculté des Lettres de l'Université de Paris,* XVIII (1904), 85–175.

Quellen zur Geschichte des Römisch-Kanonischen Processes im Mittelalter, ed. L. Wahrmund. 5 vols. Innsbruck, 1905–1931.

Recogniciones Feudorum in Aquitania. Recueil d'Actes Relatifs à l'Administration des Rois d'Angleterre en Guyenne au XIIIᵉ Siècle, ed. C. Bémont. Paris, 1914.

Recueil des Historiens des Gaules et de la France, eds. Bouquet, Delisle, *et al.* Paris, 1738–.

The Register of S. Osmund, ed. W. H. Rich Jones, R.S. 2 vols. London, 1883–1884.

"Registre des Hommages Rendus au Roi d'Angleterre dans les Sénéchaussées d'Agenais et de Condomois," ed. J. Delpit, *Arch. Gir.,* i (1859), 349–387.

Registres du Trésor des Chartes, i, ed. R. Fawtier. Paris, 1958.

Répertoire Général des Hommages de l'Évêché du Puy, 1154–1741, work of Cazalède (1740–1741), ed. A. Lascombe. Le Puy, 1882.

Responsa Doctorum Tholosanorum, ed. E. Meijers. Haarlem, 1938.

Rôles Gascons, eds. F. Michel, C. Bémont. 4 vols. Paris, 1885–1906.

Rotuli Litterarum Clausarum in Turri Londinensi Asservati, i, ed. T. Duffus Hardy. London, 1833.

Rotuli Litterarum Patentium . . . , i, ed. T. Duffus Hardy. London, 1835.

"La Somme du Code. Texte du XIII° Siècle en Dialecte Dauphinoise," eds. L. Royer, A. Thomas, *Notices et Extraits des Manuscrits . . . ,* xlii (1933), 1–138.

Le 'Te Igitur,' eds. P. Lacombe, L. Combarieu. Cahors, 1874.

Thesaurus Novus Anecdotorum, eds. E. Martin, U. Durand. 5 vols. Paris, 1717.

The War of Saint-Sardos (1323–1325): Gascon Correspondence and Diplomatic Documents, ed. P. Chaplais. London, 1954.

A. *Secondary Works Used Chiefly for Editions of Texts*

Baradat de Lacaze, C. *Astafort-en-Agenais.* Paris, 1886.

Bousquet, J. "Le Traité d'Alliance entre Hugues, Comte de Rodez, et les Consuls de Millau (6 Juin 1223)," *Annales du Midi,* lxxii (1960), 25–42.

Burdin, G. de. *Documents Historiques sur la Province de Gévaudan.* 2 vols. Toulouse, 1846–1847.

Catel, G. de. *Histoire des Comtes de Tolose, Avec Quelques Traitez, & Chroniques Anciennes, Concernans la Mesme Histoire.* Toulouse, 1623.

Compayré, C. *Études Historiques et Documents Inédits sur l'Albigeois, le Castrais et l'Ancien Diocèse de Lavaur.* Albi, 1841.

Devic, C., and Vaissete, J. *Histoire Générale de Languedoc avec des Notes et les Pièces Justificatives,* various editors. Privat edition. 16 vols. Toulouse, 1872–1904.

Ducom, A. *La Commune d'Agen; Essai sur son Histoire et son Organisation.* . . . Paris, 1892.

Dufour, É. *La Commune de Cahors.* Cahors, 1846.

Germain, A. *Histoire du Commerce de Montpellier antérieurement à l'Ouverture du Port de Cette.* . . . 2 vols. Montpellier, 1861.

Lacroix, G. de. *Series & Acta Episcoporum Cadurcensium.* . . . Cahors, 1626.

La Faille, G. *Annales de la Ville de Toulouse depuis la Réunion de la Comté de Toulouse à la Couronne.* . . . 2 vols. Toulouse, 1687–1701.

Lagarde, A. *Notice Historique sur la Ville de Tonneins.* Agen, 1882.

Limouzin-Lamothe, R. *La Commune de Toulouse et les Sources de son Histoire (1120–1249); Étude Historique et Critique Suivi de l'Édition du Cartulaire du Consulat.* Toulouse, 1932.

Marca, P. de. *Marca Hispanica, sive Limes Hispanicus.* . . . Paris, 1688.

Ménard, L. *Histoire Civile, Ecclésiastique, et Littéraire de la Ville de Nismes, avec des Notes et des Preuves.* 7 vols. Paris, 1744–1758.

Ourliac, P. *Les Sauvetés du Comminges.* . . . Toulouse, 1947.

Saint-Amans, C. de. "De la Monnaie dite Arnaldèse des Évêques d'Agen," *Rec. Trav. Soc. Agen,* VII (1855) 566–623.

Tropamer, H. *La Coutume d'Agen.* Bordeaux, 1911.

SECONDARY WORKS

Andrieu, J. *Histoire de l'Agenais.* 2 vols. Paris, 1893.

Artonne, A. *Le Mouvement de 1314 et les Chartes Provinciales de 1315.* Paris, 1912.

Babey, P. *Le Pouvoir Temporel des Évêques de Viviers au Moyen Age, 815–1452.* Paris, 1956.

Baudel, J. "Notes pour Servir à l'Histoire des États Provinciaux du Quercy," *Annuaire Statistique et Administratif du Département du Lot* (1881), part. 3, pp. 1–51.

Belperron, P. *La Croisade contre les Albigeois et l'Union du Languedoc à la France (1209–1249).* Paris 1942.

Bémont, C. *Simon de Montfort, Earl of Leicester, 1208–1265.* New ed., tr. E. F. Jacob. Oxford, 1930.

Bisson, T. "Coinages and Royal Monetary Policy in Languedoc during the Reign of Saint Louis," *Speculum,* XXXII (1957), 443–469.

———. "An Early Provincial Assembly: the General Court of Agenais in the Thirteenth Century," *Speculum,* XXXVI (1961), 254–281.

Bloch, M. "Pour une Histoire Comparée des Sociétés Européennes," *Revue de Synthèse Historique,* n.s., XX (1928), 15–50.

Bonnaud–Delamare, R. "La Légende des Associations de la Paix en Rouergue et en Languedoc au Début du XIII° Siècle (1170–1229)," *Bulletin Philol. et Hist. du Comité des Travaux Historiques et Scientifiques* (1936–1937), pp. 47–78.

Boutaric, E. "Organisation Judiciaire de Languedoc au Moyen Age," *B.É.C.,* XVI (1855), 200–230, 532–550; XVII (1856), 97–122.

———. *Saint Louis et Alfonse de Poitiers; Étude sur la Réunion des Provinces du Midi & d'Ouest à la Couronne et sur les Origines de la Centralisation Administrative. . . .* Paris, 1870.

Boutruche, R. *Une Société Provinciale en Lutte contre le Régime Féodal: l'Alleu en Bordelais et en Bazadais du XI° au XVIII° Siècle.* Rodez, 1947.

Brunel, C. "Les Juges de la Paix en Gévaudan au Milieu du XI° Siècle," *B.É.C.,* CIX (1951), 32–41.

Cadier, L. *Les États de Béarn.* Paris, 1888.

Callery, A. "Les Premiers États-Généraux, Origine, Pouvoirs et Attributions," *Revue des Questions Historiques,* XXIX (1881), 62–119.

Cathala-Coture, A. de. *Histoire Politique, Ecclésiastique et Littéraire du Querci.* 3 vols. Montauban, 1785.

Chaplais, P. "Le Duché-Pairie de Guyenne: l'Hommage et les

Services Féodaux de 1259 à 1303," *Annales du Midi*, LXIX (1957), 5–38.

Cheney, C. *English Synodalia of the Thirteenth Century*. Oxford, 1941.

Chénon, É. *Histoire Générale du Droit Français Public et Privé des Origines à 1815*. 2 vols. Paris, 1926–1929.

Coville, A. *Les États de Normandie, leurs Origines et leur Développement au XIV*^e *Siècle*. Paris, 1894.

Curie-Seimbres, A. *Essai sur les Villes Fondées dans le Sud-Ouest de la France aux XIII*^e *et XIV*^e *Siècles sous le Nom Générique de Bastides*. Toulouse, 1880.

Delcambre, É. "Le Paréage du Puy," *B.É.C.*, XCII (1931), 121–169, 285–344.

Dognon, P. *Les Institutions Politiques et Administratives du Pays de Languedoc du XIII*^e *Siècle aux Guerres de Religion*. Toulouse, 1895.

Dossat, Y. "Le Comté de Toulouse et la Féodalité Languedocienne à la Veille de la Croisade Albigeoise," *Revue du Tarn*, n.s., IX (1943), 75–90.

———. *Les Crises de l'Inquisition Toulousaine du XIII*^e *Siècle, 1233–1273*. Bordeaux, 1959.

Dupont, A. *Les Cités de la Narbonnaise Première depuis les Invasions Germaniques jusqu'à l'Apparition du Consulat*. Nîmes, 1942.

———. "Les Ordonnances Royales de 1254 et les Origines des Conseils de Sénéchaussées dans le Languedoc Méditerranéen," *Fédération Historique du Languedoc Méditerranéen et du Roussillon: XXX*^{me} *et XXXI*^{me} *Congrès, Sète-Beaucaire (1956–1957)*, pp. 227–235.

Fawtier, R. *L'Europe Occidentale de 1270 à 1380*, part 1. Paris, 1940.

Gaujal, M. A. F. de. *Études Historiques sur le Rouergue*. 4 vols. Paris, 1858–1859.

Gavrilovitch, M. *Étude sur le Traité de Paris de 1259 entre Louis IX, Roi de France et Henri III, Roi d'Angleterre*. Paris, 1899.

Géraud, H. "Mercadier. Les Routiers au Treizième Siècle," *B.É.C.*, III (1841–1842), 417–447.

————. "Les Routiers au Douzième Siècle," *B.É.C.,* III (1841–1842), 125–147.

Germain, A. *Histoire de la Commune de Montpellier.* . . . 3 vols. Montpellier, 1851.

Gierke, O. *Das Deutsche Genossenschaftsrecht.* 4 vols. Berlin, 1868–1913.

Gilles, H. "Les États de Languedoc au XV° Siècle," *École Nationale des Chartes: Positions des Thèses* . . . *de l'Année 1952*, pp. 51–54.

Gillet, P. *La Personnalité Juridique en Droit Ecclésiastique.* . . . Malines, 1927.

Giry, A. *Manuel de Diplomatique.* Paris, 1894.

Gouron, A. "Les Étapes de la Pénétration du Droit Romain au XII° Siècle dans l'Ancienne Septimanie," *Annales du Midi,* LXIX (1957), 103–120.

Gouron, M. *Les Chartes de Franchises de Guyenne et Gascogne.* Paris, 1935.

Grand, R. *Les Paix d'Aurillac.* Paris, 1945.

Guilhiermoz, P. *Essai sur l'Origine de la Noblesse en France au Moyen Age.* Paris, 1902. (New York, 1960.)

Haskins, G. L. *The Statute of York and the Interest of the Commons.* Cambridge, Mass., 1935.

Hefele, C. *Histoire des Conciles d'après les Documents Originaux,* tr. H. Leclercq. 11 vols. Paris, 1907–1952.

Hervieu, H. *Recherches sur les Premiers États Généraux et les Assemblées Représentatives pendant la Première Moitié du Quatorzième Siècle.* Paris, 1879.

Higounet, C. *Le Comté de Comminges de ses Origines à son Annexion à la Couronne.* 2 vols. Toulouse, 1949.

Hoyt, R.S. "Recent Publications in the United States and Canada on the History of Representative Institutions before the French Revolution," *Speculum,* XXIX (1954), 356–377.

Huberti, L. *Studien zur Rechtsgeschichte der Gottesfrieden und Landfrieden.* Ansbach, 1892.

Jarriand, É. "L'Évolution du Droit Écrit dans le Midi de la France," *Rev. Quest. Hist.,* XLVIII (1890), 204–216.

Keeney, B. C. *Judgment by Peers.* Cambridge, Mass., 1949.

Lacger, L. de. "L'Albigeois pendant la Crise de l'Albigéisme;

l'Épiscopat de Guilhem Peire, 1185–1227," *Revue d'Histoire Ecclésiastique,* xxix (1933), 272–315, 586–633, 849–904.

———. "L'Albigeois au Siècle de Saint Louis; Les Évêques Durant de Beaucaire et Bernard de Combret, 1228–1271," *Rev. d'Hist. Ecclés.,* lii (1957), 26–50.

Lacoste, G. *Histoire Générale de la Province de Quercy,* eds. L. Combarieu, F. Cangardel. 4 vols. Cahors, 1883–1886.

Lagarde, G. de. "Individualisme et Corporatisme au Moyen Age," *L'Organisation Corporative du Moyen Age à la Fin de l'Ancien Régime,* ii, Louvain, 1937.

Lagrèze-Fossat, A. *Études Historiques sur Moissac.* 3 vols. Paris, 1870–1874.

Langlois, C. V. "Les Doléances des Communautés du Toulousain contre Pierre de Latilli et Raoul de Breuilli (1297–1298)," *R.H.,* xcv (1907), 23–53.

———. "Les Origines du Parlement de Paris," *R.H.,* xlii (1890), 74–114.

———. *Le Règne de Philippe III le Hardi.* Paris, 1887.

Langmuir, G. I. "Counsel and Capetian Assemblies," *Études Présentées à la Commission Internationale pour l'Histoire des Assemblées d'États,* xviii (1958), 21–34.

———. " 'Judei Nostri' and the Beginning of Capetian Legislation," *Traditio,* xvi (1960), 203–239.

Lea, H. C. *A History of the Inquisition of the Middle Ages.* 3 vols. New York, 1887–1888.

Lodge, E. *Gascony under English Rule.* London, 1926.

Longnon, A. *Atlas Historique de la France.* Paris, 1885.

Lot, F., and Fawtier, R. *Histoire des Institutions Françaises au Moyen Age.* 3 vols. to date. Paris, 1957–1962.

Lousse, É. "Parlementarisme ou Corporatisme? Les Origines des Assemblées d'États," *R.H.D.F.É.,* xiv (1935), 683–706.

———. *La Société d'Ancien Régime, Organisation et Représentation Corporatives.* i, nouv. éd. Louvain, 1952.

Luchaire, A. *Manuel des Institutions Françaises.* Paris, 1892.

———. *La Société Française au Temps de Philippe-Auguste.* Paris, 1909.

———. "Une Théorie Récente sur l'Origine des États-Généraux," *Annales de la Faculté des Lettres de Bordeaux*, III-IV (1881–1882), 50–60.

McIlwain, C. H. *The High Court of Parliament and its Supremacy.* New Haven, 1910.

————. "Medieval Estates," *Cambridge Medieval History*, VII (1932), chapter 23.

McKisack, M. *The Parliamentary Representation of the English Boroughs during the Middle Ages.* London, 1932.

Maitland, F. W. Introduction to *Memoranda de Parliamento.* London, 1893.

Malinowski, J. "Notice sur les Monnaies des Évêques et des Consuls de Cahors frappées sous la Troisième Race des Rois de France," *Revue de l'Agenais*, II (1875), 224–234, 263–282, 293–298.

Merriman, R. B. "The Cortes of the Spanish Kingdoms in the Later Middle Ages," *A.H.R.*, XVI (1911), 476–495.

Michel, R. *L'Administration Royale dans la Sénéchaussée de Beaucaire au Temps de Saint Louis.* Paris, 1910.

Molinié, G. *L'Organisation Judiciaire, Militaire et Financière des Associations de la Paix; Étude sur la Paix et la Trève de Dieu dans le Midi et le Centre de la France.* Toulouse, 1912.

Molinier, A. "Catalogue des Actes de Simon et d'Amaury de Montfort," *B.É.C.*, XXXIV (1873), 153–203, 445–501.

————. "La Commune de Toulouse et Philippe III," *B.É.C.*, XLIII (1882), 5–39 (also in *H.L.*, X, 147–168).

————. "Étude sur l'Administration Féodale dans le Languedoc (900–1250)," *H.L.*, VII (1879), 132–213.

————. "Étude sur l'Administration de Louis IX & d'Alfonse de Poitiers (1226–1271)," *H.L.*, VII, 462–570.

————. "Sur la Géographie Historique de la Province de Languedoc au Moyen Age," *H.L.*, XII (1889), 130–355.

Momméja, J. "Sénéchaux de Quercy," *Rec. Trav. Soc. Agen,* 2ᵉ sér., XIII,ii (1898), 221–366.

Mundy, J. H. *Liberty and Political Power in Toulouse, 1050–1230.* New York, 1954.

Olivier-Martin, F. *Histoire de la Coutume de la Prévôté et Vicomté de Paris.* 2 vols. in 3. Paris, 1922–1930.

————. *Histoire du Droit Français.* n.p., 1948.

Parent, M. "Les Assemblées Royales en France au Temps de Saint Louis," *École Nationale des Chartes: Positions des Thèses* . . . *de l'Année 1939,* pp. 155–161.

Petit-Dutaillis, C. *Les Communes Françaises.* . . . Paris, 1947.

———. *Étude sur la Vie et le Règne de Louis VIII (1187–1226).* Paris, 1894.

Picot, G. *Histoire des États Généraux* . . . *de 1355 à 1614.* 4 vols. Paris, 1872; 2ᵉ éd., 1888.

Porée, C. *Études Historiques sur le Gévaudan.* Paris, 1919.

Post, G. "Plena Potestas and Consent in Medieval Assemblies: A Study in Romano-Canonical Procedure and the Rise of Representation, 1150–1325," *Traditio,* ɪ (1943), 355–408.

———. "Roman Law and Early Representation in Spain and Italy," *Speculum,* xvɪɪɪ (1943), 211–232.

———. "A Romano-Canonical Maxim, 'Quod Omnes Tangit,' in Bracton," *Traditio,* ɪv (1946), 197–251.

———. "The Theory of Public Law and the State in the Thirteenth Century," *Seminar* (annual extraordinary number of *The Jurist*), vɪ (1948), 42–59.

Poux, J. "Essai sur le Commun de Paix ou Pezade dans le Rouergue et dans l'Albigeois," *École Nationale des Chartes: Positions des Thèses* . . . *de l'Année 1898,* pp. 107–116.

Powicke, F. M. *The Thirteenth Century, 1216–1307.* 2nd ed. Oxford, 1962.

Regné, J. *Amauri II, Vicomte de Narbonne (1260?–1328).* . . . Narbonne, 1910.

———. *Histoire du Vivarais.* ɪɪ, Largentière, 1921.

Richardot, H. "Le Fief Roturier à Toulouse aux XIIᵉ et XIIIᵉ Siècles," *R.H.D.F.É.,* xɪv (1935), 307–359, 495–569.

Richardson, H. G. "The Origins of Parliament," *Trans. Royal Hist. Society,* 4th ser., xɪ (1928), 137–183.

———., and Sayles, G. O. *Parliaments and Great Councils in Medieval England.* London, 1961.

Riess, L. *Geschichte des Wahlrechts zum Englischen Parlament im Mittelalter.* Leipzig, 1885.

Rogé, P. *Les Anciens Fors de Béarn, Études sur l'Histoire du Droit Béarnais au Moyen Age.* Toulouse, 1908.

Rossignol, É. A. *Étude sur l'Histoire des Institutions Seign-*

euriales et Communales de l'Arrondissement de Gaillac (Tarn). Toulouse, 1866.

Stephenson, C. *Mediaeval Institutions: Selected Essays,* ed. B. Lyon. Ithaca, 1954.

Strayer, J. R. "The Crusade against Aragon," *Speculum,* XXVIII (1953), 102–113.

———. "The Development of Feudal Institutions," *Twelfth-Century Europe and the Foundations of Modern Society,* eds. M. Clagett, G. Post, R. Reynolds. Madison, 1961.

———. "The Laicization of French and English Society in the Thirteenth Century," *Speculum,* XV (1940), 76–86.

———. "The Statute of York and the Community of the Realm," *A.H.R.,* XLVII (1941), 1–22.

———., and Taylor, C. H. *Studies in Early French Taxation.* Cambridge, Mass., 1939.

Stubbs, W. *The Constitutional History of England.* 3 vols. II, 4th ed. Oxford, 1896.

Taylor, C. H. "Assemblies of French Towns in 1316," *Speculum,* XIV (1939), 275–299.

———. "An Assembly of French Towns in March, 1318," *Speculum,* XIII (1938), 295–303.

———. "The Assembly of 1312 at Lyons-Vienne," *Études d'Histoire Dédiées à la Mémoire de Henri Pirenne par ses Anciens Élèves,* Bruxelles, 1937, pp. 337–349.

———. "The Composition of Baronial Assemblies in France, 1315–1320," *Speculum,* XXIX (1954), 433–459.

———. "Some New Texts on the Assembly of 1302," *Speculum,* XI (1936), 38–42.

Tholin, G. "Notes sur la Féodalité en Agenais au Milieu du XIII° Siècle," *Rev. de l'Agenais,* XXIII-XXVI (1896–1899).

———. *Ville Libre et Barons; Essai sur les Limites de la Juridiction Comparée à Celle des Tenanciers des Seigneuries Qui en Furent Détachées.* Paris, 1886.

Tierney, B. *Foundations of the Conciliar Theory.* . . . Cambridge, 1955.

Timbal, P. *Un Conflit d'Annexion au Moyen Age; l'Application de la Coutume de Paris au Pays d'Albigeois.* Toulouse, 1950.

———. "Les Villes de Consulat dans le Midi de la France,

Histoire de leurs Institutions Administratives et Judiciaires," *Rec. Société Jean Bodin,* vi (1954), 343–370.

Trabut-Cussac, J. P. "Itinéraire d'Édouard I en France (1286–1289)," *Bulletin of the Institute of Historical Research,* xxv (1952), 160–203.

Viollet, P. *Droit Public. Histoire des Institutions Politiques et Administratives de la France.* 3 vols. Paris, 1890–1903.

Wilkinson, B. *The Constitutional History of England, 1216–1399.* 3 vols. London, 1948–1958.

Wolff, P. *Commerces et Marchands de Toulouse (vers 1350–vers 1450).* Paris, 1954.

Index

Medieval persons are indexed by Christian names, except in cases of place- or family-name designations, which, it is hoped, will facilitate the identification of dynastic or regional groups. Modern writers are indexed only for opinions or notable points. The abbreviations are: abp. = archbishop; bp. = bishop; ch. = chapter; ct. = count; cty. = county; vct. = viscount; vcty. = viscounty.

4, 67, 72; ceremonial, 64, 68, 256; consultative, 6, 56, 62, 67, 192, 218, 230, 262–64; deliberative, 218, 272; political, 48, 56, 72, 143, 185, 218, 234, 246–47, 270, 272; publicity-giving, 62, 140–41, 161, 171, 218, 220, 247, 250, 294; publicity, legal theory of, 297. *See also* armies, authoritarian use, counsel, consent, justice, legislation, taxation

G. M[o]netarii, 34n
Gaillac, 110, 152; lord of, 53
Gaillac, Bérenger de, 153
Galbert de Bruges, cited, 143n
Ganshof, F. L., 82
Garinus Abcherii, 123n
Gascony, 13, 83, 84n, 156n, 229, 238, 246, 276, 288n
Gauderiis, Petrus de, consul of Narbonne, 316
general army of Agenais, 75, 81n, 82n, 86–9, 93, 114, 134, 243
general court of Agenais, 73–101, 126, 134–35, 149–50, 155–57, 160, 176–79, 182, 234–46, 260, 263, 291, 293–94; composition and representation, 78–9, 81–92, 126, 155, 160, 176–79, 234–36, 238–41; decline, 241–46; functions, 79–97, 155–57, 176–79, 235–44, 295; origins, 74–8, 81–9, 294; sessions, 79–80, 96, 155–57, 176–79, 235–38
"general custom of Agenais," 74
generale colloquium, 55n
Genoese, 205

Géraud (de Barasc), bp. of Cahors, 124, 314
Géraud Hector, bp. of Cahors, 124
Germany, early representation in, 10
Gévaudan, 18, 21, 26, 56, 104, 111–27, 134, 136, 142, 144n, 195, 233, 250, 269, 280, 293
Gignac, 222, 223n
glossa ordinaria, cited, to *Decretales Greg. IX,* 47n, 95n, 129n, 175n, 192n, 226n; to *Decretum,* 105n, 145n, 227n, 255n
golden bull, Gévaudan, 116
Gontaut, Gasto de, 311
Gontaut, Vitalis de, 311
"good towns," 151, 158, 169, 176, 191, 197, 211
Gourdon, 126, 154n; lord of, 126
Gourdon, Fortanier de, 154
Gourdon, Géraud de, 53–4
grain, *see* exports; consultation on supply of in Rouergue and Toulousain, 260; Narbonne's right to regulate trade in, 204, 211, 219
(grain-export) assemblies of *sénéchaussées* of Beaucaire and Carcassonne, 11, 187–228, 247, 260–65, 272, 291–92, 294, 323–25; composition and representation, 220–28, 262; functions, 218–20, 262; meetings: Beaucaire (1258), 193–94; uncertain date and place, 194–95; Carcassonne (1269), 196–201; uncertain date(s) and place(s), 202–204; Béziers (1271), 202, 205–211; Carcassonne (1275), 211–18,